Practical LotusScript

Practical LotusScript

Anthony Patton

MANNING

Greenwich
(74° w. long.)

For electronic browsing and ordering of this and other Manning books, visit http://www.manning.com. The publisher offers discounts on this book when ordered in quantities. For more information, please contact:

Special Sales Department
Manning Publications Co.
32 Lafayette Place
Greenwich, CT 06830

Fax: (203) 661-9018
email: orders@manning.com

Library of Congress Cataloging-in-Publication Data

Patton, Anthony, 1969

Practical LotusScript / Anthony Patton

p. cm.

ISBN 1-884777-76-7 (alk. paper)

1. LotusScript (Computer program language) I. Title.

QA76.73.L66P38 1999

OO5.36—DC21 99-13034

CIP

Manning Publications Co.
32 Lafayette Place
Greenwich, CT 06830

Copyeditor: Elizabeth Martin
Typesetter: Dottie Marsico
Cover designer: Leslie Haimes

Printed in the United States of America

4 5 6 7 8 9 10 – VHG – 03 02 01 00

For the three women who have been there every step of the way:
Vickie (my true love),
Mammaw (happy 86th),
and most of all Mom.

Thank you for your patience, guidance, understanding, and listening.

contents

preface xvii

how this book is organized xviii

Author Online xx

special thanks xxi

1 Lotus Notes integrated development environment 1

1.1 Chapter objectives 2

1.2 Elements of the IDE 2
Colors 4, LotusScript Help 4, Errors 5, Debugging 5, Importing/Exporting 7, Printing 8, Limitations 8

1.3 Chapter summary 8

1.4 Chapter review 8

2 LotusScript basics—the foundation 11

2.1 Chapter objectives 12

2.2 Variables 13
Data Type Minimum/Maximum Value 13, Declaring and using variables 13, Constants 14, Explicit/Implicit 14, Options 15,

Converting from one type to another 16, The special variable type: Variant 17, Determining the type of a variable 17

2.3 Indentifiers 18

2.4 Looping 19

For 19, Do 20, While 21, Forall 22

2.5 Other methods to affect code execution 22

If 22, Select Case 23, Stopping execution 23, Goto 24

2.6 Interacting with the user 25

Print 25, MessageBox 25, InputBox 28

2.7 Commenting your code 29

2.8 Strings 29

Mid(String2Change, starting_position, optional_length) = String2GetCharacters 30, UCase/LCase(string) 30, Len(String) 31, Trim/LTrim/RTrim(String) 31, Left(String)/Right(String) 32, Instr(optional_starting_point, string1, string2, optional_compare_method) 32

2.9 Format function 33

2.10 Predefined constants 34

2.11 UnderScore (continuation) 34

2.12 Chapter summary 35

2.13 Chapter review 35

3 Functions and subroutines 37

3.1 Chapter objectives 38

3.2 Functions 38

3.3 Subroutines 40

Using subroutines 41, Creating your own function/subroutines 41, Built-in subs/functions 41

3.4 Scope/visibility 42

3.5 Chapter summary 44

3.6 Chapter review 44

4 Objects: working with classes 45

4.1 Chapter objectives 46

4.2 What is an object or class? 46
Dot notation 47, Defining your own classes 48

4.3 Designing classes 48
Me 49, Creating the class 49, With ... End With 50, Constructors and destructors 51, Using classes, creating objects 52, Delete 53, Is, IsA, and IsObject 53, Garbage collection 54, Property (Get/Set) 54, Arrays of objects 55

4.4 Front-end/back-end classes 56
Front-end classes 57, NotesUIWorkspace 57, NotesUIDocument 57, Back-end classes 57, NotesSession 57, NotesDatabase 58, NotesView 58, NotesDocument 58

4.5 Chapter example 59

4.6 Chapter summary 60

4.7 Chapter review 61

5 *Working with arrays, lists, collections, and items 63*

5.1 Chapter objectives 64

5.2 Arrays 64
Forall 65, LotusScript statements 66, Dynamic arrays 67, Multidimension arrays 69, Variation 70, Limitations 71

5.3 Lists 71
ListTag 71

5.4 NotesDocumentCollection 74

5.5 Working with response documents 76
Number of documents 77, Traversing a collection 77, Refining a collection 78

5.6 NotesItem 79
HasItem 81

5.7 Chapter example 82

5.8 Chapter summary 84

5.9 Chapter review 84

6 *Working with files 85*

6.1 Chapter objectives 86

6.2 Opening 86
Freefile 87

6.3 Closing 88

6.4 Reading/writing 89
Reading 89, Writing 89, EOF (filenumber) 90, LOF (filenumber) 90, LOC (filenumber) 90

6.5 Sequential access 91

6.6 Random access 94

6.7 Binary access 97

6.8 Directories 98
Dir 98, CurDrive, ChDrive, CurDir, ChDir 100, More LotusScript for working with files 101

6.9 NotesDBDirectory class 102
Methods 102

6.10 Platforms 104

6.11 Chapter example 105

6.12 Chapter summary 107

6.13 Chapter review 107

7 Error processing and activity logging 109

7.1 Chapter objectives 110

7.2 Error trapping 110
Resume 111, Handling specific errors 111, Handling user-defined errors 112, Checking objects before referencing 112, More detailed error messages 113, Err, Erl, and Error 113, Scope 114, Logging activity 114

7.3 NotesLog 115

7.4 Setting up the NotesLog object 117
Logging to a Notes database 117, Logging to a text file 118, Logging via email 118, Actions 119

7.5 Errors 119
Logging script activity via the agent log 120

7.6 Chapter summary 122

7.7 Chapter review 122

8 Events 123

8.1 Chapter objectives 124

8.2 Initialize 124

8.3 Terminate 124

8.4 Forms/subforms 125
PostOpen 125, QueryOpen 126, QuerySave 127, QueryClose 128, PostRecalc 128, QueryModeChange 128, PostModeChange 129, WebQueryOpen 129, WebQuerySave 130

8.5 Fields 130
Entering 130, Exiting 130

8.6 Database (located in the database script) 131
PostOpen 131, QueryDocumentDelete 131, PostDocumentDelete 132, QueryDocumentUndelete 132, QueryClose 132

8.7 Action/button/hotspot 132
ObjectExecute 132, Click 132

8.8 Views/folders 133
QueryOpen 133, PostOpen 133, QueryOpenDocument 133, QueryRecalc 133, QueryAddToFolder 133, QueryPaste 134, PostPaste 134, QueryClose 134

8.9 Agents 134

8.10 Creating your own events 134
The flow of events 136

8.11 Chapter summary 140

8.12 Chapter review 140

9 Working with the ACL 141

9.1 Chapter objectives 142

9.2 Seven levels of access in the ACL. 142
Manager 142, Designer 142, Editor 142, Author 143, Reader 143, Depositor 143, No Access 143

9.3 NotesACL class 146

9.4 NotesACLEntry Class 147

9.5 Roles 150

9.6 UniformAccess 153

9.7 Chapter summary 153

9.8 Chapter review 154

10 NotesItem 155

10.1 Chapter objectives 156

10.2 NotesItem class 156

Creating items 156, Removing an item 157, Copying an item 158, Checking for a value 160

10.3 NotesItem object and its values 161

GetFirstItem 161, GetItemValue 161, Checking Values 162, Other properties 162, NotesRichTextItem 163, Accessing 164

10.4 Working with text 166

NotesRichTextStyle 167

10.5 Chapter summary 171

10.6 Chapter review 171

11 Embedded objects and OLE 173

11.1 Chapter objectives 174

11.2 Attachments 174

Creating an attachment 174

11.3 OLE 179

Linking 180, Embedding 180, OLE Automation 180

11.4 Creating embedded OLE objects 181

Creating an object 182, FYI 184

11.5 Creating a linked object 184

Editing an object 184

11.6 Deleting objects 185

11.7 Chapter summary 186

11.8 Chapter review 187

12 Office 97 189

12.1 Chapter objectives 190

12.2 Object browser revisited 190

12.3 Microsoft Office 190

Microsoft Word 191, Microsoft Excel 196, Microsoft PowerPoint 200, Microsoft Outlook 200

12.4 Performance considerations 203

12.5 Accessing Lotus Notes from Visual Basic 204

12.6 Chapter summary 205

12.7 Chapter review 205

13 Searching 207

13.1 Chapter objectives 208

13.2 Full-text indexing 208
Results 208, Search string rules 209, Logical operators 209, Trimming a collection 211

13.3 Searching a view 211
FTSearch 211, GetAllDocumentsByKey 212, GetDocumentByKey 213

13.4 Searching a database 213
FTSearch/UnprocessedFTSearch 213, Search/UnprocessedSearch 215, Creating a full-text index 216

13.5 Chapter summary 217

13.6 Chapter review 217

14 Reports 219

14.1 Chapter objectives 220

14.2 Reports as documents 220
Email 222, Scheduled 223, Selective/custom reports 223, MessageBox 224, Form as a Front-End 224, Newsletter 230

14.3 Chapter summary 233

14.4 Chapter review 233

15 LotusScript data objects 235

15.1 Chapter objectives 236

15.2 Domino.Connect 236
LS:DO 237, ODBC 237

15.3 SQL 238
SELECT 238, FROM 238, WHERE 238

15.4 ODBCConnection 239

15.5 ODBCQuery 241

15.6 ODBCResultSet 241

15.7 Handling errors 242
On Error 244

15.8 Accessing data in a result set 244
15.9 Adding/deleting records 246
15.10 Domino.Connect 248
15.11 NotesSQL 248
15.12 Chapter summary 249
15.13 Chapter review 249

16 Working with date/time values 251

16.1 Chapter objectives 252
16.2 LotusScript 252
16.3 Extracting portions of time/date values 253
16.4 NotesDateTime class 255
16.5 Methods 256
Creating a NotesDateTime object 259, NotesDateRange class 260, Year 2000 issues 261, NotesInternational class 264, Properties 264
16.6 Chapter summary 266
16.7 Chapter review 267

17 Working outside the Domino/Notes environment 269

17.1 Chapter objectives 270
17.2 Shell 270
Declare 272, Windows 95/NT 273, ActivateApp 274, Evaluate 275
17.3 Chapter summary 277
17.4 Chapter review 277

18 LotusScript and the Web 279

18.1 Chapter objectives 280
18.2 Print 280
18.3 Browsers 280
18.4 Environment variables 281
DocumentContext 282
18.5 Query_String 283
Events 286, WebQueryOpen 287, WebQuerySave 287, Executing agents 287, Web Navigator database(s) 287

18.6 Chapter summary 288
18.7 Chapter review 288

19 Input validation, NotesAgent class, and script libraries 291
19.1 Chapter objectives 292
19.2 Validation 292
Input validation 292, QuerySave event 292, Field exit event 293, Unique values 294, ComputeWithForm 295
19.3 NotesAgent class 296
19.4 RunOnServer 298
19.5 Script libraries 299
Using script libraries 300
19.6 Chapter summary 300
19.7 Chapter review 301

20 Notes 5.0 303
20.1 Chapter objectives 304
20.2 Integrated development environment 305
Performance 306, Forward references 308, Variable types 309, Threads 309, Classes 309, NotesOutline 309, NotesOutlineEntry 311, NotesOutline class methods 312, NotesOutlineEntry class properties 313, NotesUIWorkspace 313, User interaction 314, File open 314, PickLists 314, Prompt 315, Spelling checker 316, NotesDocumentCollection 317, Generating HTML 318, NotesReplication 318, Replicating a database 320, NotesRichTextTab 321, NotesRichTextParagraphStyle 321, NotesViewEntryCollection 323, NotesUIView 324, NotesUIDatabase 325, NotesAgent 325, NotesACL/NotesACLEntry 326, Events 326, View 326, Document 327
20.3 Other enhancements 327
20.4 Chapter summary 327
20.5 Chapter review 328

21 Working with NotesPump 329
21.1 Chapter objectives 330
21.2 NotesPump classes 330
NPActivity 331, Creating an NPActivtiy 331, Deleting an NPActivity

object 332, NPConnect 332, Methods 332, Creating an NPConnect object 333, Deleting an NPConnect object 333

21.3 NPFieldList 333
Properties 333, Methods 333, Creating an NPFieldList object 334, Deleting an NPFieldList object 334

21.4 NPField 336
Methods 336, Creating an NPField object 336, Deleting an NPField object 337

21.5 Data types 341

21.6 Conclusion 341

appendix A Notes/Domino constants 343

appendix B Notes/Domino classes 358

appendix C LotusScript keywords 474

index 481

preface

As a developer with a background in more traditional programming languages, I was amazed to find that Lotus Notes had only a macro language in version 3 at the time I was introduced to it. It is a truly powerful product, and its strength is amplified by LotusScript which has opened up many more opportunities to build rich, robust, successful applications.

LotusScript enables developers from other environments to feel more comfortable. Its Basic syntax is so easy to use and learn that Visual Basic (VB) developers can jump right in. I say developer as opposed to programmer, because you have to be a true developer to build Notes/Domino applications. You have to know the ins and outs of the environment as well as the user requirements.

When I first began to delve deeper and deeper into Notes development I noticed there was an enormous lack of in-depth information. Yes, there are a number of books that give good introductions, but where do you go from there?

My learning process involved interactions with experienced Notes developers, VB programmers, Internet Usenet discussion groups, and various websites, hammering home the axiom: the more you learn, the less you know.

The purpose of this book is to give an overview of the core LotusScript language that is used throughout the Lotus family of products, and cover in detail power programming with LotusScript in the Notes environment.

how this book is organized

The book begins with an overview of the core LotusScript language and ends with Notes 5.0 enhancements. Appendices provide additional information.

Chapter 1 provides an overview of the Notes development environment.

Chapter 2 provides an introduction to the core LotusScript language. Looping, variables, scope, user interaction, comments, and strings are covered in detail.

Chapter 3 gives details on defining functions and subroutines.

Chapter 4 provides an in-depth look at object-oriented principles: objects, methods, and properties. Also, an introduction to the basic Notes classes is included.

Chapter 5 covers arrays and lists in LotusScript.

Chapter 6 provides the details on working with files. The different types of access, removing files, creating files, and database properties are covered.

Chapter 7 deals with handling errors and logging script activity.

Chapter 8 gives an overview of the various events in the Notes/Domino development environment.

Chapter 9 details working with database Access Control Lists.

Chapter 10 covers the NotesItem and NotesRichTextItem classes.

Chapter 11 shows how to work with embedded objects. This includes links, file attachments, and object linking and embedding (OLE) objects.

Chapter 12 shows how to integrate Lotus Notes and Microsoft Office 97.

Chapter 13 deals with searching Notes/Domino databases and handling the results.

Chapter 14 covers reporting techniques that can be used in the Notes/Domino environment.

Chapter 15 provides details on the LotusScript Data Object (LS:DO) which covers accessing Notes data through Object Database Connectivity (ODBC) and accessing external data through ODBC.

Chapter 16 covers working with Time/Date values.

Chapter 17 covers working with the Windows environment, outside of the Notes/Domino environment.

Chapter 18 deals with the Internet. LotusScript can be used with web-based clients. This chapter shows you how.

Chapter 19 ties up loose ends. It covers form validation, the NotesAgent class, and Script libraries.

Chapter 20 gives a scoop on the enhancements to LotusScript 4.0 and the Notes 5.0 environment.

Chapter 21 provides an introduction to programming Lotus NotesPump in LotusScript.

Appendix A provides the details of the constant files.

Appendix B gives a detailed list of the Notes/Domino classes with their respective properties and methods.

Appendix C provides a list of LotusScript reserved words.

Author Online

Purchase of *Practical LotusScript* includes free access to a private Internet forum where you can make comments about the book, ask technical questions, and receive help from the author and from other Swing users. To access the forum, point your Web browser to http://www.manning.com/Patton. There you will be able to subscribe to the forum. This site also provides information on how to access the forum once you are registered, what kind of help is available, and the rules of conduct on the forum.

All source code for the examples presented in *Practical LotusScript* is available to purchasers from the Manning website. The URL http://www.manning.com/Patton includes a link to the source code files.

special thanks

I want to thank Mom for her determination and perseverance, and Vickie for her constant encouragement and timely criticism.

There are so many others who have influenced my contributions to this book. This includes all of my clients past and present, colleagues, friends, and family. I want to thank Dave for introducing me to Notes, Bill for giving me a reason to leave, Mark for my first "real" job and programming experience, Jim for showing me how to schmooze, Dan for giving me another reason to leave, Kevin for his constant friendship, Brad for the moving target, Joe for his meticulous planning, Trevor for my first writing opportunity, and Chip for yet another moving target. Lastly, my family made me who I am today (so blame them): Becky (my wonderful sister), Kenny (my crazy brother), David (another crazy brother), Melanie, Steven, Tim, Megan, Andy, Alex, Jennifer, D.J., Nicole, Vickie, Donald (yes, him too), Jerry, Mary Lynn, Bobby, and Lil.

Also, I want to thank Dan, Paul, Rob, Andrea, Amy, Delores, Pam, Rick, Steve, Scott, Lori, Bobbie, Brook, George, Lee, Tonya, Don, Bruce, Bill, Tim, Ted (lotsa questions), Larry, David, Randall, Charles, Lenny, Moses, Darren, and Julius. There are so many people to mention, so I hope I did not forget anyone … if I did, I am sure they will let me know.

A number of individuals took the time to proofread the manuscript at various stages. Their feedback proved to be invaluable. This includes: Mark Boon, Anthony Davis, Michael Dennehy, Thomas Duff, Tom Faulkner, Michael Fisher, Kevin Hakanson, Dean Moore, John P. Pollard, Roselito de los Reyes, Karl Roberts, Mark Staines, Gerry Suchy, Paul Webb, Eric Wright, and Michael Zischeck.

A special thanks to the wonderful staff at Manning Publications: Dottie Marsico, Mary Piergies, Ted Kennedy, Elizabeth Martin, Helen Trimes, Lee Fitzpatrick, and Marjan Bace. I am especially grateful to Marjan for giving me the opportunity to create what you are reading.

Finally, a big hug to Branden for making me smile and providing so many laughs. The sky is the limit!

C H A P T E R   1

Lotus Notes integrated development environment

1.1 Chapter objectives 2

1.2 Elements of the IDE 2

1.3 Chapter summary 8

1.4 Chapter review 8

1.1 *Chapter objectives*

- Familiarize yourself with the script pane
- Get acquainted with the class browser
- Identify default colors and what they represent in the script pane
- Change the colors
- Disable/enable LotusScript debugging
- Set breakpoints
- Watch variables
- Step through a script
- Export a script
- Import a script
- Print a script
- Identify script limitations

The integreated development environment (IDE) included in the Lotus Notes client includes features that developers love, but lacks numerous items that many truly want and/or need. The same environment is used to develop scripts/agents with @Functions/@Commands, predefined Simple Actions, Java, and LotusScript. The selection of a radio button (Simple Action, Function, Script, or Java) determines the type of code being developed. The options in the bottom pane are driven by the selection. If Script (LotusScript) is selected, you are presented with the script pane, event drop-down list, checkbox to enable/disable class browser, and a box at the bottom of the screen that shows errors encountered during development.

1.2 *Elements of the IDE*

The top box, titled Name, allows the developer to appropriately name his/her agent. It appears only when developing agents (see figure 1.1). The same is true for the *When should this agent run* and *Which document(s) should it act on* boxes. These allow the developer to choose when and on what an agent runs. The Shared check box signals whether this agent is for private use (not checked) or available to all (checked).

The bottom of the IDE is the same no matter what type of script you are creating. It could be an agent, `QueryClose` event on a form, or a database script. It is commonly called the script pane (figure 1.2). The very bottom of the window is where errors appear during your development. It is a drop-down list, so there can be more than one error.

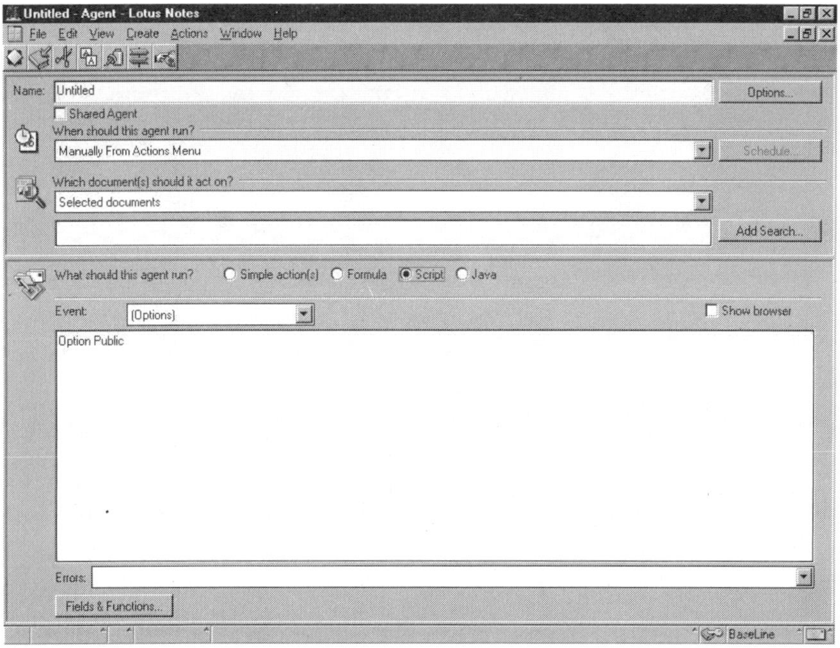

Figure 1.1 Notes 4.6 IDE

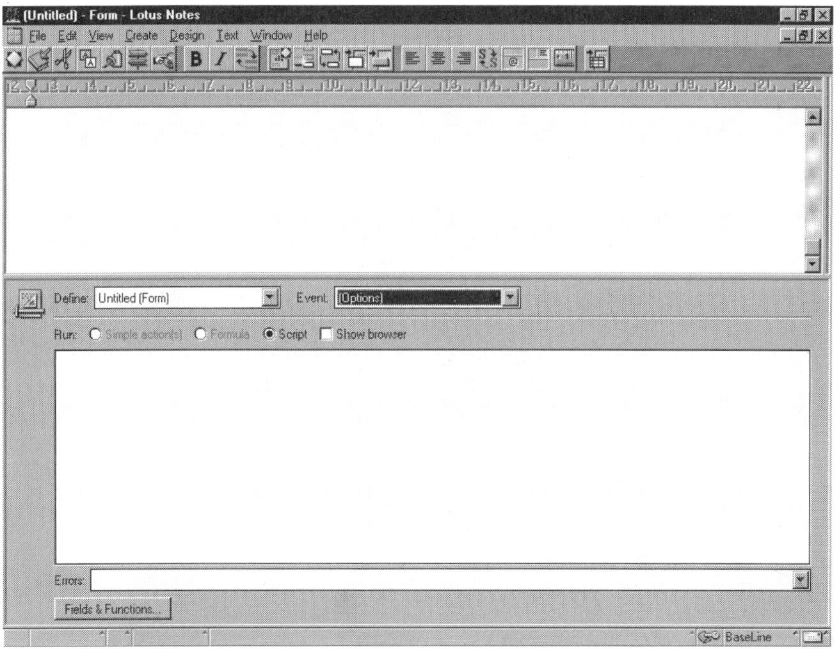

Figure 1.2 The script pane as seen when developing a form

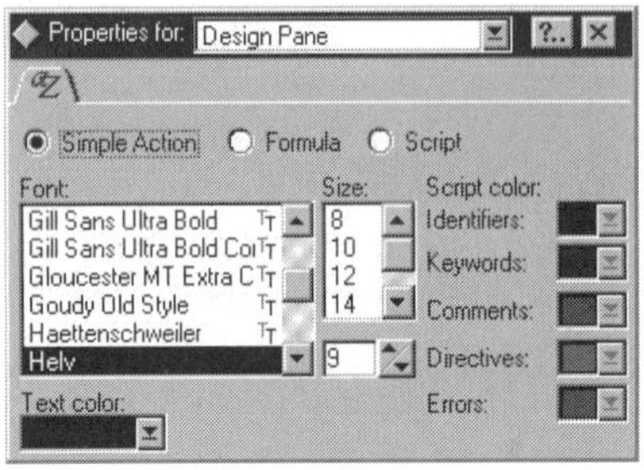

Figure 1.3
Design Pane design properties

1.2.1 Colors

The colors used in the IDE default to black for identifiers (items created by the user). Reserved LotusScript keywords are blue, comments are green, directives (%Include) and errors are red. Right-click the script pane and the properities for the design pane appear (figure 1.3). Colors, font size, and face can be selected if changes are desired.

1.2.2 LotusScript Help

The browser checkbox (figure 1.4) allows the developer to quickly look up syntax for the LotusScript language. Select the check box and the browser pane appears. It works just like a view with twisties that expand/collapse the choices. The drop-down list, which drives the browser pane, is just above the browser pane and lets you view different sets of items. You can select All, Notes Classes, Notes Constants, Notes Subs and Functions, Notes Variables, and OLE Classes.

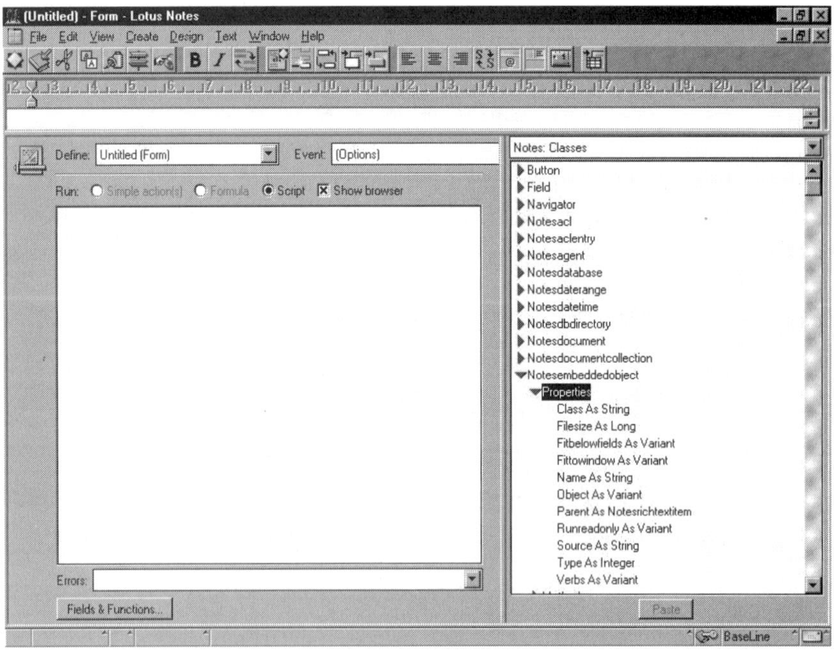

Figure 1.4 Browser pane

Once an item has been selected (highlighted) in the browser, F1 opens the Notes Help database to the topic highlighted (if Notes Help is installed). Double-clicking on an item places it into the design pane.

1.2.3 Errors

The environment does not allow a script to be saved until all syntax errors have been resolved. Syntax errors are comprised of improper use of any aspect of the language including the mispelling of statements, missing parentheses, or illegal comparisons. Remember, errors appear in red in the script pane. The error drop-down list (just below the script pane) lists all errors in the order encountered and describes each. Clicking the down arrow expands the drop-down list to show additional errors (if there is more than one). The format of the error box is:

```
<Object Name> : <Section/Event> : <Line Number> : <Error Message>
```

An error in the `Initialize` event could appear like this:

Example 2.1

```
LSTest : Initialize : 3: Unexpected: Chr; Expected: End-of-statement; _
  Operator;,
```

Explanation

There was an error in line 3 of the script LSTest in the `Initialize` event. The problem line of code looked like this:

```
Messagebox "Hello"  Chr(10) & Chr(13) & "How are you?"
```

The line is missing a concatenation character (&) after "Hello", so the script didn't know what to do. Adding the proper character (&) fixes this error.

The object name corresponds to the section/event that contains the script. Section is the section of code containing the error (Initialize, Declarations, Click, etc.). The error number is an integer that corresponds to the error description. The code causing the problem shows where the error occurred in the highlighted (in red) line. The error box is not always helpful, because the description can be a little arcane. It does show where the error occurred, and double-clicking on the error in the error box highlights the questionable line in the design pane. Logical or program design errors are caught during the testing and/or debugging phase.

1.2.4 Debugging

The environment allows the developer to debug a script by stepping through its execution, watching variables, and setting breakpoints. Debugging is enabled/disabled from the File drop-down menu in the Lotus Notes client (File | Tools | Debug LotusScript). Once this option is selected, every script is opened for the user to watch its execution.

The debugging option allows the user to step through a script (move through the program one line at a time), step over a call to subroutine/function (the script will not step into and through the code in the function or subroutine), stop execution, or continue, which runs the script to the end or any breakpoints that are encountered. *Breakpoints* are points in a script where a developer wants the script to stop execution until he/she says continue. Breakpoints are set by double-clicking on a line of code. Once it has been double-clicked, a red ball/circle appears to the left of the line. The line can be double-clicked again to turn it off, at which time the red ball/circle appears with a line through it. Once breakpoints are set, they appear in the breakpoint tab in the debugging mode of the design pane. It shows all breakpoints set with line number and where it is defined (subroutine/function). Also, breakpoint functionality can be achieved with a `Stop` statement.

Breakpoints, as I said earlier, are points in a script where execution stops. The developer can set breakpoints, click the Continue button in debugging mode, and the script will run until a breakpoint or an error occurs. Once it has stopped at a breakpoint, the developer can step through the rest of the code, select the Continue button, or set more breakpoints and continue. Breakpoints can be set only on code that is executed. They cannot be set on comments or `Dim` statements.

Watching variable activity (figure 1.5) is another requirement for developers. We need to watch how objects/variables are manipulated during the execution of a script.

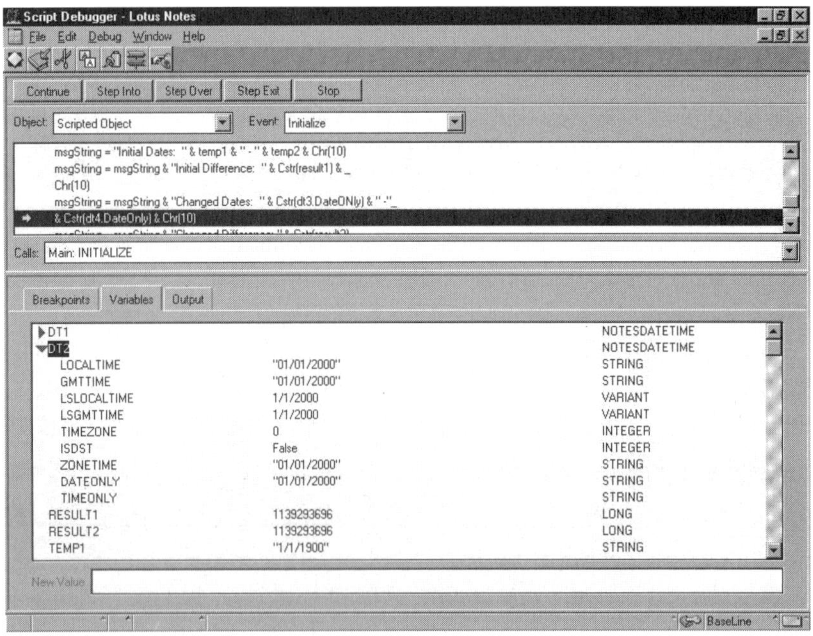

Figure 1.5 Watching variables while debugging a script

The variables tab in the debugging mode of the design pane shows all variables that are defined within the scope of the current object and their values, if any.

The last tab is labeled output. It receives any output from `Print` statements. This allows the developer to place strategic `Print` statements (for debugging) within a script and this pane will show their output.

1.2.5 Importing/Exporting

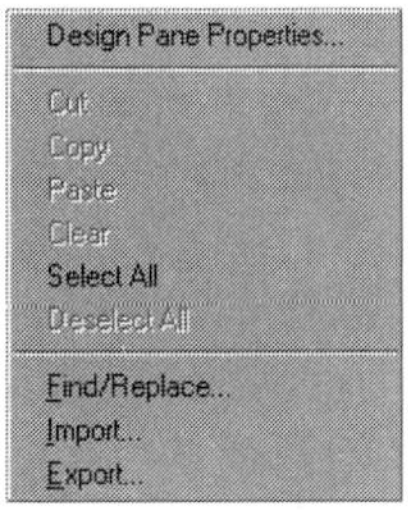

Figure 1.6 Script pane pop-up

Code can be exported from the script pane to a text file. Also, code can be imported into the environment from a text file. Right-click anywhere within the script pane, and a pop-up menu (figure 1.6) appears with the import and export choices.

Selecting Import presents the user with a file dialog box to select the file to import. Once that has been selected, the file is brought into the environment. If there are any conflicts between code in the import file and the current script (duplicate objects, methods, events, etc.), the user is presented with the Import Option (figure 1.7) dialog box.

This box describes the conflict and allows the user to replace this occurrence (Yes), all occurrences (Yes to All), skip the conflict (No), or stop the import process (Stop). Once the process is completed, the imported code appears in the script pane. It is not final until the script has been saved.

Export is the reverse of the import process. Select Export from the Script pane pop-up. Once again, a file dialog box is presented that allows the user to signify where to save the exported file and to give it a name. The standard extension for text files containing LotusScript code is .lss, but any extension can be used. Make sure you remember it. Once the path and name have been specified, the option to export the Current Object, Current Section, or All objects is presented in a MessageBox (figure 1.8).

The Current Object option exports everything associated with the currently open section of code. For example, if an action button's click method is currently open and the current object is exported, everything associated with the action button is exported. This would include the Options, Declarations, Initialize, Terminate, and Click sections along with any user-defined subroutines and/or functions.

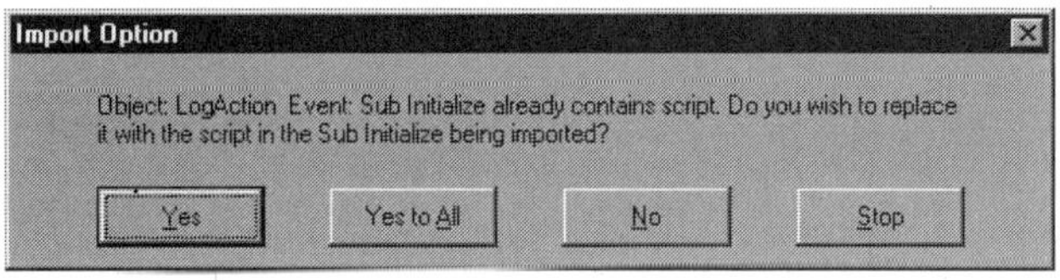

Figure 1.7 Import options

Figure 1.8 Export options

The Current Section option exports what is currently open in the script pane. If the same action button's click method is currently open, the click section will be the only part of the script that is exported.

The All Objects selection exports everything associated with the currently open object. The object can be a script library, form, agent, subform, view, or database script. All sections and user-defined function/subroutines are exported.

1.2.6 Printing

The Export option is used to overcome a weakness in the development environment: lack of support for printing code. Developers love to get a printout of their code so they can trace the logic; besides, staring at a computer screen is very tiring on the eyes. Once the code has been exported to a text file, it can be opened and printed from any text editor such as the MS-DOS-based editor, Windows Notepad, or any word processing software.

1.2.7 Limitations

In addition to printing, the development environment has many limitations that must be recognized by the developer. As previously stated, no direct printing of scripts is supported. Also, there is no easy way to look at all of the scripts/code included in an application. Domino/Notes Release 5.0 will facilitate this through the design synopsis. The size of a script and arrays is limited to 64K. The use of script libraries is sluggish because they must be loaded when they are used.

1.3 Chapter summary

The development environment included in the Lotus Notes client is not the most full-featured development environment, but it has steadily improved with each incremental release of Domino/Notes. Many of the limitations discussed are being addressed in Domino/Notes 5.0, including support for the development of Java code.

1.4 Chapter review

- The script pane is used to develop Simple Actions, Formulas, Scripts, and Java code.
- A class pane is included in the development environment for quick look up of LotusScript syntax.

- LotusScript code can be debugged by enabling the Debug LotusScript option from the File | Tools menu. It is disabled the same way.
- Debugging gives the options of stepping through code, stepping over subroutines/functions, or stopping execution.
- Breakpoints can be set during debugging by double-clicking on a line of code.
- The debugging pane allows the watching of variables through the variable tab.
- Exporting/importing script facilitates code reuse and printing.
- Syntax errors appear in the error box just below the script pane during code design.
- Script size is limited to 64K.

CHAPTER 2

LotusScript basics—the foundation

2.1 Chapter objectives 12
2.2 Variables 13
2.3 Indentifiers 18
2.4 Looping 19
2.5 Other methods to affect code execution 22
2.6 Interacting with the user 25
2.7 Commenting your code 29
2.8 Strings 29
2.9 Format function 33
2.10 Predefined constants 34
2.11 UnderScore (continuation) 34
2.12 Chapter summary 35
2.13 Chapter review 35

2.1 Chapter objectives

- Introduce syntax of the LotusScript language
- Variable types
- Constants
- Options section
- Declarations section
- Converting data from one type to another
- Public/Private/Static identifiers
- `For` loops
- `Do` loops
- `While` loops
- `Forall`
- Branching (If/Then and Select Case)
- Displaying messages
- User input
- Commenting your code
- Strings
- The Format function
- Predefined constants
- Continuation

Learning a Basic-like language is much easier than grasping arcane languages like C or C++. Basic has English-like statements. It was designed with ease of use in mind. This has led to the enormous popularity of languages like QBasic and Visual Basic from Microsoft Corporation.

The syntax of LotusScript is almost identical to Visual Basic which makes it easy for Visual Basic developers to move to LotusScript although they still have to learn the environment. Working with Lotus Notes/Domino requires a thorough understanding of such elements as views, databases, forms, and agents.

This chapter gives an overview of the basics of developing with LotusScript and Lotus Notes/Domino. If you are familiar with Visual Basic, you may want to skim the material. You may be able to skip this section if you are already familiar with the environment, but that decision is up to you.

2.2 Variables

LotusScript has seven data types: variant, integer, double, long, single, string, and currency. Integer and long hold numbers with no decimal places. Single and double store decimal numbers (real numbers); string variables store text and currency holds monetary values.

2.2.1 Data Type Minimum/Maximum Value

LotusScript defines the following range of values for each numeric data type:

Table 2.1

Date Type	Minimum Value	Maximum Value
Integer	-32,768	32,767
Long	-2,147,483,648	2,147,483,647
Single	-3.402823E+38	3.402823E+38
Double	-1.7976931348623158E+308	1.7976931348623158E+308
Currency	-922,337,203,685,477.5666	922,337,203,685,477.5666

The string type is limited as well. The size of a string value is limited to 64K, and a string literal is limited to 32K.

Note E represents scientific notation, it signals the number of leading (-) or trailing (+) zeroes.)

2.2.2 Declaring and using variables

The Dim keyword (dimension) is used to declare a variable. Once the variable has been declared, it can be used.

```
Dim variable_name As variable_type
```

Variables can be declared anywhere within a script. The As keyword and variable_type are not required when declaring variables of the type variant. Variant, a special type of variable, will be addressed in an upcoming section.

To declare an integer called index:

```
Dim index As Integer
```

To declare a string called name, and set its value:

```
Dim Name As String
Name = "Tony Patton"
```

Multiple variables of the same type can be declared on one line (they are separated by commas), but the type of each must be included.

```
Dim index1 As Integer, index2 As Integer, index3 As Integer
Dim Name1 As String, Name2 As String
```

Note If multiple variables are declared on one line and any of the variables is missing a type declaration, it is declared as a `Variant` data type. `Variant` is the default data type. For instance, the following line

```
Dim var1, var2 As String
```

declares `var1` as a `Variant` and `var2` as a String variable.

2.2.3 Constants

Constants are variables whose value does not change; it is constant. The keyword CONST is used to define a constant in a script.

Note LotusScript constants are usually defined in all capitals.

```
Const CONSTANT_NAME = constant_value
```

There are a number of built-in constants in LotusScript:

Table 2.2

EMP	The initial value for a variable of the type Variant.
FALSE	Returned by comparison or logical operations; it has the numeric value of 0.
NOTHING	Objects are initialized to Nothing. This is used extensively in loops or condition statements when working with Notes objects.
NULL	A variant variable that has no data. It can be used to retrieve memory occupied by a variant by setting the Variant to this.
PI	3.14159265358979...
TRUE	Returned by comparison or logical operations; it has the numeric value of -1.

2.2.4 Explicit/Implicit

By default, LotusScript allows a variable to be referenced/used before it has been declared. If this happens, the variable is declared as a `variant`. This can lead to messy code. This type of *freedom* is called implicit declarations. The developer is allowed to implicity use a variable whenever he or she likes.

Explicit declaration is the opposite of implicit. It demands that a variable be declared before it is ever used. That is, it must have a line with a `Dim` statement that declares it. This leads to much more readable and manageable code. The `Option Explicit` line can be entered into the Options section of a script to enforce explicit declarations. `Implicit` declarations is the default.

```
[Options]
Option Explicit
```

If a script is set up to use explicit declarations, a compile-time error is generated if a variable is referenced before it is declared.

Example 2.1

```
[Options]
Option Explicit

[Initialize]
Sub Initialize
     For x = 1 To 10
          Msgbox x
     Next
End Sub
```

Explanation

Attempting to save this script generates a compile-time error. The Errors box contains the following statement:

```
ExplicitTest: Initialize:  2:  Variable not declared:  X
```

- The name of the script is ExplicitTest
- The error occurred in the `Initialize` event.
- The error number is 2.
- The error is `Variable not declared: X`.

The variable `X` must be declared before it is used as the index in the `For` loop.

2.2.5 Options

In addition to setting implicit/explicit variable declarations, the options section of a script allows other items to be set up. The default lower bound for an array is zero (just like languages such as C or Java), but the `Option Base` statement is used to reset the lower bound.

```
Option Base X
```

This statement sets the default lower bound for arrays to the number X. Chapter 5 covers arrays in more detail. `Option Compare` is used to configure the way string comparisons are handled. The following list shows its various formats.

- `Option Compare Binary` says that string comparisons will be performed at the bit level. A case-sensitive, pitch sensitive comparison will be performed. This is used alone, no other `Option Compare` statements can exist.

- `Option Compare Case/NoCase` allows you to specify if string comparisons will be case-sensitive. This can be used with other `Option Compare` statements, but only one option compare `Case/NoCase` can exist.
- `Option Compare Pitch/NoPitch` specifies if pitch-sensitive comparisons are used. This can be used with other `Option Compare` statements, but only one `Pitch/NoPitch` can exist.

`Option Public`

If `Explicit` variable declarations are used, the `Option Public` statement tells the system that each variable declared is `Public` unless otherwise specified. This overrides the system default of `Private`.

`Option Declare`

Another way to signal `Explicit` variable declarations is the use of `Option Declare`. This tells the system that implicit declarations are not allowed. It performs the same function as `Option Explicit`.

2.2.6 Converting from one type to another

LotusScript includes a number of functions to handle the conversion of one data type to another.

- *`CCur`(number or string)* Converts numeric value rounded to a four decimal place currency value
- *`CDat`(number or string)* Converts value to a date/time value
- *`CDbl`(number or string)* Converts numeric value to a double value
- *`CInt`(number or string)* Converts numeric value to a rounded integer value
- *`CLng`(number or string)* Converts numeric value to long value
- *`CSng`(number or string)* Converts numeric value to single value
- *`CStr`(number or string)* Converts value to a string value
- *`CVar`(any value)* Converts value to a variant value

Example 2.2

```
    Dim var1, var2 As Integer
    Dim var3 As Double
    Dim var4 As Currency
    Dim var5 As String
    var2 = 250
    var3 = 20.00
1   var4 = CCur(var2)
2   var1 = CInt(var3)
```

```
3    var5 = CStr(var2)
```

Explanation

1. The value of `var2` is converted to a currency value and stored in `var4`.
2. The value of `var3` is converted to an integer value and stored in `var1`.
3. The value of `var2` is converted to a string value and stored in `var5`.

2.2.7 The special variable type: Variant

If you are ever unsure of what type of data a variable may need to store, declare it as a `Variant`. `Variants` can store any type of variable but a user-defined type. It can store all types of numbers, string values, arrays, dates, lists, or objects. `Variant` is the default data type in the Notes environment. If a variable is defined with no type (`Dim` variable) or implicity used, it is set to a `Variant`. To declare a `Variant`:

```
Dim var
```
- or –
```
Dim var As Variant
```

If a variable is implicitly used, it is set to a `Variant`.

Note `Variants` require more resources than other data types. This includes memory, disk space, and processing time. Always specify a data type for variables whenever possible.

2.2.8 Determining the type of a variable

You may find yourself working with a `Variant` variable and need to know immediately what type of data it contains. This could occur for a number of reasons, but it is easily overcome. Two statements in LotusScript identify the type of value(s) stored in a `Variant` object: `DataType` and `TypeName`. Both accept the variable name and return the variable type. The difference lies in the format of the returned value. `DataType` returns an integer that corresponds to the data type, and `TypeName` returns a string identifying the type.

Example 2.3

```
1    Dim index
2    index = 2
3    Print DataType(index)
4    Print TypeName(index)
```

Details:

1. A `Variant` called `index` is declared
2. The `Variant` is set to the integer `2`.

3 The `DataType` statement is used to determine `Variant`'s data type. It prints `2` for integer.

4 The `TypeName` statement is used to determine `Variant`'s data type. It prints `INTEGER`.

The LotusScript online Help contains more details concerning the return values for both functions.

2.3 Indentifiers

Identifiers precede variable declarations to signal the visibility of the variable. The two types of visibility for variables in LotusScript are `Public` and `Private`. `Private` is the default identifier, and it is used if no identifier is specified. `Private` restricts access to a variable to the section of code in which it is defined. If a private variable is in a function or subroutine, it is only visible within that function or subroutine. On the other hand, `Public` opens a variable to everything.

The static keyword signals that a function/subroutine's local variables will retain their value(s) between calls to it. Normally, a variable defined in a function/subroutine will exist in memory only when the function/subroutine is accessed in the script.

Note Functions and subroutines are covered in chapter 4.

Example 2.4

```
1       Public varPublic
2       Private varPrivate
```

Explanation

1 The variable `varPublic` is declared as visible to everything in the script in which it is used.

2 The variable `varPrivate` is declared as visible to only those objects in its section of code.

Example 2.5

```
Static Public Sub TrackHits
   Private count As Integer
   count = count + 1
End Sub
```

Explanation

This function tracks the number of times an item is accessed. We don't want the counter reset each time the code is accessed, so the static keyword is used to make sure the variables will retain their values between calls.

1. The subroutine TrackHits is declared so that it can be accessed by all (`Public`) and the values of its local variables will be retained between calls to it (Static).
2. The local variable count is declared as an Integer.
3. The count variable is incremented each time the subroutine is accessed.

2.4 Looping

Four types of loops can be used in LotusScript: `For`, `Do`, `While`, and `Forall`.

2.4.1 For

The `For` loop allows you to execute a block of code a certain number of times.

Syntax

```
For [count variable] = [start value] to [end value] step [increment value]
  <block of code>
Next [count variable]
```

The count variable, start value, end value, and increment value are all numeric values. The step and its corresponding increment value are optional, as is the count variable on the next statement. Example 2.6 prints integers 1 through 5.

Example 2.6

```
For x = 1 to 5
       Print "x = " & x
Next x
```

Output

x=1

x=2

x=3

x=4

x=5

You will notice that implicit declarations are used, since the variable x is used before it is declared. Example 2.7 prints the multiples of two up to twenty.

Example 2.7

```
For x = 0 to 20 step 2
       Print "x = " & x
Next x
```

Output

x=0

x=2

x=4
x=6
x=8
x=10
x=12
x=14
x=16
x=18
x=20

The loop counts from 0 to 20, but it does so in increments of 2 (steps). `For` loops can be nested to achieve numerous results.

Example 2.8

```
For x = 1 to 2
      For y = 1 to 5
             Print "x = " & x " and y = " & y
Next y, x
```

Output

x= 1 and y= 1
x= 1 and y= 2
x= 1 and y= 3
x= 1 and y= 4
x= 1 and y= 5
x= 2 and y= 1
x= 2 and y= 2
x= 2 and y= 3
x= 2 and y= 4
x= 2 and y= 5

2.4.2 Do

The `Do` loop allows the execution of a block of code until a condition is met. Its main strength is in allowing the execution of code before a condition is checked. The `Do` statement is used in conjuction with the `While`, `Until`, and `Loop` statements. It has four variations:

1
```
Do While [condition]
   <block of code>
Loop
```

2
```
Do Until [condition]
    <block of code>
```

```
    Loop
```

3
```
    Do
        <block of code>
    Loop Until [condition]
```

4
```
    Do
        <block of code>
    Loop While [condition]
```

Example 2.9

```
Dim response As String
response = "Continue"
Do While (response <> "Done")
     response = InputBox$("Please enter response")
Loop
```

This loop will continue until the word Done is entered by the user. It could have been coded a different way.

Example 2.10

```
Do
     response = InputBox$("Please enter response.")
Until (response = "Done")
```

Example 2.10 accomplishes the same task, but with two fewer lines of code. The beauty of the `Do` loop lies in Example 2.10; it allows the execution of a block of code before a condition is checked. We had to initialize the variable in 2.9, but 2.10 allows us to let the user set the variable before it is checked.

2.4.3 While

The `While` loop executes a block of code until a condition is validated as `true`. The block of code in the loop begins with the `While` statement and ends with the `wend` statement.

```
While [condition]
     <code>
Wend
```

Examples 2.9 and 2.10 could have been coded using a `While` loop; it strongly resembles example 2.9.

Example 2.11

```
Dim response As String
response = ""
Whilc (rcoponoc <> "Donc")
    response = InputBox$("Please enter response.")
Wend
```

2.4.4 *Forall*

The `Forall` statement executes a block of code repeatedly for each item in an array or list. It has the following syntax:

```
Forall <variable> In <array/list name>
   <do something>
End Forall
```

Chapter 5 uses the `Forall` statement extensively.

2.5 *Other methods to affect code execution*

2.5.1 *If*

The `If` statement checks a condition first, and executes a block of code *if* the condition evaluates to `true`. It can be used to check a number of conditions with additional conditions contained in `ElseIf` statements, and a default action(s) contained in an `else` block. It has the following syntax:

```
If [condition] Then
   <code>
ElseIf [condition]
   <code>
Else
   <default action>
End If
```

There can be any number of `ElseIf` statements, but only one `If` and `Else`. The `else` condition is not required; there does not have to be a default action. The `If` loop differs in the fact that it is executed only one.

Example 2.12

```
Dim response As String
response = InputBox$("Please enter response.")
If (response = "1") Then
     Print "Reponse was 1."
ElseIf (response = "2") Then
     Print "Response was 2."
ElseIf (response = "3") Then
     Print "Response was 3."
Else
     Print "Response was neither 1, 2, or 3."
End If
```

Explanation

Example 2.12 accepts input from the user, and checks the input for certain values and performs certain actions depending on the value entered (or not entered).

2.5.2 *Select Case*

The `select case` statement mimics the behavior of the `if` statement. `Select case` will execute a block of code depending on the value of an expression. It has the following syntax:

```
Select Case variable
   Case condition :
      <statements to execute>
   Case Else
      <statements to execute>
End Select
```

Here is the select case representation of example 2.12.

Example 2.13

```
Dim response As String
response = InputBox$("Please enter response.")
Select Case response
   Case "1"   :  Print "Response was 1."
   Case "2"   :  Print "Response was 2."
   Case "3"   :  Print "Response was 3."
   Case Else :  Print "The response was neither 1, 2, or 3."
End Select
```

2.5.3 *Stopping execution*

The `Exit` and `End` statements are used to stop execution, but `Exit` stops execution of the current block of code and `end` stops the current script altogether. There are many variations of the `Exit` statement:

- `Exit Do`
- `Exit For`
- `Exit Forall`
- `Exit Function`
- `Exit Property`
- `Exit Sub`

Each stops execution of the loop that follows it. Of course, they are only valid if they are contained within the type of loop specified.

Example 2.14

```
For x = 1 to 10
   value = InputBox$("Enter a value.")
   If (value = "") Then
1     Exit For
```

```
   End If
Next x
```

Explanation

1 The script exits the `For` loop if a blank value is entered by the user.

2.5.4 Goto

No command has received more negative comments than the `Goto` statement. This statement allows the execution of a script to be transferred to another point in the script. Often it is linked to spaghetti code, but this is due to its use in procedural programming. The `Goto` can be a great aid in development if appropriately used.

Syntax

```
Goto <Label>
```

The label designates a point in a script. A label resides on its own line with a colon appended. It looks like this:

```
Handle_goto:
MsgBox "This was accessed with a goto statement."
```

Handle_goto: is a label. Once a label is defined, control can be transferred to that point in the script from anywhere else using a `Goto` statement. Many developers view the use of the `Goto` statement as bad programming, because it can make a program hard to read and debug. Of course, this is true if the `Goto` statement is used to jump all around a script. On the other hand, LotusScript requires that it be used when handling errors (see chapter 7).

Example 2.15

```
     response = InputBox$("Please enter a name.")
     If (response = "") Then
1       Goto No_Response
     End If
     ...
2    Exit Sub
3    No_Response:
        MsgBox "You entered a blank name.  Aborting...."
4    End
```

Explanation

1 If the response variable is empty, control is transferred to the section of code with the No_Response label.

2 The `Exit Sub` statements are placed before the No_Response label, so that its contents are executed only when it is called.

3 The No_Response label.

4 The script ends.

2.6 *Interacting with the user*

Numerous situations arise where user input is needed, or information must be displayed to the user. LotusScript provides the `Print`, `MessageBox`, and `InputBox` statements to handle these situations.

2.6.1 *Print*

LotusScript defines the `Print` statement as sending output to the screen. In the Notes/Domino environment, the `Print` statement sends its output to the status line at the bottom of the Notes Workspace. If it is used in scheduled agents, the output is sent to the Notes Log. Finally, when used with web-related applications, it sends the output to the web browser (so it acts like the definition in LotusScript Help). Chapter 18 gives more details about interacting with web browser clients. The format is very simple.

```
Print <expression>
```

Expression can be a string, number, or date/time value. `Print` is great for keeping users informed when a script is running in the foreground.

2.6.2 *MessageBox*

MessageBox has two variations: one returns a value (a function) and the other does not (statement). The format of the two is almost identical, the function has the following syntax:

```
return_value = MessageBox ( message_to_the_user, (buttons + icon + default +
mode), messagebox_title)
```

The format without a return value has the same syntax minus the parentheses:

```
MessageBox message_to_the_user, (buttons + icon + default + mode),
messagebox_title
```

The only item required in each variation is the the message to be displayed. A title for the box is not necessary, and the default OK button will be displayed with no icon if nothing is specified.

Note The MessageBox keyword can be abbreviated to MsgBox with no errors.

Note Constant values can be used for the buttons, icon, default, and mode parameters of the `MessageBox` statement/function. This is detailed later in the chapter.

Figure 2.1 MessageBox with Hello message

Example 2.16

```
MessageBox "Hello"
```

The second parameter determines the buttons that appear on the MessageBox, the icon that is displayed, the default button (if the user clicks Return), and the modality. Various integer values correspond to different button combinations, icons, default buttons, and modality. The numbers for each setting are added together to set the second parameter of the `MessageBox` statement/function. The numbers and their settings follow.

Table 2.3

Buttons	
Button Type	**Integer Value**
OK	0
OK and Cancel	1
Abort, Retry, and Ignore	2
Yes, No, and Cancel	3
Yes and No	4
Retry and Cancel	5
Icons	
Icon Name	**Integer Value**
Stop Sign	16
Question Mark	32
Exclamation Mark	48
Information	64
Default Button	
Button Designation	**Integer Value**
First Button	0
Second Button	256
Third Button	512
Modality	
Modal Type	**Integer Value**
Application Modal	0
System Modal	4096

So, make a selection for each category (buttons, icon, default button, and modality) and add each integer value together for a final integer value that is used in the MessageBox statement/function.

Example 2.17

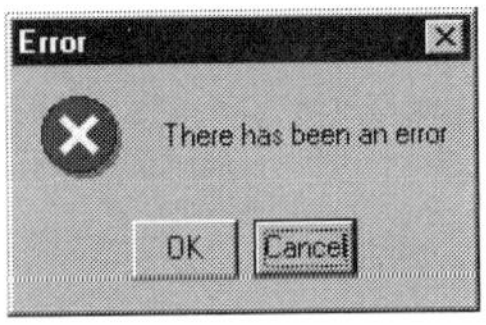

Figure 2.2 MessageBox

Let's say I want to display a warning message to the user with OK and Cancel buttons (figure 2.2). The default button will be Cancel, and the modality will be application modal. This means the the current application will stop running until the user responds, system modality stops all applications on the system until the user responds. Finally, a message will be displayed with the title of Error.

```
MessageBox "There has been an error", (1 + 16 + 256 + 0), "Error"
```

If I want to know which button a user selects, I would use the MessageBox function as shown in figure 2.3.

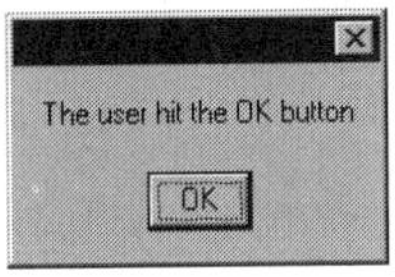

Figure 2.3 User selected OK button in MessageBox

```
value = MessageBox("There has been an error.",273,"Error")
If (value = 1) Then
  MsgBox "The user hit the OK button"
ElseIf (value = 2) Then
  MsgBox "The user hit the CANCEL button"
End If
```

A return value of one signals the OK button was selected, and two signals the Cancel button. A list of return codes is in table 2.4.

Table 2.4

Return value	Button	Constant
1	OK	IDOK
2	Cancel	IDCANCEL
2	Abort	IDABORT
4	Retry	IDRETRY
5	Ignore	IDIGNORE
6	Yes	IDYES
7	No	IDNO

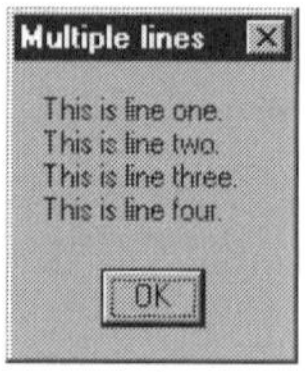

Figure 2.4 Multiple line messages

Multiple lines can be displayed as well (figure 2.4). The `Chr` function can be used to insert carriage returns in the message displayed in the message box.

Example 2.18

```
MessageBox "This is line one." & Chr(10) & "This is line two." _
   & Chr(10) & "This is line three." & Chr(10) & "This is line" _
   & "four.", 0, "Multiple lines"
```

`MessageBox` is great for presenting information to the user, but retrieving data is another function.

2.6.3 InputBox

There is only one format for the InputBox function, but it accepts from one to five parameters. The format is like this.

```
value = InputBox(message_to_user, title, default_value, display_column,
  display_row)
```

The only item required is the message to the user; it can be used to tell the user what type of information to enter.

Example 2.19

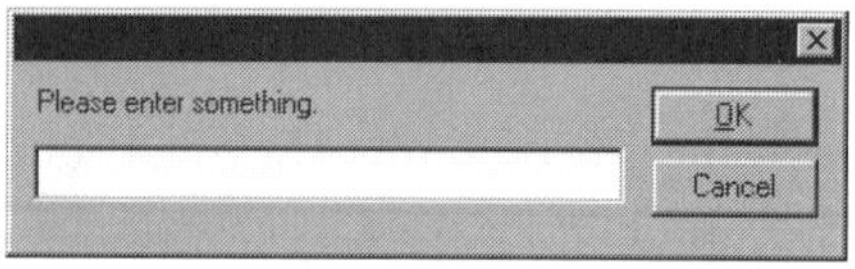

Figure 2.5 InputBox

```
something = InputBox("Please " _&
  "enter  something.")
```

The box from example 2.19 can be "cleaned up" by adding a title and a default value, and telling the system where to display it on the screen (figure 2.5).

Example 2.20

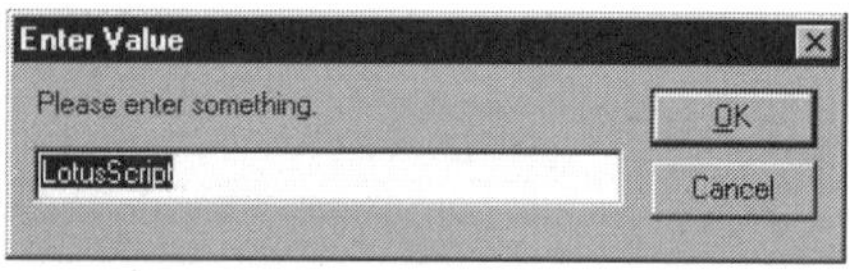

Figure 2.6 InputBox

```
something = InputBox("Please " _&
  "enter  something.","Enter Value", _
  "LotusScript",30,30)
```

The last two parameters signal the `x` and `y` coordinates for the upper left corner of the `InputBox`. Example 2.21 tells the system to display an input box (figure 2.6) with its upper left corner starting at the coordinate (30,30).

Note The return value of the `InputBox` function is a variant, but a dollar sign can be appended to the `InputBox` statement to signal a string value:

Example 2.21

```
something = InputBox$("Please enter a string value.")
```

This accepts input from the user in the form of a string.

2.7 Commenting your code

Good programming practice involves the insertion of comments that describe the purpose of code and give specific details on items that may be tricky. Good comments can serve the purpose of refreshing your memory six months from now, or providing a roadmap for a new developer on the job once you have moved on to a new project. Be aware that the overuse of comments can be as bad as no comments at all. Comments are inserted in LotusScript using two methods: The %REM..%END REM block or using an apostrophe.

Example 2.22

```
%REM
   Author:  Tony Patton
   Date:  3/14/1998
   Description:  This script shows how comments can be used.
%END REM
For x = 1 to 10
   Print "x = " & x           ' print the loop index
Next x
```

' This comment was inserted to show use of apostrophes for commenting.

Example 2.22 shows both comment methods in action. You should notice that the apostrophe style of comments can be placed at the end of a line or on a separate line. The %REM...%END REM block is best suited for large comments that span multiple lines. Either method achieves the same result, but the `%REM` statements can be easier to spot than apostrophes.

2.8 Strings

Dealing with strings is a common occurrence. Fortunately, LotusScript provides numerous functions to handle strings. The following list shows a few.

- `Mid`
- `UCase`
- `LCase`
- `Len`
- `Trim`
- `LTrim`

- `RTrim`
- `Left`
- `Right`
- `Instr`

2.8.1 Mid(String2Change, starting_position, optional_length) = String2GetCharacters

The `Mid` function allows you to replace all or a portion of one string with characters from another.

- *`String2Change`* Designates the variable to alter.
- *`starting_position`* The character position within `String2Change` to use as the starting point for the replacement characters.
- *`optional_length`* Signals how many characters to retrieve from `String2GetCharacters` and place in the `String2Change` variable. If this parameter is omitted, all of `String2GetCharacters` is used.

Example 2.23

```
Dim string1 As String, string2 As String
string1 = "Today was a good day."
string2 = "slow day."
Print "Before:  " & string1
Mid(string1,13,9) = string2
Print "After:  " & string1
```

Output

Before Today was a good day.
After Today was a slow day.

Explanation

The system is directed to start at position thirteen within the string "Today was a good day.", which is the g in good, and replace it with the first four characters from the string "slow day." If the optional length parameter (`4`) had been left out, string1 would contain "Today was a slow one." after execution of the script.

2.8.2 UCase/LCase(string)

These two functions change the case of the string passed to them. `UCase` stands for uppercase and `LCase` is lowercase.

Example 2.24

```
Dim string1 As String, string2 As String
string1 = "Tony Patton"
```

```
Print LCase(string1)
Print UCase(string1)
```

Output

tony patton
TONY PATTON

Explanation

The two perform opposite functions. `LCase` changes every character in string to lowercase, and UCase converts every character to uppercase. These functions are excellent when checking for exact values entered by a user. We cannot guarantee the format of data entered, so converting it to lowercase or uppercase allows for easier comparisons.

Example 2.25

```
Dim answer as String
answer = InputBox("Please enter Yes or No.")
If (LCase(answer) = "no") Then
  MsgBox "No was entered."
ElseIf (UCase(answer) = "YES") Then
 MsgBox "Yes was entered."
End If
```

Explanation

The user is prompted to enter "yes" or "no." We cannot control the format of the input, so it is converted to lowercase to check for "no" and uppercase to check for "YES".

2.8.3 Len(String)

The `len` function returns the number of characters in the string passed into it.

Example 2.26

```
Dim entry As String
entry = InputBox("Please enter your name.")
If (Len(entry) < 1) Then
  MsgBox "You entered nothing!"
End If
```

Explanation

The user enters a string, and the `len` function is used to check for actual input.

2.8.4 Trim/LTrim/RTrim(String)

The `Trim` function removes all leading and trailing spaces from the string passed to it. `LTrim` removes leading spaces, and `RTrim` removes all trailing spaces.

Example 2.27

```
Dim string1 As String
```

```
string1 = "  This has spaces on both ends  "
Print Len(string1)
Print Len(Trim(string1))
Print Len(LTrim(string1))
Print Len(string1)
Print Len(RTrim(string1))
```

Output

33
29
31
33
31

Explanation

The `len` function is used to print the length of the variables with and without the `trim` functions. `Trim` removes the two spaces in the front and the end of string1. The `LTrim` function removes the two leading spaces from string2. The `RTrim` function removes the two trailing spaces from string3.

2.8.5 Left(String)/Right(String)

Left and Right are used to pull out a number of characters from a string.

Example 2.28

```
Dim answer As String
answer = InputBox$("Please enter yes or no.")
If (Left(UCase(answer),1) = "Y") Then
   MsgBox "You entered yes."
ElseIf (Right(LCase(answer),1) = "o") Then
   MsgBox "You entered no."
End If
```

Explanation

The `Left` and `Right` functions are used to check user input.

2.8.6 Instr(optional_starting_point, string1, string2, optional_compare_method)

The `Instr` function searches one string (string1) for the first occurrence of another string (string2). The optional_starting_point parameter is used to signal the point within the string (string1) to start the search. Also, the optional_compare_method is used to signal if a case-sensitive or insensitive search should be conducted (`1` signals case-insensitive and the default, if no method is signaled, is `0` for case-sensitive). The `Instr` function returns the position within string1 that string2 was found. It returns `0` if there is no match.

Example 2.29

```
Dim string1 As String, string2 As String
string1 = "Lotus Notes rules!"
string2 = "notes"
position = Instr(string1, string2, 1)
Print "The string was found at position " & position
```

Output

The string was found at position 7.

Explanation

The string "Lotus Notes rules!" was searched for "notes" starting at position one using a case-insensitive search. A match is found at position seven.

2.9 Format function

The `format` function allows a string, number, or date value to be specifically formatted for output. This is an excellent function to use when creating reports or displaying data that must have a certain appearance. The syntax of the function is:

```
Format(variable, optional_format)
```

The `optional_format` parameter controls how the variable will be formatted. Numbers can be displayed as a General Number, Currency, Fixed, Standard, or Percent. Date/Time values can be displayed as General Date, Long Date, Medium Date, Short Date, Long Time, Medium Time, or Short Time. LotusScript help gives more detailed descriptions of the options for the format parameter.

Example 2.30

```
Dim dateNow
dateNow = Now
MessageBox "Different date/time formats. " & Chr(10) & Chr(10) &_
   Format(dateNow, "General Date") &_
   Chr(10) & Format(dateNow, "Long Date") & Chr(10) &_
   Format(dateNow, "Medium Date") & Chr(10) &_
   Format(dateNow, "Short Date") & Chr(10) & Format(dateNow, "Long Time") &_
   Chr(10) & Format(dateNow, "Medium Time") & Chr(10) &_
   Format(dateNow, "Short Time")
```

Output

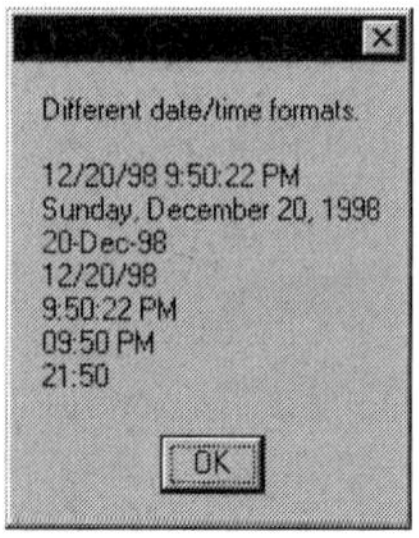

Figure 2.7 Format function

2.10 *Predefined constants*

Lotus Notes provides a set of constants with predefined names that can be used in your scripts. The constants are defined in a few files: LSCONST.LSS, LSERR.LSS, LSXUIERR.LSS, and LSXBEERR.LSS. The first file, LSCONST.LSS, contains constants that are used with various LotusScript functions/statements like `MessageBox`. The remaining three contain error messages. Each file is located in your Notes data directory and appendix A lists the contents of each.

Note The files mentioned should be located in the root Notes directory. For example, they are located in the `C:\Notes` directory on my laptop.

To take advantage of the files, your script(s) must be told to use them. This is accomplished with the `%INCLUDE` statement. This statement tells the system to insert the contents of an external file into the script. The insertion occurs at compile time. If the file to be included is not in the default Notes data directory, you must include its complete path.

Example 2.31

```
[Options]
%INCLUDE "LSCONST.LSS"
Sub Initialize
   MsgBox "This message was generated with constants.",MB_OK + _
      MB_ICONQUESTION,"Test"
End Sub
```

Explanation

This script takes advantage of the constants file. It uses predefined constants with the `MessageBox` statement instead of integer values that have to be used if the constant file has not been included.

2.11 *UnderScore (continuation)*

The underscore character (_) serves a special purpose in LotusScript. It allows a single statement to continue over multiple lines. The underscore character is the continuation character. Example 2.31 took advantage of it because the `MessageBox` statement had numerous lines.

2.12 Chapter summary

The purpose of this chapter was to build a foundation for the rest of the book. The syntax of the basic language constructs of LotusScript like looping, user interaction, and declaring variables is almost identical to Visual Basic, but not quite. This makes LotusScript a quick study for experienced Visual Basic developers, but they still have to learn the Notes/Domino environment. The topics covered in this chapter will be used extensively throughout the remainder of this book.

2.13 Chapter review

- Declaring variables
- Converting variables from one type to another
- The Options and Declarations section of a script.
- Looping with the `For`, `While`, `Do`, and `Forall` loops.
- Branching with `If` and `Select Case`.
- Displaying messages to the user with `MessageBox` and `Print` statements.
- Using the `InputBox` statement/function to get information from the user.
- Commenting scripts with the %`REM..%END REM` block and apostrophe.
- Dealing with strings.
- Accessing predefined constants.

CHAPTER 3

Functions and subroutines

3.1 Chapter objectives 38
3.2 Functions 38
3.3 Subroutines 40
3.4 Scope/visibility 42
3.5 Chapter summary 44
3.6 Chapter review 44

3.1 Chapter objectives

- What is a function?
- What is a subroutine?
- What is the difference between the two?
- How are functions used?
- How are subroutines used?
- Scope of functions and subroutines
- Proper function and subroutine syntax
- Passing values to functions/subroutines
- Subroutines and functions within classes
- Code reuse

The reuse of code is a strong point of emphasis in object-oriented development, but it is only common sense. If you have a block of code that is repeatedly used, what do you do? Do you type it over and over every time it is needed, or place it in a location where it can be referenced when needed? The place to put it is called a subroutine or possibly a function.

At the risk of restating the obvious, functions and subroutines are unique blocks of code that can be used repeatedly by an application. These blocks of code reduce the work of the developer (typing and debugging), and make him/her more efficient. Functions and subroutines reduce the size of an application; make it much more readable and easy to follow; and reduce debugging time. Rather than debug many lines of redundant code, you debug a single block. Changes to that code affect every place it is used (called).

3.2 Functions

LotusScript defines a *function* as a named procedure that returns a single value. The LotusScript language contains numerous functions, such as `Round`, `Tan`, or `Sin`, all math related. They are named procedures that return a single value. Functions may accept arguments that are used to return a value. (The previously mentioned math functions accept arguments.)

The `Round` function has the following syntax:

```
ReturnValue = Round(number, places)
```

`ReturnValue` is defined as a Double. `Round` accepts the number to round and the number of decimal places to keep to the right of the decimal point.

`ReturnValue` will contain 3.14 for the following code:

```
ReturnValue = Round(PI, 2)
```

Functions do not have to accept parameters. The following user-defined function returns the current date in a set format:

Note Pi is a built-in constant in LotusScript. Its value is 3.141592654...

Example 3.1

```
Function getDate As Variant
        getDate = Format(Date, "Long Date")
End Function
```

Explanation

When the function is called, it returns the current date in long format. The function could be used as follows:

```
MsgBox "Todays date is " & getDate
```

Syntax

We have eluded to the format of a function block, but here is the specific notation:

```
1    (Public/Private/Static) Function functionName(parameter1..parameterN)_
       As Variable Type
       <body of the function>
2      functionName = <some code>
3    End Function
```

Details

1 The function is declared. It is given a name, parameter list, and variable type. The scope of the variable is declared with the `Public` or `Private` identifiers. `Private` is the default. Refer to chapter 1 for more details. The parameter list consists of variable names and their types (For example: parameter `As String`). Multiple parameters are separated by commas. The function is given a variable type as well.

2 The return value of the function is set.

3 The end of the function block.

Example 3.2

```
1    Public Function greaterThan(number1 As Integer, number2 As Integer) _
       As Integer
2    If (number1 > number2) Then
3      greaterThan = number1
     Else
4      greaterThan = number2
     End If
5    End Function
```

Details

1 A function called greaterThan is declared. It is available to everything in the application (Public), and it accepts two integers. The return value is an integer as well.

2 The two numbers passed into the function are compared.

3 Sets the return value to number1 if it is the larger of the two.

4 Otherwise the return value is set to number2.

5 The end of the function.

Let's use the function from the previous example.

```
Dim rValue As Integer
rValue = greaterThan(20,5)
```

If we run this piece of code, rValue will contain 20.

3.3 Subroutines

A subroutine is the same as a function in all areas except it does not return a value. It can accept multiple or no parameters, just like a function. The following subroutine mimics the getDate function from example 3.1:

Example 3.3

```
Sub getDate
  MsgBox "Todays date is " & Format$(Date, "Long Date")
End Sub
```

Explanation

The output of this subroutine and the previous function is the same, but the two are not always interchangeable. Use a function if you need to return a value. A subroutine can be used if no return value is needed. A subroutine accepts parameters just like a function. The following variation of the getDate subroutine shows it accepting two variables:

```
Sub getDate(passedTitle As String, passedName As String)
  MsgBox "Hello, my name is " & passedName & " and the date is " &_
  Format$(Date, "Long Date"),0, passedTitle
End Sub
```

Explanation

The MsgBox statement displays a message that uses the two variables passed into the subroutine getDate. The first parameter is used as the title for the message box, and the second is used in the message in the output.

3.3.1 *Using subroutines*

The actual use of subroutines (syntax) differs from functions. This makes sense because one returns a value and the other does not. The `Call` statement can be used to execute a subroutine. The `getDate` subroutine could be called like this:

```
Call getDate("The Date", "Tony Patton")
```

Output

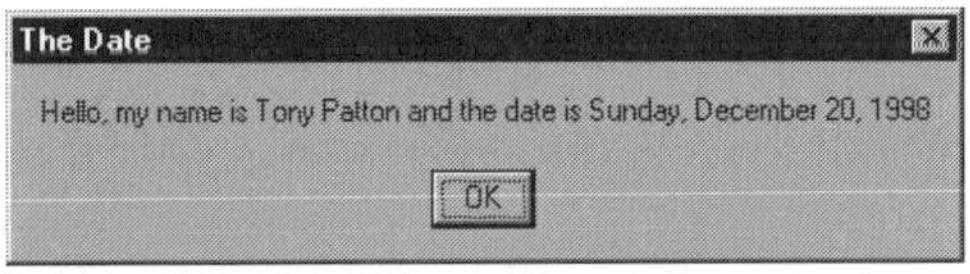

Figure 3.1 Output of user-defined function

Syntax

The proper syntax for a subroutine:

```
1  (Public/Private/Static) _
     Sub NameOfSub (parameters)
     <body of subroutine>
2  End Sub
```

Details

1 The Sub keyword is used to identify the starting point for a subroutine block of code. It is preceded by the optional `Public`, `Private`, or `Static` identifiers. A name is required, and parameters are optional. The parameters are defined in the same way as those for functions.

2 The subroutine block of code is terminated by the `End Sub` statements.

3.3.2 *Creating your own function/subroutines*

You can start typing your own functions/subroutines almost anywhere within the development environment. Once you type the first line of the subroutine/function declaration and press return, LotusScript will move you to a blank script pane and automatically insert the ending tags (`End Sub`/`End` Function). After the function or subroutine has been entered with no compile errors, its name appears in the event drop-down list. Basically, a user-defined function or subroutine is seen as an event.

3.3.3 *Built-in subs/functions*

Your own functions/subroutines appear in the event list with the other subroutines that are standard with any script: `Initialize` and `Terminate`. The `Initialize` subroutine lets you specify tasks to be completed when an item is loaded. It exists for everything in the environment including forms, agents, and buttons.

If you want a Boolean flag called MyFlag to be set to `true` when a form is loaded, you would enter the following:

Example 3.4

```
Sub Initialize
```

```
        MyFlag = True
End Sub
```

Of course, you do not have to enter the beginning and ending sub block identifiers. If this is saved in a form, the variable MyFlag will be set to `true` every time a document created with the form is loaded. The `Terminate` subroutine performs the opposite function.

Example 3.5

```
Sub Terminate
        MsgBox "The object is terminating."
End Sub
```

The terminate block of code is executed when its corresponding object (form, agent, button, etc.) is unloaded or closed. It can be thought of as a cleanup routine. The previous code would present a message box to the user every time an item is closed.

3.4 Scope/visibility

The scope or visibility of a function or subroutine is determined by where it is defined. It is limited to the object in which it is contained. For example, if a subroutine is declared in an action button's script, it will be unavailable to other action buttons. If it is defined in the globals section of a form, it is available to all action buttons and any other script within that form. Script libraries can be used to overcome these limitations. Chapter 19 provides more information on script libraries.

> *Note* The following example uses concepts (Notes classes) presented in chapter 4.

Example 3.6

Scenario I have a Lotus Notes database that stores sales orders. I want to quickly find the largest sales order. This is determined by the total sale amount on the sales order (TotalSales field).

Solution A LotusScript agent that scans every document tracking the largest sales order. When all sales orders have been examined, a message box presents the largest sales order and salesperson number to the user.

```
     [Declarations]
1    Public TopSalesAmount As Double

2    Function compareSalesAmount(passedSalesAmount As Double) As Double
3    If (passedSalesAmount > TopSalesAmount) Then
4          compareSalesAmount = passedSalesAmount
     Else
5          compareSalesAmount = TopSalesAmount
     End If
```

```
   End Function

6     Sub checkDoc (passedDoc As NotesDocument, passedCount As Integer)
7        If (passedCount = 1) Then
            TopSalesAmount = passedDoc.TotalSales(0)
         Else
8           TopSalesAmount = compareSalesAmount(passedDOc.TotalSales(0))
         End If
   End Sub

Sub Initialize
         Dim s As New NotesSession
         Dim db As NotesDatabase
         Dim dc As NotesDocumentCollection
         Dim doc As NotesDocument
         Dim x As Integer
9        Set db = s.CurrentDatabase
10       Set dc = db.AllDocuments
11       For x = 1 to dc.Count
12          Set doc = dc.GetNthDocument(x)
13          Call checkDoc(doc, x)
      Next x
14    MessageBox "The top sales amount is " & TopSalesAmount & " sold by " &_
         TopSalesPerson
   End Sub
```

Explanation

1 The variable `TopSalesAmount` is declared as a double. It will be used to track the largest sales amount.

2 The function that will be used to compare values is declared. It accepts a double value and returns a double value.

3 The value of the double value passed into the function is compared with the value in the `TopSalesAmount` variable.

4 If the value passed is larger than `TopSalesAmount`, the function is set to the value that was passed into the function.

5 Otherwise, the function is set to the value in `TopSalesAmount`.

6 The subroutine `checkDoc` is declared. It accepts a NotesDocument object and an integer.

7 If the integer passed into the subroutine equals `1`, the `TopSalesAmount` variable is initialized to the value from the TotalSales field on the document passed into the subroutine.

8 Otherwise the `CompareSalesAmount` function is called, and the return value of the function is stored in the `TopSalesAmount` variable.

9 The NotesDatabase object `db` is set to the current database. The `CurrentDatabase` property of the NotesSession object is referenced.

10 The NotesDocumentCollection object `dc` is set to all documents in the database. The `AllDocuments` property of the NotesDatabase object is used.

11 A `For` loop is used to scroll through all documents in the document collection.

12 The document corresponding to the loop index is retrieved from the collection. The `GetNthDocument` method of the NotesDocumentCollection object is used.

13 The `checkDoc` subroutine is called with the current document and loop index value passed to the subroutine.

14 The results of the script are displayed.

3.5 Chapter summary

Defining your own functions and/or subroutines allows code reuse and reduces development and maintenance time. Variables/objects can be passed into functions/subroutines, and they are passed by reference which means you are dealing with the actual objects. They can be typed into any area in your script. After you type the first function or sub line the environment inserts the ending tags.

3.6 Chapter review

- A function is a block of code contained within the function heading and `End Function` statement. It performs a specific task and returns a value to the code that referenced it.
- A subroutine is a block of code contained within the `Sub` and `End Sub` statements. Unlike functions, a subroutine does not return values.
- The major difference between a function and subroutine is that functions return a value. A subroutine does not.
- Both subroutines and functions accept parameters.
- The Lotus Notes/Domino environment includes numerous built-in functions and subroutines.
- The `Initialize` and `Terminate` subroutines are standard for every object in Lotus Notes.
- The `Initialize` subroutine is executed when its associated object is loaded; the `Terminate` subroutine when the object is closed.
- User-defined subroutines/functions are created by entering the sub/function declaration and clicking Enter. LotusScript inserts the ending tag, and presents a blank script pane.
- Functions/subroutines foster the reuse of code, and result in more readable and manageable code.

CHAPTER 4

Objects: working with classes

4.1 Chapter objectives 46
4.2 What is an object or class? 46
4.3 Designing classes 48
4.4 Front-end/back-end classes 56
4.5 Chapter example 59
4.6 Chapter summary 60
4.7 Chapter review 61

4.1 Chapter objectives

- What is a class?
- Define properties. How do you access an object's properties?
- Define methods. How do you access an object's methods?
- What is dot notation? How is it used?
- Dealing with objects
- Me, With, Set, and New
- Encapsulation
- Create your own classes
- Use your own classes
- Lotus Notes front-backend classes.

The use of object-oriented principles in the software development life cycle has gained momentum over the last few years. The introduction of the Java programming language has added fuel to the growth. Java is an object-oriented language like C++. It supports object-oriented principles as well as procedural development. LotusScript includes object-oriented features as well.

The Lotus Notes/Domino database can be described as a database of objects. The objects are represented by the database container, forms, fields, views, agents, and so forth. The Notes Objects are defined as the notes object interface (NOI). The NOI gives developers access to the numerous objects in the Notes environment.

4.2 What is an object or class?

The most popular way to explain object-oriented programming is to compare it to the real world. Objects can be thought of as a noun. That is, a person, place, or thing. This object has certain characteristics called properties, and certain behaviors called methods. A class can be thought of as a group of related objects. A mailman is a person object, he/she delivers the mail (methods), and is male or female (property). On the other hand, a person class can be used to define a mailman, programmer, bus driver, or any other type of person. A class is a template for an object. An object is an instance of a class. The terms object and class are often used interchangeably, but it can be confusing. I will stick with the previous definition for consistency.

Also, you will often hear the words encapsulation and inheritance to describe the greatness of object-oriented programming. *Encapsulation* describes the way a object can contain its own methods, properties, and data. These elements are contained (encapsulated) within the object, so nothing else is needed. *Inheritance* refers to a class getting (inherited) properties or methods from another class (parent class). Examples of both base (parent) and derived (child) classes can be found throughout the chapter.

You may not have realized it, but working with LotusScript and Lotus Notes involves objects every step of the way. If we need to access a NotesDatabase, we might first create an instance of the NotesSession class. We create a database object from the NotesDatabase class, and instantiate it with the `CurrentDatabase` property of the NotesSession object previously declared. From there we work with collections, views, and documents which are all objects.

> *Note* An overview of the basic Lotus Notes classes is presented later in this chapter.

4.2.1 Dot notation

Dot notation is the technical term used by Lotus (look it up in the Help) that describes the access of an object's properties/methods by a developer.

Example 4.1

```
    Dim s As New NotesSession
    Dim db As NotesDatabase
1   Set db = s.CurrentDatabase
    Dim dbTitle As String
    Dim dbSize As Double
2   dbTitle = db.Title
3   dbSize = db.Size
```

Explanation

1 The database object `db` is set to the `CurrentDatabase` property of the NotesSession object.

2 The string variable `dbTitle` is set to the database object title. The title property of the database object is accessed via dot notation.

3 The double variable `dbSize` is set to the database object's size. The size property of the database is accessed via dot notation.

The methods of an object are accessed in a similar fashion:

Example 4.2

```
    Dim s As New NotesSession
    Dim db As NotesDatabase
    Dim dc As NotesDocumentCollection
    Dim doc As NotesDocument
    Set db = s.CurrentDatabase
1   Set dc = db.AllDocuments
2   If (dc.Count > 0) Then
3      For x = 1 to dc.Count
4         Set doc=dc.GetNthDocument(x)
5         doc.FieldName = "New Value"
6         Call doc.Save(True, False)
```

```
7        Next x
8     End If
```

Explanation

1 The document collection object is set to the `AllDocuments` property of the NotesDatabase object.

2 The `count` property of the NotesDocumentCollection is used to determine if the collection contains any documents.

3 The `count` property is used as the ceiling in the `For/Next` loop.

4 NotesDocument object doc is set to a document in the collection using the `GetNthDocument` method of the NotesDocumentCollection object.

5 A field on the NotesDocument is accessed just like a property, and its value is set.

6 The `save` method of NotesDocument is used to save the document.

4.2.2 *Defining your own classes*

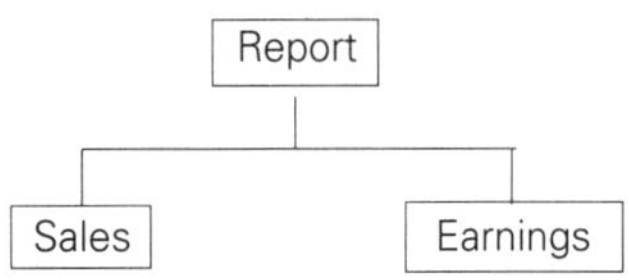

Figure 4.1

In addition to the classes included in Lotus Notes, you can develop your own. There are two types of classes to work with: base and derived. A base class is defined and its methods and properties can be inherited by derived classes. For example, we can create a generic reports class that is used to create more specific reports like a sales or a report of earnings. Figure 4.1 shows the relationship between the base report class and the derived sales report and sales per salesperson classes.

The methods and properties of the Report class are now methods and properties of the derived classes. Also, they can add their own attributes and override methods and/or properties of the base class.

4.3 *Designing classes*

The work involved in designing good object-oriented applications is far beyond the scope of this book. There are a great number of methodologies in place today that foster the object-oriented design. The uniform modeling language (UML) is just one of the many in existence. These methodologies help create solid reusable classes. The examples in this chapter are fairly straightforward, but proper planning and design go a long way toward a good application.

4.3.1 Me

The keyword `Me` can be used within a property or method of an object to access its attributes. This is a real time saver, because you do not have to repeatedly type a class name when using it within itself.

4.3.2 Creating the class

The following syntax is used to define a class in LotusScript:

Example 4.3

```
1    Public Class Report
2       Private title As String
3       Public Sub setTitle(passedVariable as String)
           Me.title = passedVariable
        End Sub
        Public Function getTitle As String
4          GetTitle = Me.title
        End Function
     End Class
```

Explanation

1 A class named Report is declared, and the `Public` identifier says it is available to all.

2 The class variable title is declared: It is visible only within the class (`Private`).

3 The subroutine `setTitle` is declared as visible to the world. It sets the class variable called `title` to what value(s) is passed into it.

4 The function `getTitle` is declared to provide access to the class variable title.

Do you notice the keywords `Public` and `Private` that precede declaration? They define the scope of who can see and/or access the objects being created. `Public` says that the whole world can see and use it. `Private` states that only the object which contains it can use it (that includes any derived classes). In the previous example, the variable title is accessible only by the Report class. The methods `setTitle` and `getTitle` are available to the world, so other objects can reach the title variable through these methods. The methods assure that `title` is used the way it was designed. If `Public` or `Private` is not stated, it defaults to `Private`.

Now, we have created the base Reports class. It has the title which is common to all of our reports. We will use this class to create our Sales and Earnings reports. Our sales class contains `SalesToDate`, `ProjectSales`, and `PastSales`.

Example 4.4

```
1    Public Class Sales As Report
        Private SalesToDate As Currency
        Private ProjectedSales As Currency
        Private PastSales As Currency
```

```
2       Public Sub setSalesToDate(passedSales As Currency)
3         If (passedSales >= 0) Then
4           Me.SalesToDate = passedSales
          End If
        End Sub
        Public Sub setProjectedSales(passedProjected As Currency)
          If (passedProjected >= 0) Then
            Me.ProjectedSales = passedProjected
          End If
        End Sub
        Public Sub setPastSales(passedPast As Currency)
          If (passedPast >= 0) Then
            Me.PastSales = passedPast
          End If
        End Sub
        Public Function getSalesToDate As Currency
          GetSalesToDate = Me.SalesToDate
        End Function
        Public Function getProjectedSales As Currency
          GetProjectedSales = Me.ProjectedSales
        End Function
        Public Function getPastSales As Currency
          GetPastSales = Me.PastSales
        End Function
5       Public Sub setTitle(passedTitle As String)
          Me.Title = "Sales Report:  " + passedTitle
        End Sub
    End Class
```

Explanation

1. The class named Sales is declared as a dervied class from Report. It inherits all properties and methods (unless overridden) of the Report class, and it adds it own properties and methods.
2. The subroutine `setSalesToDate` is declared as usable by all (`Public`).
3. The `setSalesToDate` subroutine checks for a valid sales amount before using the value. This is good practice, because you never are certain what values may be entered.
4. The `Me` keyword is used to set the `SalesToDate` property of the current object.
5. The `setTitle` subroutine of the parent Report class is overridden to accommodate the proper title for a Sales report.

4.3.3 With … End With

The `With` statement, like the `Me` keyword, is a time saver and can be used in conjunction with the `Me` keyword. It allows access to numerous methods and/or properties of an object. Everything within a With/End With block preceded by a dot will be associated with the specified `Object`.

Example 4.5

```
  With <Object>
1    .property = "Test1"
2    Call .method …
3    Object2.property = "Test3"
  End With
```

Explanation

1 The property of the Object is set to `Test1`.

2 The method of the object is called.

3 Sets the property of `Object2` not `Object` to `Test3`. This happens because the object name is identified.

4.3.4 Constructors and destructors

A constuctor is a method that is automatically executed when an object is created, and a destructor is automatically called when an object is detroyed. In LotusScript, the method called `New` is the constructor and `Delete` is the destructor. These special methods can be utilized to perform initialization and cleanup tasks. The following class uses the constructor to initialize variables, and the destructor to clean things up.

Example 4.6

```
  Public Class Sample
     Private name As String
     Public description As String
     Private donation as Double
1    Sub New
2       With Me
3          .name = ""
           .description = "none"
           .donation = 5.00
4       End With
     End Sub
5    Sub Delete
6       Print "Deleting the Sample object."
     End Sub
  End Class
```

Explanation

1 The constructor is declared.

2 The `With` keyword is used to perform multiple operations on one object.

3 Variable names are set to initial values. These will always be set when an object is created. The `New` method will not be explicitly called. It will be called automatically by the system.

4 This closes the `With` statement, it is required.

5 The destructor is declared.

6 Nothing special is accomplished in the destructor, but a message is sent to the user telling them that the object has been deleted.

4.3.5 Using classes, creating objects

The `New` and `Set` keywords are used to create objects from classes you have defined. The following code creates and uses a Programmer class.

Example 4.7

```
1   Public Class Programmer
       Private Name As String
       Private Age As Integer
       Private Language As String
       Public Sub setName(s As String)
          Me.Name = s
       End Sub
       Public Sub setAge(i As Integer)
          If (i > 0) Then
             Me.Age = I
          End if
       End Sub
       Public Sub setLanguages(s As String)
          Me.Language = s
       End Sub
    End Class

2   Public Class NotesProgrammer As Programmer
       Private LatestVersion As String
       Private YearsExperience As Integer
       Private LotusScript As String
       Public Sub setLatestVersion(s As String)
          Me.LatestVersion = s
       End Sub
       Public Sub setYearsExperience(I As Integer)
          Me.YearsExperience = I
       End Sub
       Public Sub setLotusScript(s As String)
          Me.LotusScript = s
       End Sub
       Function getLatestVersion As String
          GetLatestVersion = Me.LatestVersion
       End Function
       Function getYearsExperience As Integer
          GetYearsExperience = Me.YearsExperience
       End Function
       Function getLotusScript As String
          GetLotusScript = Me.LotusScript
       End Function
    End Class

3   Dim NotesPerson As NotesProgrammer
4   Set NotesPerson = new NotesProgrammer
```

```
5    With NotesPerson
        .setLotusScript("Yes")
        .Name = "Tony Patton"
        .Age = "28"
        .Language = "Java"
        .setYearsExperience(4)
     End With
     MsgBox NotesPerson.Name + " has been working with Notes for " + _
        NotesPerson.getYearsExperience + " , and has experience with " + _
        NotesPerson.getLanguage + "."
```

Output

Tony Patton has been working with Notes for 4 years, and has experience with Java.

Explanation

1 The base class called Programmer is defined/declared.

2 The derived class NotesProgrammer is declared as a subclass of Programmer. It inherits all methods and properties of the Programmer class (unless overridden in the subclass), and defines its own.

3 An object called NotesPerson is declared as the user type NotesProgrammer.

4 The NotesPerson object is instantiated.

5 Properties of the NotesPerson object are set using the `With` statement.

4.3.6 Delete

An object is deleted from memory with the Delete command.

```
Delete <object>
```

4.3.7 Is, IsA, and IsObject

The `Is` statement is used to test equality between two objects. It evaluates to `true` if—and only if—the two objects refer to the same object.

```
If (object1 IS object2) Then
  MsgBox "The two objects are equal."
End If
```

The `IsA` statement checks to see if one object is derived (subclassed) from another object.

```
If (subclass ISA parentclass) Then
  MsgBox "Subclass is derived from parentclass."
End If
```

The `IsObject` statement checks whether or not a variable is an object. An object can be created by the user or any one of the objects in the Notes environment.

```
If (IsObject(item)) Then
  MsgBox "Item is an Object."
End If
```

4.3.8 Garbage collection

The memory associated with objects is handled by LotusScript. No effort is required of the developer to allocate memory or take back memory from objects that are no longer in use. The usage of objects is tracked internally by LotusScript, so memory associated with an object is freed when it is no longer referenced.

4.3.9 Property (Get/Set)

Languages like Java and C++ preach the use of object-oriented programming (Java more than C++). One nuance of object-oriented programming is the use of accessor methods. The use of accessor methods when creating classes says that all variables should be declared `Private` (accessible only to the class), and `get` and `set` methods are implemented to retrieve or set the value of the variables. At first glance, it appears that the `get/set` methods only add a layer of complexity when accessing variables. Upon further investigation, it is clear that the `set` and `get` methods can be used to control what happens to the variables. For instance, the values can be verified as valid before assigning them to a variable.

LotusScript provides the same functionality through the `Property Set` and `Property Get` statements. A `Property` can be defined as `Public`, `Private`, or `Static` (just like functions and subroutines). Also, the use of the `Property` statements is not restricted to classes. `Propery Get` and `Set` are just like subprocedures. They can be placed almost anywhere within the LotusScript environment.

Syntax

```
Property Set name_of_property As type_of_data
  < body of the property >
End Property

Property Get name_of_property As type_of_data
  < body of the property >
End Property
```

Once a `Property Get` and `Set` have been defined, the name of the property is used whenever its contents are retrieved or altered (attempt to alter). LotusScript knows to run the `Get` or `Set` routine.

Example 4.8

```
(Declarations)
Dim actualCounter As Integer

Property Set counter As Integer
```

```
2       actualCounter = counter
     End Property

3    Property Get counter As Integer
4       If (actualCounter < 0) Then
5          counter = 0
        Else
           counter=actualCounter
        End If
     End Property

     Sub Initialize
6       counter = Cint(InputBox("Please enter a count."))
7       MsgBox "Counter = " & counter
     End Sub
```

Explanation

1 The set property procedure for counter is declared.

2 The variable `actualCounter` is set to the contents of the counter property.

3 The get property procedure for counter is declared.

4 If the `actualCounter` variable is zero then the counter property is set to zero.

5 The `Property Set` procedure for counter is called.

6 The `Property Get` procedure for counter is called.

The `Property` statements are used to store and retrieve values in `actualCounter`. When a value is assigned to `acutalCounter`, LotusScript executes the `Property Set` procedure for `actualCounter`. When the `actualCounter` variable is accessed (`Msg-Box`), the system calls the `Property Get` procedure to get its value. In this example, the `Property` procedures use a variable called `actualCounter` to check for a zero value.

4.3.10 Arrays of objects

Declaring an object and using its methods and properties is good, but the real power is realized when multiple objects are created through the use of arrays. Arrays of objects are created the same as regular arrays, but instead of using one of the built-in variable types you use your own.

> *Note* More information on arrays can be found in chapter 5.

Example 4.9

```
1    Public Class Student
        Public Name As String
        Public Tuition As Currency
2    Public Sub calcTuition(I As Integer)
3    Me.Tuition = 2000 * I
        End Sub
     End Class
```

```
     Dim x As Integer
4    Dim StudentObject() As Student
5    For x = 1 to 4
6    Redim Preserve StudentObject(x) As Student
7    Set StudentObject(x) = New Student
8    With StudentObject(x)
        .Name = "Student #" + Cstr(x)
        .calcTuition(x)
     End With
  Next x
```

Explanation

1 The class Student is declared.

2 The method `calcTuition` of the Student class is declared.

3 The `calcTuition` sets the value of the `Tuition` property of the Student class.

4 An array of Student objects is declared as StudentObject.

5 A `For` loop is used to create four StudentObjects to show the use of an array of objects.

6 The size of the array of Student objects is resized to the `For` loop index with the contents of the array remaining intact (Preserve).

7 The Student object for the current array element (loop index) is instantiated.

8 Properties of the current object are set using the `With` statement.

Although this is a very simple example, it shows the power that classes can bring to your applications. The calculation of the tuition and storage of the tuition is encapsulated into the Student object in the example.

The use of classes produces more manageable and readable code and facilitates code reuse if properly designed

4.4 *Front-end/back-end classes*

The numerous LotusScript classes that are available to work with Notes/Domino data/objects can be divided into two types: front-end and back-end. The difference between the two is simple. Front-end classes allow Notes user interface objects/data to be manipulated. Back-end classes allow Notes objects/data to be accessed without user intervention.

This section gives a very brief overview of the two types of classes and the common classes in each. It is not meant to be an exhaustive review, but an introduction. Everything mentioned is used extensively throughout the remainder of the book.

Note The Lotus Notes classes (front-end and back-end) cannot be used as a base class to create subclasses.

4.4.1 *Front-end classes*

All classes associated with the front-end have the letters U and I, for user interface, in their names. When a user opens a database, document, or view, these classes allow the objects to be accessed.

4.4.2 *NotesUIWorkspace*

The NotesUIWorkspace class is used for one and only one thing: setting up the environment in which front-end objects will be accessed/manipulated. The syntax for it follows:

```
Dim variable_name as New NotesUIWorkspace
```

Note Notes 5.0 will allow the current database and view to be accessed from a NotesUIWorkspace object.

This class allows access to the currently open document.

4.4.3 *NotesUIDocument*

The NotesUIDocument class is used to access the currently open document.

```
Dim uiw As New NotesUIWorkspace
Dim uidoc As NotesUIDocument
Set uidoc = uiw.CurrentDocument
```

Note The `ComposeDocument` method of the NotesUIWorkspace class can be used to create a new document in the UI.

The code shows that the CurrentDocument property of the NotesUIWorkspace class is used to access the current document.

4.4.4 *Back-end classes*

All classes that do not have UI in their titles are said to be back-end classes. These classes require no direct interaction in the UI to access objects. The basic classes show how to work with documents, views, and databases.

4.4.5 *NotesSession*

The NotesSession class corresponds to the NotesUIWorkspace's role; it is used to set up the environment in which back-end scripts will operate. Once a NotesSession object is declared, it allows the current database to be accessed, which leads to accessing documents and views among other objects. Also, it allows access to information pertaining to the current environment such as username, platform, and Notes version.

Declaring a new NotesSession object:

```
Dim variable_nama As New NotesSession
```

4.4.6 *NotesDatabase*

The NotesDatabase object allows a database to be accessed. The `CurrentDatabase` property can be used to access a database, or the specific location of a database can be used.

Accessing the current database:

```
Dim s As New NotesSession
Dim db As NotesDatabase
Set db = s.CurrentDatabase
```

Accessing another database:

```
Dim db As New NotesDatabase("Server Name", "database filename and path")
```

4.4.7 *NotesView*

Views with Notes databases can be accessed in the back-end through a NotesDatabase object because views are contained with databases.

The next snippet of code shows how a NotesView object is set up and initialized.

```
Dim s As New NotesSession
Dim db As NotesDatabase
Dim view As NotesView
Set db = s.CurrentDatabase
Set view = db.GetView("View Name")
```

4.4.8 *NotesDocument*

The NotesDocument object is used to access documents within databases. Documents can be retrieved in numerous ways including through NotesView or NotesDatabase objects.

This piece of code shows how a document is accessed through a view. It accesses the last document in a view.

```
Dim s As New NotesSession
Dim db As NotesDatabase
Dim view As NotesView
Dim doc As NotesDocument
Set db = s.CurrentDatabase
Set view = db.GetView("View Name")
Set doc = view.GetLastDocument
```

The back-end representation of the currently open document can also be accessed through the `Document` property of the NotesUIDocument class. This is most useful considering the back-end NotesDocument class allows document fileds to be accessed more easily than using the NotesUIDocument methods/properties. The next piece of code shows it in action.

```
Dim uiw As New NotesUIWorkspace
Dim uidoc As NotesUIDocument
Dim doc As NotesDocument
Set uidoc = uiw.CurrentDocument
Set doc = uidoc.Document
```

4.5 Chapter example

Scenario

I have a Notes database that stores sales amounts for field salespeople. There is one record per sale, so there are numerous documents per salesperson. I want a recap of the sales for each. The only thing I want to track is each salesperson's name, ID, and total sales. The ID is needed because it is a unique identifying value for a salesperson, a key.

Solution

A class will be created to store the information (name, ID and total sales). The class will contain methods to tally total sales, and store and retrieve the name, ID, and total sales values. I will traverse the sales documents in the database and track a salesperson's sales using an array of the classes. Every time a new salesperson is encountered, a new object will be created. In the end, I will have an array of objects that has a salesperson and the total sales.

```
Public Class SalesPerson
  Private Name As String
  Private ID As String
  Private TotalSales As Currency
  Sub New
    With Me
      .Name = ""
      .ID = ""
      .TotalSales = 0
    End With
  End Sub
  Public Sub setName(s As String)
    Me.Name = s
  End Sub
  Public Function getName As String
    getName = Me.Name
  End Function
  Public Sub setID(s As String)
    Me.ID = s
  End Sub
  Public Function getID As String
    getID = Me.ID
  End Function
  Public Sub setTotalSales(c As Currency)
    Me.TotalSales = c
  End Sub
  Public Function getTotalSales As Currency
```

```
    getTotalSales = Me.TotalSales
  End Function
  Public Sub incTotalSales(amount As Currency)
    Me.TotalSales = Me.TotalSales + amount
  End Sub
End Class
' Initialize Section
Dim sp() As SalesPerson
Dim s As New NotesSession
Dim db As NotesDatabase
Dim dc As NotesDocumentCollection
Dim doc As NotesDocument
Set db = s.CurrentDatabase
Set dc = db.AllDocuments
Dim x As Integer
Dim y As Integer
Dim z As Integer
For x = 1 To dc.Count
  Set doc = dc.GetNthDocument(x)
  If (x=1) Then
    Redim sp(0) As SalesPerson
    sp(0).setName(doc.name(0))
    sp(0).setID(doc.ID(0))
    sp(0).setTotalSales(doc.Sales(0))
  Else
    Found = False
    For y = 0 To Ubound(sp)
      If (sp(y).getID = doc.Name(0)) Then
        sp(y).incTotalSales(doc.Sales(0))
        Found = True
      End If
    Next y
    If Not (found) Then
      Redim Preserve sp(Ubound(sp) + 1) As SalesPerson
      sp(Ubound(sp) + 1).setName(doc.Name(0))
      sp(Ubound(sp) + 1).setID(doc.ID(0))
      sp(Ubound(sp) + 1).setTotalSales(doc.Sales(0))
    End If
  End If
Next x
For z = 1 To Ubound(sp)
  Msgbox "Total sales for " + sp(z).getName + " is " + Cstr(sp(z).getTotalSales) + "."
Next z
```

4.6 Chapter summary

The proper use of classes leads to much more efficient and readable code. Effective subclassing (base and derived classes) fosters reusable code. For example, reports may have the same basic information with some custom aspects. The basic information can be declared as a base class with derived classes created for each report type. Reusable code reduces development time, which results in happy developers and customers.

4.7 *Chapter review*

- Object-oriented development with LotusScript.
- A class can be described as a person, place, or thing.
- Methods are behaviors of a class.
- Properties are characteristics of a class.
- Dot notation is used to access properties and methods of an object.
- There are two types of classes: base and derived.
- Derived classes inherit a portion of its methods and/or properties from a base class
- Everything in the Notes environment is an object: database, form, document, view, agent, and so forth.
- `Public` and `Private` denote the scope of an object.
- The `New` method of a class is a constructor. It is executed automatically when an object is instantiated.
- The `Delete` method of a class is a destructor. It is executed automatically when an object is deleted.
- The `Set` and `New` statements are used to create objects.
- The `With` statement facilitates easy access to multiple items in an object.
- Arrays of objects are created just like arrays of any other type.
- `Property Get` and `Set` can be used to build truly object-oriented applications.
- Front-end classes allow the currently open elements to be accessed/manipulated.
- Back-end classes allow Notes objects/data to be accessed without actually opening them.
- Lotus Notes classes cannot be subclassed.

CHAPTER 5

Working with arrays, lists, collections, and items

5.1 Chapter objectives 64

5.2 Arrays 64

5.3 Lists 71

5.4 NotesDocumentCollection 74

5.5 Working with response documents 76

5.6 NotesItem 79

5.7 Chapter example 82

5.8 Chapter summary 84

5.9 Chapter review 84

5.1 *Chapter objectives*

- What is an array?
- What is a list?
- What is a collection?
- Why is NotesItem special?
- Declaring an array
- Declaring a list
- Obtaining a collection
- Accessing values, properties of a NotesItem
- Dynamic arrays
- Accessing elements of an array
- Accessing elements of a list
- Accessing elements of a collection
- Dealing with NotesItems

Declaring a variable and assigning it a value is a very simple and straightforward process. Unfortunately, a lot of the items dealt with in programming are not as simple. Many have multiple values and your script needs to access those values. For instance, the values may need to be sorted or a search of the values may need to be conducted to check for a certain value.

5.2 *Arrays*

The array is the basic multivalued storage mechanism in LotusScript. An `array` is a set of consecutive memory locations used to store data. The items in an array are called elements, and the size of an array is the dimension. Items in an array are referenced by using the index value for the item's position within the array. Arrays are defined as a type just like single value variables (Single, Double, Variant, etc.).

Syntax

The following syntax is used to declare an array:

```
Dim array_name(dimension) As type
```

The array name can be any legal variable name. Dimension is an integer value that sets the number of elements in the array; `type` signals what type of values are contained within the array. If we wanted to declare an array to hold ten integers, we would do it like this:

```
Dim numbers(9) As Integer
```

The numbering of the index of an array starts at zero, so the dimension used to declare an array actually declares it with the number of elements equal to the dimension plus one. Elements are accessed by giving the array name and the index of the value to retrieve. This is true for both retrieving and assigning values.

Likewise, we could declare an array called `names` to store five names like this:

Example 5.1

```
Dim names(4) As String
```

It would look like this in memory:

```
names(0)  =  ""
names(1)  =  ""
names(2)  =  ""
names(3)  =  ""
names(4)  =  ""
```

We could have used a `For` loop to populate the array from example 5.1.

Example 5.2

```
1    Dim names(4) As String
     Dim x,y As Integer
2    For x = 0 to 4
3       names(x) = InputBox$("Please enter a name.","Data Entry")
     Next x
     For y = 0 to 4
4       Print names(y)
     Next y
```

Explanation

1 An array of five string values is declared.

2 The loop will execute five times.

3 The `For` loop index is used as the array index to store a value in that element in the array. The value is set by the user via an `InputBox$` statement.

4 The values from the array are displayed.

5.2.1 Forall

The `Forall` statement is used to loop through all elements in an array without prior knowledge of the number of elements in it. `Forall` executes a block of statements (comprised by the `Forall` and `End Forall` tags) for each element in an array. Example 5.2 could be rewritten using `Forall` like this.

Example 5.3

```
Dim names(4) As String
For x = 0 to 4
```

```
      names(x) = InputBox$("Please enter a name","Name")
   Next
1  Forall y in names
2     print y
3  End Forall
```

Explanation

The names array is set up and populated just like example 5.2.

1 The beginning of the `Forall` block. It tells the system to loop through every item in the names array.

2 The current value being accessed from the names array is printed.

3 The end of the `Forall` block.

5.2.2 LotusScript statements

There are a number of other statements in LotusScript that are specific to arrays.

- *`Lbound`* Returns an integer representing the lower bound (smallest index value) for an array.
- *`Ubound`* Returns an integer representing the highest bound (largest index value) of an array.
- *`IsArray`* Is a Boolean (True or False) signaling whether a variable is an array or not.

Example 5.4

```
   Dim names(2) As String
   Dim onename As String
1  Print Ubound(names)
2  Print Lbound(names)
3  If (IsArray(onename)) Then
      Print "The onename variable is not an array."

   Else
        Print "The onename variable is an array."
   End If
```

Explanation

1 The upper bound of the names array is printed.

2 The lower bound of the names array is printed.

3 Checks to see if the `onename` variable is an array or not.

Output

2

0

The `onename` variable is not an array.

5.2.3 *Dynamic arrays*

In a perfect world we always know how many items will be stored in an array, so it is easy to set up. The world is not so perfect and situations arise where the number of elements to be stored in an array is unknown. There are two LotusScript statements to help with this dilemma: `Redim` and `Preserve`:

- *`Redim`* Resizes an array, it redimensions an array.
- *`Preserve`* Used in conjuction with `Redim`, tells the system to resize an array but keep the current elements of an array intact. If `Redim` is used without preserve, the elements in an array are erased.

The key to using `Redim` and `Preserve` is the initial declaration of the array. In order to be allowed to use `Redim` and `Preserve`, the array must be initially dimensioned with no index value like this:

```
Dim names() As String
```

This tells the system that you want an array to store string values, but you are not sure how many names you will need to store. After declaring the array, it can be redimensioned to any size needed:

```
Redim names(2) As String  - or - Redim Preserve names(2) As String
```

The first one sets the index value for names to `2` and erases anything in the array. The second one has the `Preserve` keyword that tells the system to reset the index, but the contents of the array remain intact.

Example 5.5

All documents in a database will be searched for the ones with a field named salesID equal to "1234". If a match is found, the sales amounts are stored in an array:

```
Dim s As New NotesSession
Dim db As New NotesDatabase("","")
Dim doc As NotesDocument
Dim dc As NotesDocumentCollection
Dim sales()
If  db.Open("server/US","filename.nsf") Then
   Set dc = db.AllDocuments
   For x = 1 to dc.Count
         Set doc = dc.GetNthDocument(X)
         If doc.salesID(0) = "1234" Then
            If (x=1) Then
               Redim sales(0)
               sales(0) = doc.salesAmount(0)
            Else
               Redim Preserve sales(Ubound(sales) + 1)
```

```
15              sales(Ubound(sales)) = doc.salesAmount(0)
             End If
          End If
      Next
16    MessageBox "There were " & Ubound(sales) &_
         " documents found for 1234",0,"Count"
      Dim total
      total = 0
17    Forall y In sales
18       Msgbox "Sales amount #" & x & " is $" & y
19       total = total + y
20    End Forall
21       MsgBox "Total sales:  " & total
   End If
```

Explanation

1 NotesSession object is declared and instantiated.

2 NotesDatabase object is declared.

3 NotesDocument object is declared.

4 NotesDocumentCollection object declared. It allows us to scroll through all documents in the database.

5 A dynamic sales array is declared. No type is signaled, so it will be an array of variants.

6 The database object is set to a specific database, and the rest of the script is executed if and only if the database exists. The `Open` method of the NotesDatabase object returns `false` if it does not exist, and `true` otherwise.

7 The document collection is set to all documents in the database.

8 A `For` loop is used to scroll through all documents in the collection.

9 The document object is set to a document in the collection using the loop value as the index.

10 The sales field on the document is checked for a match to “1234”.

11 If there is a match and the value of `x` is `1`, it is the first document, so the array is initialized.

12 The sales array index is set to `0` (`1` element) using the `Redim` statement.

13 The first element in the sales array (`index = 0`) is set to the value from the document.

14 If there is a match and it is not the first document (`x > 1`), the sales arrays index is reset and the contents of the array remain intact.

15 The new array item is set to the sales value from the array.

16 A message box displays the number of matches.

17 A `Forall` loop is used to scroll through all elements in the sales array without knowing how many it contains.

18 A message box displays each individual sales amount.

19 The variant total tallies the total sales amount.

20 The end of the `Forall` loop.

21 The total sales amount is diplayed with a message box.

5.2.4 Multidimension arrays

Up to this point, we have dealt strictly with one-dimensional arrays. That is, arrays with only one column of values. Arrays can be thought of as matrices with columns and rows. A one-dimensional array has one column and a number of rows equaling its dimension.

Example 5.6

```
Dim names(5) As String
```

Table 5.1

	Column#0
Row#0	names(0)
Row#1	names(1)
Row#2	names(2)
Row#3	names(3)
Row#4	names(4)
Row#5	names(5)

Note The `Redim` statement can be used only with the last element of a multi-dimensional array. You cannot have a multidimensional array in which every index is dynamic.

Remember, just like in other programming languages, the numbering of the elements in an array starts at zero. The first element is always zero unless specified differently.

A matrix with more than one column can be declared a multidimensional array.

Example 5.7

```
Dim names(5,1) As String
```

Table 5.2

	Column#0	Column#1
Row#0	names(0,0)	names(0,1)
Row#1	names(1,0)	names(1,1)
Row#2	names(2,0)	names(2,1)
Row#3	names(3,0)	names(3,1)
Row#4	names(4,0)	names(4,1)
Row#5	names(5,0)	names(5,1)

The elements in a mulitdimensioned array are accessed just like a single-dimension array, except that one column is added.

Example 5.8

We are going to create an array to hold five first- and last-name pairs.

```
    Dim x As Integer
1   Dim name(4,1) As String
2   For x = 0 to 4
3      name(x,0) = InputBox$("Enter first name.","Enter")
4      name(x,1) = InputBox$("Enter last name.","Enter")
    Next x
```

Explanation

1 An array with five rows and two columns (10 elements total) is declared to hold string values.

2 The `For` loop is used to set the five value pairs.

3 Column one of the current index row is set.

4 Column two of the current index row is set.

5.2.5 Variation

The index values of an array can be specified rather than using the default of starting at zero. The syntax gives a better idea:

```
Dim array_name(lower to higher) As Type
```

Lower assigns the starting value of the index of the array (lower bound), and `higher` assigns the ending index value (higher bound). Both lower and higher are integer values, and lower must be less than higher. A compile time error is generated if it is not. This gives greater flexibility when using arrays. You may want to assign an index value that is related to the data stored at that location.

Example 5.9

```
    Dim names(5 to 7) As String
    Dim x As Integer
1   x = Lbound(names)
2   Forall y In names
3      names(x) = InputBox$("Enter customer name.")
4      x = x + 1
    End Forall
```

Explanation

1 An array of String values is set with index values of `5`, `6`, and `7`.

2 The integer variable `x` is initialized to the lower bound of the array (`5`).

3 The `Forall` loop is used to loop through all elements in the array. This is a variation on the normal `For` loop.

4 The element at index `x` is set to the value entered by the user.

5 The index variable is incremented.

5.2.6 Limitations

The Lotus Notes/Domino LotusScript environment has limitations on arrays in versions prior to and including 4.6. The maximum number of dimensions (columns) is limited to eight, and the maximum storage size for an array is 64K. The number of elements (rows) is limited to the amount of memory on the machine using the array.

5.3 Lists

Lists are similar to arrays, but the index value(s) in a list are textual, not numeric (they can contain numbers, but they are stored as text), and lists can contain only one dimension (column). Actually, lists resemble dynamic arrays with their ability to grow and shrink as the application runs. The dynamic nature of lists is its strong point, and it does not require special keywords (`Redim` and `Preserve`) like arrays. Perhaps the greatest strength of a list is its ability to pull out a value from a list based on a string value (a unique string value). The unique string value is called a ListTag. Items are added to a list by specifying a list tag and assigning a value.

Syntax

Lists are declared just like any other variable with one exception: the `List` keyword follows the variable name. Items are added to a list by specifying the list tag and assigning a value.

Example 5.10

```
1    Dim theList List As String
2    theList("This is the ListTag") = "whatever"
3    Print theList("This is the ListTag")
```

Explanation

1 The variable `theList` is declared as a List to store string values.

2 The value `whatever` is added to the list with a corresponding `ListTag` of `This is the ListTag`.

3 A value from the list is printed by specifying its `ListTag`.

5.3.1 ListTag

ListTag corresponds to an item's index value in a array. An array may have a value at location (index) 1, whereas a List has a value at a location specified by a `ListTag` value.

The ListTag values must be unique. If a ListTag value is set twice, the second value overwrites the first. As a result, there are no duplicate ListTags.

Example 5.11

```
1   Dim theList List As String
2   theList("element1") = "One"
3   theList("element2") = "Two"
4   theList("element1") = "Two"
```

Explanation

1 The list is declared.

2 A value is stored with ListTag element1.

3 A value is stored with ListTag element2.

4 A new value is stored with ListTag element1.

Both element1 and element2 contain the same values once the code is executed.

Example 5.12

```
1   Dim thelist List As String
2   theList("One") = "Element One"
    theList("Two") = "Element Two"
    theList("Three") = "Element Three"
3   Forall x In theList
4     print ListTag(x) & " - " & x
5   End Forall
```

Output

One - Element One
Two - Element Two
Three - Element Three

Explanation

1 The list is declared to store String values.

2 Item added to the list.

3 The Forall loop is used to scroll through all elements in the list.

4 The ListTag and element value are printed.

5 End of the Forall loop.

Example 5.12 shows that the Forall statement functions the same way for lists as it does with arrays. The DataType and TypeName functions from chapter 2 can be used with lists as well. Use them to check the list as a whole or individual elements like this:

Example 5.13

```
1   Dim ex613 List
2   ex613("Element1") = "One"
3   ex613("Element2") = "Two"
4   Print TypeName(ex613)
5   Print TypeName(ex613("Element1"))
6   Print DataType(ex613)
7   Print DataType(ex613("Element1"))
```

Explanation

1 The List `ex613` is declared to hold any type of data (variant).

2 A string value is stored with `ListTag` of `Element1`.

3 A string value is stored with `ListTag` of `Element2`.

4 The `TypeName` function returns the keyword `List` and the data type for the `List`. This prints as List Variant

5 The `TypeName` function returns the data type for the element at `Element1` in the list. This prints as String.

6 The `DataType` function returns an integer value representing a `List` and the data type of the `List`. This will print `2060`.

7 The `DataType` function returns an integer value representing the datatype of `Element1` of the `List`. This will print `8` for String.

Other List related keywords

- *`IsList(variable name)`* Returns a Boolean value signaling whether a variable/object is a list or not.
- *`IsElement(NameOfList(ListTagName))`* Returns a Boolean value signaling whether a list contains the specified ListTag. This is used to search a list for a specified value.
- *`Erase(NameOfList)`* Removes all contents of the specified list.
- *`Erase(NameOfList(ListTag))`* Removes contents of a specified element in a list.

Example 5.14

```
Dim myList List
Dim search As String
myList("Spotts") = "One"
myList("Wathen") = "Two"
myList("Hamilton") = "Three"
myList("Campbell") = "Four"
If (IsList(myList)) Then
  search = InputBox$("Enter name to delete.","Enter Name")
  If (IsElement(myList(search))) Then
    Erase myList(search)
```

```
    End If
End If
```

Explanation

1 The body of the `If ... Then` statement is executed only if `myList` is a `List`.

2 The search variable is set by the user.

3 The body of the `If ... Then` statement is executed only if the value entered by the user exists as a `ListTag` in the `List`.

4 If there is a match, the item is removed from the list.

5.4 NotesDocumentCollection

A NotesDocumentCollection object resembles an array. It is a group of documents from a database. The group of documents is assembled using various methods available to LotusScript in the Lotus Notes/Domino objects A collection of documents can be assembled with all documents from a database, a subset of documents from a view (based on a key), or as a result of a search.

The NotesDatabase object contains a property that is a NotesDocumentCollection that represents all documents in a database. This method is used throughout this book.

Example 5.15

```
1   Dim s As New NotesSession
2   Dim db As NotesDatabase
3   Dim dc As NotesDocumentCollection
4   Set db = s.CurrentDatabase
5   Set dc = db.AllDocuments
```

Explanation

1 A new session object is instantiated.

2 Database object is declared.

3 Collection object is declared.

4 The database object is set to the current database.

5 The collection is set to contain all documents from the database object.

The NotesView object can be used to form a collection as well. The NotesView class contains a method called `GetDocumentsByKey`, and it returns a collection of objects whose sorted columns contain values that match a search string.

Example 5.16

```
    Dim s As New NotesSession
    Dim db As NotesDatabase
1   Dim view As NotesView
```

```
    Dim dc As NotesDocumentCollection
    Set db = s.CurrentDatabase
2   Set view = db.GetView("All")
3   Set dc = view.GetDocumentsByKey("match", True)
```

Explanation

1. A NotesView object is declared.
2. The NotesView object is set to the `All` view in the database object.
3. The document collection is formed containing documents from the view whose first sorted column matches the search string ("match"). The `True` paramater signals that exact case should match. `False` would indicate a case insensitive search.

The `UnprocessedDocuments` property of the NotesDatabase returns a collection of documents as well. Its main use is with agents. It returns a collection of objects that the current agent has not processed. This is perfect for mail/paste or modified/new documents agents that need a way to signal which documents it has processed.

Search methods can be used to form collections of documents from a database. Two methods exist for databases with a full text index and those without.

- `db.Search("Search Formula", Cutoff Date, Maximum number of matches to return)`
- `db.UnprocessedSearch("Search Formula", Cutoff Date, Maximum number of matches to return)`
- `db.FTSearch("Search String", Maximum number of matches to return)`
- `db.UnprocessedFTSearch("Search String", Maximum number of matches to return)`

Details

- Search Formula performs standard search on the database. The search formula uses standard search syntax (it can contain @formulas). This is used on databases without a full text index. It is more restrictive than a full text indexed database due to the fact that field names must be specified and @functions can and sometimes must be used.
- Cutoff date is the oldest date of a document to return.
- Maximum number of matches to return
- Search string is used on databases that have been full text indexed. It is much more flexible than databases without a full-text index. It allows the entry of one word, and the whole database is searched for documents that contain that one word.

Example 5.17

```
Dim s As New NotesSession
Dim db As NotesDatabase
Dim doc As NotesDocument
Dim dc As NotesDocumentCollection
Dim thedate As New NotesDateTime("1/1/87")
Dim stringtofind As String
Dim x As Integer
Set db = s.CurrentDatabase
If (db.IsFullText) Then
   stringtofind = InputBox$("Enter word(s) to seek.")
   Set dc = db.FTSearch(stringtofind,0)
Else
   fieldname = InputBox$("Enter field name to search")
   fieldstring = InputBox$("Enter value to seek.")
   stringtofind = |@Contains("| & fieldname & |";"| & fieldstring & |")|
   Set dc = db.Search(stringtofind,thedate,0)
End IF
MsgBox "There were " & dc.Count & " matches to your query."
```

Explanation

Note Using two DocumentCollections in a script can cause unexpected results, such as losing object pointers. If two collections are used, access one of the collections using the `GetNthDocument` method and a `For` loop and access the other using the `GetFirstDocument`, `GetNextDocument`, and so forth methods.

5.5 Working with response documents

A collection can be formed with all response documents to a certain document. It will assemble a collection of all *direct* responses, not all documents underneath a document which may include many levels of responses and response to responses.

Example 5.18

```
   Dim s As New NotesSession
   Dim db As NotesDatabase
   Dim dc1 As NotesDocumentCollection
   Dim dc2 As NotesDocumentCollection
   Dim index As Integer
   Set db = s.CurrentDatabase
1  Set dc1 = db.AllDocuments
   Set doc = dc1.GetFirstDocument
2  While Not (doc Is Nothing)
3     Set dc2 = doc.Responses
4     MsgBox "This document has " & dc2.Count & " responses."
5     Set doc = dc1.GetNextDocument(doc)
   Wend
```

Explanation

1 The collection will contain all documents in the database.

2 Process all documents.

3 The second collection will contain all responses to a document (if any).

4 Tell the user the number of responses.

5 Get the next main document from the collection.

5.5.1 Number of documents

The number of documents in a collection turns out to be a value that is used quite frequently. It is easily accessed through the count property of the NotesDocumentCollection object.

```
NotesDocumentCollection.count
```

It returns an integer count of the total number of documents contained in the collection (greater than or equal to zero).

5.5.2 Traversing a collection

Once a collection has been assembled, the documents in it can be accessed individually using various methods in the NotesDocumentCollection class. All of the methods return NotesDocument objects.

- `GetFirstDocument` Returns the first document from a collection.
- `GetNextDocument(NotesDocument)` Returns the next document in a collection. The current position in the collection is passed into it as a NotesDocument object. It returns the document that follows that document.
- `GetLastDocument` Returns the last document from a collection.
- `GetNthDocument(Integer)` Returns the document at the postion passed to it as an Integer in the collection. This is often used with a `For` loop and the count property of a collection to scroll through all documents in a collection.
- `GetPrevDocument(NotesDocument)` Returns the previous document in the collection. The current position is passed into it as a NotesDocument object. It returns the document previous to the document passed.

Example 5.19

```
Dim s As New NotesSession
Dim db As NotesDatabase
Dim dc As NotesDocumentCollection
Dim doc As NotesDocument
Dim SalesReceipts As Integer
Set db = s.CurrentDatabase
```

```
1   Set dc = db.AllDocuments
2   Set doc = dc.GetFirstDocument
    SalesReceipts = 0
3   Do While Not (doc Is Nothing)
4      If (doc.HasItem("SalesReceipt")) Then
          SalesReceipts = SalesReceipts + 1
       End If
5      Set doc = dc.GetNextDocument(doc)
6   Loop
```

Explanation

1. NotesDocumentCollection object set to all documents in the current database.
2. NotesDocument object set to first document in the collection
3. The `Do` loop will continue until there are no more documents (Nothing). Nothing is a reserved word in LotusScript.
4. If the document contains a field called SalesReceipt, the body of the `If` block is executed.
5. The NotesDocument object is set to the next document in the collection. The current document is passed into this method to let it know its starting point.
6. The end of the `Do` loop.

5.5.3 Refining a collection

The number of documents in a collection can be reduced by conducting a search. The `FTSearch` method of the NotesDocumentCollection class allows a collection to be searched for specific items, and only those documents that meet the search criteria will remain in the collection. A database does not need to have a full-text index to use this method, but it does affect its performance. It runs much faster on a full-text indexed database. The syntax of the `FTSearch` method follows.

Syntax

```
Call NotesDocumentCollection.FTSearch(search string, maximum number of docs to return)
```

The first parameter is a string containing the search criteria, the second parameter signals the maximum number of documents to return (zero signals to return all matches). The next example shows how to reduce a collection to only those documents that contain a certain name.

Example 5.20

```
    Dim s As New NotesSession
    Dim db As NotesDatabase
    Dim dc As NotesDocumentCollection
    Dim doc As NotesDocument
1   Dim searchString As String
    Set db = s.CurrentDatabase
```

```
2    Set dc = db.AllDocuments
3    searchString = InputBox$("Enter name to find.")
4    Call dc.FTSearch(searchString, 0)
     If (dc.Count > 0) Then
        ...... do something ...
     End If
```

Explanation

1 The variable to store the search criteria is declared as a String.

2 The document collection is set to contain all documents from the current database.

3 The search string is set by the user via the `InputBox` function.

4 The document collection is refined using the search string entered by the user.

5.6 NotesItem

The NotesItem class is another example of where the use of arrays is imperative to their proper handling. There are two variations of this class that will be covered in this chapter: `Items` property of the NotesDocument class and items (fields) on a NotesDocument.

The `Items` property of the NotesDocument class returns an array of items (fields) on a document. The array is returned as a NotesItem object. This NotesItem object contains the list (array) of all fields on that document.

Example 5.21

```
1    Sub Click(Source As Button)
2       Dim uiw As New NotesUIWorkspace
3       Dim uid As NotesUIDocument
        Dim ub As Integer
4       Set uid = uiw.CurrentDocument
5       ub = Ubound(uid.Document.Items)
6       MessageBox "There are " & ub & " fields on this document.",0,_
           "Attention"
     End Sub
```

Explanation

1 Code is contained within an action button. It is executed when the button is selected.

2 A NotesUIWorkspace object is instantiated.

3 A NotesUIDocument object is declared.

4 The NotesUIDocument object is set to the currently open document.

5 The `Ubound` of the `Items` property (array of fields) is stored in the variable `ub`. The items property is retrieved by accessing the `NotesDocument` (Docu-

Note Remember that dot notation is used to access elements of an object. Lines 4 and 5 from the previous example demonstrate it.

ment) property of NotesUIDocument property, and the Items property is retrieved from this.

6 A message box displays the count of fields on the current document to the user.

This is a very simple example, but it does show that the Items property is an array. This powerful property could be used to search for a specific field and its value.

Example 5.22

```
  Dim s As New NotesSession
  Dim db As New NotesDatabase("","")
  Dim doc As NotesDocument
  Dim dc As NotesDocumentCollection
  Dim JonesCount As Integer
  JonesCount = 0
1 If (db.Open("server_name","database.nsf")) Then
2    Set dc = db.AllDocuments
3       If (dc.Count > 0) Then
4          For x = 1 to dc.Count
5             Set doc = dc.GetNthDocument(x)
6             Forall i In doc.Items
7                If (i.Name = "LastName") Then
8                   If (doc.LastName(0) = "Jones") Then
9                      JonesCount = JonesCount + 1
                    End If
                 End If
              End Forall
           Next x
        End If
     End If
```

Explanation

This script scans all documents in a database for documents that have the string "Jones" stored in the LastName field.

1 The block of code is executed only if the database can be accessed (opened).

2 DocumentCollection object set to all documents in the database.

3 Proceed only if the number of documents in the collection is greater than zero.

4 A For loop is used to loop through all documents in the collection.

5 NotesDocument object is set to document from collection using For loop index and GetNthDocument method from the NotesDocumentCollection object.

6 Forall loop is used to access all fields on the document.

7 The name property (name of the field) is checked for existence on the document.

8 If the LastName field does exist, its value is checked to see if it is "Jones".

9 If there is a match, the counter variable is incremented.

The last example shows that fields on a NotesDocument are themselves arrays, called value arrays. Whether the field is accessed as a NotesItem object or a property of the document, they are arrays. Of course this does not apply to Rich Text fields which are a special type. Fields on documents are created as arrays with the first element starting at zero. If you are looking for a value in a field, you will almost always access the first element (zero) of the array. On the other hand, multivalued fields will contain multiple values. Line 8 from example 5.21 shows how fields can be accessed—just like properties of the Notes Document object. This is only true when accessing documents through the back end, it is not allowed when working with documents with front-end classes. Fields can be obtained from a document by using an instance of the NotesItem class as well. The next example illustrates this point.

Example 5.23

```
    Dim uiw As New NotesUIWorkspace
    Dim uid As NotesUIDocument
    Set uid = uiw.CurrentDocument
1   Dim item As NotesItem
    Dim JonesCount As Integer
    JonesCount = 0
2   Set item = uid.Document.GetFirstItem("LastName")
3   Forall v in item.Values
4     If (v = "Jones") Then
5       JonesCount = JonesCount + 1
      End If
    End Forall
```

Explanation

1 A NotesItem object is declared.

2 The NotesItem object is set to the LastName field on the current document. The `GetFirstItem` method exists in the NotesDocument object, so the NotesDocument object of the current document is accessed through its document property.

3 The `Forall` loop allows us to access all values from the LastName field. The `Values` property of the NotesItem class returns a value array containing all of its values.

4 The current value from the field is checked to see if it is Jones.

5 The counter variable is incremented if it matches.

5.6.1 HasItem

If you are unsure if a field exists on a document, the `HasItem` method can be used to verify that a field exists on a document.

```
If (NotesDocument.HasItem("FieldName")) Then
```

This is useful for error handling or error avoiding. You don't want to try to access a field that does not exist, this will generate a run-time error. Example 5.19 takes advantage of this method.

5.7 *Chapter example*

Scenario

I want to retrieve a quick list of sales amounts (with the name of the salesperson) from a Notes database.

Solution

```
   Dim s As New NotesSession
   Dim db As New NotesDatabase("","")
   Dim dc As NotesDocumentCollection
   Dim doc As NotesDocument
1  Dim sales List As Currency
2  If (db.Open("","Test2.nsf")) Then
     Set dc = db.AllDocuments
3      If (dc.Count > 0) Then
4        Call dc.FTSearch(|FIELD Form =| & "Sales", 0)
5        For x = 1 To dc.Count
           Set doc = dc.GetNthDocument(x)
6          If (doc.HasItem("SalesAmount") And _
             doc.HasItem("SalesPerson")) Then
7            If (IsElement(sales(doc.SalesPerson(0)))) Then
8              sales(doc.SalesPerson(0)) = sales(doc.SalesPerson(0)) +_
                 doc.SalesAmount(0)
             Else
9              sales(doc.SalesPerson(0)) = doc.SalesAmount(0)
             End If
           End If
         Next x
       End If
10     Forall y In sales
11       soutput$ = soutput$ + Listtag(y) + " - " + Cstr(y) + Chr(13)
       End Forall
12     MessageBox soutput$, 0, "Results"
     End If
```

Explanation

1 A list called `sales` is declared to hold currency values.

2 The database is checked to make sure it is accessible.

3 If the number of documents in collection is greater than zero, the script is executed.

4 The collection of all documents is refined.

5 Loop through all documents in the collection.

6 The document is checked for the proper fields.

7 Check to see if the salesperson already exists in the list.

8 If the salesperson is in the list, the sales amounts from the current document are added.

9 If the salesperson does not exist in the list, he/she is added to the list with the sales amount from the current document.

10 All elements of the list will be accessed by the `Forall` loop.

11 The string for the results message box is formatted.

12 The results of the search are presented to the user.

Notes The code could have easily used arrays instead of lists. The `If` block starting at line 7 would be coded like this:

```
1    If (x = 1) Then
2       Redim salesamount(x) As Currency
3       Redim salesperson(x) As String
4       salesamount(x) = doc.SalesAmount(0)
5       salesperson(x) = doc.SalesPerson(0)
     Else
6       Found = False
7       For z = 1 to Ubound(salesperson)
8          If (salesperson(z) = doc.SalesPerson(0)) Then
              salesamount(z) = salesamount(z) + doc.SalesAmount(0)
              Found = True
           End If
        Next z
9       If Not Found Then
           Redim Preserve salesamount(Ubound(salesamount) + 1)
           Redim Preserve salesperson(Ubound(salesperson) + 1)
           salesamount(Ubound(salesamount)) = doc.SalesAmount(0)
           salesperson(Ubound(salesperson)) = doc.SalesPerson(0)
        End If
     End If
```

Explanation

1 A value of one in x signals the first time through the loop. The array needs to be initialized if it is the first time.

2 The `salesamount` array is set to hold one value.

3 The `salesperson` array is set to hold one value.

4 The current sales amount is stored in the `salesamount` array.

5 The current salesperson is stored in the `salesperson` array.

6 The Boolean variable `Found` signals if a salesperson was found in the array.

7 Loop through all values in the `salesperson` array to search for a match.

8 If the current salesperson matches the one from the current position in the array, add the sales amount to their total and set the match flag to `true` to signal a match was found.

9 The found variable is checked for a `false` value after searching the array. If it is `false`, then the current salesperson and their sales amount are added as new elements in their respective arrays.

As you can see, the code is a bit more complex. In this situation, Lists were much easier and more efficient to implement. Lists cannot always be used; arrays are much more flexible in the amount of data that can be stored and performing operations such as sorting. These topics will be covered in more detail in chapter 14.

5.8 Chapter summary

Multivalued objects are the norm in Lotus Notes/Domino development. All fields are stored as multivalued arrays (with the exception of Rich Text fields), documents from a database can be "collected" into an array of documents, and the list goes on and on. Familiarity with array syntax is essential to successful Notes/Domino development. Lists are similar to arrays because they hold multiple values, but their strength and key difference lies in the unique key for each element in a list. This makes searching much faster. Arrays and lists have a strong presence in the remaining examples in the book.

5.9 Chapter review

- The size of an array can be specific or dynamic.
- Lists are dynamic by nature.
- Items are added to lists with the `addElement` method.
- Items are added to an array by specifying the element number in the array.
- `Dim`, `Redim`, and `Preserve` are used to declare arrays.
- `Dim` and `List` are used to declare lists.
- Multiple documents are retrieved from a database using the NotesDocumentCollection object.
- Working with collections is similar to working with Lists and Arrays.
- `GetNextDocument`, `GetPrevDocument`, `GetFirstDocument`, `GetLastDocument`, and `GetNthDocument` are the methods used to work with documents in a collection.
- Notes treats fields like arrays with the exception of Rich Text fields. They are called value arrays.

CHAPTER 6

Working with files

6.1 Chapter objectives 86
6.2 Opening 86
6.3 Closing 88
6.4 Reading/writing 89
6.5 Sequential access 91
6.6 Random access 94
6.7 Binary access 97
6.8 Directories 98
6.9 NotesDBDirectory class 102
6.10 Platforms 104
6.11 Chapter example 105
6.12 Chapter summary 107
6.13 Chapter review 107

6.1 Chapter objectives

- Accessing external files from LotusScript
- Opening/closing files
- Reading data from files
- Writing data to files
- Sequential access
- Random access
- Binary access
- Directories (accessing, deleting, creating)
- File properties
- Deleting files
- NotesDatabase properties (file name, path, server, etc.)
- Import example
- Export example

Working with files in LotusScript is a routine task. LotusScript provides the necessary functionality to access files sequentially or randomly, or work with bytes (binary). Accessing a file sequentially means that each record in the file is read one after the other, the order in which they were originally written to the file. Files that contain unstructured data (i.e., no defined length) should be accessed sequentially, because you can never be certain where one record will start and another may end. Random access allows any record in a file to be accessed, thus it is more flexible, but the size of the record(s) must be known (fixed). Binary access allows any byte in a file to be accessed. A number specifies the byte.

Basically, there are two actions you will want to perform with files: read and write. Data will be written to a file, and data will be retrieved from a file. In addition to reading and writing files, LotusScript provides the means to work with directories, delete files, retrieve Notes database paths and file names, work with Notes database directories, and access the various properties of a file.

6.2 Opening

Whether you are working with files as sequential, random, or binary access, the file must be opened before it can be read from or written to. The `Open` statement handles the opening of files for reading and/or writing data.

Syntax (Everything within brackets—[]—is optional.)

```
1    Open filename
2    [ For { Random | Input | Output | Append | Binary } ]
3    [ Access { Read | Read Write | Write } ]
4    [ { Shared | Lock Read | Lock Read Write | Lock Write } ]
5    As [#] fileNumber
6    [ Len = recordLength ]
```

Explanation

1 *Required* Instructs the system to open the designated file name.

2 *Optional* designates whether the file will be opened for random, binary, or sequential (input, output, append) access. Random is used if this is not specified.

3 *Optional* Designates whether the file will be opened for reading, writing, or both. If this is not specified, it is set to Write for output, append, and binary modes; Read for input mode; and Read Write for Random mode. Specifying Read Write says that both read and write operations are permitted; Write signals that only write operations are allowed, and Read says that only reading from the file is permitted.

4 *Optional* Designates how the file can be shared. The default is Shared. Lock Read prevents other processes from reading from the file, although they can write to it; Lock Read Write prevents other processes from reading or writing to the file; and Lock Write prevents other processes from writing to the file.

5 *Required* The file number to associate with this file. The next section on *Freefile* provides a more complete explanation.

6 *Optional* Designates the record length, but it has a different meaning depending on how the file is opened (sequential, binary, or random). If the file is opened as sequential (input, output, or append) this tells the system how many characters to read from the file into the internal buffer. If the file is opened as random, it designates the length of the file. Finally, it is ignored when dealing with binary access.

Therefore, the only required information is the fileNumber. A file number is specified when a file is opened; LotusScript limits the number of open files to 255. You can designate the file number to open as any integer between 0 and 255, but it is better to retrieve an available file number from the system. A better term than file number is file handle. The number gives a handle to a file that both you and the system agree to use to access that file.

6.2.1 Freefile

The freefile function returns an unused file number. Use this function and you will not encounter any errors trying to use a file number that is already in use. If there are no more file numbers available, LotusScript generates an error. Therefore, if we want to open a file:

```
freeNumber = FreeFile
Open NewFile As freeNumber
```

Example 6.1

We will open a file for reading and writing, as random access, and we will not lock it.

```
    Dim filename As String
    Dim filenum As Integer
1   filename = "c:\test.txt"
2   filenum = FreeFile()
3   Open filename For Random Access Read Write As filenum
```

Explanation

1 Sets the file name to open.

2 Obtains available file number from the system.

3 Opens the file for reading and writing as random access.

Example 6.2

Now, we will open a sequential file for reading.

```
    Dim filename As String
    Dim filenum As Integer
    filename = "c:\text.txt"
1   filenum = FreeFile()
2   Open filename For Input Access Read As filenum
3   Close filenum
```

Explanation

1 Obtains available file number from the system.

2 Opens the file for reading as sequential access.

3 Closes the file.

6.3 Closing

Of course once a file has been opened, it must be closed. The LotusScript `Close` statement provides this functionality.

Syntax

```
Close [file number]
```

The file number is optional. If it is not specified, all open files are closed. Also, separating the file numbers with commas can close more than one file. Example 6.2 shows how the `Close` statement is used. The remainder of the examples in this chapter that use files will use it as well.

6.4 Reading/writing

LotusScript provides definite statements for dealing with sequential file access, but the commands for random and binary access overlap. Two lists follow that give a brief explanation of the LotusScript commands associated with reading and/or writing data to files. Each item indicates which type of access they work with (sequential, random, or binary). A more detailed discussion of each command is available in the Notes Help database.

6.4.1 Reading

- `Line Input # filenumber, variable`
  Access: sequential
  One line is read from the file. Characters are read from the file until a newline character is encountered, the newline character is not read into the variable. The variable must be a `string` or `Variant`.

- `Input # filenumber, variables`
  Access: sequential
  Data is read from the file into a variable or list of variables. Commas separate the variables in the list.

- `Input number_of_characters, filenumber`
  Access: sequential
  The number of characters specified is read from the file. The number of characters to read must not exceed 32K.

- `Get # filenumber, position_number, variable`
  Access: random and binary
  Reads data from a file into a variable. The `position_number` parameter is optional. If it is included, it tells the system where (record number when used with random files, and byte number for binary files) to start reading the data from the file. If it is omitted, the current record position is used as the starting point.

6.4.2 Writing

The `Print #` and `Write #` statements can be used to write data to a sequential file. A file must be opened in Output or Append mode to write to it.

- `Print # filenumber, expression`
  Access: sequential

Data is written to the file associated with the filenumber file handle. The `expression` parameter is optional; if it is omitted a blank line is written to the file. It can include one or more variables separated by commas, semicolons, or spaces.

- `Write # filenumber, expression`
  Access: sequential
  Data is written to the file associated with the filenumber file handle. Commas separate the items in the expression and a newline character is inserted when the data is saved to the file. If the expression is left out, a blank line is written to the file.

- `Put # filenumber, position_number, variable`
  Access: random and binary access
  Writes data to the file associated with the filenumber file handle. The `position_number` parameter is optional. If it is used, it tells the system where (record number if used with random files and byte number when used with binary files) to write the data. If it is left out, the current record position is used.

Lets cover a few other important items before we move into examples. The EOF, LOF, and LOC functions can be used to check where you are in a file.

6.4.3 EOF (filenumber)

This function returns an integer indicating whether the end of file (EOF), specified by the filenumber file handle, has been reached. A value of `-1` indicates that the end of the file has been reached, and a zero (`0`) signals that the end has not been reached. The circumstances of the return value vary depending on the file access used. A return value of `-1` with binary access infers the last `Get` statement could not read the amount of data requested; a return value of `-1` with random access signals that the last `Get` statement could not read the entire record; and a `-1` with sequential access indicates that the end of the file has been reached. A zero with all three access types means there is more data to read.

6.4.4 LOF (filenumber)

This function returns the length of file (LOF) as a long value, in bytes associated with the file handled passed to it.

6.4.5 LOC (filenumber)

The LOC function returns the current position of the file pointer in the file specified by the filenumber file handle. Actually, the return value of this function varies (slightly) depending on the access type used. The LOC returns the position of the last read or written file for random access; the byte position (divided by 128 and truncated to zero decimal places) for sequential access; and the position of the last bytes read or written to the file for binary access.

Now let's cover a few examples to see what we have been discussing.

Example 6.3

```
    Dim filenum As Integer
    Dim filename As String
    Dim lineIn As String
1   filename = "c:\test.txt"
2   filenum% = FreeFile()
3   Open filename For Input As filenum
4   MsgBox "The size of the file is " & LOF(filenum)
5   Do Until EOF(filenum)
6   Line Input #filenum, lineIn
7     MsgBox "Current position in the file " & LOC(filenum)
    Loop
8   Close filenum
```

Explanation:

1 The name and path of the file to be opened is set.

2 Retrieves a file handle from the system.

3 Opens the file for input as a sequential access file.

4 Displays the length of the file in a message box.

5 A `Do` loop is used to loop through the file until the end of the file is reached.

6 Reads a line of text into the `lineIn` variable.

7 Displays the current position in the file.

8 Closes the file.

At this point we will cover each access mode independently.

6.5 Sequential access

Data is stored in sequential files as a continuous stream of characters, your basic text files. Everything stored in a sequential file is stored as a character or its ASCII equivalent. For this reason, sequential files are not well suited for storing numbers. When reading from a sequential file, the data is retrieved in the order it was written to the file. Likewise, data is written to the file in the order specified. Of course, data can be appended (Append) or written over top of existing data (Output).

Example 6.4

We will open a file as sequential and add data to it. The data will be appended to the existing data in the file.

```
Dim filename As String
Dim filenum As Integer
Dim userdata As String
```

```
1   filename = "c:\test.txt"
2   filenum = FreeFile
3   Open filename For Append Access Write As filenum
4   Do
5      userdata = InputBox$("Please enter a name.")
6      Write #filenum, userdata
7   Loop Until (userdata = "")
8   Close filenum
```

Explanation

1 Sets the file to be opened.

2 Obtains a file handle from the system.

3 Opens the file to append data to it.

4 A `Do` loop is used to write data to the file.

5 Obtains data to write to the file from the user.

6 Writes the data to the file. The `Print#` statement could have been used.

7 The end of the `Do` loop. We continue until the user enters nothing. Of course, the blank line will be written to the file.

8 Closes the file.

Example 6.5

Now we want to read the data from the file from example 6.4. After reading it, we display the data in a message box.

```
    Dim filename As String
    Dim filenum As Integer
1   Dim outstring As String
2   Dim instring As String
3   filename = "c:\test.txt"
    filenum = FreeFile
4   Open filename For Input Access Read As filenum
5   Do Until EOF(filenum)
6      Line Input #filenum, instring
7      outstring = outstring + instring + Chr(10) + Chr(13)
    Loop
8   MsgBox outstring, 0, "Contents of " & filename
```

Explanation

1 Declares string used to hold output.

2 Declares string to receive line of input from the file.

3 Opens the file for sequential reading.

4 Loops through the contents of the file until the end of the file is reached.

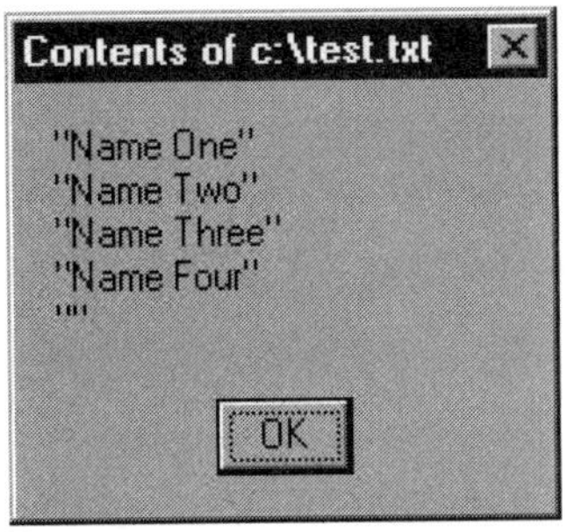

Figure 6.1 Example 6.5 output

5 Reads one line from the file into the `instring` variable.

6 Creates the outstring by concatenating lines from the file and separating multiple lines with newline characters.

7 Once all data has been read from the file, displays the contents in a message box. Figure 6.1 shows one possible outcome.

I will close the section on sequential files with a simple example of copying the contents of one file to another.

Example 6.6

```
     Dim destFile As String, sourceFile As String
     Dim destNum As Integer, sourceNum As Integer
     Dim copyString As String
1    Do
2       sourceFile = Inputbox$("Enter text file to copy.")
     Loop Until (sourceFile <> "")
3    If (Dir$(sourceFile, 0) = "") Then
4       Msgbox "The file to copy does not exist. Aborting...",64,"Error"
        Exit Sub
     End If
     Do
5       destFile = Inputbox$("Enter text file to copy " & sourceFile & " to.")
     Loop Until (destFile <> "")
6    sourceNum = Freefile
7    Open sourceFile For Input Access Read As sourceNum
8    destNum = Freefile
9    Open destFile For Append As destNum
10   Do Until Eof(sourceNum)
11         Line Input #sourceNum, copyString
12         Print #destNum, copyString
     Loop
13   Close #sourceNum, #destNum
```

Explanation

1 A `Do` loop is used to retrieve a value for the name of the file to copy. If the user enters a blank name, they are prompted to enter it again.

2 Stores the input value in the `sourceFile` string variable.

3 A new function: the `dir` function. `Dir` is used to obtain a list of files from a directory, or determine if a file exists. In this case, it checks to make sure that the file to copy does exist. It makes no sense to copy a file that does not exist. The `dir` function is covered later in the chapter.

4 If the file does not exist, the user is notified and the script ends.

5 Gets the name of the destination file for the copying.

6 Obtains file handle from the system for the source file.

7 Opens the source file for reading.

8 Obtains file handle from the system for the destination file.

9 Opens the destination file for appending.

10 Loops through the source file until the end of the file is reached.

11 Reads a line from the source file into the `copyString` variable.

12 Copies the line read from the source file to the destination file.

13 Closes the files.

6.6 Random access

Random access files, like sequential files, contain text. There is a major difference: random access files have some defined structure. Each record in a random access file has the same length, whereas record size in sequential files is not set in any way. The use of the Type data structure is extensive when working with random files. They give the flexibility of defining a data structure and declaring the length. Get, Put, and Seek are used to read and write data to and from a random access file. The best way to learn is through examples.

Example 6.7

```
1    Type Person
        Name As String * 25
        Address As String * 40
        Phone As String *16
     End Type

     Dim filename As String
     Dim filenum As Integer
2    Dim personInfo As Person
3    filename = "c:\random.txt"
4    filenum = Freefile
5    Open filename For Random As filenum Len = Len(personInfo)
6    For x = 1 To 5
7    personInfo.Name = Inputbox$("Name")
8    personInfo.Address = Inputbox$("Address")
9    personInfo.Phone = Inputbox$("Phone")
10   Put # filenum,x , personInfo
     Next x
11   Close #filenum
```

Explanation

1 Declares the data structure for the file. It contains three string variables: `name`, `address`, and `phone`. The lengths of each string variable is set using the `* num-`

ber notation. The length of the name variable is set to 25, address is 40, and phone is 16.

2 Declares a variable name to be of the user type defined in step one.

3 Declares the file name and path.

4 Retrieves a file handle from the system.

5 Opens the file as a Random access file, and the record length is set to the length of the user defined data type (using the `Len` function).

6 `For` loop saves five records to the file.

7 The user sets the name.

8 The user sets the address.

9 The user sets the phone number.

10 Writes the record (name, address, and phone) to the file. The record number to write is specified using the `For` loop index variable (`x`). This writes records starting at the beginning of the file, which is position one (`1`).

11 Closes the file.

Now that we have written five records to the file, let's read them back. We will use the same record structure from the previous example.

Example 6.8

```
    Dim filenum As Integer
    Dim personInfo As Person
    filename = "c:\random.txt"
    filenum = Freefile
1   Open filename For Random As filenum Len = Len(personInfo)
2   Do Until Eof(filenum)
3        Get # filenum, ,personInfo
4        Messagebox "Name:  " & personInfo.Name & Chr(13) & "Address:  " &
         personInfo.Address & Chr(13) & "Phone:  " & personInfo.Phone
    Loop
5   Close #filenum
```

Explanation

1 Opens the file for random access and sets the record length to the length of the user-defined data type `personInfo`.

2 Loops through the file until the end of the file is reached.

3 Reads one record from the file. No record number is specified, so uses the current position.

4 Displays the contents of the record to the user.

5 Closes the file.

The last example is nice, but it doesn't display any advantages over sequential files. The next example uses the `Seek` statement. The syntax of it follows.

Syntax

```
Seek file_number, position_number
```

The record position pointer is moved to the position_number specified. If you try to move beyond the end of the file, the record pointer will be positioned at the last position referenced.

Example 6.9

```
    Dim filenum As Integer
    Dim personInfo As Person
    filename = "c:\random.txt"
    filenum = Freefile
1   Open filename For Random As filenum Len = Len(personInfo)
2   Seek # filenum, 3
3   Get # filenum, ,personInfo
4   Messagebox "Name:  " & personInfo.Name & Chr(13) & "Address:  " &
      personInfo.Address & Chr(13) & "Phone:  " & personInfo.Phone
5     Seek # filenum, 6
6     Get # filenum, ,personInfo
7     Messagebox "Name:  " & personInfo.Name & Chr(13) & "Address:  " &
        personInfo.Address & Chr(13) & "Phone:  " & personInfo.Phone
8   Close #filenum
```

Explanation

1 Opens the file for random access with the record length set to the length of the user-defined data type.

2 Moves the record pointer to three (3).

3 Reads the record at the current position (3 from the previous step) into the user-defined data type.

4 Displays the contents of the record read.

5 Moves the record pointer to six (6).

6 Reads the record at the current position. The previous step moved the pointer beyond the length of the file, so the position is reset to its previous position, that is three (3). Consequently, the same record is read.

7 Displays the contents of the record.

8 Closes the file.

6.7 Binary access

The Lotus Help describes the binary file as providing the ultimate in control over the organization of data in your files. The drawback to this ultimate freedom is that you must know *exactly* how the file was written when you prepare to read it. Essentially, binary files are random access files without the structure to let you know what is going on. The record size is variable. The main benefit of binary files over random is the fact that binary files waste less space, resulting in smaller size.

Example 6.10

```
  Dim filename As String
  Dim filenum As Integer
  Dim inputName As String
  Dim x As Integer
1 filename = "c:\binary.txt"
2 filenum = Freefile
3 Open filename For Binary As filenum
4 inputName = Inputbox("Please enter a name.")
5 Put #filenum,1,inputName
6 Close #filenum
```

Explanation

1 Defines the file name and path.

2 Obtains the file handle from system.

3 Opens the file as a binary file.

4 A name is entered by the user and stored in the `inputName` string variable.

5 Writes the data entered by the user to the file.

6 Closes the file.

Example 6.11

```
  Dim filename As String
  Dim filenum As Integer
  Dim char
  Dim charString As String * 12
  Dim x As Integer
  filename = "c:\binary.txt"
  filenum = Freefile
1 Open filename For Binary As filenum
2 char = Input(1,filenum)
3 Msgbox "Name:  " & char
4 Get #filenum,1,charString
5 Msgbox "Name:  " & charString
6 Close filenum
```

Explanation

1 Opens the file as binary.

2 The `Input` function reads in a byte at position one in the file.

3 Displays the character.

4 The `Get` statement reads in a string value. The variable `charString` was defined with a length of twelve (12), so the length of the variable is read from the file.

5 Displays the string.

6 Closes the file.

Output

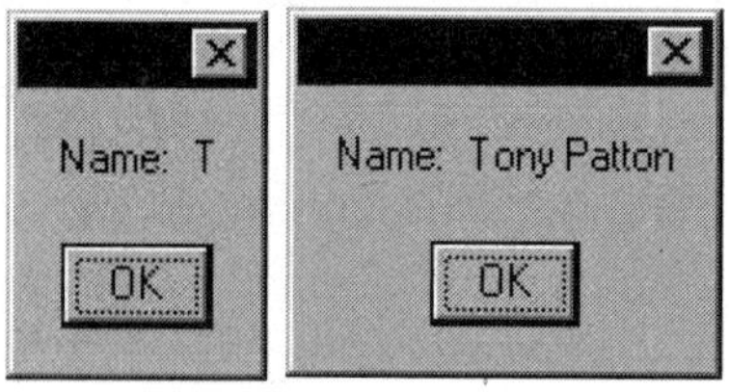

Figure 6.2 Output of example 6.11 - Two messageboxes

If I entered my name (Tony Patton) into the file in example 6.10, the output for example 6.11 looks like figure 6.2.

Binary files give an abundance of freedom, but high maintenance makes them the least used of the three.

6.8 Directories

Example 6.6 gave a glimpse of working with directories. It used the `Dir` function to check for the existence of a file. This is a must when reading files, because you must be certain the file exists before attempting to read data from it. Attempting to read a non-existent file results in a run-time error.

6.8.1 Dir

The `Dir` function returns file, directories, or the volume label from a specified directory.

Syntax

```
Dir (filename, attribute_mask)
```

- *File Name* Specifies the name of the file or directory. It can include path information.
- *Attibute_mask* Is optional. It tells the system what type(s) of items should be retrieved. The values can be summed to include more than one file type.
- *0* Normal files
- *2* Hidden files
- *4* System files
- *8* Volume label
- *16* Directory

Example 6.12

Retrieve a list of all normal and hidden files from drive C directory.

```
Dir("c:\",2)
```

Retrieve the volume label for drive D.

```
Dir("d:\",8)
```

Retrieve directories and hidden files from drive E.

```
Dir("e:\",18)
```

Example 6.13

I want to search a directory for a certain file (test.txt), which could be hidden or a system file.

```
    Dim path As String
    Dim filename As String
1   path = "c:\test.txt"
2   filename = Dir(path,6)
3   If (filename <> "") Then
4         Msgbox "The file was found."
    End If
```

Explanation

1 Sets the directory and file name to search for.

2 Uses the `Dir` function to search for the file. We are interested in normal, system, and hidden files (0 + 4 + 2 = 6).

3 Finds the file if the file name variable is not empty.

4 Displays message if the file was found.

Example 6.14

The `Dir` function can be used to scroll through all files in a directory as well.

```
    Dim path As String
    Dim info As String
    path = "c:\"
1   info = Dir(path, 22)
2   Do While (info <> "")
3      MsgBox "File:  " & info
4      info = Dir()
    Loop
```

Explanation

1 Retrieves the first item from the path. We are interested in everything but volume label (0 + 2 + 4 + 16 = 22).

2 A `Do` loop scrolls through the items from the path.

3 Displays the item.

4 Retrieves the next item from the path. Once the `Dir` function has been used the first time, the next call to it without parameters performs the same lookup.

After checking for the existence of a directory, we may want to remove it or create it depending on what we find. The `MkDir` and `RmDir` statements provide this functionality.

Example 6.15

```
    Dim info As String
    Dim path As String
1   path = "c:\test"
2   info = Dir(path, 16)
3   If (info <> "") Then
4        Rmdir(path)
    Else
       Mkdir(path)
    End If
```

Explanation

1 Sets the path to find.

2 The `Dir` function checks for existence of directory.

3 Deletes the directory if it is found.

4 Creates the directory if it doesn't exist.

6.8.2 CurDrive, ChDrive, CurDir, ChDir

Four functions—`CurDrive`, `ChDrive`, `CurDir`, and `ChDir`—access the current drive and/or directory on the system. When you start Lotus Notes the current directory is set to your Lotus Notes directory (Ex: `\notes`), and the current drive is the one where Lotus Notes is installed. The `ChDir` and `ChDrive` functions are used to change these settings.

Example 6.16

```
Print "Current Drive:  " & Curdrive
Print "Current Directory:  " & Curdir
Chdrive("D")
Chdir("\temp")
Print "Current Drive:  " & Curdrive
Print "Current Directory:  " & Curdir
```

Output

On my system:
Current Drive: C:
Current Directory: C:\notes

```
Current Drive: D:
Current Directory: D:\temp
```

6.8.3 More LotusScript for working with files

Example 6.6 copied one text file to another one line at a time. It has no real purpose other than instruction, because LotusScript provides the `FileCopy` command. Example 6.17 shows it and a few others.

Example 6.17

```
  Dim sourcefile As String
  Dim destfile As String
  Dim renamefile As String
1 sourcefile = "c:\test1.txt"
2 destfile = "c:\test2.txt"
3 renamefile = "c:\new.txt"
4 FileCopy sourcefile, destfile
5 Kill sourcefile
6 Print destfile & " was created on " & FileDateTime(destfile)
7 Print "The size of " & destfile & " in bytes is " & FileLen(destfile)
8 Name destfile As renamefile
```

Explanation

1 Sets name of the file to be copied; it is the source file.

2 Sets name of the file to copy source file into.

3 Sets the new name of the file.

4 The `FileCopy` statement copies the contents of one file to another. If the destination file exists, its contents are overwritten. The path information in the file names is optional. The syntax for FileCopy is.

```
FileCopy  source_file As destination_file
```

5 The `Kill` command deletes the file. Use this command with extreme caution, because a file cannot be brought back once it has been deleted with `Kill`.

```
Kill filename
```

6 The `FileDateTime` function prints the date and time the file was created.

```
FileDateTime(filename)
```

7 The `FileLen` function prints the size of the file (in bytes).

```
FileLen(filename)
```

8 The `Name` command renames the file. `Name` can be used to rename files and directories, but the new name must not currently exist and the current directory cannot be renamed.

```
Name oldName newName
```

We have now covered the various ways to work with files and directories in LotusScript. Lotus Notes/Domino adds a few other techniques.

6.9 NotesDBDirectory class

The NotesDBDirectory class is used to obtain a list of databases on a Domino server or local workstation. You can restrict the list to contain only databases, template databases, replica candidates, or template candidates.

Syntax

```
Dim variable_name As New NotesDBDirectory(server_name)
```

or

```
Dim variable_name As NotesDBDirectory
Set variable_name = New NotesDBDirectory(server_name)
```

or

```
Dim session As New NotesSession
Dim variable_name As NotesDBDirectory
Set variable_name = session.GetDBDirec-
tory(server_name)
```

Note The server_name is left blank ("") when accessing the local Notes directory.

6.9.1 Methods

There are two methods associated with the NotesDBDirectory class: `GetFirstDatabase` and `GetNextDatabase`. `GetFirstDatabase` accepts a parameter that signals what type of databases to list.

- *DATABASE* Any Lotus Notes/Domino database.
- *TEMPLATE* Any Lotus Notes/Domino template database (.ntf)
- *REPLICA_CANDIDATE* Any Lotus Notes/Domino database that does not have replication disabled.
- *TEMPLATE_CANDIDATE* Any Lotus Notes/Domino database.

Example 6.18

```
Dim s As New NotesSession
Dim db As NotesDatabase
Dim dbdir As NotesDBDirectory
Set dbdir = s.GetDBDirectory("")
Set db = dbdir.GetFirstDatabase(TEMPLATE_CANDIDATE)
Print db.Title
Do
   Set db = dbdir.GetNextDatabase
```

```
7       If Not (db Is Nothing) Then
8          Print db.Title
        Else
9          Exit Do
        End If
      Loop
```

Explanation

1. Declares a NotesDBDirectory.
2. Instantiates the NotesDBDirectory object using the `GetDBDirectory` method of the NotesSession object.
3. Sets the NotesDatabase object to the first database from the GetDBDirectory list. The `TEMPLATE_CANDIDATE` parameter tells the system to get the first database no matter what.
4. Displays the title of the database in the status bar.
5. Uses a `Do` loop to repeat the process of getting more databases.
6. Sets the NotesDatabase object to the next database from the NotesDBDirectory list.
7. Checks the database object returned for validity.
8. Displays the title in the status line if the database object exists.
9. Exits the `Do` loop if the database object does not exist (it is nothing), because an empty database object signals the end of the databases in the NotesDBDirectory object.

Example 6.19

```
     Dim dbdir As NotesDbDirectory
     Dim db As NotesDatabase
     Dim temp As Long
     Dim tempTitle As String, tempFileName As String
1    Set dbdir = New NotesDbDirectory("")
2    Set db = dbdir.GetFirstDatabase(DATABASE)
3    Call db.Open("","")
4    tempSize = db.Size
5    tempTitle = db.Title
6    tempFileName = db.FileName
     Do
7       Set db = dbdir.GetNextDatabase
     If Not (db Is Nothing ) Then
        Call db.Open("","")
8       If (db.Size > tempSize) Then
           tempSize = db.Size
           tempTitle = db.Title
           tempFileName = db.FileName
        End If
     Else
```

```
9       Exit Do
      End If
   Loop
   If (tempTitle <> "") Then
10    Msgbox "The largest database on the system is..." & Chr(13) &_
        "Title:  " & tempTitle & Chr(13) &    "Filename:  " & tempFileName &_
        Chr(13) & "Size:  " & tempSize, 64, "Database"
End If
```

Explanation

1 Sets the NotesDBDirectory object to the local directory.

2 Sets the NotesDatabase object to the first database in the directory. The `DATABASE` parameter specifies that only databases are returned.

3 Opens the database. This must be done to access properties like size and file name.

4 Stores the size of the database in a holding variable.

5 Stores the title of the database in a holding variable.

6 Stores the file name of the database in a holding variable.

7 Sets the database object to the next database in the directory object.

8 Resets the holding variables to hold the current database values if the size of the current database is larger than the value in holding variable.

9 Exits if there are no more databases.

10 Displays the information on the largest database (in size) if one was found.

Possible output

Figure 6.3 6.19 Output

6.10 Platforms

The file separator is different depending on the platform used. UNIX uses the forward slash (/) and DOS/Windows uses the back slash (\). LotusScript supports both methods, but care must be taken when using either character in strings. For example, Unix allows the Windows/DOS separator (\) in file names, but this will generate an error in LotusScript. Also, the use of drives differs in the UNIX, DOS/Windows, and Apple worlds. DOS/Windows uses a drive letter, but UNIX does not. These are just a couple of examples of the differences that need to be addressed for your application to take advantage of the platforms supported by Lotus Notes/Domino. The Notes Help contains more details on platform differences.

6.11 Chapter example

A text file will be imported into a Lotus Notes database. Each record from the file will be stored as a record in the database. The file will be read as random access.

```
[Declarations]
1     Type Product_Info
         Name As String * 20
         Price As Currency
         Description As String * 40
      End Type

2     Sub Initialize
3        On Error Goto Handle_Errors
         Dim sess As New NotesSession
         Dim filename As String
         Dim filenum As Integer
4        Dim inputRecord As Product_Info
         Dim db As New NotesDatabase("","")
5        If (db.Open("server","products.nsf")) Then
            Dim newdoc As NotesDocument
            filename = "c:\import.txt"
6           If (Dir(filename) <> "") Then
               filenum = Freefile
7              Open filename For Random Access Read As _
                  #filenum Len = Len(inputRecord)
               Do
8                 Get # filenum, ,inputRecord
9                 Set newdoc = db.CreateDocument
10                With newdoc
                     .Form = "Product"
                     .Name = inputRecord.Name
                     .Price = Ccur(inputRecord.Price)
                     .Description = inputRecord.Description
                  End With
11                Call newdoc.Save(True,False)
12             Loop Until Eof(filenum)
13             Close(filenum)
            Else
14             Messagebox "The file to import does not exist. _
                  Import failed.",64,"Error"
               Exit Sub
            End If
```

```
     Else
15      Messagebox "The database could not be opened. _
           Import failed.",64,"Error"
     End If
     Exit Sub
16   Handle_Errors:
     Messagebox "An error has occurred.  Import failed.",64,"Error"
     Exit Sub
17 End Sub
```

Explanation

1 Declares the data type to be used to read the data from the file. It has a name, price, and description. It is defined in the Declarations section of the script.

2 Starts the `Initialize` event.

3 Instructs the system to transfer control to the `Handle_Errors` label if an error is encountered.

4 Declares a variable of the user-defined data type.

5 Proceeds if the database was successfully opened.

6 Checks for the existence of the file before starting the import, an attempt to predict errors, so the script won't crash during run time.

7 Opens the file for reading as a random access file. The record length is set to the user-defined type.

8 Gets the first line from the file.

9 Creates a document in the database.

10 Uses the `With` statement to set the form variables to values read from the file. It saves some typing, so it is a good thing. Less typing means fewer errors.

11 Saves the new document.

12 The `Do` loop continues until the end of the file is reached.

13 Closes the file because the `Do` loop has completed. There are no more records to read from the file.

14 Displays a message to the user if the file to import could not be found, and exits the script. This is the `Else` portion of the `If` statement in step 6.

15 Displays a message to the user if the database could not be opened, and exits the script. This is the `Else` portion of the `If` statement from step 5.

16 The `Handle_Errors` label. The script knows to transfer execution to this point if any runtime errors occur.

17 Ends the `Initialize` event.

The script imports the contents of the file into a Notes database; it could be set up to check to see if a document exists for the data from the file before saving records. The chapter that covers searching will give more details on searching for values.

Note The file in the chapter example was created with the following short script. The purpose of the script was to set up a file to test the script from the chapter example. It is straightforward, utilizing commands covered to this point.

```
[Declarations]
Type Product_Info
      Name As String * 20
      Price As Currency
      Description As String * 40
End Type

Sub Initialize
Dim filename As String
Dim filenum As Integer
Dim export As Product_Info
filename = "c:\import.txt"
filenum = Freefile
Open filename For Random Access Write As filenum Len = Len(export)
limit = CInt(InputBox("Enter number of records to enter.","Input"))
For x = 1 To 10
   export.Name = Inputbox$("Enter Name","Data Entry")
   export.Price = Ccur(Inputbox("Enter Price","Data Entry"))
   export.Description = Inputbox$("Enter Description","Data Entry")
   Put # filenum,,export
Next x
Close (filenum)
End Sub
```

6.12 Chapter summary

The text file is a common item in every office. Applications such as Microsoft Excel and Lotus 1-2-3 allow the user to save data as a text file. This is true for database applications such as Microsoft Access and Lotus Approach as well. LotusScript provides all of the functionality needed to bring data into Notes, and export the data into a format readable by other applications

6.13 Chapter review

- Files can be opened for random, sequential, or binary access.
- Sequential files are a continuous stream of characters with no formalized or consistent structure (ordinary text files).

- Random files have a set record length. Records are accessed by number (ordered, starting at one). Data must be read the same as it was written.
- Binary files are accessed at the byte level. Extreme care must be taken when dealing with files as binary.
- Various commands are available to view, create, rename, or remove directories.
- Various commands, such as renaming and deleting, are available to work with files.
- The NotesDBDirectory class provides access to the list of Notes/Domino databases on a server or workstation. It can be used to find a database or template.
- The NotesDatabase class provides properties that correspond to the database file name, size, and directory.
- The numerous platforms supported by Lotus Notes must be considered when working with files in LotusScript.

C H A P T E R 7

Error processing and activity logging

7.1 Chapter objectives 110

7.2 Error trapping 110

7.3 NotesLog 115

7.4 Setting up the NotesLog object 117

7.5 Errors 119

7.6 Chapter summary 122

7.7 Chapter review 122

7.1 Chapter objectives

- Handling run-time errors.
- Handling user errors.
- Using the error description files for more informative error messages
- Logging script activity to a Notes database
- Logging script activity via email.
- Logging script activity to a text file.
- Logging script activity via the Agent Log

Errors occur no matter what language or environment you choose to develop applications. Hopefully, these errors will appear during development and/or testing, but as we all know this is not the case. The key to dealing with errors lies in program design. A good program/script takes errors into account.

Errors fall into three categories: user, system, and programmer. Such things as entering the wrong type of data, selecting the wrong option, or hitting the wrong key generate user errors. On the other hand, system errors are beyond the control of the user. These occur when a server is unavailable or the system runs out of memory. Finally, yes programmers do make mistakes, errors occur when data is not validated or an object is referenced before it is created.

Programmer errors can be caught by rigorously testing an application. Get users who have no clue about the application, so they can do things you would never do. Also, these errors can be handled during code execution by checking anything and everything.

There are two ways to monitor script activity for errors and gracefully handle errors during execution: error trapping and activity logging. They can be used together or seperately.

7.2 Error trapping

Creating a block of code to handle errors and trapping errors with `On Error` statements is the best way to appropriately handle user, programmer, and system errors.

Example 7.1

```
1    On Error Goto HandleErrors
        ....
        <code>
        ....
     Exit Sub
2    HandleErrors:
        MessageBox "An error has occurred"
```

```
        <code to handle error>
        ...
3    End
```

Explanation

1 Notifies the script to switch control to the HandleErrors section if any error is encountered. The `On Error` statement can be used with a specific error number or none at all. If no error number is specified, it handles all errors.

2 Begins the section of code to handle errors. You will notice `Exit Sub` statements just before the section. This ensures that the error handling code is only executed when it is called. This is called a label in LotusScript. Labels define points in a program where execution can be passed to using `goto` statements.

3 Ends execution after handling the error. This could say Resume to continue execution of the script at the point immediately following the line where the error occurred.

Notice the Exit Sub line before the start of the section of code to handle errors? It keeps the code in the section from running every time the script runs. Therefore, it runs only when called. Also, the script did not have to end once an error occurred. Line 3 could have told the script to continue execution with the `Resume` statement.

7.2.1 Resume

`Resume` tells the script to continue execution at the point of the error, the statement following the error, or transfer control similar to the `On Error` statement.

- *`Resume 0`* Continues execution at the point of the error.
- *`Resume <Label>`* Transfers execution to a specified section of code (section marked with the label).
- *`Resume Next`* Continues execution with the line immediately following the error.

7.2.2 Handling specific errors

`On Error` statements facilitate the capturing of specific errors. For example, if I want to catch error number 4084 (File Not Found), line 1 from the previous example would read as follows:

```
On Error 4084 Goto HandleErrors
```

Example 7.2

```
On Error 4084 Goto HandleFileNotFound
...
<code>
...
HandleFileNotFound:
```

```
MsgBox "Error, File Not Found"
End
```

7.2.3 Handling user-defined errors

In addition to handling predefined errors, custom errors can be created and used. First, define the error number. Next, raise the error whenever appropriate.

Example 7.3

```
1  On Error 88888 Goto ZeroError
   Dim uiw As NotesUIWorkspace
   Dim uidoc As NotesUIDocument
   Set uidoc = uiw.CurrentDocument
2  If (uidoc.Document.Field(0) = "0") Then Error 88888
   ….
   Exit Sub
3  ZeroError:
   MsgBox "The field is zero, aborting…)
   End
```

Explanation

1 Transfers control to the section of code with the label ZeroError when error 88888 occurs.

2 If the statement is `false`, error 88888 is raised. At this point, the script knows to transfer control to ZeroError.

3 Defines a section of code that tells the user an error has occurred, and the program is terminated.

7.2.4 Checking objects before referencing

Good error handling involves anticipation as well. Always check the existence of an object or variable before utilizing it in any way. If the contents of a field will be used in a calculation, the contents should be checked for validity before using.

Example 7.4

```
   Dim uiw As New NotesUIWorkspace
   Dim uidoc As NotesUIDocument
   Dim item As NotesItem
   Set uidoc = uiw.CurrentDocument
1  If (uidoc.Document.HasItem("FieldName")) Then
      <code that relies on the field>
   End If
```

Line 1 uses the `HasItem` method of the NotesDocument class to make sure a field exists before using it. This technique can be used to check for a database before using it. The database may not exist, or the server may not be reachable.

Example 7.5

```
   Dim db As New NotesDatabase("","")
1  If (db.Open("Server Path","Database Path")) Then
      < code that relies on database >
   End If
```

Line 1 uses the `Open` method of the NotesDatabase class (it returns a Boolean value) to determine if a database exists.

7.2.5 More detailed error messages

Catching errors and informing the user that an error has occurred is good, but giving the user more information about the error is even better. He/she can take this information and relay it to the developer. The more information you have when debugging is *always* better.

%Include

LotusScript has a standard set of errors and their corresponding error numbers defined in files in the root Notes directory. There are three files included with Notes 4.5/4.6: lserr.lss, lsxbeerr.lss, and lsxuierr.lss. The lsxuierr.lss contains error numbers/messages related to the user interface. You can view the contents of the files with any text editor such as the DOS editor, Notepad, or Wordpad. The files contain LotusScript constant statements. Files referenced using the `%Include` directive must include only LotusScript statements. The file extension does not have to be .lss, but if no extension is specified it is assumed to be .lss. Another .lss file that is included in the Notes installation is lsconst.lss, which contains all of the constants utilized by Lotus Notes. The `%include` directive is entered into the Options section of a script.

```
[Options]
Option Explicit
%INCLUDE "lserr.lss"
%INCLUDE "lsxbeerr.lss"
%INCLUDE "lsxuierr.lss"
```

You may develop your own .lss files. These are called LotusScript Extensions. The LotusScript Extension toolkit is available for free download from the Lotus website (http://www.lotus.com).

7.2.6 Err, Erl, and Error

Once the `%Include` directive has been used to bring in the error information from the .lss files, the error descriptions from the files can be used to provide more detailed error messages. The `Err`, `Erl`, and `Error` statements facilitate their use. The `Err` function returns the current error number (0 signals no error). `Erl` returns the line number where the error occurred. `Error` returns the error message associated with an error.

Example 7.6

The following code uses the `%Include`, `Err`, `Erl`, and `Error` statements.

```
[Options]
1    %Include "lserr.lss"
2    %Include "lsxbeerr.lss"

[Initialize]
3    On Error Goto HandleErrors %Include "lsxbeerr.lss"
4    Dim s As New NotesSession
     Dim db As NotesDatabase
     Dim dc As NotesDocumentCollection
     Set db = s.CurrentDatabase
     MsgBox "There are " & dc.Count & "documents in the " & db.Title & " _
        database."
     Exit Sub
     HandleErrors:
5    Beep
6    MsgBox "Error number " & Err & " occurred at line number " & Erl & _
        " due to " & Error(Err)
     End
```

Explanation

1. Places the contents of the lserr.lss file into the script at compile time.
2. Places the contents of the lxbeerr.lss file into the script at compile time.
3. Tells the script to transfer control to the `HandleErrors` label when any type of error occurs.
4. Sends a beep to signal an error.
5. Displays a message on the screen that tells what error number occurred, the line number of the error, and the text description of the error from the .lss files from the `%Include`.

7.2.7 Scope

Scope refers to the visibility of an object. An `On Error` statement remains in effect from the time a script is started until it ends.

7.2.8 Logging activity

The previous examples work very well for scripts that interact with users. The user runs a script, an error is encountered, and the script notifies the user of the problem and either exits or continues execution. An agent running in the background can gracefully exit using these techniques, but how does the developer and/or administrator know why an agent did not run as planned? The log option for an agent (highlight agent name in list, and right-click on the agent; select log from the bottom of the list) gives only minimal information. It tells when an agent last ran, how many documents were affected, and if any errors occurred. It gives no signal to why an agent may have failed to run (see figure 7.1).

7.3 NotesLog

The NotesLog class provides a means to monitor agent and other script activity. Information is logged during code execution. The log has four formats: text file, Notes database, email notifications, or an agent log. A script can be configured to email a message if and only if an agent fails to run as planned. The same agent could log activity to a text file or possibly a Notes database, which is monitored to see the activity. This provides an easy way to centralize the monitoring of script activity in several databases, thus easing the burden on developers and/or administrators. Instead of opening every database and checking every agent log (or worse yet, waiting for users to call with problems), a NotesLog object can be used to notify you via email or store information in one central location (text file or Notes database).

Two types of information are logged to a NotesLog: action and error. Both are recorded using methods of the NotesLog class (`LogAction` and `LogError`). `LogAction` accepts a text description of the action, and `LogError` accepts an error number and description. The difference between the two is how they appear in the Agent Log database. Errors appear with a red x and actions with a blue lightbulb. Figure 7.2 shows each item in the default view of an Agent Log database.

The entries are categorized by the name of the originating agent. The first entry recorded an action, the second, an error. A NotesLog object is declared, instantiated, and methods are called to record activity or errors. The NotesLog should be closed once the script has completed.

Example 7.7

```
1    Dim aLog As NotesLog
     Dim s As New NotesSession
     Dim db As NotesDatabase
     Dim dc As NotesDocumentCollection
     Dim x As Integer
2    On Error Goto HandleErrors
```

Figure 7.1 Agent log (right-click on agent in agent list and select log)

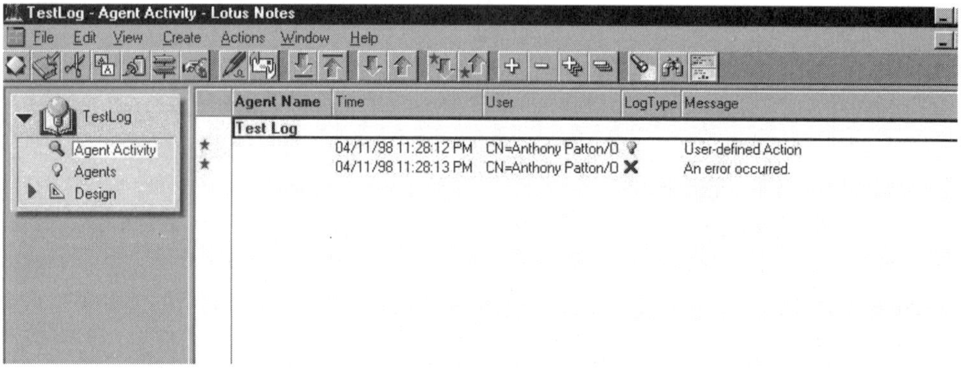

Figure 7.2 Action and error entries in agent log

```
     Set db = s.CurrentDatabase
     Set dc = db.AllDocuments
3    Set aLog = New NotesLog( "Database log" )
4    Call aLog.OpenNotesLog(db.Server,"log4a.nsf")
5    Call aLog.LogEvent("The script has started…")
     If (dc.Count > 100) Then
       Call aLog.LogAction("There are over 100 documents in this database.")
     Else
       Call aLog.LogAction("There are 100 or fewer documents in this database
     End If
6    Call aLog.LogAction("Script has finished running.")
7    Call aLog.Close
     Exit Sub
8    HandleErrors:
9    Call aLog.LogError(Err,"There has been an error at line#" & Erl &_
       ".  Error:  " & Error(Err))
10   Call aLog.Close
11   Resume Next
```

Explanation

1. Declares the NotesLog object.
2. Transfers execution to `HandleErrors` routine if errors are encountered.
3. Sets up the NotesLog object.
4. Opens the NotesLog database.
5. Logs an event in the Log.
6. Logs an action in the Log.
7. Closes the Log.
8. Begins the error handling routine.
9. Logs an error in the log. The `LogError` method accepts two parameters: `error number` and `description`.

10 Closes the Log.

11 Continues execution with the statement immediately following the error.

7.4 Setting up the NotesLog object

There are two ways to create a NotesLog object:

Create a NotesLog object and use the methods New and OpenNotesLog.

```
Dim log As NotesLog
Set log = New NotesLog( "Test Agent" )
```

Use the CreateLog method of the NotesSession object.

```
Dim s As New NotesSession
Dim log As NotesLog
Set log = s.CreateLog("Test Agent" )
```

Once the NotesLog object has been set up, it is instructed to log information to a text file, Notes database, or NotesMail.

7.4.1 Logging to a Notes database

Errors and actions can be logged to a Notes database. The NotesLog database is created from a template: StdR4AgentLog (file name: alog4.ntf). The new database may be placed wherever you desire. Once the file has been created, a NotesLog object can utilize it. Every action and/or error logged to the NotesLog database is written as a separate document.

Example 7.8

```
    Dim aLog As NotesLog
    Dim db As NotesDatabase
    Set db = s.CurrentDatabase
    Set aLog = New NotesLog( "Database log" )
1   Call aLog.OpenNotesLog(db.Server,"agentlog.nsf")
2   Call aLog.LogAction("The script has started...")
    ...
3   Call aLog.Close
```

Explanation

1 Sets the log object to log to a Lotus Notes database. The `OpenNotesLog` method accepts two parameters: `server` path (blank if local) and the `filename` for the agent log database. The `server` parameter is passed using the `Server` property of the NotesDatabase object.

2 Records an action in the database.

3 Closes the agent log.

The `LogAction` method can be a great aid when debugging an agent and/or script. Debugging text can be logged at various points in a script. LotusScript provides a way to turn off (or on) the logging of actions.

7.4.2 Logging to a text file

Logging errors and actions to a text file is the same as a Notes database except how the `OpenFileLog` method is used instead. Every action and/or error logged to the NotesLog object is written on a separate line in the text file. The following example shows how example 7.8 can be rewritten to use a text file instead of a Notes database.

Example 7.9

```
    Dim aLog As NotesLog
    Dim db As NotesDatabase
    Set db = s.CurrentDatabase
    Set aLog = New NotesLog( "Database log" )
1   Call aLog.OpenFileLog( "c:\log.txt" )
2   aLog.OverwriteFile = True
    Call aLog.LogAction("The script has started…")
    …
    Call aLog.Close
```

Explanation

1 The script is the same as example 7.8 except for this line. The `OpenFileLog` method tells the script to log to a text file. The method accepts one parameter: the name and path of the text file.

2 The `OverwriteFile` property of the NotesLog class provides a mechanism to tell the system to overwrite or append the text file. It contains a Boolean value which when set to `True` says overwrite the file; `False`, appends the file.

7.4.3 Logging via email

Logging errors and/or actions via email is the same except the opening of the NotesLog object. The `OpenMailLog` method is used to open an email for logging, and the close method sends it. Every action and/or error logged to the NotesLog object is written on a separate line in the mail memo.

Example 7.10

```
    Dim Log As NotesLog
    Dim db As NotesDatabase
    Set db = s.CurrentDatabase
    Set aLog = New NotesLog( "Database log" )
1   Call aLog. OpenMailLog("Tony Patton","Subject line …")
    Call aLog.LogAction("The script has started…")
    …
    Call aLog.Close
```

Explanation

1 Creates a mail memo for logging purposes. Actions and errors are added to the mail memo, and the memo is mailed once it is sent. The `OpenMailLog` method accepts two parameters: recipient(s) email addresses and the subject line of the mail message.

7.4.4 Actions

The `LogAction` method of the NotesLog object is used to record actions. All of the examples up to this point have taken advantage of this method. It accepts one parameter: a string that describes the action.

```
Call NotesLogObject.LogAction("Action description")
```

Also, the `NumActions` and `LogActions` properties can be used in conjunction with the `LogAction` method. The `NumActions` property returns the number of actions logged so far.

```
Integer_Value = NotesLogObject.NumActions
```

The `LogActions` property indicates whether action logging is on or off. Example 7.11 shows how to use it.

Example 7.11

```
    Dim s As New NotesSession
    Dim aLog As NotesLog
    Set aLog = s.CreateLog("Test Agent" )
    Call aLog.OpenFileLog( "c:\log.txt" )
1   Call aLog.LogAction("The script is starting …")
2   MsgBox "Number of actions logged so far:  " & aLog.NumActions
3   aLog.LogActions = False
4   Call aLog.LogAction("An action occurred.")
    Call aLog.Close
```

Explanation

1 Sends an action to the file.

2 Displays the number of actions logged so far (1).

3 Disables the logging of actions.

4 This action will not be logged to the text file, since action logging has been turned off.

7.5 Errors

The `LogError` method of the NotesLog object is used to log errors.

```
Call NotesLogObject.LogError(Error_Number, "Error Description")
```

The NotesLog object contains the `LogErrors` and `NumErrors` properties. These properties perform the same functions as their counterparts for actions. The `Err` function (returns the current error number) can be used with the `LogError` method to record the error number and description to the NotesLog.

Example 7.12

```
   Dim s As New NotesSession
   Dim aLog As NotesLog
   Set aLog = s.CreateLog("Test Agent" )
   Call aLog.OpenFileLog( "c:\log.txt" )
1  Call aLog.LogError(Err,Cstr(Err))
2  MsgBox "Number of errors logged so far:  " & aLog.NumErrors
3  aLog.LogErrors = False
4  Call aLog.LogErrors(0,"Another error has occurred.")
5  aLog.LogErrors = True
   Call aLog.Close
```

Explanation

1 Records an error in the log file.

2 Displays the number of errors logged so far (1).

3 Displays the logging of errors.

4 This error message will not be logged to the file, since the logging of errors has been disabled.

5 The logging of errors is enabled.

7.5.1 Logging script activity via the agent log

Another useful method for debugging/monitoring agents is through the use of the agent log. Instead of storing information in a text file or Notes database, the Agent itself has its very own log. To view an agent log select Agent | Log from the drop-down menu, or right-click on an agent and select Log (Figure 7.3).

The data stored in this log is limited by space, and it is overwritten each time the agent is run. As a result, it has limitations but it does have its usefulness. The `OpenAgentLog` and `LogAction` methods of the NotesLog class are used to utilize it.

Example 7.13

```
   Dim s As New NotesSession
   Dim db As Notesdatabase
   Dim dc As NotesDocumentCollection
1  Dim aLog As New NotesLog("Agent Log")
   Set db = s.CurrentDatabase
   Set dc = db.AllDocuments
2  Call aLog.OpenAgentLog
   If (dc.Count > 0) Then
3     Call aLog.LogAction(Cstr(dc.Count) & " documents were processed.")
   Else
4      Call aLog.LogAction("No documents found.")
```

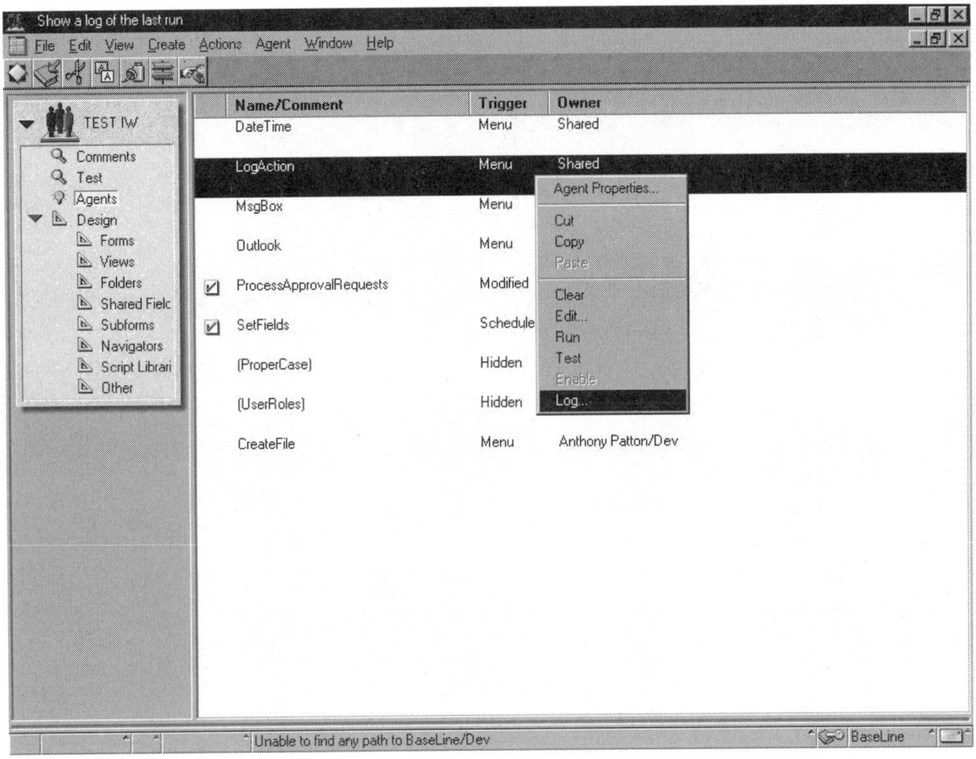

Figure 7.3 Viewing an agent log

```
    End If
5   Call aLog.Close
```

Explanation

1 Declares NotesLog object.

2 Sets up the NotesLog to log to the agent log.

3 If documents are found, the total number is sent to the agent log.

4 If no documents are found, a message is sent to the agent log.

5 Closes the NotesLog.

Output

To view the results of the previous example, right-click on the agent and select log to view the results. Figure 7.4 shows the fact that fifty-eight documents were found.

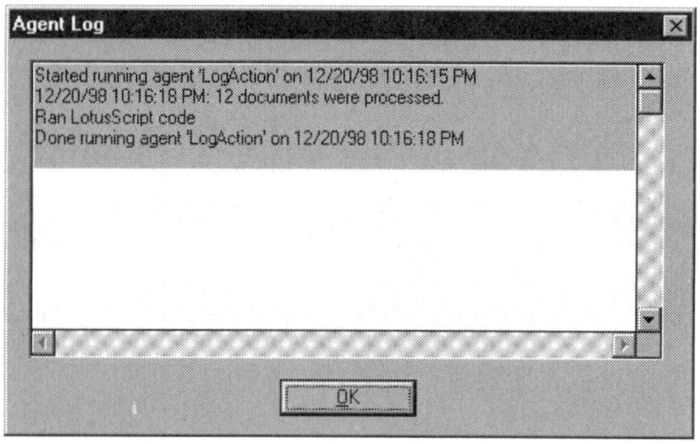

Figure 7.4 Results of logging to the agent log

7.6 Chapter summary

Building solid applications requires careful planning and extensive testing, but errors still creep into a system. For this reason, extensive error checking and handling must be incorporated into an application. The use of error handling and logging either separately or together helps achieve the goal of a smooth running application that gracefully handles errors.

7.7 Chapter review

- Errors result from system problems, user errors, or programming mistakes.
- `On Error`, `Goto`, and `Labels` are used to handle all errors or specific errors including user-defined errors.
- Once an error has occurred, execution of a script can be stopped or resumed.
- The `%Include` directive allows the importing of external files that contain LotusScript code.
- Three .lss files included with the installation of Notes contain definitions of Error numbers.
- The NotesLog class allows script activity to be recorded in a Notes database or text file, or send email messages.
- `LogAction` and `LogError` is used to record activities to the NotesLog object.
- `NumErrors` and `NumActions` contain a count of the number of errors and actions.
- `LogErrors` and `LogActions` are Boolean properties of the NotesLog class that tell the system to log errors and/or actions or not.

CHAPTER 8

Events

8.1 Chapter objectives 124
8.2 Initialize 124
8.3 Terminate 124
8.4 Forms/subforms 125
8.5 Fields 130
8.6 Database (located in the database script) 131
8.7 Action/button/hotspot 132
8.8 Views/folders 133
8.9 Agents 134
8.10 Creating your own events 134
8.11 Chapter summary 140
8.12 Chapter review 140

8.1 Chapter objectives

- Event-based programming in the Notes/Domino environment.
- Form/subform events
- Field events
- Database events
- Action/button/hotspot events
- View/folder events
- Creating your own events
- Flow of events

The LotusScript environment in Notes/Domino is event-driven. An event is an indication that something has occurred. Events can be triggered by user actions or the system. They are generated by everything from the opening of a database to selecting a button. This chapter details various events within the Notes/Domino environment, and includes numerous examples.

All objects (database, form, view, etc.) have `Initialize` and `Terminate` events.

8.2 Initialize

The `Initialize` event is executed when on object is loaded. For example, the `Initialize` event of a form would be triggered when a document created with that form is loaded. This event should be used to declare objects/variables that need to be available during the life of the object. The next example declares variables in the `Initialize` event of a form. The variables will be available in all other events on the form.

Example 8.1

```
Sub Initialize
  Dim s As New NotesSession
  Dim db As NotesDatabase
  Set db = s.CurrentDatabase
End Sub
```

Note The `Initialize` event for an agent is an exception. Agents have only two events: `Initialize` and `Terminate`. For this reason, an agent's code/script is placed in the `Initialize` event.

8.3 Terminate

The `Terminate` event is the `Initialize` event's counterpart. It is triggered/executed when a object is unloaded or closed. To see when/how the event is triggered, place a

MessageBox statement in the terminate event and load/unload on object (view, database, document, etc.) to see when/if the message box appears.

Example 8.2

```
Sub Terminate
  MsgBox "Object terminating."
End Sub
```

The Initialize and Terminate events are unique because they exist for each and every object. The remaining events can exist in more than one object, but it is not consistent. The rest of the chapter covers each object and its corresponding events.

8.4 *Forms/subforms*

8.4.1 *PostOpen*

The PostOpen event is triggered immediately after a form/subform has been opened. The currently open document is passed into the event as a NotesUIDocument object. The PostOpen script has read/write access to the document.

Note Subform events execute before the events of the form that contains it.

Format

```
PostOpen(Source As NotesUIDocument)
```

Example 8.3

The PostOpen event can be used to set values for fields on the document. This example mimics the DBColumn @function.

```
   Sub PostOpen(Source As NotesUIDocument)
     Dim uiw As New NotesUIWorkspace
     Dim uidoc As NotesUIDocument
     Dim lookupDoc As NotesDocument
     Dim db As NotesDatabase
     Dim view As NotesView
     Set uidoc = uiw.CurrentDocument
1    Dim NameList() As String
2    Set view = db.GetView("Names")
3    Set lookupDoc = view.GetFirstDocument
4    FirstTime = True
     While Not (lookupDoc Is Nothing)
       If (FirstTime) Then
         Redim NameList(0) As String
         FirstTime = False
       Else
         Redim Preserve NameList(Ubound(NameList) + 1) As String
       End If
5      NameList(Ubound(NameList)) = lookupDoc.Name(0)
       Set lookupDoc = view.GetNextDocument(lookupDoc)
     Wend
6    uidoc.Document.Names = NameList
```

```
    Call db.Close
End Sub
```

Explanation

1 Declares the array that will be used to retrieve field values.

2 The view that gets documents.

3 Gets the first document in the view.

4 The `FirstTime` variable tells the script how it needs to be intialized.

5 Stores the name from the document as a new element in the array.

6 Sets the field on the current document to the array.

8.4.2 QueryOpen

The `QueryOpen` event is executed just before a document is opened. The document being opened is passed into the event as a NotesUIDocument object. Also, a variable called `mode` is passed. `Mode` signals whether the document is being opened in read mode (value of `0`) or edit mode (value of `1`). A Boolean variable called `IsNewDoc` signals whether a newly created document is being opened/created. The last parameter is `Continue`. `Continue` is a Boolean variable signaling whether a document should be open or not. The default value for `Continue` is `true`.

Format

```
QueryOpen(Source As NotesUIDocument, Mode As Integer, IsNewDoc As Variant,
Continue As Variant)
```

Example 8.4

The `QueryOpen` event can be used to create a trial copy of your application. Code placed in the `QueryOpen` event can allow/disallow an item to be opened based on a date.

```
  Sub Queryopen(Source As Notesuidocument, Mode As Integer, _
     Isnewdoc As Variant, Continue As Variant)
1    If (Now < DateValue("01/01/87")) Then
2       Continue = False
     End If
  End Sub
```

Explanation

1 If the current date is less than the date value (01/01/87), then do not allow the document to be opened.

2 Sets the `Continue` variable to `false`, so the form will not be opened.

8.4.3 *QuerySave*

The `QuerySave` event is triggered when a document is being saved. The script runs before the document is actually saved, so it can affect whether or not the document is actually saved. The currently open document is passed into the event as a NotesUIDocument object. The other parameter is called `Continue` and it signals whether or not the document should be saved. The default value for `Continue` is `true`. The script has only read/write access to the document and `Continue` flag.

Format:

```
QuerySave(Source As NotesUIDocument, Continue As Variant)
```

Example 8.5

The `QuerySave` event can be used to replace `Input Validation` formulas. Numerous validation formulas result in numerous message boxes, but a `QuerySave` script can be used to check a number of fields and tell the user which fields he/she needs to re-enter.

```
    Sub Querysave(Source As Notesuidocument, Continue As Variant)
       Dim FieldList List As String
       Dim checkItem As NotesItem
       Dim MsgString As String
1      FieldList("Brand") = "Brand"
       FieldList("AdName") = "Ad Name"
       FieldList("MarketingType") = "Marketing Type"
2      Forall i In FieldList
3         Set checkItem = Source.Document.GetFirstItem(Listtag(i))
4         If (Isempty(checkItem.Text)) Then
             MsgString = MsgString + Chr$(13) & " - " & i
          End If
       End Forall
       If (MsgString <> "") Then
5         Msgbox "The following required fields were not entered:  " & _
          Chr$(13) & MsgString & Chr$(13) & Chr$(13) & _
          "Please enter values in these fields and save again.", _
          16, "Missing required information"
6         Continue = False
          Exit Sub
       End If
    Exit Sub
```

Explanation

1 A list is used to assemble a list of required fields.

2 A `Forall` loop is used to check for all required fields.

3 Gets the field from the current document.

4 If the field is empty, adds it to a string variable to display to the user.

5 Tells the user which fields are missing values.

6 Sets the `Continue` variable to false, so the form cannot be closed.

8.4.4 *QueryClose*

The `QueryClose` event is executed when a document is closed. It is run just before a document is closed. The current document, and a Boolean variable to signal whether or not to close the document, is passed into the event script. The script has read/write access to the document object and continue flag.

Format

```
QueryClose(Source As NotesUIDocument, Continue As Variant)
```

Example 8.6

The `QueryClose` event can be used to force a user to select an action button to close a document. The action button can set the field to the proper value to allow closing.

```
  Sub Queryclose(Source As Notesuidocument, Continue As Variant)
1      If Not (Source.Document.CloseFlag(0) = "Yes") Then
2         Continue = False
3         MsgBox "Please use the close button to close this document."
       End If
  End Sub
```

Explanation

1 If the `CloseFlag` variable is not `Yes` then does not allow the document to be closed.

2 The `Continue` variable is set to `False`, so the document will not be closed.

3 Tells the user why the document was not closed.

8.4.5 *PostRecalc*

The `PostRecalc` event is executed when a document is recalculated/refreshed. The current open document is passed into the script as a NotesUIDocument object.

Note All formulas on a form are calculated before the `PostRecalc` script is run.

Format

```
PostRecalc(Source As NotesUIDocument.
```

8.4.6 *QueryModeChange*

The `QueryModeChange` event is executed before a document changes modes. The modes are reading or editing a document. The currently open document is passed into the script as a NotesUIDocument object. Also, a Boolean variable signaling whether or not the document will change modes is passed into the script. The default value for the

Boolean variable is `True`. The script has only read access to the document, but read/write access to the Boolean variable.

Format

`QueryModeChange(Source As NotesUIDocument, Continue As Variant)`

Example 8.7

I have a form that will be used to create reports. All field values on the form are computed, and I do not want users to have the ability to change values on the reports. As a result, the `QueryModeChange` event can be used to negate any type of editing.

```
  Sub QueryModeChange(Source As NotesUIDocument, Continue As Variant)
     Dim s As New NotesSession
1    If (Not (Source.EditMode)) Then
2       Continue = False
     End If
  End Sub
```

Explanation

1 The `EditMode` property of the NotesUIDocument class signals `True` if the document is currently in `edit` mode and `false` otherwise. If the document is not currently in `edit` mode, which means the user is trying to switch to it, then do not allow the document to be edited.

2 Sets the `Continue` variable to `False`, so the mode cannot be changed.

8.4.7 PostModeChange

The `PostModeChange` event is triggered after a document changes modes. The modes include reading and editing a document. The current document is passed into the script as a NotesUIDocument object.

Format

`PostModeChange(Source As NotesUIDocument)`

Note The difference between the `PostModeChange` and `QueryModeChange` events is *when* they run. `PostModeChange` runs *after* a document changes modes, and `QueryModeChange` runs *before* a document changes modes.

8.4.8 WebQueryOpen

The `WebQueryOpen` event was introduced with version 4.6. It is specific to web browser clients accessing Domino databases. The event is triggered before a document is loaded into a web browser. The script uses an `@Command` to run an agent on the Domino server.

Format

```
@Command([ToolsRunMacro]; "<Agent Name goes here>")
```

Note LotusScript is not supported by *any* browser in the market, so LotusScript must be run on the Domino server. This is the reason the web events call agents on the server.

8.4.9 WebQuerySave

The `WebQuerySave` event was introduced in version 4.6. It is specific to web browser clients accessing Domino databases. The event is triggered just before a document is submitted (saved) by a browser client. The event uses an `@Command` to run an agent on the Domino server.

Note Chapter 18 gives more details about using web events and accessing the document attached to the event.

Format

```
@Command([ToolsRunMacro], "<Agent name goes here>")
```

8.5 Fields

8.5.1 Entering

`Entering` is triggered when a field on a document in edit mode gains focus. The `entering` event for the default field will be triggered when a document is opened.

Format

```
Entering(Source As Field)
```

8.5.2 Exiting

`Exiting` is triggered when a field on a document in edit mode loses focus. The `exiting` event is triggered when a user leaves a field.

Format

```
Exiting(Source As Field)
```

Example 8.8

The `exiting` event will be used to make certain a value has been entered into the field. Focus is returned to the field until a value is entered.

```
   Sub Exiting(Source As Field)
      Dim uiw As New NotesUIWorkspace
      Dim uidoc As NotesUIDocument
      Set uidoc = uiw.CurrentDocument
1     If (uidoc.Document.FieldName(0) = "") Then
         MsgBox "Please enter a value in the field."
```

```
2       Call uidoc.GotoField("FieldName")
    End If
End Sub
```

Explanation

1 Checks the contents of the field, and notifies the user if it is empty.

2 Focus returns to the field until a value is entered.

Note One field's `exiting` event is another's `entering` event. If one field checks to make sure it has a value during its `exiting` event and returns to that field if it is empty, the `entering` event will be triggered before moving focus back to the first field. This can cause unusual problems when using field events for input validation.

8.6 Database (located in the database script)

Every event in the database object accepts the current database as the `source` parameter. This gives easy access to all of the database properties and methods.

8.6.1 PostOpen

The `PostOpen` event is executed immediately after a database has been opened.

Format

```
PostOpen(Source As NotesUIDatabase)
```

Example 8.9

The `PostOpen` event can be used to display a database opening a window with title, copyright information, and so forth.

```
Sub PostOpen(Source As NotesUIDatabase)
   MsgBox "Welcome to the database...." & Chr(13) & "@1998, BaseLine, Inc."
End Sub
```

8.6.2 QueryDocumentDelete

The `QueryDocumentDelete` event executes just after a document has been marked for deletion and before the trash can is placed next to the document. It has a Boolean variable called `Continue` in addition to the database object. The `Continue` variable signals `true` or `false` as to whether a document can be deleted.

Format

```
QueryDocumentDelete(Source As NotesUIDatabase, Continue As Variant)
```

Example 8.10

This event can be used to disallow documents to be deleted from a database.

```
Sub QueryDocumentDelete(Source As NotesUIDatabase, Continue As Variant)
   Continue = False
End Sub
```

8.6.3 PostDocumentDelete

The `PostDocumentDelete` event executes after a document has been selected for deletion and after the trash can is placed next to the document.

Format

```
PostDocumentDelete(Source As NotesUIDatabase)
```

8.6.4 QueryDocumentUndelete

`QueryDocumentUndelete` is triggered just after a document has been selected to be undeleted and just before the trash can is removed from the document. In addition to the database object, it has one Boolean variable (`Continue`) that signals whether or not an item should be undeleted.

Format

```
QueryDocumentUndelete(Source As NotesUIDatabase, Continue As Variant)
```

8.6.5 QueryClose

The `QueryClose` event executes when a database is closing, but before it is closed. The `Continue` variable allows the closing of a database to be canceled by setting it to `false`, the default value is `true`.

```
QueryClose(Source As NotesUIDatabase, Continue As Variant)
```

8.7 Action/button/hotspot

Every event for actions, hotspots, and buttons has a `Source` parameter that returns a handle to the object that triggered the event.

8.7.1 ObjectExecute

The `ObjectExecute` event is executed when an object is activated via OLE. The `data` parameter returns a handle to the OLE Server Dispatch/Automation interface.

```
ObjectExecute(Source As Button, Data As Variant)
```

8.7.2 Click

The `click` event executes when a button or hotspot is selected. This is the main event for these objects and all code for the object is placed in this event.

```
Click(Source As Button)
```

8.8 Views/folders

Every event for view and folder objects has a `Source` parameter which returns a handle to the current view as a NotesUIView object.

8.8.1 QueryOpen

The `QueryOpen` event executes just before a view is opened. The Boolean variable `Continue` allows the opening of a view/folder to be canceled. The default value for `Continue` is `true`.

Format

```
QueryOpen(Source As NotesUIView, Continue As Variant)
```

8.8.2 PostOpen

The `PostOpen` event executes immediately after a view has been opened.

Format

```
PostOpen(Source As NotesUIView)
```

8.8.3 QueryOpenDocument

The `QueryOpenDocument` event runs immediately before a document is opened from a view/folder. The Boolean variable `Continue` signals whether or not the opening of the document can occur.

Format

```
QueryOpenDocument(Source As NotesUIView, Continue As Variant)
```

8.8.4 QueryRecalc

The `QueryRecalc` event is triggered immediately before a view is refreshed. The Boolean variable `Continue` signals whether or not the refresh should continue.

Format

```
QueryRecalc(Source As NotesUIView, Continue As Variant)
```

8.8.5 QueryAddToFolder

The `QueryAddToFolder` event runs just before a document is added to a folder. The Boolean variable `Continue` signals whether or not the item can be added to the folder. Also, the `Target` parameter contains the name of the folder to which the document is attempting to be added.

Format

```
QueryAddToFolder(Source As NotesUIView, Target As Variant, _
Continue As Variant)
```

8.8.6 QueryPaste

The `QueryPaste` event is triggered just before a document is pasted into a view or folder. The Boolean variable `Continue` signals `true` to allow the pasting and `false` to disallow.

Format

```
QueryPaste(Source As NotesUIView, Continue As Variant)
```

8.8.7 PostPaste

The `PostPaste` event runs immediately after a document has been pasted into a view or folder.

Format

```
PostPaste(Source As NotesUIView)
```

8.8.8 QueryClose

The `QueryClose` event executes just before a view/folder is closed. The closing of the view/folder can be canceled by setting the `Continue` variable to `false`; the default value is `true`.

Format

```
QueryClose(Source As NotesUIView, Continue As Variant)
```

8.9 Agents

Agents have only two events: `Initialize` and `Terminate`. The code for an agent is entered in the `Initialize` event.

8.10 Creating your own events

The `On Event` statement facilitates the creation of your own events. That is, it allows the binding of a user-defined event to one of the numerous events in the Lotus Notes environment. The syntax for defining an event is.

```
On Event <system event> From <object name> Call <user-defined subroutine>
```

- *<system event>* The user-defined event is associated with a known event such as `QuerySave`, `QueryClose`, `PostOpen`, and so forth.
- *<object name>* The object to which the event is associated. This can be a NotesDocument, NotesUIDocument, or whatever. It must be the same object with which the object event is associated.
- *<user-defined subroutine>* The subroutine that is called when the event is fired. The parameters (objects/variables) passed into the subroutine must match

exactly the parameters passed into the object event tied to it. If you associate an event with the `QuerySave` event, the subroutine must accept NotesUIDocument and Variant objects just like the `QuerySave` routine.

Events can be set up/declared within any event associated with an object. The `Initialize`, `PostOpen`, or `QueryOpen` events are good locations for event set up since they are called when an object is opened. Therefore, the event will be registered/used throughout the life of the object.

Example 8.11

I want to send a message to the administrator each time a form is saved.

First, we set up our routine.

```
Sub sendMemo(puidoc As NotesUIDocument, pflag As Variant)
  Dim db As NotesDatabase
  Dim message As NotesDocument
  Set db = puidoc.Document.Parentdatabase
  Set message = db.CreateDocument
  With message
     .Form = "Memo"
     .SendTo = "Admin"
     .Subject = "Document Saved"
     Call .Send(False)
  End With
End Sub
```

Next, we add the code to the form's `Initialize` event that will trigger our routine when/if the document is saved.

```
Sub Initialize
  Dim uiw As New NotesUIWorkspace
  Dim uidoc As NotesUIDocument
  Set uidoc = uiw.CurrentDocument
  On Event QuerySave From uidoc Call sendMemo
End Sub
```

Finally, we don't place anything in our `QuerySave` event. Nothing is needed.

```
Sub Querysave(Source As Notesuidocument, Continue As Variant)

End Sub
```

Explanation

Each time a document is saved, a message will be sent to the designated individual. The same functionality provided in example 8.11 can be provided by just calling the subroutine in the `QuerySave` event.

```
Sub Querysave(Source As Notesuidocument, Continue As Variant)
```

```
   Call sendMessage(Source, Continue)
End Sub
```

The `On Event` setup allows you to define/set up everything from within the Initialize event, but either way gets the job done.

Example 8.12

We want to send a message each time a database is closed.

First, we set up the routine to send the message. The parameters passed into it match the parameters passed into the associated `QueryClose` event.

```
Sub sendMemo(pDB As NotesUIDatabase, pFlag As Variant)
   Dim db As NotesDatabase
   Dim s As New NotesSession
   Dim message As NotesDocument
   Set db = pDB.Database
   Set message = db.CreateDocument
   With message
      .Form = "Memo"
      .SendTo = "Admin"
      .Subject = "Database " & db.Title & " closed by " & s.UserName
      Call .Send(False)
   End With
End Sub
```

The `On Event` line is added to the `PostOpen` event to register the user-defined event.

```
Sub PostOpen(Source As NotesUIDatabase)
   On Event QueryClose From Source Call sendMemo
End Sub
```

Once again, there is no need for anything extra in the `QueryClose` event.

```
Sub QueryClose(Source As NotesUIDatabase, Continue As Variant)
End Sub
```

Setting up and using your own events puts even more power in the hands of you, the developer. Examples 8.10 and 8.11 are simple, but they do show you how to get started. Using your own events is limited only by your imagination.

8.10.1 The flow of events

At this point, we have covered the various events within the Notes/Domino environment. I want to close this chapter with a look at how and when events are triggered. This is demonstrated with pictures and words. A solid understanding of the intricacies of events can only lead to better designed applications.

Opening a database

Figure 8.1 shows the events (and their order) triggered when a Notes database is opened by a Notes client.

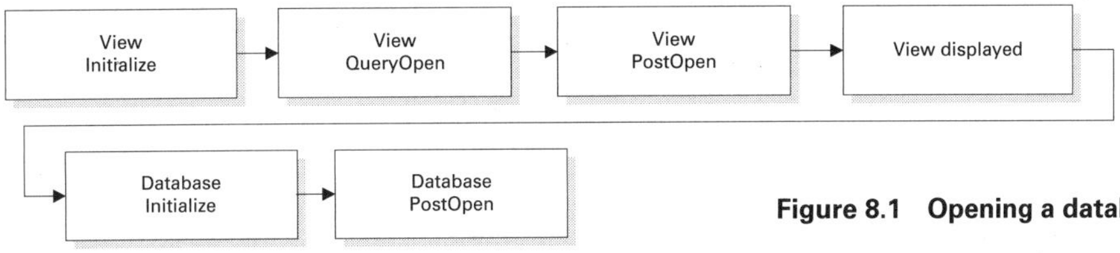

Figure 8.1 Opening a database

Note The boxes in the figures list the object name, or sentence explaining action, on top with the event name underneath.

First, the `Initialize` event for the default view (or last view displayed for user) is fired. This is followed by the view's `QueryOpen` and `PostOpen` events. At this point, the view is displayed to the user. Next, the database `Initialize` event executes followed by the database `PostOpen` event.

Closing a database.

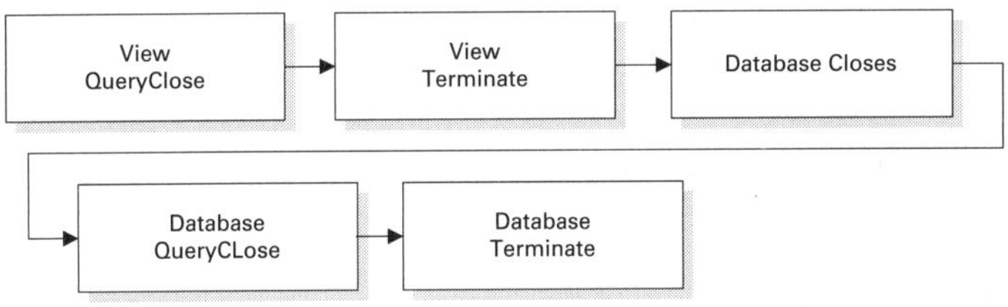

Figure 8.2
Closing a database

Opening a document.

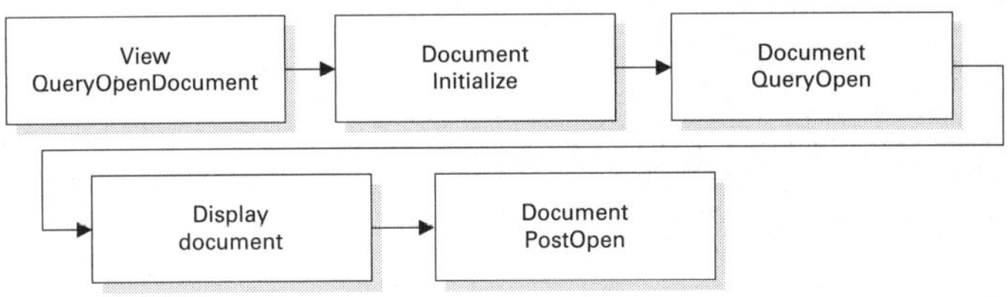

Figure 8.3
Open a document

Closing a document.

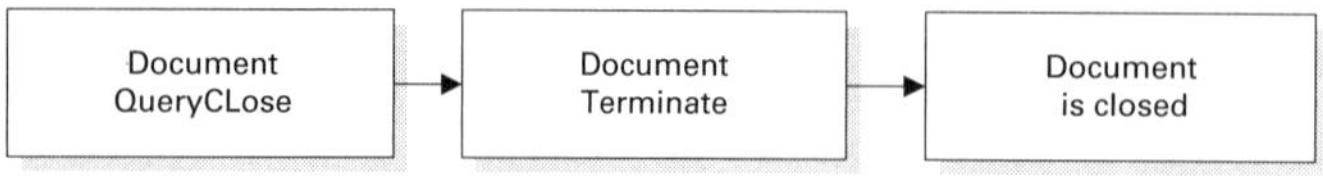

Figure 8.4 Closing a document

Opening a document containing a subform.

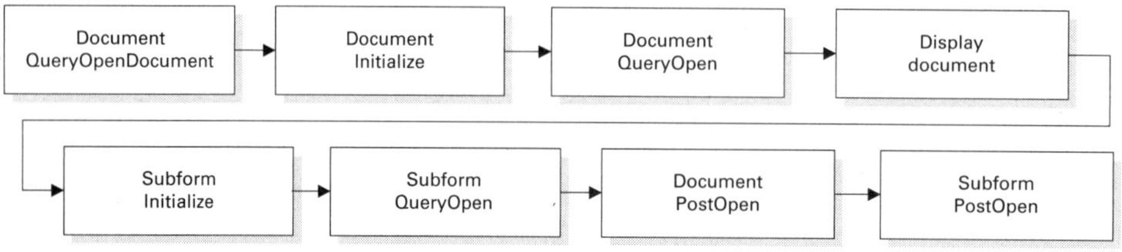

Figure 8.5 Opening a document containing a subform

Closing a document containing a subform.

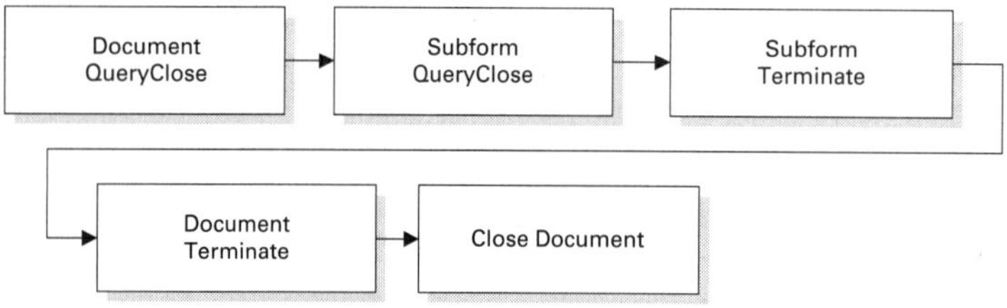

Figure 8.6 Closing a document containing a subform

Marking a document for deletion.

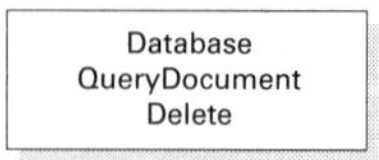

Figure 8.7 Marking a document to be deleted

Unmarking a document for deletion.

Figure 8.8 Unmarking a document for deletion

Refreshing a view.

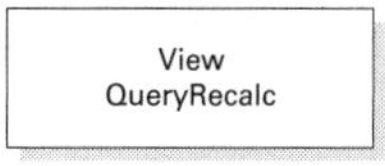

Figure 8.9 Refresh a view (F9)

Change from `edit` *to* `read` *mode (and vice versa).*

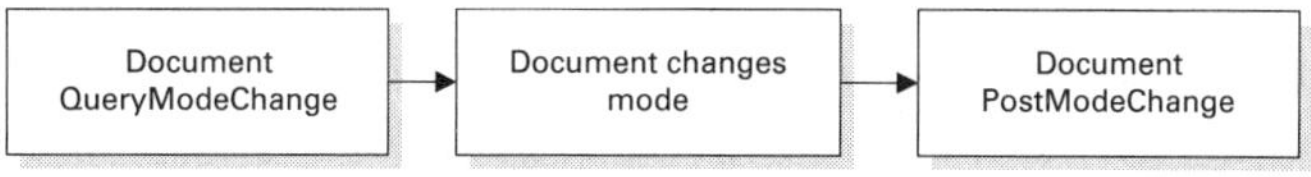

Figure 8.10 Change document mode

Change from `edit` *to* `read` *mode (and vice versa)*

(In a document containing a subform.)

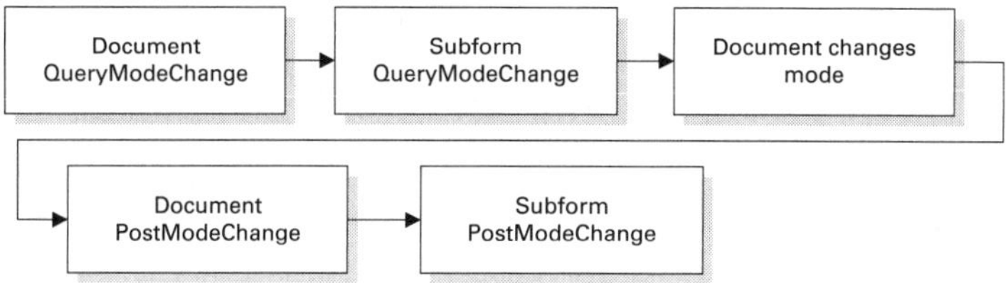

Figure 8.11 Change document with subform mode

Saving a document.

Figure 8.12 Saving a document

Saving a document containing a subform.

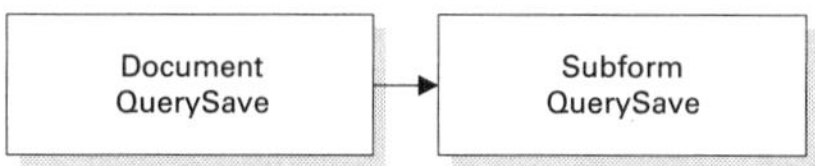

Figure 8.13 Saving document containing subform

Deleting a document.

Figure 8.14 Deleting a document

Copying/pasting a document.

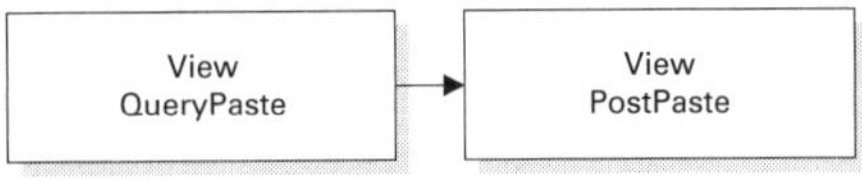

Figure 8.15 Copying/pasting a document

8.11 Chapter summary

The release of version 4 brought event-driven programming to Notes developers. This allows applications to easily interact with the user. Events are attached to each object type in the Notes environment. All objects have `Initialize` and `Terminate` events. From there the events attached to each object varies.

8.12 Chapter review

- Events were introduced in release 4 of Lotus Notes.
- Events are generated by users and by the Notes system. The click of a button generates a click event.
- Every object in the Notes environment contains `Initialize` and `Terminate` events.
- Agents contain `Initialize` and `Terminate` events.
- Views/folders, forms/subforms, agents, buttons/hotspots, and database objects each have their own set of events
- The `On Event` statement facilitates the creation of your own events.

CHAPTER 9

Working with the ACL

9.1 Chapter objectives 142

9.2 Seven levels of access in the ACL. 142

9.3 NotesACL class 146

9.4 NotesACLEntry Class 147

9.5 Roles 150

9.6 UniformAccess 153

9.7 Chapter summary 153

9.8 Chapter review 154

9.1 Chapter objectives

- What is the ACL?
- Seven access levels
- NotesACL
- NotesACLEntry class
- Roles
- Uniform Access

The access control list (ACL) is one of the most important aspects of a Lotus Notes/Domino database. It determines who can (or cannot) access an application. In addition, it determines what tasks a user (or server) can perform in the database. Users can be listed by their names in the ACL or as a part of a group. Groups are defined in the name and address book; the groups allow multiple users to be grouped together. The ACL is just one level of security implemented in Lotus Notes/Domino.

9.2 Seven levels of access in the ACL.

9.2.1 Manager

Users with Manager access can modify ACL settings, encrypt a database for local security, modify replication settings, and delete a database—tasks permitted by no other access level. Managers can also perform all tasks allowed by other access levels. Notes requires each database to have at least one Manager. It's best to assign two people Manager access to a database in case one manager is absent.

9.2.2 Designer

Users with Designer access can modify all database design elements (fields, forms, views, public agents, the database icon, Using This Database document and About This Database document), can modify replication formulas, and can create a full text index. Designers can also perform all tasks allowed by lower access levels, assign Designer access to the original designer of a database or to a user responsible for updating the design after a database is in use.

9.2.3 Editor

Users assigned Editor access can create documents and edit all documents, even those created by others. Assign Editor access to a user responsible for maintaining all data in a database.

9.2.4 Author

Users assigned Author access can create documents and edit documents they create. Assign Author access to allow users to contribute to a database but not edit documents created by others.

When possible, use Author access rather than Editor access to reduce replication or save conflicts.

9.2.5 Reader

Users assigned Reader access can read documents in a database but cannot create or edit documents. Assign Reader access to users who must be able to read the contents of a reference database such as a company policy database.

Anyone with at least Reader access to a database can create personal agents in the database if the database manager selects the ACL "Create personal agents" option. However, users can only run agents that perform tasks allowed by their access levels. For example, someone with Reader access can create a private agent that deletes documents, but the agent won't delete documents when the user runs it.

9.2.6 Depositor

Users assigned Depositor access can create documents but can't see any documents in the database views, even the documents they create. Assign Depositor access to allow users to contribute to a mail-in database or to a database used as a ballot box.

9.2.7 No Access

Users assigned No Access cannot access the database. Assign No Access as the default access to prevent most users from accessing a confidential database.

The database ACL can be accessed from the Notes workspace by right-clicking the mouse on the database icon (or select File | Database | Access Control list) and selecting Access Control List. A dialog box (figure 9.1) will appear.

The box shows who has access to the database and what level of access they possess. The ACL can contain user names, group names, or servers. Server access determines what a server can replicate.

Accessing a database ACL in script involves the NotesDatabase and NotesACL classes. The NotesDatabase class contains an ACL property that returns an instance of the NotesACL class for the database.

Example 9.1

```
    Dim s As New NotesSession
    Dim db As NotesDatabase
1   Dim dbacl As NotesACL
    Set db = s.CurrentDatabase
2   Set dbacl = db.ACL
3   MsgBox "The current user's level of access is " & db.CurrentAccessLevel
```

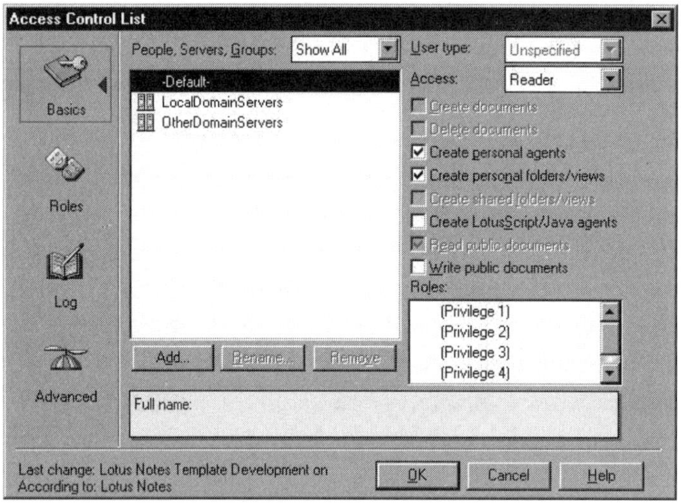

Figure 9.1
Database Access Control List dialog box

Explanation

1 Declares a NotesACL object.

2 Sets the NotesACL object to the current database's ACL. This class will be used more extensively in the next section.

3 The `CurrentAccessLevel` property of the NotesDatabase class is used to display the current user's access level.

Example 9.2

```
1   On Error Resume Next
    Dim s As New NotesSession
    Dim db As NotesDatabase
    Set db = s.CurrentDatabase
2   If (db.CurrentAccessLevel = ACLLEVEL_MANAGER) Then
3         Call db.GrantAccess("Tony Patton",ACLLEVEL_EDITOR)
4         Call db.RevokeAccess("Joe Smith")
    End If
```

Explanation

1 Tells the system to execute the next statement if an error is encountered.

2 Checks to see if the current user's access level is Manager. Only the user with Manager access can add or remove users from the database ACL.

3 If the user's access is Manager, adds a user with editor access to the database ACL. The `GrantAccess` method accepts two parameters: `username` and `access level`.

4 If the user's access is Manager, removes the user from the database ACL. The `RevokeAccess` method accepts only the `username` to revoke.

The seven legal access levels for the database ACL have the following values that are used in the NotesACL and NotesACLEntry classes:

Table 9.1

Value	Integer Value	Access Level
ACLLEVEL_NOACCESS	0	No Access
ACLLEVEL_DEPOSITOR	1	Depositor
ACLLEVEL_READER	2	Reader
ACLLEVEL_AUTHOR	3	Author
ACLLEVEL_EDITOR	4	Editor
ACLLEVEL_DESIGNER	5	Designer
ACLLEVEL_MANAGER	6	Manager

You will see these constant values used throughout the examples in this chapter.

Example 9.2 used the `GrantAccess` and `RevokeAccess` methods of the NotesDatabase class to give a person access and remove another's access privileges. The `GrantAccess` method will add the user to the database ACL if they are not in the ACL currently, or change their access if they are in the ACL. The `RevokeAccess` method will return an error if the user specified does not exist in the ACL. That is the reason for the `On Error Resume Next` line.

Also, the `QueryAccess` method of the NotesDatabase class allows the access level of a user to be retrieved.

Example 9.3

```
    Dim s As New NotesSession
    Dim db As NotesDatabase
    Set db = s.CurrentDatabase
1   If (db.CurrentAccessLevel = ACLLEVEL_MANAGER) Then
2     If (db.QueryAccess("Joe Smith") = ACLLEVEL_AUTHOR) Then
3       Call db.GrantAccess("Joe Smith",ACLLEVEL_EDITOR)
      End If
    End If
```

Explanation

1 Checks the access level for the current user to see if it is Manager. Only a user with Manager access can alter the database ACL.

2 The `QueryAccess` method of the NotesDatabase class checks the access level for a user. If the user is not listed in the ACL, it returns the default access level for the database.

3 Gives the user access to the database.

Note If the `QueryAccess` method is used for a user who is a member of a group or groups listed in the database ACL, the method returns the access level for the group, or the highest access level if there is more than one group.

9.3 NotesACL class

Example 9.1 showed how an object of the NotesACL class is used. The example did not do anything with the object, but there are plenty of tasks it can perform. The NotesACL class represents a database's ACL, and it can perform the same tasks as the NotesDatabase class.

The `CreateACLEntry` method allows a new user, server, or group to be added to a database ACL and set its access level.

Example 9.4

```
    Dim s As New NotesSession
    Dim db As NotesDatabase
    Dim nACL As NotesACL
    Dim newUser As String
    Set db = s.CurrentDatabase
1   Set nACL = db.ACL
2   newUser = InputBox$("Please enter the user to add to the ACL and _
       give Editor rights for " & db.Title)
3   If Not (newUser = "") Then
4   Call nACL.CreateACLEntry(newUser,ACLLEVEL_EDITOR)
5   Call nACL.Save
End If
```

Explanation

1 Sets the NotesACL object to the ACL for the current database.

2 Prompts the user to enter another user to add to the database ACL.

3 Continues only if a name was entered.

4 The `username` entered is added to the database ACL with editor access.

5 Saves the ACL, so the changes will take effect.

Note The `NotesACL Save` method must be called for changes to a database ACL to take effect. If it is not called, changes are lost.

In addition to creating new entries, the ACL for a database can be traversed. This involves the NotesACLEntry class as well.

9.4 *NotesACLEntry Class*

The NotesACLEntry class represents an entry in the ACL of a Domino database. It allows specific information regarding an ACL entry to be accessed.

Example 9.5

```
1   Sub entryOutput(passedEntry As NotesACLEntry)
       Dim user As String
       Dim level As String
       Dim deleteIt As String
       Dim create As String
       Dim folders As String
       Dim agents As String
       Dim outString1 As String, outString2 As String, outString3 As String
2      user = passedEntry.Name
3      level = passedEntry.Level
4      If (passedEntry.CanCreateDocuments) Then
          create = "Yes"
       Else
          create = "No"
       End If
5      If (passedEntry.CanCreatePersonalAgents) Then
          agents = "Yes"
       Else
          agents = "No"
       End If
6      If (passedEntry.CanCreatePersonalFolders) Then
          folders = "Yes"
       Else
          folders = "No"
       End If
7      If (passedEntry.CanDeleteDocuments) Then
          deleteIt = "Yes"
       Else
          delete = "No"
       End If
8      outString1="User: " & name & Chr(13) & "Access: " & level & Chr(13)
       outString2 = "Create docs: " & create & Chr(13) & _
          "Create personal agents: " & agents & Chr(13)
       outString3 = "Create personal folders: " & folders & Chr(13) & _
          "Delete docs:  " & deleteIt
9      MsgBox outString1 & outString2 & outString3
    End Sub

10  Sub Click (Source As Button)
       Dim s As New NotesSession
       Dim db As NotesDatabase
       Dim nACL as NotesACL
       Dim aclEntry As NotesACLEntry
       Set db = s.CurrentDatabase
11     Set nACL = db.ACL
12     Set aclEntry = nACL.GetFirstEntry
13     Call entryOutput(aclEntry)
```

```
14      While Not (aclEntry Is Nothing)
15          Set aclEntry = nACL.GetNextEntry(aclEntry)
16         Call entryOutput(aclEntry)
        Wend
    End Sub
```

Explanation

1 A separate subroutine handles the output of the user information to the screen. This eliminates the need to type the code twice, thus reducing the risk of errors. The routine accepts a NotesACLEntry object.

2 The `Name` property of the NotesACLEntry class gets the name associated with the ACL entry. This could be a user, group, or server name.

3 The `Level` property of the NotesACLEntry class gets the access level associated with the ACL entry. This has seven possible values.

4 The `CanCreateDocuments` property signals `true` if an ACL entry is allowed to create documents in the database and `false` otherwise. The `create` variable is set accordingly.

5 The `CanCreatePersonalAgents` property signals `true` if an ACL entry can create personal agents in the database and `false` otherwise. The `agents` variable is set accordingly.

6 The `CanCreatePersonalFolders` property signals `true` if an ACL entry can create personal folders in the database and `false` otherwise. The `folders` variable is set accordingly.

7 The `CanDeleteDocuments` property signals `true` if an ACL entry can delete documents from the database and `false` otherwise. The `delete` variable is set accordingly.

8 Sets the strings used to display the values.

9 Displays the results for the ACL entry in a message box.

10 The main part of the script is contained in an action button.

11 Instantiates the NotesACL object to the current database's ACL.

12 Sets the NotesACLEntry object to the first entry in the NotesACL object.

13 Calls the sub, and the values for the entry are displayed by the subroutine.

14 A `While` loop traverses the entries in the ACL.

15 The NotesACLEntry object is set to the next entry in the database ACL. The `GetNextEntry` method accepts a NotesACLEntry object that is used as a pointer to get the next entry.

16 Calls the sub again, and the values associated with the entry are displayed by the subroutine.

Example 9.5 showed how to access the various properties of an ACL entry, but these properties can be set as well. Example 9.6 shows the `GetEntry` method of the NotesACL class and setting properties.

Example 9.6

```
     Sub Click(Source As Button)
     Dim s As New NotesSession
     Dim db As NotesDatabase
     Dim nACL As NotesACL
     Dim aclEntry As NotesACLEntry
     Set db = s.CurrentDatabase
     Set nACL = db.ACL
1    Set aclEntry = nACL.GetEntry("Tony Patton")
2    If Not (aclEntry Is Nothing) Then
3       aclEntry.CanDeleteDocuments = False
4       aclEntry.CanCreatePersonalAgent = False
5       aclEntry.CanCreateDocuments = True
6       aclEntry.Level = ACLLEVEL_AUTHOR
7       Call nACL.Save
     Else
8          Call nACL.CreateACLEntry("Tony Patton",ACLLEVEL_AUTHOR)
           Call nACL.Save
     End If
  End Sub
```

Explanation

1 Uses the `GetEntry` method of the NotesACL class to retrieve an ACL entry for a specific person, group, or server. The method accepts only one parameter, which is the name to retrieve.

2 The GetEntry method returns `Nothing` if the entry does not exist.

3 If the entry does exist, sets the `DeleteDocuments` property to `true`. The entry will not be allowed to delete documents from the database.

4 If the entry does exist, sets the `CreatePersonalAgents` property to `false`. The entry will not be allowed to create personal agents in this database.

5 If the entry does exist, sets the `CreateDocuments` property to `true`. The entry will be allowed to create new documents in the database.

6 Sets the access level to author.

7 Saves the ACL so the changes will take effect.

8 If the entry was not found, creates it using the `CreateACLEntry` method of the NotesACL class.

9.5 Roles

Roles are an enhancement to the access control list. They allow database-specific subgrouping within the ACL; that is, they allow a sort of group specific to a database. Roles are defined in the ACL, and are not listed in the name and address book. In figure 9.1, the ACL dialog box, there is a Roles button on the left side of the dialog box that allows all roles defined for a database to be viewed. Also, Roles can be accessed through LotusScript.

The NotesACL and NotesACLEntry classes provide various methods and properties for working. The NotesACL class allows Roles to be added, removed, and renamed.

Example 9.7

```
    Dim s As New Session
    Dim db As NotesDatabase
    Dim nACL As NotesACL
    String rolesList As String
    Set db - s.CurrentDatabase
    Set nACL = db.ACL
    rolesList = "List of roles for " & db.Title & Chr(13)
1   Forall v in nACL.Roles
      rolesList = rolesList & v & Chr(13)
    End Forall
2   MsgBox rolesList, 0, "Roles"
```

Explanation

1 The `Roles` property of the NotesACL class returns an array of strings with the names of the `Roles` defined in the database. The `Roles` are listed in square brackets. (If a `Role` is named Tony, it is listed as [Tony].)

2 Displays the list of `Roles` for the current database. The `Roles` are stored in the string variable `RolesList` and separated by the newline character Chr(13).

Example 9.8

```
Sub Click (Source As  Button)
1   On Error Resume Next
    Dim session As New NotesSession
    Dim db As NotesDatabase
    Dim nACL As NotesACL
    Dim newRole As String, oldRole As String, oldName As String, newName _
      As String
    Set db = session.CurrentDatabase
    Set nACL = db.ACL
2   oldRole = InputBox$("Please enter the name of the role to delete.")
    If Not (oldRole = "") Then
3         Call nACL.DeleteRole(oldRole)
    End If
4   newRole = InputBox$("Please enter the name of the role to add.")
    If Not ((newRole = "") Or (Left(newRole,1) = "[") Or _
      (Right(newRole,1) = "]")) Then
```

```
5        Call nACL.AddRole(newRole)
      End If
6     oldName = InputBox$("Please enter the name of the role to rename.")
      If Not (oldName = "") Then
7         newName = InputBox$("Please enter the new name for the role named "_
            & oldName)
8         Call nACL.RenameRole(oldName, newName)
      End If
      Call nACL.Save
   End Sub
```

Explanation

1 If an error is raised in the script, continues execution with the line following the line that generated the error.

2 The user enters the name of the `Role` to remove from the current database ACL.

3 Calls the `DeleteRole` method of the NotesACL class to remove the Role entered by the user. If the Role does not exist in the database ACL, a “Role Name Not Found” error is raised.

4 The user enters the name of the Role to add to the database ACL.

5 Adds the new Role to the database ACL if the new name entered by the user is not blank or does not contain leading or trailing square brackets. Role names are enclosed by square brackets by the system, so they cannot exist in the name. Also, the Role name cannot be enclosed in parentheses.

6 The user enters the name of the Role to rename.

7 The user enters the new name for the Role given the fact that an old name was entered.

8 The old Role name is renamed to the new name, if it exists.

The NotesACLEntry class allows you to check if an entry in the database ACL belongs to a Role, and it allows a role to be enabled.

Example 9.9

```
     On Error Resume Next
     Dim s As New NotesSession
     Dim db As NotesDatabase
     Dim nACL As NotesACL
     Dim aclEntry As NotesACLEntry
     Set db = s.CurrentDatabase
     Set nACL = db.ACL
1    Set aclEntry = nACL.GetFirstEntry
2    While Not (aclEntry Is Nothing)
3       If (aclEntry.IsRoleEnabled("TestRole")) Then
4          Call aclEntry.DisableRole("TestRole")
        Else
5          Call aclEntry.EnableRole("TestRole")
```

```
      End If
      Set aclEntry = nACL.GetNextEntry(aclEntry)
    Wend
  Call nACL.Save
```

Explanation

1 Sets the NotesACLEntry object to the first ACL entry in the database ACL.

2 Loops through the entries in the database ACL.

3 Uses the `IsRoleEnabled` method to check if the entry is a member of a role.

4 Removes the entry if it is a member of the role. The role is disabled for the entry. The `DisableRole` method of the NotesACLEntry class is used to achieve this, it accepts the role name as its only parameter.

5 Adds the entry if it is not a member of the role, and enables the role for the entry. The `EnableRole` method of the NotesACLEntry class is used for this. It accepts the role name to enable as its only entry.

Example 9.10

```
    Dim ns As New NotesSession
    Dim ndb As NotesDatabase
    Dim nacl As NotesACL
    Dim nentry As NotesACLEntry
    Dim entryName As String, roleList As String
    Dim addRole As String, removeRole As String
    Set ndb = ns.CurrentDatabase
    Set nacl = ndb.ACL
1   entryName = InputBox$("Enter entry name to edit.")
2   Set nentry = nacl.GetEntry(entryName)
    If Not (nentry Is Nothing) Then
      roleList = nentry.Name & " is in the following roles..." & Chr(13)
      Forall roles in nacl.Roles
3       If (nentry.IsRoleEnabled(roles)) Then
4         roleList = roleList & roles & Chr(13)
        End If
      End Forall
5     MsgBox roleList,0,"Roles"
6     addRole = InputBox$("Enter name of the role to enable for " & _
        nentry.Name)
      If Not (addRole = "") Then
7         Call nentry.EnableRole(addRole)
      End If
8     removeRole = InputBox$("Enter the name of the role to disable for " & _
        nentry.Name)
      If Not (removeRole = "") Then
9       Call nentry.DisableRole(removeRole)
      End If
    End If
```

Explanation

1 The user enters an entry name to display and edit.

2 Retrieves the entry name (if it exists) from the database ACL using the `GetEntry` method of the NotesACL class.

3 Traverses the `Roles` property of the NotesACLEntry class using a `Forall` loop. Checks the ACL entry to see if it has the roles enabled.

4 Assembles the string containing all of the roles for the entry.

5 Displays the list of roles in a message box.

6 The user enters the name of the role to enable for the entry.

7 Adds to the role, if a new role name is entered.

8 The user enters the name of the role to disable for the entry.

9 Removes the entry from the role, if a role name has been entered.

9.6 UniformAccess

The last item we will cover in this chapter is the `UniformAccess` property of the NotesACL class. This property allows you to specify whether a uniform ACL is to be enforced across all replicas of a database. If this is set to `true`, then all replicas of the database will have the same ACL. `False` turns off this feature.

Example 9.11

```
    Dim s As New NotesSession
    Dim db As NotesDatabase
    Dim nACL As NotesACL
    Set db = s.CurrentDatabase
    Set nACL = db.ACL
1   If Not (nACL.UniformAccess) Then
2   nACL.UniformAccess = True
3   Call nACL.Save
    End If
```

Explanation

1 The user proceeds only if the `UniformAccess` property is not `True`.

2 Sets the `UniformAccess` property to `true`.

3 Saves the new ACL settings.

9.7 Chapter summary

The database ACL is one of the most powerful elements of the Lotus Notes/Domino environment. Unlike other development tools, the security is built in. A few clicks of a button and a user is given access to an application and their access level is set. In addition, roles add an extra layer of functionality to a database. They allow ACL entries to be grouped together and used throughout an application, thus centralizing the point where access changes are made to the ACL.

9.8 Chapter review

- The access control list is the security list for a database.
- Users, groups, and servers are listed in the database ACL.
- The NotesDatabase class provides access to its ACL.
- The NotesDatabase class makes it easy to grant or revoke access for a user.
- The NotesACL class is used to work with the database ACL.
- The `GetEntry`, `GetFirstEntry`, and `GetNextEntry` methods of the NotesACL class allow easy access to all entries in an ACL.
- There are seven levels of access in the database ACL.
- The NotesACLEntry class allows manipulation of entries in an ACL.
- The NotesACLEntry class provides methods to get the name associated with an ACL entry, the access level, and many other properties.
- Roles are like database-specific groups.
- The NotesACL and NotesACLEntry classes allow the roles for a database to be manipulated.
- The `UniformAccess` property of the NotesACL class signals whether a uniform ACL is enforced on all replicas for a database.
- The `save` method of the NotesACL class must be called when changes are made to a database ACL. If it is not called, the changes will not be reflected.

CHAPTER 10

NotesItem

10.1 Chapter objectives 156
10.2 NotesItem class 156
10.3 NotesItem object and its values 161
10.4 Working with text 166
10.5 Chapter summary 171
10.6 Chapter review 171

10.1 *Chapter objectives*

- Overview of the NotesItem class
- Accessing fields on documents using the NotesItem class
- Creating fields
- Changing the contents of a field
- Multivalued fields
- Determining the type of data stored in a field
- What is a Rich Text field?
- How are Rich Text fields differ from other fields?
- NotesRichTextItem class
- NotesRichTextStyle class

Every piece of information (field) on a Notes document is accessible with LotusScript. This information is accessed through fields on the Notes document, and the NotesItem class is used in LotusScript. This class was introduced in chapter four where accessing field values was covered. This chapter gives a more in depth look at the NotesItem class with details on its various methods and properties.

10.2 *NotesItem class*

A piece of information on a document is called a field, so a Memo in the Lotus Notes Mail database has the following fields of information: subject, from, to, cc, bcc, body, and so forth. Along with the known fields, there are many hidden pieces of information maintained by the Lotus Notes/Domino environment. These include $UpdatedBy (list of past editors of the document), $Revisions (list of dates the document has been edited), and form (the form used to create the document). The system-maintained fields can be accessed just as user-defined fields. They are all accessed (or can be) via the NotesItem class. In addition to accessing fields of information, new fields can be created on documents with the NotesItem class.

10.2.1 *Creating items*

New fields are created on a Notes document using either of two methods:

```
Dim NameOfVariable As New NotesItem(NotesDocument, field_name, value,
optional_type)
Dim NameOfVariable as NotesItem
Set NameOfVariable = New NotesItem(NotesDocument, field_name, value,
optional_type)
```

Both methods require three parameters and accept one optional parameter. The three required values are:

- `NotesDocument` The document to contain the new item.
- `field_name` The name of the field on the form.
- `value` The value to store in the field.

Both accept an optional fourth value. If used, it signals whether the item will be a reader, author, or names field.

Example 10.1

```
    Dim session as New NotesSession
    Dim db As NotesDatabase
1   Dim doc As NotesDocument
2   Dim newName As NotesItem
3   Set db = session.CurrentDatabase
4   Set doc = db.CreateDocument
5   Set newName = New NotesItem(doc, "name", "Tony Patton")
6   Call doc.Save(True,False)
```

Explanation

1 Declares NotesDocument object that will contain new item.

2 Declares new NotesItem object.

3 Sets the NotesDatabase object to the current database.

4 Sets the NotesDocument object to a new document in the database.

5 Creates the new field on the NotesDocument. It is a field called `name` with the value `Tony Patton`.

6 Saves the document. The new field is not created until the document which contains it is saved.

10.2.2 Removing an item

Removing an item from a document is very easy, perhaps too much so. The `remove` method allows an item to be removed. The syntax for it is very simple.

```
Call item.Remove
```

The item must be set to the field to remove.

Example 10.2

```
    Dim session As New NotesSession
    Dim db As NotesDatabase
    Dim dc As NotesDocumentCollection
    Dim doc As NotesDocument
1   Dim item As NotesItem
```

```
   Set db = session.CurrentDatabase
2  Set dc = db.AllDocuments
   If (dc.Count > 0) Then
      For x = 1 to dc.Count
         Set doc = dc.GetNthDocument(x)
3        Set item = doc.GetFirstItem("Test")
4        Call item.Remove
5        Call doc.Save(True,False)
      Next x
   End If
```

Explanation

This script removes a field called Test from every document in the database.

1 Declares an NotesItem object.

2 Instantiates document collection with all documents from the database.

3 Sets the NotesItem object to the Test field from the document.

4 Removes the Test field from the document.

5 Saves the document, so the Test field will be permanently removed.

The NotesDocument object contains a method called `RemoveItem` that performs the same function. Lines 3 and 4 from the previous example could be replaced with this line.

```
Call doc.RemoveItem("Test")
```

This tells the system to remove the field named Test from the doc NotesDocument object.

10.2.3 Copying an item

In addition to removing items, the need to copy information is a frequent requirement. The NotesItem class makes it easy to copy information from one document to another. The `CopyItemToDocument` method facilitates it.

```
Call item.CopyItemToDocument(NotesDocument,field_name)
```

The NotesItem object item is copied to the NotesDocument and given the field_name on the new document. If the field_name is blank, the same field name is used.

Example 10.3

```
   Dim uiw As New NotesUIWorkspace
   Dim db As NotesDatabase
   Dim uidoc As NotesUIDocument
   Dim doc As NotesDocument
1  Dim item As NotesItem
   Dim s As New NotesSession
   Set db = s.CurrentDatabase
```

```
2     If (uidoc.Document.HasItem("Name")) Then
3           Set item =  uidoc.Document.GetFirstItem("Name")
            Set doc = db.CreateDocument
4           Set formItem = New NotesItem(doc,"Form","Test")
5           Call item.CopyItemToDocument(doc,"")
6           Call doc.Save(True,True)
      End If
```

Explanation

1 Declares a new NotesItem object.

2 Checks to see if the current document contains the Name field.

3 If it does, sets the NotesItem object to it.

4 Creates a field on the new document called Form and sets its value to `Test`.

5 Copies the `Name` field to the new document retaining the field name.

6 Saves the new document.

In addition to `CopyItemToDocument`, there are two methods of the NotesDocument class that can be used to copy items from one document to another: `CopyItem` and `CopyAllItems`. The `CopyItem` method of the NotesDocument class does just what its name suggests; the `CopyAllItems` method copies every item from one document to another.

Example 10.4

```
1     Sub QuerySave(Source As NotesUIDocument, Continue As Variant)
         Dim session As New NotesSession
         Dim db As NotesDatabase
         Dim newDoc As NotesDocument
2        Dim nameItem As NotesItem, addressItem As NotesItem
3        Call uidoc.Save
         Set db = session.CurrentDatabase
         Set newDoc = db.CreateDocument
4        Set nameItem = Source.Document.GetFirstItem("Name")
5        Set addressItem = Source.Document.GetFirstItem("Address")
6        Call newDoc.CopyItem(nameItem,"")
7        Call newDoc.CopyItem(addressItem, "")
8        newDoc.Form = "Test"
9        Call newDoc.Save(True, False)
    End Sub
```

Explanation

1 This script, located in the `QuerySave` event of a form, runs whenever a document created with the form is saved.

2 Declares two NotesItem objects.

3 Saves the current document before progressing. The document must be saved to ensure all fields will be accessible.

4 Sets the nameItem NotesItem object to the Name field on the current document.

5 Sets the addressItem NotesItem object to the Address field on the current document.

6 Copies the nameItem is to the new document. The field name for the item will be the same.

7 Copies the addressItem to the new document.

8 Sets another field on the new document, but the other notation is used.

9 Saves the new document.

Every item from the document in example 10.4 could have been copied into the new document with this line.

```
Call Source.Document.CopyAllItems(newDoc)
```

10.2.4 Checking for a value

The `contains` method of the NotesItem class allows the contents of a NotesItem object to be searched for a specific value. The `contains` method accepts one parameter: the value to find. The value to find can be a string, date value, or number. This method cannot be used to search an item for a phrase or word. It is used to check if one of an item's values matches a value *exactly*. It doesn't search for variances of a word, it wants an exact match. Therefore, a search for ham will not yield a match for a value containing hamburger. This method should be used to search the values in a multivalued field.

Example 10.5

```
     Dim session As New NotesSession
     Dim db As NotesDatabase
     Dim doc As NotesDocument
     Dim dc As NotesDocumentCollection
     Dim item As NotesItem
     Dim match As Double, x As Double
     Dim searchString As String
     Set db = session.CurrentDatabase
     Set dc = db.AllDocuments
1    searchString = "Tony Patton/Baseline/Dev"
     match = 0
     For x = 1 to dc.Count
        Set doc = dc.GetNthDocument(x)
2       Set item = doc.GetFirstItem("$UpdatedBy")
3       If (item.Contains(searchString)) Then
4          match = match + 1
        End If
5       MsgBox "There are " & match & " documents in " & db.Title & _
           " touched by " & searchString
     Next x
```

Explanation

1 Create the string to find.

2 Sets the NotesItem object to the $UpdatedBy field. The $UpdatedBy field is a system field maintained by Domino. It is read-only, and it contains a list of all persons who have edited the document.

3 Searches the NotesItem object for the string.

4 If the string is found, increments the count variable.

5 Displays the results of the search. Every document in the database is processed.

10.3 NotesItem object and its values

All of the examples in this chapter have accessed values on Notes documents. The values in a field can be accessed in various ways.

10.3.1 GetFirstItem

`GetFirstItem`, used extensively up to this point, is a method contained in the NotesDocument class. It accepts one parameter, which is the field name.

10.3.2 GetItemValue

`GetItemValue`, another method in the NotesDocument class, is used to get the values stored in a field. If the field is a Rich Text object, this method will return the text. Otherwise, an array of the values in the field is returned.

Example 10.6

```
    Dim doc As NotesDocument
    Dim fieldValues As Variant
1   fieldValues = doc.GetItemValue("$UpdatedBy")
2   For x = 1 to Ubound(fieldValues)
3      Print fieldValues(x)
    Next x
```

Explanation

1 Sets the variant fieldValues object to the contents of the $UpdatedBy field.

2 The `For ... Next` loop traverses the value array.

3 Displays every value in the item.

The `Values` property of the NotesItem class performs the same function as the `GetItemValue` method of the NotesDocument class. Lines 1, 2, and 3 from the previous example could be replaced with the following code.

```
Dim field As NotesItem
field = doc.GetFirstItem("$UpdatedBy")
Forall v in field.Values
```

```
   Print v
End Forall
```

Note System fields (those that begin with the dollar sign $), such as $UpdatedBy, can be accessed as properties by placing a tilde (~) in front of the dollar sign. For example, Print doc.~$UpdatedBy.

10.3.3 Checking Values

There are numerous methods available to check the contents of an item.

1. `IsAuthors` Signals whether or not an item is an Authors field.
2. `IsEncrypted` Signals whether or not an item is encrypted.
3. `IsNames` Signals whether or not an item is a Names field.
4. `IsProtected` Signals whether or not a user needs Editor access to edit an item.
5. `IsReaders` Signals whether or not an item is a Readers field.
6. `IsSigned` Signals whether or not an item is signed.
7. `IsSummary` Signals whether or not an item can appear in a view.

10.3.4 Other properties

1. `Type` Returns the type of values stored in a field. This property can contain numerous values. It is covered in greater detail in the NotesRichItem section.
2. `Text` A text representation of the values stored in an item; multiple values are separated by semicolons.
3. `Name` Returns the name of an item.
4. `DateTimeValue` Returns a NotesDateTime object if the field contains a NotesDateTime value. Otherwise, it returns nothing.

Example 10.7

```
     Dim uiw As New NotesUIWorkspace
     Dim db As New NotesDatabase("","")
     Dim uidoc As NotesUIDocument
     Dim doc As NotesDocument
     Dim newdoc As NotesDocument
1    Dim nameItem As NotesItem
2    Dim addressItem As NotesItem
     Set uidoc = uiw.CurrentDocument
3    Set doc = uidoc.Document
4    If (doc.HasItem("Name")) Then
5       If (db.Open("server","other_db")) Then
6          Set nameItem = doc.GetFirstItem("Name")
7          If Not ((nameItem.IsReaders) Or (nameItem.IsAuthors) Or_
              (nameItem.IsNames)) Then
8             Set addressItem = doc.GetFirstItem("Address")
9             Set newdoc = db.CreateDocument
```

```
10           Call nameItem.CopyItemToDocument(newdoc, "")
11           Call addressItem.CopyItemToDocument(newdoc, "")
12           Call nameItem.Remove
13           Call addressItem.Remove
           End If
         End If
       End If
```

Explanation

1 Declares NotesItem object. This will be used to get the name.

2 Declares NotesItem object. This will be used to get the address.

3 Sets NotesDocument object to the document property of the current document.

4 Checks NotesDocument for the existence of the name field.

5 Checks to see if the Notes database exists before proceeding.

6 Sets the nameItem NotesItem to the name field on the Notes document. The `GetFirstItem` method of the NotesDocument class is used.

7 Proceeds only if the field is not a Readers, Authors, or Names field.

8 Sets the addressItem NotesItem to the address field on the Notes document. The `GetFirstItem` method of the NotesDocument class is used.

9 Creates a document in the database.

10 Copies the name field to the new document. The `name` parameter is left blank, so the same field name will be used.

11 Copies the address field to the new document. The `name` parameter is left blank, so the same field name will be used.

12 Removes the name field from the document.

13 Removes the address field from the document.

The NotesItem class is just one way to deal with the fields of data in a Notes document. The NotesRichTextItem class is available as well. Its job is to handle the catch all fields: the Rich Text field.

The NotesRichTextItem class is a subclass of the NotesItem class. Therefore, all methods and properties of the NotesItem class are available to the NotesRichTextItem (refer to the chapter on classes if this is confusing). All examples up to this point apply to the NotesRichTextItem as well as the NotesItem class.

10.3.5 NotesRichTextItem

If you are unsure of the type of data to be entered into a field in your application, create it as a Rich Text field. These fields can store anything from regular text to file attachments. The flexibility given the user adds more work to the developer. As the developer, you need to decide what type of data is in the Rich Text field before you begin to work with it; this is where the RichTextItem, RichTextStyle, and NotesEmbeddedObject classes come into play. The first two will be covered in this chapter. The NotesEmbeddedObject class is a chapter unto itself.

The NotesRichTextItem class is used to deal with Rich Text Items which users love because they can hold almost anything: graphics, file attachments, OLE objects, tables, formatted text, and so forth. The body of a Notes mail message is one example of a Rich Text Field.

10.3.6 Accessing

Because the NotesRichTextItem class is derived from the NotesItem class, a Rich Text field can be accessed using either class (remember, a derived class has access to all of its parent class's methods and properties). This is legal if the field contains only text. The NotesRichTextItem class must be used if a field contains attachments, OLE objects, graphics, or other objects.

Example 10.8

```
1   Sub Initialize
       Dim uiw As New NotesUIWorkspace
       Dim uidoc As NotesUIDocument
       Dim doc As NotesDocument
       Set uidoc = uiw.CurrentDocument
       Set doc = uidoc.Document
2      Dim item As NotesItem
3      Set item = doc.GetFirstItem("Body")
4      If (item.Type = RICHTEXT) Then
5         Msgbox item.Name & " is a Rich Text field."
       End If
    End Sub
```

Explanation

1 This action button script executes when the button is selected (clicked).

2 Creates a NotesItem object.

3 Instantiates the NotesItem object as the body field on the current document.

4 Utilizes the `type` property of the NotesItem class to find out if the field is a Rich Text field or not.

5 Uses the `name` property to print the name of the field.

Example 10.9

```
Sub Initialize
   Dim uiw As New NotesUIWorkspace
   Dim uidoc As NotesUIDocument
   Dim doc As NotesDocument
   Set uidoc = uiw.CurrentDocument
```

```
    Set doc = uidoc.Document
1   Dim item As NotesRichTextItem
    Set item = doc.GetFirstItem("Body")
    If (item.Type = RICHTEXT) Then
      Msgbox item.Name & " is a Rich Text field."
    End If
  End Sub
```

Explanation

1 This is the same code as example 10.3, but the item has been declared as a NotesRichTextItem object. The script works just like the previous script.

The previous examples took advantage of the `type` property. It is used extensively when dealing with Rich Text fields. It must be used, because the field can contain numerous types of objects. As a developer, you need to know what type of object you are dealing with.

The type property has the following legal values:

Table 10.1

Type	Description
ATTACHMENT	File attachment
AUTHORS	Authors
DATETIMES	Date/time value or range of date/time values
EMBEDDEDOBJECT	Embedded object
ERRORITEM	An error occurred while accessing the type
FORMULA	Notes formula
HTML	HTML source text
ICON	Icon
NAMES	Names
NOTELINKS	Link (to a database, view, or document)
NOTEREFS	Reference to the parent document
NUMBERS	Number or number list
OTHEROBJECT	Other object
READERS	Readers
RICHTEXT	Rich Text
SIGNATURE	Signature
TEXT	Text or text list
UNAVAILABLE	The item type isn't available
UNKNOWN	The item type isn't known
USERDATA	User data
USERID	User ID name

The `embeddedobject` type is one of the key types when dealing with Rich Text items, it is covered later in the chapter.

10.4 Working with text

The most basic type of information stored in a Rich Text field is text. The `GetFormattedText` method of the NotesRichTextItem class can be used to get a handle on text stored in an item.

Example 10.10

```
     Dim session As New NotesSession
     Dim db As NotesDatabase
     Dim doc As NotesDocument
     Dim dc As NotesDocumentCollection
     Dim x As Long, bodyText As String
1    Dim rtitem As NotesRichTextItem
     Set db = session.CurrentDatabase
     Set dc = db.AllDocuments
     For x = 1 to dc.Count
        Set doc = dc.GetNthDocument(x)
        If (doc.HasItem("TypeOfLetter")) Then
2          If (doc.TypeOfLetter(0) = "Business") Then
3             Set rtitem = doc.GetFirstItem("Body")
4             If (rtitem.Type = RICHTEXT) Then
5                bodyText = rtitem.GetFormattedText(False, 25)
6                MsgBox bodyText, 0, "Business Letter"
              End If
           End If
        End If
     Next x
```

Explanation

1 Declares a NotesRichTextItem object.

2 Proceeds only if the TypeOfLetter field on the document is set to Business Letter.

3 Sets the NotesRichTextItem object to the body field from the document.

4 Determines if the body field is a Rich Text item.

5 If it is Rich Text, retrieve the text from it and stores it in the `bodyText` String variable. The `GetFormattedText` method accepts two parameters. The first signals whether or not to strip tabs from the text. The second paramater sets the line length of the text read into the string variable.

6 Displays the text from the field in a message box.

In addition to getting a handle on the text, new text can be added to a Rich Text Field. The `AddNewLine`, `AddTab`, and `AppendText` methods of the NotesRichTextItem class help you do this.

Example 10.11

```
    Dim session As New NotesSession
    Dim db As NotesDatabase
    Dim dc As NotesDocumentCollection
    Dim doc As NotesDocument
1   Dim rtitem As NotesRichTextItem
    Dim x As Long
    Set db = session.CurrentDatabase
    Set dc = db.AllDocuments
    For x = 1 to dc.Count
       Set doc = dc.GetNthDocument(x)
       If (doc.HasItem("Body")) Then
2         Set rtitem = doc.GetFirstItem("Body")
3         Call rtitem.AddNewLine(4, False)
4         Call rtitem.AppendText("Copyright")
5         Call rtitem.AddTab(1)
6         Call rtitem.AppendText("@1998")
7         Call doc.Save(True,False)
       End If
    Next x
```

Explanation

The script adds copyright information to every document in the database that has a body field.

1 Declares a NotesRichTextItem object.

2 Sets the object to the Body field.

3 Adds four lines to the end of the text in the Body field. The `AddNewLine` method accepts two parameters: number of lines to add and whether the new line should be a new paragraph separator (`true` or `false`).

4 Adds new text to the end of the body field. The `AppendText` method accepts only one parameter: the text to add to the field. The text is appended to the end of the existing text in the field.

5 Adds a tab to body field. The `AddTab` method accepts only the number of tabs to create.

6 Adds more text to the body field.

7 Saves the document; the changes will be reflected only if the document is saved.

10.4.1 NotesRichTextStyle

Adding text, tabs, and carriage returns is nice, but a Rich Text field gives so much more power. For example when I compose a mail memo, I can set the color, font, and special effects such as bold, italics, or underline. The NotesRichTextStyle class was added to version 4.6 of Notes/Domino. It lets these charactertistics of text be set in LotusScript.

Before attributes can be set using this class, it must be created. The `CreateRichTextStyle` method of the NotesSession class is used to create a new instance of the NotesRichTextStyle class so attributes can be set.

```
Dim rtstyle as NotesRichTextStyle
Set rtstyle = session.CreateRichTextStyle
```

Once the style has been set and defined, it is applied to a NotesRichTextItem. The `AppendStyle` method of the NotesRichTextItem class handles this.

```
Dim rtitem As NotesRichTextItem
Call rtitem.AppendStyle(rtstyle)
```

That is a quick overview of how it is done. The style is created, attributes are set, and the style is applied to a Rich Text item. The setting of attributes is where everything gets done. The NotesRichTextStyle class has eight properties that are used to control the appearance of text.

Table 10.2

Property	Possible Values
Bold	True False STYLE_NO_CHANGE
Italics	True False STYLE_NO_CHANGE
~~Strikethrough~~	True False STYLE_NO_CHANGE
<u>Underline</u>	True False STYLE_NO_CHANGE
FontSize	Legal integer font size. STYLE_NO_CHANGE
Effects	EFFECTS_EMBOSS EFFECTS_EXTRUDE EFFECTS_NONE EFFECTS_SHADOW EFFECTS_SUBSCRIPT EFFECTS_SUPERSCRIPT STYLE_NO_CHANGE
NotesFont	FONT_COURIER FONT_HELV FONT_ROMAN STYLE_NO_CHANGE

Table 10.2

Property	Possible Values
NotesColor	COLOR_BLACK COLOR_BLUE COLOR_CYAN COLOR_DARK_BLUE COLOR_DARK_CYAN COLOR_DARK_GREEN COLOR_DARK_MAGENTA COLOR_DARK_RED COLOR_DARK_YELLOW COLOR_GRAY COLOR_GREEN COLOR_LIGHT_GRAY COLOR_MAGENTA COLOR_RED COLOR_WHITE COLOR_YELLOW STYLE_NO_CHANGE

Notice that every property has `STYLE_NO_CHANGE` as a possible value. This tells it to maintain its previous state.

The properties can be combined in numerous ways to give the text the appearance that you desire. Example 10.12 should make everything a little more clear.

Example 10.12

```
   Dim session As New NotesSession
   Dim db As NotesDatabase
   Dim doc As NotesDocument
   Dim titleItem As NotesItem
1  Dim bodyItem As NotesRichTextItem
2  Dim rtStyle As NotesRichTextStyle
   Set doc = db.CreateDocument
   doc.Form = "Posting"
3  Set titleItem = New NotesItem(doc, "Title", "Test Posting")
4  titleItem.IsSummary = True
5  Set rtStyle = session.CreateRichTextStyle
6  rtStyle.Bold = False
7  rtStyle.Italic = False
8  rtStyle.Strikethrough = False
9  rtStyle.Underline = False
10 rtStyle.FontSize = 12
11 rtStyle.NotesFont = FONT_COURIER
12 rtStyle.FontColor = COLOR_BLUE
13 rtStyle.Effects = EFFECTS_NONE
14 Set bodyItem = New NotesRichTextItem(doc, "Body")
15 Call bodyItem.AppendStyle(rtStyle)
16 Call bodyItem.AppendText("Line one")
17 Call bodyItem.AppendNewLine(2, False)
```

```
18  rtStyle.Bold = True
19  rtStyle.FontColor = COLOR_RED
20  Call bodyItem.AppendStyle(rtStyle)
21  Call bodyItem.AppendText("Line Two")
    Call doc.Save(True,True)
```

Explanation

1 Declares NotesRichTextItem object

2 Declares NotesRichTextStyle object

3 Creates Title field on the new document.

4 Sets the `IsSummary` property to `true` for the Title field. This lets the field be displayed in view columns.

5 Instantiates the NotesRichTextStyle object.

6 Disables `Bold`.

7 Disables `Italics`.

8 Disables `strikethrough`.

9 Disables `Underline`.

10 Sets `font` size to 12 points.

11 Sets `font` face to Courier.

12 Sets the color of the text to blue.

13 Applies no special effects.

14 Creates new Body Rich Text field on the document.

15 Applies the style to the body field.

16 Adds text to the body field. This text will be formatted according to the NotesRichTextStyle object.

17 Adds two lines to the body field.

18 Enables bold.

19 Sets the font color to red.

20 Applies the new settings for the NotesRichTextStyle object to the body field.

21 Adds more text to the body field. The new text will have the new settings of the NotesRichTextStyle object.

The NotesRichTextStyle class gives you the power to present text as you see fit. You can use any combination of fonts, colors, sizes, and other effects.

The NotesRichTextItem class allows attachments, links, and OLE objects to be included in their contents as well. These items are handled with the aid of the NotesEmbeddedObject class, and it has its own chapter. Chapter 11 details the handling of attachments, links, and OLE objects in Rich Text fields.

10.5 Chapter summary

Fields on documents can be accessed as properties of the NotesDocument object using dot notation or through the use of the NotesItem and/or NotesRichTextItem classes. Also, new fields can be created using the same methods. Methods of the NotesUIDocument and NotesDocument classes are provided to work with these items.

10.6 Chapter review

- Fields of data in Notes documents can be accessed with the NotesItem class, or they can be accessed using dot notation (NotesDocument.FieldName).
- The NotesItem class can be used to access, create, alter, delete, or copy fields.
- Methods are provided to check the type of data in a field.
- The NotesRichTextItem class is a subclass of the NotesItem class. All methods and properties of the NotesItem class are available to the NotesRichTextItem class.
- The NotesRichTextItem class allows a script to work with text in a Rich Text field, attachments, links, or OLE objects.
- The NotesRichTextStyle class allows text in a Rich Text field to be formatted.

CHAPTER 11

Embedded objects and OLE

11.1 Chapter objectives 174
11.2 Attachments 174
11.3 OLE 179
11.4 Creating embedded OLE objects 181
11.5 Creating a linked object 184
11.6 Deleting objects 185
11.7 Chapter summary 186
11.8 Chapter review 187

11.1 Chapter objectives

- Working with file attachments
- Accessing attachment properties
- What is OLE?
- Working with links
- Working with OLE objects
- Activating OLE objects
- Accessing link properties
- Accessing object properties

Inevitably, Lotus Notes cannot provide all of the functionality needed/wanted by the user community. Software such as Microsoft Office and Lotus SmartSuite performs tasks that will never be a part of Lotus Notes, but combining them produces powerful results. You could combine the workflow, email, and database features of Lotus Notes with the number crunching of Microsoft Excel to build a powerful application. Data is entered into word processers and spreadsheets every day (databases are covered later), and they can be embedded into a Lotus Notes form or document or attached to a document.

This chapter relies heavily on the last chapter's treatment of Rich Text fields. The Rich Text field is where an embedded object will reside. File attachments and OLE objects can be inserted into Rich Text fields as well as formatted text. The NotesEmbeddedObject class provides the necessary tools to work with these items.

Note This class is useful when working with the Windows platforms only. It is not supported by UNIX, OS/2, or the Macintosh.

11.2 Attachments

A file attachment is a file that is physically inserted into a document. A file attachment can only be inserted into Rich Text fields. From the Notes workspace, users insert file attachments with the paper clip symbol, or by selecting File | Attach. Figure 11.1 shows the box which appears when they do so.

On the other hand, attachments can be created through LotusScript by using the `EmbedObject` method of the NotesRichTextItem class.

11.2.1 Creating an attachment

```
Set eobject = NotesRichTextItem.EmbedObject(EMBED_ATTACHMENT, "", filepath,_
  optional_name)
```

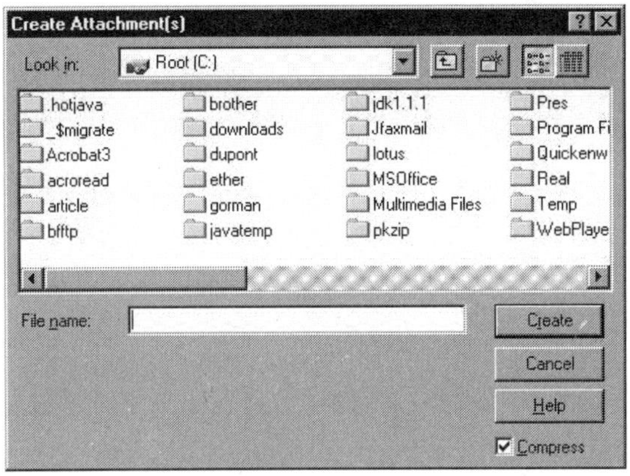

Figure 11.1
Inserting an attachment in the UI

The `filepath` parameter should include the full path (including drive letter) for the file to attach. The `optional_name` parameter allows you to assign a name to the object for future use in the script.

Note The `optional_name` parameter is very important if you are attaching multiple files that have the same name, but different paths. If you attempt to attach a file with the same file name and no optional name assigned, LotusScript will insert only the first file.

Example 11.1

```
1    Sub Initialize
        Dim session As New NotesSession
        Dim db As NotesDatabase
        Dim doc As NotesDocument
        Dim rtf As NotesRichTextItem
2       Dim eo As NotesEmbeddedObject
        Set db = session.CurrentDatabase
        Set doc = db.CreateDocument
        doc.Form = "Attachment"
        doc.Title = "Temp"
3       Set rtf = New NotesRichTextItem(doc, "attach")
4       Set oe = rtf.EmbedObject(EMBED_ATTACHMENT,"","c:\temp.txt","temp")
        Call doc.Save(True, False)
     End Sub
```

Explanation

1 Script resides in the `Initialize` event of an agent.

2 Declares a NotesEmbeddedObject object.

3 Instantiates a new Rich Text item on the document.

4 Embeds the file (`c:\temp.txt`) in the Rich Text field on the form. It is given the name `temp`.

Note Files attached in a Notes document are saved in system fields named $File. One $File field is created for every attached file. So, one way to check for the existence of attachments on a document is to check for any $File fields.

Once a file has been attached to a document, certain properties of it can be accessed. The following list shows properties relevant to attachments:

- `FileSize` The size of the attachment in bytes.
- `Parent` The Rich Text item that holds the attachment.
- `Source` The name of the original file attachment.
- `Type` Signals what type of object it is; it returns `EMBED_ATTACHMENT` for attachments.

Example 11.2

```
    Dim session As New NotesSession
    Dim db As NotesDatabase
    Dim doc As NotesDocument
    Dim dc As NotesDocumentCollection
1   Dim rtitem As NotesRichTextItem
    Dim loopIndex As Long
    Set db = session.CurrentDatabase
    Set dc = db.AllDocuments
    For loopIndex = 1 to dc.Count
       Set doc = dc.GetNthDocument(loopIndex)
2      If (doc.HasItem("$File")) Then
3         Set rtitem = doc.GetFirstItem("Body")
4         Forall eo In rtitem.EmbeddedObjects
5            If (eo.Type = EMBED_ATTACHMENT) Then
6               MsgBox "Filename:  " & eo.Source & Chr(13) & "File size:  " & _
                   eo.FileSize
7               Call eo.ExtractFile("C:\TEMP\" & eo.Source)
             End If
          End Forall
       End If
    Next loopIndex
```

Explanation

1 Declares NotesRichTextItem object.

2 Determines if the document has an attachment. If it does, it will have one or more fields named $File.

3 Sets the NotesRichTextItem object to the body field on the document. The body field will contain the attachments.

4 The `EmbeddedObjects` property of the NotesRichTextItem class accesses the embedded objects in the body field. The Embedded Objects returns an array of the

embedded objects in a Rich Text field. The `Forall` loop allows easy access to all of the embedded objects.

5 The `Type` property allows us to determine if the embedded object is an attachment or not.

6 If the embedded object is an attachment, displays its file name and size in a message box.

7 Detaches the attachment to the Temp directory on drive C.

The last example showed how to access multiple attachments on a document, but if we know for sure that there is only one attachment on a document we can easily access it. The `embeddedobjects` property of the NotesRichTextItem class returns an array of objects, so designate the number the element you want to access. If we know there is only one attachment, we would access element zero (`0`).

```
Line#4 from the previous example would be replaced with this line.

Set eo = doc.EmbeddedObjects(0)
```

This would give us access to the first attachment.

The NotesDocument and NotesRichTextItem classes provide methods to access embedded objects by name. The problem with these methods is the fact that you don't always know the name. It would be a pain if you had to know the file name for an attachment before you could work with it in script.

Example 11.3

We want to allow our users to search an entire database for a specific file attachment. The search will be conducted by file name, and we are only interested in the first match. If a match is found, the user enters where to save (detach) it.

```
   Dim session As New NotesSession
   Dim db As NotesDatabase
   Dim doc As NotesDocument
   Dim dc As NotesDocumentCollection
1  Dim eo As NotesEmbeddedObject
2  Dim filename As String, path As String
   Dim x As Long
3  filename = InputBox$("Please enter the name of the file to find.")
4  If (filename <> "") Then
      Set db = session.CurrentDatabase
      Set dc = db.AllDocuments
      For x = 1 to dc.Count
         Set doc = dc.GetNthDocument(x)
5        Set eo = doc.GetAttachment(filename)
6           If Not (eo Is Nothing) Then
```

```
7               path = InputBox$("The file has been found."  & _
                   "Please enter the path (<drive letter>:\<directory>)" & _
                   "to save it.")
8               If Not (path = "") Then
9                  If ((Dir(path,16)) <> "") Then
10                    Call eo.ExtractFile(path & "\" & eo.Source)
11                    Exit Sub
                  End If
               End If
            End If
         Next x
      End If
```

Explanation

1 Declares NotesEmbeddedObject object.

2 Declares variables to store the name of the file to find and the location (path) to save it if it is found.

3 The user enters the name of the file attachment to find in the database.

4 Continues only if the user enters a file name.

5 Uses the `GetAttachment` method of the NotesDocument class to check for the existence of the file attachment entered by the user. The `GetAttachment` method accepts one parameter: the file name.

6 Detaches the file only if it has been found. The NotesEmbeddedObject object will be Nothing (empty) if the file attachment was not found in the current document.

7 Asks the user to enter the location to save it, if the file was found.

8 Continues only if the path was not empty.

9 Uses the `Dir` command to make sure the path entered by the user exists.

10 Uses the `ExtractFile` method of the NotesEmbeddedObject class to detach the file.

11 Exits the routine we were only interested in the first match.

The NotesRichTextItem class contains a method called `GetAttachment` as well, but it searches only a Rich Text field for an attachment. It works the same way as its counterpart in the NotesDocument class. In addition, the NotesRichTextItem class contains the `GetEmbeddedObject` method that is used the same way as the `GetAttachment` method. The difference lies in the fact that `GetAttachment` is specific to file attachments, but the `GetEmbeddedObject` can be used with any type of embedded object.

Example 11.4

```
Dim ns As New NotesSession
```

```
    Dim ndb As NotesDatabase
    Dim ndoc As NotesDocument
    Dim neo As NotesEmbeddedObject
    Dim nrtf As NotesRichTextItem
    Dim ndc As NotesDocumentCollection
    Dim filename As String
    Dim count As Long
    Set ndb = ns.CurrentDatbase
    Set ndc = ndb.AllDocuments
    For count = 1 to ndc.Count
       Set ndoc = ndc.GetNthDocument(count)
1      If (ndoc.HasItem("Body") & (ndoc.HasEmbedded)) Then
2         Set nrtf = ndoc.GetFirstItem("Body")
3         filename = InputBox("Please enter the name of the file.")
          If (filename <> "") Then
4            Set neo = nrtf.GetEmbeddedObject(filename)
5            If Not (neo Is Nothing) Then
6               MsgBox "The file was found.",0,"Found"
7                  Exit Sub
             End If
          End If
       End If
    Next count
```

Explanation

1 Checks the document for the existence of the body field and embedded objects. The `HasEmbedded` property of the NotesDocument class signals `true` if a document contains one or more embedded objects such as file attachments, links, or OLE objects.

2 The NotesRichTextItem object is assigned to the body field on the current document.

3 Gets the file name to find from the user.

4 Sets the NotesEmbeddedObject object to the item entered by the user. The `GetEmbeddedObject` method of the NotesRichTextItem class searches for it. It accepts only one parameter: the name of the object to find.

5 If the object was not found, the NotesEmbeddedObject will be empty or Nothing.

6 Signals that the item was found.

7 Exits the script when and if a match is found.

11.3 OLE

OLE is an acronym for object linking and embedding. OLE is a technology from Microsoft that allows the sharing of data between applications. For example, all or a part of a Microsoft Excel or Lotus WordPro document can be embedded in a Notes document. New or blank objects can be inserted into Notes documents and the object's application can be used to enter data into it.

11.3.1 Linking

The Lotus Notes Help defines a *linked object* as a pointer to data in a source file. When and if the data in the source file changes, the changes are reflected in Notes. There are a few requirements for linking that often make it undesirable: linking involves a source file located on some drive, so users who access the link must have access to the file and the same directory mappings to get to the file, and the user must have the application that created the linked file installed on his/her system. If the source file for a link is deleted or moved, the link must be recreated. This goes against all of the features of Lotus Notes, especially the mobility piece. For this reason, I do not use linking.

11.3.2 Embedding

An *embedded* object is a copy of the data from a source file. It is not *linked* to a file, so source file changes are not reflected in Notes. The user does have to have the source application installed on his/her system to work with the embedded object. The lack of a link to an external file makes this the most appealing type of OLE use for Lotus Notes.

11.3.3 OLE Automation

OLE Automation is an OLE service for integrating development tools and applications. It enables an application to expose its functionality, or to control the functionality of other applications on the same computer or across networks. Microsoft says that applications can be automated and integrated with programming code creating virtually endless possibilities.

The two key elements of OLE Automation are:

- Applications or software components, called OLE Automation servers, that can be controlled because their functionality has been exposed and made accessible to other applications. All of the products in the Microsoft Office suite are OLE Automation servers. These OLE Automation servers expose their functionality through object models.
- Other applications or development tools, called OLE Automation controllers, that can control OLE Automation servers through programming code, by accessing the functionality exposed by the OLE Automation servers. Microsoft Visual Basic and C++ are just two examples. Microsoft Visual Basic can be used to work with Lotus Notes objects.

OLE objects can be created manually (Create | Object) or through LotusScript (see figure 11.2). An embedded object stores its data in Lotus Notes, but uses its OLE Server application to edit it.

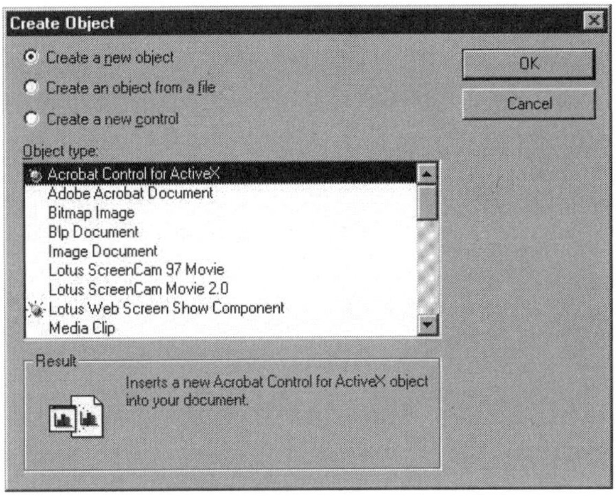

Figure 11.2
Embedding an object manually

11.4 Creating embedded OLE objects

The NotesUIDocument class contains a `CreateObject` method that can be used to embed an object into a document.

Example 11.5

This script embeds a Microsoft Word document in a Notes document.

```
1    Sub Click (Source As Button)
        Dim uiw As New NotesUIWorkspace
        Dim uidoc As NotesUIDocument
2       Set uidoc = uiw.CurrentDocument
        Dim embedFile as String
3       embedFile = InputBox$("Please enter the path and filename of the" & _
           "file to embed.","Filename")
4       If (Dir(embedFile,0) = "") then
5          MsgBox "The file entered does not exist.....aborting.",64,"Error"
6          Exit Sub
        Else
7          Call uidoc.GotoField("EmbeddedObject")
8          Call uidoc.CreateObject("Word Document","",embedFile)
           MsgBox "The file has been embedded.",0,"Success"
        End If
     Exit Sub
```

Explanation

1 Activates the script by an action button.

2 Sets the NotesUIDocument to the current document that is open.

3 The user enters the path and name of the file to embed.

4 Uses the `Dir` function to make sure the file name entered exists.

5 Ends the script if the file does not exist.

6 Exits the script.

7 Sets the pointer to the field named EmbeddedObject; this is where the file will be embedded.

8 Uses the `CreateObject` method of the NotesUIDocument class to create an OLE Automation object. The method accepts three parameters: an optional name that will be used to refer to the object in your code; the type of object to create (it must correspond to an entry in the OLE registry); and the path and name of the source file to use to create an object. The `type` and `filepath` parameters are exclusive. That is, if a `type` is declared then a `filepath` is not needed and vice versa.

The important note from the example is that the file path and type parameters are not used together. The type parameter is used to create an object, and the file path parameter is used to create an object from an existing file.

11.4.1 Creating an object

Example 11.6

```
1    Sub Click(Source As Button)
        Dim uiw As New NotesUIWorkspace
        Dim uidoc As NotesUIDocument
        Set uidoc = uiw.CurrentDocument
2       Call uidoc.GotoField("Body")
3       Call uidoc.CreateObject("Excel Example","ExcelWorksheet")
     End Sub
```

Explanation

1 Locates the script (in an action button on the Memo form in my mail database).

2 Sets the pointer to the body field, so the object will be created in this field.

3 Uses the `CreateObject` method of the NotesUIDocument class to insert a Microsoft Excel spreadsheet in the document. Notice that the `file` parameter was omitted since we are creating an object.

Example 11.7

```
   Sub Click(Source As Button)
      Dim uiw As New NotesUIWorkspace
      Dim uidoc As NotesUIDocument
      Set uidoc = uiw.CurrentDocument
      Call uidoc.GotoField("Body")
1     Call uidoc.CreateObject("Word Example","WordDocument")
   End Sub
```

Explanation

1 Uses the `CreateObject` method to create a Microsoft Word object.

The `EmbedObject` method of the NotesRichTextItem class can be used to embed an object as well.

Example 11.8

```
    Dim s As New NotesSession
    Dim db As NotesDatabase
    Dim rtf As NotesRichTextItem
1   Dim eo As NotesEmbeddedObject
    Dim doc As NotesDocument
    Set db = s.CurrentDatabase
    Set doc = db.CreateDocument
    doc.Form = "Memo"
    doc.Subject = "Word Document"
2   Set rtf = New NotesRichTextItem(doc,"Body")
3   Set eo = rtf.EmbedObject(EMBED_OBJECT,"","C:\oletest.doc",_
      "Word Document")
    Call doc.Save(True,True)
```

Explanation

1 Declares a new NotesEmbeddedObject object.

2 Creates a new Rich Text field on the document.

3 Uses the `EmbedObject` method of the NotesRichTextItem class to embed the Word document in the body field.

Example 11.9

This bit of code inserts a new Word document into a new document.

```
    Dim s As New NotesSession
    Dim db As NotesDatabase
    Dim doc As NotesDocument
    Dim rtf As NotesRichTextItem
    Dim eo As NotesEmbeddedObject
    Set db = s.CurrentDatabase
    Set doc = db.CreateDocument
    doc.Form = "Memo"
    doc.Subject = "Empty Word Document"
    Set rtf = New NotesRichTextItem(doc, "Body")
1   Set eo = rtf.EmbedObject(EMBED_OBJECT,"WordDocument","","Word Document")
    Call doc.Save(True,True)
```

Explanation

1 Uses the `EmbedObject` method of the NotesRichTextItem class to embed a new Word document in the body field. The object type (WordDocument) is specified and the source (file path) is left off since it is a new object.

11.4.2 FYI

The names specified in the `type` parameter (ExcelWorksheet and WordDocument) can be found in your registry on the Windows 95 and NT platforms. You can quickly find OLE Server Automation objects that can be inserted into Notes documents by searching the registry for OLE1Class. To bring up your registry, run regedit.exe, and use Edit | Find (ctrl F) to search. Use F3 to find the next match after a match is found. The items returned can be used as object types on your system.

The `EmbedObject` method of the NotesDocument class should be used when working with documents through the back end (documents not open). The `CreateObject` method of the NotesUIDocument class should be used when working with documents in the front end.

11.5 Creating a linked object

As noted earlier, linked objects differ from embedded objects in that the data in the object is not stored in Notes. It is stored in the file specified, so if the file changes, they are reflected in Note. On the other hand, if the file is deleted, the link is broken.

Example 11.10

```
    Dim s As New NotesSession
    Dim db As NotesDatabase
    Dim doc As NotesDocument
    Dim rtf As NotesRichTextItem
1   Dim eo As NotesEmbeddedObject
    Set db = s.CurrentDatabase
    Set doc = doc.CreateDocument
    doc.Form = "Memo"
    doc.Subject = "OLE Link"
2   Set rtf = New NotesRichTextItem(doc,"Body")
3   Set eo = rtf.EmbedObject(EMBED_OBJECTLINK,"","C:\oletest.doc",_
       "Word Document")
    Call doc.Save(True, False)
```

Explanation

1 Declares a new NotesEmbeddedObject object.

2 Creates a new Rich Text field on the document. This field will hold the linked object.

3 Uses the `EmbedObject` method of the NotesRichTextItem class to create the linked object. The type of object is set to `EMBED_OBJECTLINK` to specify a linked object.

11.5.1 Editing an object

An embedded or linked object can be edited through the `Activate` method in the NotesEmbeddedObject class.

Example 11.11

```
  Sub Click (Source As Button)
     Dim session As New NotesSession
     Dim db As NotesDatabase
     Dim doc As NotesDocument
     Dim rtf As NotesRichTextItem
     Dim eo As NotesEmbeddedObject
     Set db = session.CurrentDatabase
     Set doc = db.CreateDocument
     doc.Form = "Memo"
     doc.Title = "Test"
     Set rtf = New NotesRichTextItem(doc,"Body")
1    Set eo = rtf.EmbedObject(EMBED_OBJECT,"","c:\oletest.doc",_
        "Word Document")
     Call doc.Save(True,True)
2    Call eo.Activate(True)
  End Sub
```

Explanation

1 A Word document is embedded in the body Rich Text field.

2 The `Activate` method of the NotesEmbeddedObject class is used to activate the object. It accepts one parameter that signals `true` to show the application interface and `false` to not show it. We told the system to show the Microsoft Word interface with the `True` parameter.

Note The behavior of the `Activate` method can be a little erratic, so you may have to experiment with it to get it to work properly on your system.

11.6 Deleting objects

The NotesEmbeddedObject class contains a `remove` property to handle the task of removing items from documents.

Example 11.12

This code removes every embedded object (object link, embedded object, or attachment) from every document in the database.

```
Sub Initialize
     Dim session As New NotesSession
     Dim db as NotesDatabase
     Dim doc As NotesDocument
     Dim dc As NotesDocumentCollection
     Dim x As Long
     Set db = session.CurrentDatabase
     For x = 1 to dc.Count
        Set doc = dc.GetNthDocument(x)
1       Forall object in doc.EmbeddedObjects
2            Call object.Remove
        End Forall
```

```
3       Call doc.Save(True,True)
     Next x
   End Sub
```

Explanation

1 Uses a `Forall` loop and the `EmbeddedObjects` property of the NotesDocument class to access every embedded object in the current document.

2 Uses the `Remove` method to delete the embedded object from the current document.

3 Saves the document so the changes (deletions) take effect.

An embedded object can also be accessed by its name. That is, the name that is assigned to it when it is created. Example 11.11 created an embedded object named Word Document, so it can be accessed by this name. The `GetObject` method of the NotesUIDocument class retrieved objects by name. It accepts the object name as its only parameter.

Example 11.13

```
   Dim uiw As New NotesUIWorkspace
   Dim uidoc As NotesUIDocument
   Dim eo As Variant
   Dim objectName as String
   Set uidoc = uiw.CurrentDocument
1  objectName = InputBox$("Please enter the name of the object.")
2  If Not (objectName = "") Then
3     Set eo = uidoc.GetObject(objectName)
4     If (eo Is Nothing) Then
         MsgBox "The object does not exist"
      Else
         MsgBox "Object found!"
      End If
   End If
```

Explanation

1 The user enters the name of the object to retrieve.

2 Continues only if the user enters a value.

3 Uses the `GetObject` method of the NotesUIDocument class to retrieve the object, if it exists.

4 If the object does not exist on the document, it will be empty or Nothing.

11.7 Chapter summary

The NotesRichTextItem and NotesEmbeddedObject classes facilitate working with embedded objects such as attachments, links, and OLE objects. OLE is a Microsoft technology that allows the sharing of data between applications. Notes/Domino is an

OLE Client, not an OLE Server. OLE allows development of powerful applications that take advantage of other products like Microsoft Office or Lotus SmartSuite.

11.8 Chapter review

- File attachments can be inserted into documents using the `EmbedObject` method of the NotesRichTextItem class.
- One $File field is created for every file attached to a Notes document.
- The `filename`, `size`, and `type` are properties of file attachments. The created date is not a property, it can be accessed by detaching the file and using the `FileDateTime` function on the detached file.
- The NotesEmbeddedObject class can be used to work with file attachments and OLE objects in Notes documents.
- Every object embedded in a Notes document can be accessed through the `EmbeddedObjects` property of the NotesDocument class. It returns an array of objects.
- OLE is a Microsoft solution for sharing data between applications.
- Linking an object involves inserting a pointer to a file.
- Embedding copies data from a source file.
- The `CreateObject` method of the NotesUIDocument class can be used to insert an OLE object into a Notes document.
- The `EmbedObject` method of the NotesRichTextItem class can be used to insert OLE objects into Notes documents as well.
- The `Activate` method of the NotesEmbeddedObject class activates an OLE object.
- The `Remove` method of the NotesEmbeddedObject class removes an embedded object from a Notes document.

CHAPTER 12

Office 97

12.1 Chapter objectives 190

12.2 Object browser revisited 190

12.3 Microsoft Office 190

12.4 Performance considerations 203

12.5 Accessing Lotus Notes from Visual Basic 204

12.6 Chapter summary 205

12.7 Chapter review 205

12.1 Chapter objectives

- Viewing OLE object properties/methods in the Lotus Notes IDE
- Integrate Microsoft Word and Lotus Notes
- Integrate Microsoft Excel with Lotus Notes
- Integrate Microsoft PowerPoint with Lotus Notes
- Integrate Microsoft Outlook and Lotus Notes in an application
- Access Lotus Notes objects from Visual Basic
- Optimize OLE code

Lotus Notes is a very powerful environment for building robust applications, but it does have its limitations. For example, it does not possess the number-crunching capabilities inherent in a spreadsheet application such as Lotus 1-2-3 or Microsoft Excel. In addition, it cannot help you give a presentation like Microsoft PowerPoint, and the printing capabilities cannot match full-featured word processors like Microsoft Word. Each brings its own set of tools to the table. The power of each can be tapped by combining them to form full-featured applications.

Chapter 11 introduced OLE with simple examples. All office suites on the market today, Lotus SmartSuite, WordPerfect Office, and Microsoft Office, are OLE compatible. This chapter takes OLE a bit further by demonstrating the integration of Microsoft Office, the market leader, and Lotus Notes. The chapter contains numerous examples, but these do not, and cannot, cover the wide range of possibilities. They are limited only by your imagination.

12.2 Object browser revisited

Chapter 1 introduced the object browser in the Notes IDE. In addition to LotusScript classes, it allows you to view all OLE classes on the current machine as well. Select the show browser check box to enable the browser, and choose OLE classes from the drop-down list. Figure 12.1 shows the outcome on my machine.

The list of OLE classes will vary, depending on the applications installed. It allows you to view all pertinent properties and methods for the OLE objects. These are invaluable since you may not be as familiar with the OLE application as you would like.

12.3 Microsoft Office

The Microsoft Office suite consists of five applications: Word, Excel, PowerPoint, Access, and Outlook. Microsoft Office Professional contains all of the applications. Also, each application can be purchased separately. OLE allows tight integration

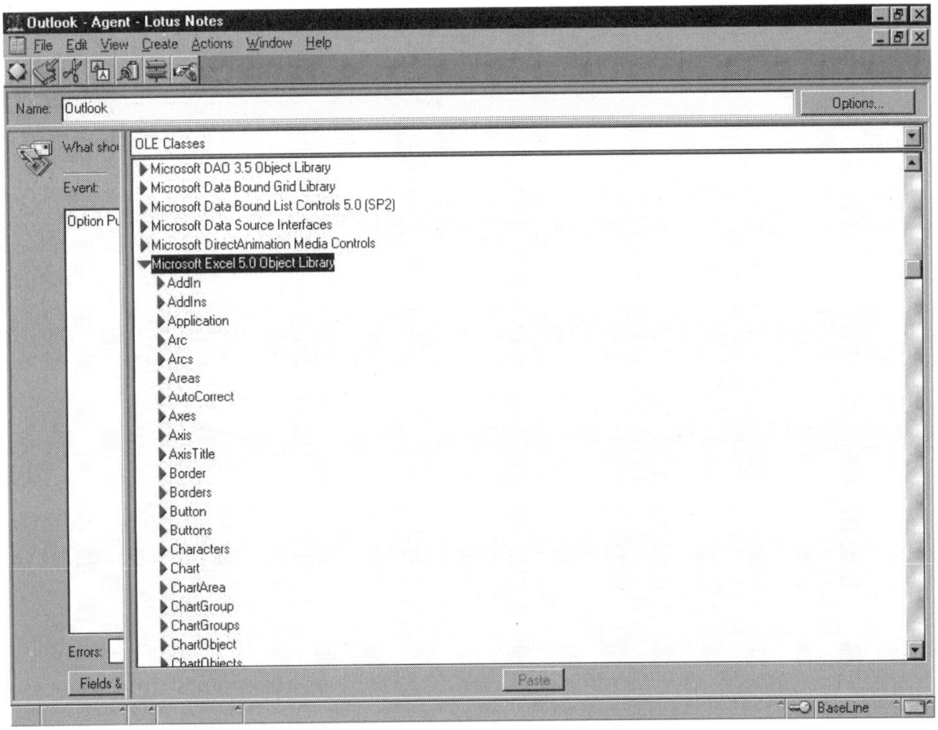

Figure 12.1 Viewing OLE properties/methods via object browser

between the applications, and also tight integration with non-Microsoft products like Lotus Notes.

Remember OLE can go both ways. That is, Lotus Notes can use an Office object and vice versa. Word, Excel, and PowerPoint will be covered separately. Access is covered with LS:DO in chapter 15. Let's start by examining the integration of Microsoft Word and Lotus Notes.

12.3.1 Microsoft Word

Note All examples in this chapter were created using Microsoft Office 97.

Embedding a Word object in a Notes document is a straightforward process (refer to chapter 11 for more details).

Example 12.1

```
    Sub Click(Source As Button)
       Dim uiw As New NotesUIWorkspace
1      Dim wordObj As Variant
       Dim uidoc As NotesUIDocument
       Set uidoc = uiw.CurrentDocument
2      Call uidoc.GotoField("body")
```

```
3     Set wordObj = uidoc.CreateObject("Word Document","Word.Document.8")
4     Call wordObj.Application.ActiveDocument.Range(0,0)._
         InsertBefore(uidoc.FieldGetText("title"))
   End Sub
```

Explanation

1 Declares Variant object to use as a handle to the Word object.

2 Moves the cursor to the body field on the currently open document. The cursor must be on a Rich Text field when the `CreateObject` method is used in the next line.

3 Creates an embedded Word 97 object. The first parameter assigns a name to the object. The second parameter, the most important, tells the system what type of OLE object to create. In this case we create a Word.Document.8 object which is a Microsoft Word 97 object.

4 Uses the methods/properties of the embedded Word object. This line inserts text from the title field on the current Notes document into the first line on the embedded Word document.

The previous example gives you an idea of the power of using Word and Notes together. The inserting of text into an embedded Word object enables the creation of such items as form letters. Portions of the form letter, such as address, can be populated with data from a Notes document. The next example uses data from a Lotus Notes document to assemble a letter in Microsoft Word. This example uses the Word object model. The Notes object browser can be used to view the various objects, methods, and properties of Microsoft Word. In addition, there are numerous books at your local bookstore that focus on programming with Visual Basic and Microsoft Office.

Example 12.2

```
   Sub Click(Source As Button)
      Dim uiw As New NotesUIWorkspace
1     Dim wordObj As Variant, handle As Variant, csz As String
2     Dim app As Variant
      Dim uid As NotesUIDocument
      Set uid = uiw.CurrentDocument
3     Call uid.GotoField("letter")
4     Call uid.CreateObject("Word Document","","C:\formletter.doc")
5     Set handle = uid.GetObject( "Word Document" )
6     Call handle.Activate
7     Set app = handle.Application
8     Call app.ActiveDocument.Paragraphs(7).Range.InsertBefore_
         (uid.FieldGetText("Name"))
9     Call app.ActiveDocument.Paragraphs(8).Range.InsertBefore_
         (uid.FieldGetText("Address"))
10    csz = uid.FieldGetText("City") + ", " + uid.FieldGetText("State") +_
         "  " + uid.FieldGetText("Zip")
```

```
11    Call app.ActiveDocument.Paragraphs(9).Range.InsertBefore(csz)
12    Call app.ActiveDocument.PrintOut
   End Sub
```

Explanation

1 Declares Variant object to work with Word object and a String variable.

2 Declares Variant object that will be used to work with embedded Word object.

3 Positions the cursor in the Rich Text field that will contain the Word object.

4 Creates the Word object using a file from the local hard drive. There is no handle to the object returned using this method.

5 Sets the Variant object to the newly created embedded Word object.

6 Activates the embedded object.

7 Sets the Variant to the application portion of the Word object. This is an object within the Word object model that is used to access the embedded document. This variable is declared and set to save typing.

8 Inserts text from the current Notes document into the seventh paragraph of the Word document.

9 Inserts text from the current Notes document into the eighth paragraph of the Word document.

10 Assembles a String variable containing the city, state, and ZIP code from the currently open Notes document.

11 Inserts the String variable into the ninth paragraph of the embedded Word document.

12 Prints the embedded Word document. This will use the default Printer.

The last example allows us to use the printing capabilities of Microsoft Word to print form letters with information from a Notes document.

There is one major difference between example 12.1 and 12.2: the first example creates a Word document, the second uses an existing one. The difference lies in how to get a handle on the embedded Word objects. If you are creating an object (not from an existing file), then a handle is returned when it is created.

```
Set wordObj = uidoc.CreateObject("Word Document","Word.Document.8")
```

Embedding an existing Word document requires an extra step.

```
Call uidoc.CreateObject("Word Document","","C:\formletter.doc")
Set handle = uidoc.GetObject( "Word Document" )
```

So, the style depends on whether you are creating an object or using an existing file.

Note The format for creating objects or using existing files is consistent for all types of OLE objects. It could be a Lotus WordPro, Microsoft Excel, or a Visio diagram object.

It doesn't matter what environment is used to develop applications, you always encounter a situation where data must be translated from one format to another. The data must be exported/imported. The next example demonstrates creating Notes documents from data in a Microsoft Word document. The data has a set format.

Format of the Word document

```
Name:  <data>
Address:  <data>
City:  <data>
State:  <data>
Zip:  <data>
Phone:  <data>
```

The next example shows how a LotusScript agent can create Notes documents from a Word document.

Example 12.3

```
     Sub Initialize
        Dim session As New NotesSession
        Dim db As NotesDatabase
        Dim coc As NotesDocument
1       Dim rangeHandle As String
2       Dim handle As Variant, app As Variant
        Set db = session.CurrentDatabase
3       Set handle = GetObject("c:\import.doc", "Word.Document.8")
4       Set app = handle.Application.Documents(1)
5       Forall p In app.Paragraphs
6          rangeHandle = v.Range.Text
7          If (rangeHandle <> "") Then
8             If(Left(Ucase(rangeHandle),5) = "NAME") Then
9                If Not (doc Is Nothing) Then
10                  Call doc.Save(True,False)
                 End If
11               Set doc = db.CreateDocument
12               doc.Form = "frmPersonInfo"
13               pos = Instr(rangeHandle,"NAME")
14               doc.name = removeCRLF(Trim(Right(rangeHandle,Len(rangeHandle) -_
                    (pos + 3))))
              Elseif (Left(Ucase(rangeHandle),7) = "ADDRESS") Then
                 pos = Instr(rangeHandle,"ADDRESS")
                 doc.addr = removeCRLF(Trim(Right(rangeHandle,Len(rangeHandle) -_
                    (pos + 3))))
              Elseif (Left(Ucase(rangeHandle),4) = "CITY") Then
                 pos = Instr(rangeHandle,"CITY")
                 doc.city = removeCRLF(Trim(Right(rangeHandle,Len(rangeHandle) -_
                    (pos + 2))))
              Elseif (Left(Ucase(rangeHandle),5) = "STATE") Then
```

```
            pos = Instr(rangeHandle,"STATE")
            doc.st = removeCRLF(Trim(Right(rangeHandle,Len(rangeHandle) -_
               (pos + 3))))
         Elseif (Left(Ucase(rangeHandle),3) = "ZIP") Then
         pos = Instr(rangeHandle,"ZIP")
         doc.zip = removeCRLF(Trim(Right(rangeHandle,Len(rangeHandle) -_
            (pos + 2))))
         Elseif (Left(Ucase(rangeHandle),5) = "PHONE") Then
            pos = Instr(rangeHandle,"PHONE")
            doc.phone = removeCRLF(Trim(Right(rangeHandle,Len(rangeHandle) -_
               (pos + 3))))
         End If
      End Forall
15    Call handle.Close
16    Set handle = Nothing
   End Sub
```

Explanation

1 Declares String variable that will be used to retrieve text from paragraphs in the Word document.

2 Declares Variants that will be used to access the contents of the Word document.

3 Sets the Variant to the Word document specified by file name.

4 Sets the Variant app to the first document in the Word document. The file contains only one document, so it is the first and only document.

5 Loops through all paragraphs in the Word document. Text in a Word document is divided into paragraphs. This allows us to access the Word document line by line.

6 Sets the String variable to the text from the current paragraph.

7 Processes the paragraph only if it is not empty. An empty line on a document is seen as a paragraph, so this check must be performed.

8 Determines if the current line of text starts with NAME. If it does, this signals a new document in the Notes database (start of a record).

9 Allows creation of multiple documents while we loop through all paragraphs. When a line starting with NAME is encountered, this signals a new record. Also, the first time through the paragraphs, a document will created. Nevertheless, we must determine if a document is currently open.

10 Saves the document if it is open. The document must be saved, because the existence of NAME in the current line signals the start of a new record/document.

11 Creates a document.

12 Sets the form used to create the document.

13 Uses the `Instr` function to determine the position of NAME within the text. This is repeated for each field in the record.

14 Uses the position from the previous line to set the name field on the new Notes document. The `removeCRLF` function is used to remove unwanted characters from the line (the complete listing of removeCRLF follows this example). This is repeated for each field in the record.

15 Closes the Word document.

16 Sets the Word object to `nothing` to destroy it.

The function to remove carriage returns and line feeds is listed next.

```
1     Function removeCRLF (passedString As String) As String
         Dim tempString As String
2        For i = 1 To Len(passedString)
3           If Asc(Mid(passedString,i,1)) = Clng(13) Or _
               Asc(Mid(passedString,i,1)) = Clng(10) Then
4              tempString = tempString + Space(1)
            Else
5              tempString = tempString + Mid(passedString,i,1)
            End If
         Next i
6        removeCRLF = tempString
   End Function
```

Explanation

1 Removes function declaration, carriage returns, and line feeds from the String passed into the function.

2 Loops through all characters in the string passed into the function.

3 Uses the `Mid` and `Asc` functions to determine if the current character in the string is a carriage return or line feed.

4 Inserts a space in its place if the current character from the string is a carriage return or line feed.

5 Does not alter the current character if it is not a carriage return or line feed.

6 Returns the string assembled by the function to the code that called the function.

12.3.2 Microsoft Excel

Spreadsheet programs like Microsoft Excel or Lotus 1-2-3 contain the number-crunching functionality that Lotus Notes lacks. Data is presented in a series of rows and columns. Embedding an Excel spreadsheet into a Notes document is no different than the procedure for a Word document.

Example 12.4

```
Sub Click(Source As Button)
   Dim uiw As New NotesUIWorkspace
   Dim wordObj As Variant, csz As String
```

```
      Dim uidoc As NotesUIDocument
      Set uidoc = uiw.CurrentDocument
1     Call uidoc.GotoField("body")
2     Set handle = uidoc.CreateObject("Excel Spreadsheet","Excel.Sheet.8","")
3     Call handle.Activate
    End Sub
```

Explanation

1 Positions the cursor in the Rich Text field that will contain the embedded Excel spreadsheet object.

2 Creates the Excel spreadsheet. The `Excel.Sheet.8` parameter signals the creation of a Microsoft Excel version 8.0 object which is Excel 97. The number corresponds to the version with which you are working.

3 Activates the Excel spreadsheet.

After embedding a spreadsheet in a Notes document you may need to save it to a local or network drive. Embedded objects differ from attachments in that they have no associated file name. Also, there is no method of the NotesEmbeddedObject class that facilitates saving or detaching them. For this reason, you must turn to the object model of the embedded object. The next example loops through all documents in a database saving the embedded Excel spreadsheets locally. The file name is created using a special field from the Notes form.

Note An excellent source of information for programming with Microsoft Office 97 is *Microsoft Office 97 Visual Basic Programmer's Guide* from Microsoft Press.

Example 12.5

```
    Sub Initialize
      Dim s As New NotesSession
      Dim db As NotesDatabase, doc As NotesDocument
      Dim dc As NotesDocumentCollection
      Dim rtitem As NotesRichTextItem
      Dim sheet As Variant, handle As Variant, wb As Variant
1     Const drive = "C:\"
      Set db = s.CurrentDatabase
      Set dc = db.AllDocuments
      Set doc = dc.GetFirstDocument
      While Not (doc Is Nothing)
2       Set rtitem = doc.GetFirstItem("eObject")
3       Set handle = rtitem.GetEmbeddedObject("Microsoft Excel Worksheet")
4       Set sheet = handle.Activate(True)
5       If ((Not (sheet Is Nothing)) And (doc.HasItem("FileName"))) Then
6         Set wb = IDisp.Application.ActiveWorkbook
7         Call wb.SaveAs(drive & doc.FileName(0))
        End If
        Set doc = dc.GetNextDocument(doc)
```

```
  Wend
End Sub
```

Explanation

1 Uses a constant variable to define the target drive for saving the spreadsheets.

2 Sets the Rich Text item to the field containing the embedded object.

3 Sets the `Variant` variable handle to the embedded spreadsheet. We use the name "Microsoft Excel Worksheet," the name used when the object was created, to retrieve it.

4 Activates the spreadsheet and sets the Variant Object to it.

5 Continues only if we have a handle on the spreadsheet object and the document contains the field named FileName.

6 Sets the Variant variable `wb` to the ActiveWorkbook object of the embedded object.

7 Utilizes the `SaveAs` method of the Excel Workbook object to save the spreadsheet. The constant variable drive and a field from the current document is used to define the path and file name for the saved spreadsheet.

Embedding spreadsheets in a Notes document allows them to be easily distributed to field personnel via replication. The field personnel can make changes to the embedded spreadsheets, and replicate their changes to the server copy.

In addition, the calculating power of Excel can be accessed in Notes. Cells in a spreadsheet can be used to perform certain calculations, and these cells can be used to populate fields on a Notes document. The next example embeds a spreadsheet in a Notes document and retrieves cell values storing them in fields on the document.

Example 12.6

```
     Dim uiw As New NotesUIWorkspace
     Dim uidoc As NotesUIDocument
1    Dim handle As Variant, app As Variant
     Set uidoc = uiw.CurrentDocument
2    Call uidoc.GotoField("object")
3    Call uidoc.CreateObject("excelObject","","filename")
     Call uidoc.Save
4    Set handle = uidoc.GetObject("excelObject")
5    If Not (handle Is Nothing) Then
6       Call handle.Activate
7       Set app = handle.Worksheets(1)
8          If Not (app Is Nothing) Then
9             Call setFields(uidoc.Document,app)
           End If
10         Call handle.Save
11         Call handle.Close
12         Set handle = Nothing
     End If
```

```
Call uidoc.Refresh
Call uidoc.Save
```

Explanation

1 Declares variables that will be used to work with the Excel object.

2 Moves focus to the Rich Text field that will contain the embedded spreadsheet.

3 Creates an Excel object using a file name. The object will be named excelObject, the name which will be reused when accessing it.

4 Sets the Variant object to the embedded spreadsheet. The name of it (excelObject) is used to access it.

5 Executes the next block of code only if the Excel object exists.

6 Calls the `activate` method of the OLE Excel object, which allows the objects properties/methods to be accessed in script.

7 Sets the `app` Variant object to the first worksheet in the Excel object.

8 Executes the `If` ... `Then` block only if the worksheet object exists.

9 Calls the `setFields` subroutine, a function which sets fields on the Notes document with values from the spreadsheet. The subroutine is listed next.

10 Saves the embedded Excel spreadsheet via its `Save` method.

11 Closes the embedded Excel spreadsheet via its `Close` method.

12 Disposes of the Excel object by setting it to Nothing.

The `setFields` function takes advantage of the `Range` property of the Excel object.

```
1      Public Sub setFields(passedDoc As NotesDocument, app As Variant)
2         With passedDoc
3            .Field1 = app.Range("A4").Value
4            .Field2 = app.Range("B3").Value
5            .Field3 = app.Range("C6").Value
6            .Field4 = app.Range("A6").Value
       End With
   End Sub
```

Explanation

1 Declares subroutine which accepts a NotesDocument and a Variant object.

2 Uses `With/End With` block to access fields on the document passed into the subroutine.

3 Populates the field named Field1 on the NotesDocument with the contents of cell A4 from the spreadsheet object passed into the subroutine.

4 Populates the field named Field2 on the NotesDocument with the contents of cell B3 from the spreadsheet object passed into the subroutine.

5 Populates the field named Field3 on the NotesDocument with the contents of cell C6 from the spreadsheet object passed into the subroutine.

6 Populates the field named Field4 on the NotesDocument with the contents of cell A6 from the spreadsheet object passed into the subroutine.

12.3.3 Microsoft PowerPoint

Microsoft PowerPoint is an application that facilitates the creation of powerful slide presentations. Lotus Notes and PowerPoint can be used together by populating a PowerPoint presentation with data from a Notes database, or a PowerPoint presentation can be embedded in a Notes document.

Once again, we will start by embedding/creating an object in a Notes document. Creating a PowerPoint object is no different from an Excel or Word object. The main difference is the object class type used.

Example 12.7

```
   Sub Click(Source As Button)
      Dim uiw As New NotesUIWorkspace
1     Dim handle As Variant
      Dim uidoc As NotesUIDocument
      Set uidoc = uiw.CurrentDocument
2     Call uidoc.GotoField("body")
3     Set handle = uidoc.CreateObject("Powerpoint Presentation",_
         "PowerPoint.Show.8")
   End Sub
```

Explanation

1 Declares a `Variant` variable that will be used to get a handle on the PowerPoint object.

2 Positions the cursor in the field that will contain the embedded object.

3 Creates a PowerPoint presentation object in the body field.

12.3.4 Microsoft Outlook

The rivalry between Microsoft Outlook and Lotus Notes is well publicized. As a developer, sooner or later you will be confronted with a mixed environment that utilizes both products. For example, a company may utilize Lotus Notes/Domino as an Intranet server and Microsoft Outlook as its standard mail client. The Notes server needs to send out emails to the administrator on a regular basis. The next example demonstrates sending an email from an agent via Microsoft Outlook.

Example 12.8

```
   Sub Initialize
1     Dim outlookObject As Variant
      Dim newMemo As Variant
2     Set outlookObject = CreateObject("Outlook.Application.8")
3     If Not (outlookObject Is Nothing) Then
4        Set newMemo = outlookObject.CreateItem(0)
5        If Not (newMemo Is Nothing) Then
6           NewMemo.To = baseline@aye.net
7           NewMemo.Subject = "Test message from Lotus Notes"
8           NewMemo.Body = "This is the body of the message."
9           Call NewMemo.PrintOut()
10          Call NewMemo.Send()
         End If
11       Call outlookObject.Quit()
      End If
   End Sub
```

Explanation

1. Declares `Variant` variables to use in the script.
2. Creates an OLE object for Outlook 98.
3. Proceeds only if the object was successfully created.
4. Calls the `CreateItem` method of the Outlook Application object to create a mail memo. It accepts a parameter that signals what type of item to create. A mail memo is `0` and a contact item is `2`. All other types can be found in an Outlook VBA reference.
5. Continues only if the mail memo object was successfully created.
6. Sets the `To` property of the mail memo to the recipient of the mail memo.
7. Sets the `Subject` property of the mail memo.
8. Inserts text into the body of the mail memo.
9. This line was added for demonstration purposes. It sends the mail memo to the default printer.
10. Sends the memo using the Outlook mail engine.
11. Closes the Outlook object.

That was a good example, but it showed no integration with Lotus Notes. The next example forwards all documents in a view to an Outlook recipient. The database used in the application allows users to compose comments/suggestions. The person responsible for monitoring the database uses Outlook. This example keeps that person up-to-date.

Example 12.9

```
   Sub Initialize
```

```
1     Dim outlook As Variant
      Dim NewMemo As Variant
      Dim session As New NotesSession
      Dim db As NotesDatabase
      Dim view As NotesView
      Set db = session.CurrentDatabase
      Set view = db.GetView("Comments")
      If Not (view Is Nothing) Then
2        Set outlook = CreateObject("Outlook.Application.8")
         If Not (outlook Is Nothing) Then
3           Set doc = view.GetFirstDocument
4           While Not (doc Is Nothing)
5              Set NewMemo = outlook.CreateItem(0)
6              If Not (NewMemo Is Nothing) Then
                  NewMemo.To = baseline@aye.net
                  NewMemo.Subject = doc.Subject(0)
                  NewMemo.Body = doc.body(0)
7                 Call NewMemo.Send()
               End If
               Set doc = view.GetNextDocument(doc)
            Wend
8           Call outlook.Quit()
         End If
      End If
   End Sub
```

Explanation

1 Declares variables to be used.

2 Creates a Microsoft Outlook 98 OLE object.

3 Gets the first document from the view.

4 Processes all documents in the view.

5 Creates an Outlook mail memo.

6 Sets the memo fields only if the memo was successfully created.

7 Sends the mail memo.

8 Closes the instance of Outlook.

In addition to mail memos, you can create any other item type in Outlook. The next example creates an appointment in Outlook.

Example 12.10

```
   Sub Initialize
      Dim outlook As Variant
      Dim appt As Variant
1     Set outlook = CreateObject("Outlook.Application.8")
      If Not (outlook Is Nothing) Then
2        Set appt = outlook.CreateItem(1)
         If Not (appt Is Nothing) Then
```

```
3          appt.CreateTime = TimeValue(Now)
4          appt.Start = "2/1/1999 06:00 AM"
5          appt.End = "2/1/1999 10:00 AM"
6          appt.AllDayEvent = False
7          appt.Body = "Meet with sales rep."
8          appt.Location = "Conference Room A"
9          Call appt.Save()
        End If
     End If
  End Sub
```

Explanation

1 Creates an OLE Outlook object.

2 Creates an Outlook Appointment item (the parameter `1` signals appointment).

3 Sets the `CreateTime` property to now.

4 Sets the Start time/date.

5 Sets the End time/date.

6 Shows the appointment is not an all-day event.

7 Sets the body of the appointment.

8 Sets the location of the appointment.

9 Saves the new appointment.

12.4 Performance considerations

OLE calls consume system resources and valuable time. Each property and/or method that you reference or call will add to the overhead of the application. For this reason, the number of dots in your code statements should be minimized if possible. The next line illustrates a line with several dots:

```
Call handle.Application.ActiveDocument.Paragraphs(7).Range._
     InsertBefore("test")
```

The above line contains five method/property calls (the number is equal to the number of dots or periods). The number can be reduced one of two ways: variables or the `with` statement. You can set up a variable and assign it to a certain level, property, or method. The following line could be used to reduce the number of calls from the previous line of code:

```
Set aDoc = handle.Application.ActiveDocument
With aDoc
   Call .Paragraphs.Range.InsertBefore("test")
End With
```

This reduces the number of calls by two. By setting a Variant object (aDoc) the code has to make that call only once, and then it is stored in memory. In addition, the code shows the use of the `With` statement that reduces the number of calls and the typing! In addtion, you can loop through a multivalued item quickly using a `Forall` loop.

12.5 Accessing Lotus Notes from Visual Basic

Up to this point, we have accessed other objects via OLE from within the Lotus Notes environment. Before closing this chapter, I want to demonstrate accessing Lotus Notes objects from the Visual Basic environment using OLE.

The next snippet of code sends a Notes email message from a Visual Basic program.

Example 12.11

```
   Sub main()
1     Dim session As Object
      Dim db As Object
      Dim doc As Object
      Dim rtf As Object
2     Set session = CreateObject("Notes.NotesSession")
3     Set db = NotesSession.GetDatabase("","")
4     Call db.OpenMail
5     Set doc = db.CreateDocument
6     With doc
7          .Form = "Memo"
8          .SaveMessageOnSend = True
9          .SendTo = "Tony Patton"
10         .Subject = "Message sent from Visual Basic"
11         Set rtf = .CreateRichTextItem("Body")
12         Call rtf.AppendText("Body of message goes here…")
13         Call .Send(True)
      End With
14    Set rtf = Nothing
      Set doc = Nothing
      Set db = Nothing
      Set session = Nothing
   End Sub
```

Explanation

1 Declares variables to be used to create Lotus Notes objects. They are declared using the generic Object data type.

2 Creates a NotesSession via CreateObject. The object name is Notes.NotesSession.

3 Uses the methods/properties of the NotesSession class once we have the session created. Uses the GetDatabase method to get a handle on a NotesDatabase object.

4 Calls the `OpenMail` method of the NotesDatabase object.

5 Uses the methods/properties of the NotesDatabase class once the NotesDatabase is created. Uses the CreateDocument method to create a new document.

6 Uses a `With/End With` block to access various properties (fields) of the NotesDocument object.

7 Sets the form field to "Memo".

8 Sets the SaveMessageOnSend to `True`. This ensures that the message will be saved.

9 The SendTo field is set to the recipient's name of the email.

10 Sets the Subject field for the email message.

11 Creates a New Rich Text item on the email message, the body field.

12 Inserts text in the newly created body field. The `AppendText` method of the NotesRichTextItem class is used.

13 Uses the `Send` method to send the mail message.

14 Sets the Notes objects to `Nothing` to destroy them since they are no longer in use or needed.

12.6 Chapter summary

OLE facilitates the development of very robust applications by combining the power of Lotus Notes with other applications such as Microsoft Excel or Word. The number-crunching capabilities of Excel or Lotus 1-2-3 can be incorporated into your application, or format a form letter in Word with Notes data. If you are working in a mixed environment that consists of Microsoft Outlook and Lotus Notes, OLE allows you to use both. Also, OLE goes the other way by allowing Visual Basic, Delphi, or other environments to access Notes objects/data. The possibilities are endless.

12.7 Chapter review

- The methods and properties of all registered OLE objects on a machine can be viewed using the object browser in the Lotus Notes IDE.
- All applications in the Microsoft Office Suite can be inserted as objects into a Rich Text field on a Notes document.
- All methods and properties of the Microsoft Office Suite applications can be accessed in Notes via OLE.
- Microsoft Word can be used to create a form letter with data from a Notes application.
- Values from cells in a Microsoft Excel spreadsheet can be used to populate fields on a Notes document.
- The Microsoft Outlook object model can be used to compose Outlook messages, journal entries, etc. from within Lotus Notes.
- Visual Basic can easily access Lotus Notes objects.

CHAPTER 13

Searching

13.1 Chapter objectives 208
13.2 Full-text indexing 208
13.3 Searching a view 211
13.4 Searching a database 213
13.5 Chapter summary 217
13.6 Chapter review 217

13.1 *Chapter objectives*

- Full-text indexed databases
- Search string rules
- Using logical operators in your searches
- Searching a database
- Searching a view
- Seaching a collection
- Is a database full-text indexed or not?
- Including fields in searches

As a database grows, the need to locate a certain document or subset of documents grows as well. Thankfully, searching is a standard feature of Lotus Notes/Domino. In addition, LotusScript exposes the power of searching to be used in your applications.

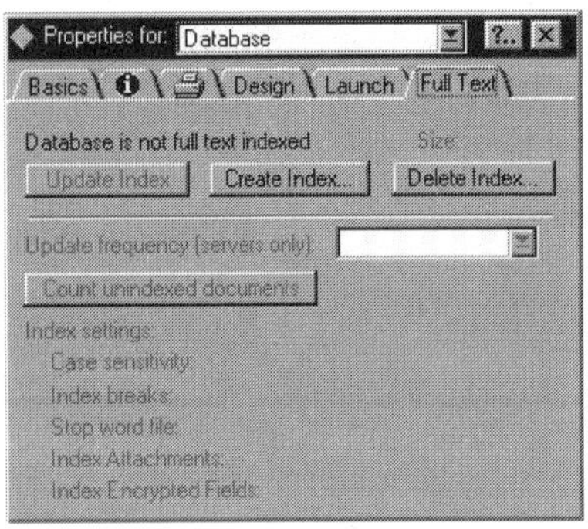

Figure 13.1 Database properties

13.2 *Full-text indexing*

Full-text indexing a database adds more power to your searching capabilities for that database. There is a tab in the database properties pop-up (figure 13.1) that contains the index settings for a database.

The NotesDatabase object contains a method, `IsFTIndexed`, for determining if a database is full-text indexed or not. It is a read-only property that returns a Boolean value: `true` if indexed and `false` if not.

Example 13.1

```
Dim s As New NotesSession
Dim db As NotesDatabase
Set db = s.CurrentDatabase
If (db.IsFTIndexed) Then
  MsgBox db.Title & " is full-text indexed.",0,"Index Info"
Else
  MsgBox db.Title & " is not full-text indexed.", 0, "Index Info"
End If
```

13.2.1 *Results*

The results of most searches are returned as a NotesDocumentCollection object. The collection may be empty or contain thousands of documents. The NotesDocumentCollection object does contain an `FTSearch` method that can be used to trim down the collection by performing a search on it.

13.2.2 Search string rules

Searches are conducted by assembling a search string. This string is used to search an object (database, view, collection, etc.). The string is a parameter in every search method within LotusScript.

There are a few rules for creating strings that are useful when creating search strings.

- Strings can be delimited by double quotation marks (""), vertical bars (||), or braces ({}).
- To include a quotation mark, vertical bar, or brace in a string, double it (two back to back).
- Strings can include any characters.

Example 13.2

```
Dim string1 As String, string2 As String, string3 As String
string1 = "LotusScript is very powerful!"
string2 = |LotusScript is very powerful!|
string3 = {LotusScript is very powerful}
```

Explanation

All three strings are equal.

Note I like to use the vertical bars as the beginning and ending delimiters for search strings. I use quotes for anything that needs quotes within the string. This makes the string much easier to read/understand, and it works!

13.2.3 Logical operators

Logical operators allow multiple conditions to be included in a search. The OR operator returns `true` if one or more of the conditions are true. The AND operator returns `true` if and only if all conditions are met. The NOT operator returns the opposite of a condition.

Example 13.3

```
     Sub Initialize
        Dim Condition1, Condition2, Condition3, Condition4
        Dim Output1 As String, Output2 As String, Output3 As String
        Dim Output4 As String, Output5 As String, Output6 As String
1       Condition1 = True
        Condition2 = True
        Condition3 = False
        Condition4 = False
2       Output1 = (Condition1) And (Condition2)
```

```
3    Output2 = (Condition2) And (Condition4)
4    Output3 = (Condition1) OR (Condition3)
5    Output4 = (Condition3) OR (Condition4)
6    Output5 = Not (Condition1)
7    Output6 = (((Condition1) AND (Condition4)) Or (Not Condition3))
     MsgBox Output1 & Chr(10) & Output2 & Chr(10) & Output3 & Chr(10) & _
     Output4 & Chr(10) & Output5 & Chr(10) & Output6, 0, "Logical Operators"
  End Sub
```

Explanation

1 Sets the conditions.

2 Returns `true`, because both conditions are true.

3 Returns `false`, because both are not true.

4 Returns `true`, because one of the conditions is true.

5 Returns `false`, because neither condition is true.

6 Returns `false` which is the opposite of true.

7 Uses parentheses to group items. The AND condition is evaluated first due to its parentheses. After it is evaluated, the result is evaluated with the OR condition. So it is false OR true which returns `true`.

Output:

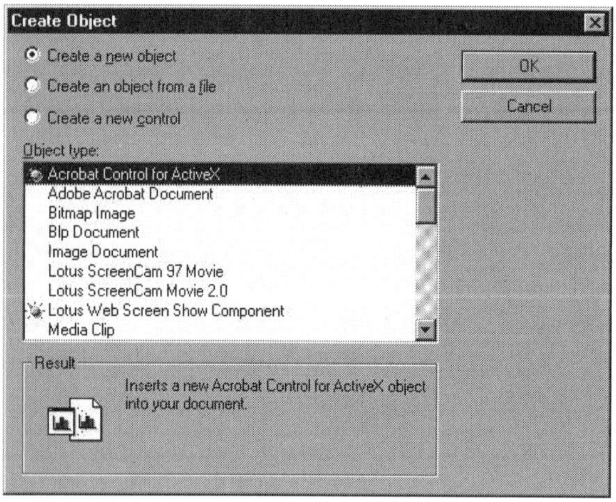

Figure 13.2 Example 13.3 Output

Note The use of parentheses serves a functional as well as cosmetic purpose. I use them extensively because it makes the code much easier to read. Also, the use of them forces the system to evaluate the statement as you expect. The guesswork is removed!

Now let's move into the actual searching. The last few sections covered topics that are important to proper searching, so let's see them in action.

13.2.4 Trimming a collection

The NotesDocumentCollection contains a method called `FTSearch` which can be used to reduce the number of documents in the collection. The method accepts a search string and an integer signaling the maximum number of documents to return. All documents are returned if the number of return documents is zero. This method is used extensively in the chapter covering reports.

Example 13.4

```
  Sub Initialize
     Dim s As New NotesSession
     Dim db As NotesDatabase
     Dim dc As NotesDocumentCollection
     Dim searchString As String
1    searchString = |FIELD FORM = "Memo"|
     Set dc = db.AllDocuments
2    Call dc.FTSearch(searchString,0)
     ...
  End Sub
```

Explanation

1 Creates the search string. This will search for all documents composed with the Memo form.

2 Trims the document collection to only those documents that match the search criteria.

Note The `FTSearch` method works whether or not the database is Full Text Indexed, but it is much more efficient (faster) if it is.

13.3 Searching a view

A NotesView can be searched a variety of ways: `FTSearch`, `GetAllDocumentsByKey`, and `GetDocumentByKey` methods. All methods reduce the number of documents in the view to those that match the search criteria.

13.3.1 FTSearch

Example 13.5

```
     Dim s As New NotesSession
     Dim db As NotesDatabase
     Dim view As NotesView
     Dim doc As NotesDocument
     Dim searchString As String
     Dim numDocs As Integer, x As Integer
     Dim totalSales As Double
     Set db = s.CurrentDatabase
1    Set view = db.GetView("Sales by Name")
2    searchString = |FIELD LastName = "Barkley"|
```

```
3    numDocs = view.FTSearch(searchString,0)
4    For x = 1 to numDocs
        Set doc = view.GetNthDocument(x)
5       totalSales = totalSales + doc.Sales(0)
     Next x
```

Explanation

1 Instantiates the NotesView object.

2 Sets the search string to return only those documents with a defined last name.

3 The FTSearch method of the NotesView object returns an integer representing the number of matches.

4 Loops through all documents found; returns only documents returned from the collection.

5 Accumulates the total sales.

13.3.2 GetAllDocumentsByKey

The `GetAllDocumentsByKey` method of the NotesView class takes advantage of the first sorted column in a view. It accepts key values and searches a view for all matches. The key value can be one string value or multiple in an array. If more than one value is included, the first value is searched for in the first sorted column, the second in the second sorted column, and so on.

Example 13.5 could be changed to take advantage of this method. If we have a view that sorts documents according to a person's last name, we do this:

Example 13.6

```
     Dim s As New NotesSession
     Dim db As NotesDatabase
     Dim doc As NotesDocument
     Dim dc As NotesDocumentCollection
     Dim view As NotesView
     Dim x As Integer, totalSales As Double
     Set db = s.CurrentDatabase
1    Set view = db.GetView("by Last Name")
2    Set dc = view.GetAllDocumentsByKey("Barkley",True)
     If (dc.Count > 0) Then
        For x = 1 to dc.Count
           Set doc = dc.GetNthDocument(x)
           totalSales = totalSales + doc.Sales(0)
        Next x
     End If
```

Explanation

1 Instantiates the view object.

2 Uses the `GetAllDocumentsByKey` method to search a sorted view for a certain value. The second parameter signals whether the match should be exact (`True`) or not (`False`). We want only exact matches. The method returns a NotesDocumentCollection object containing the documents that meet the criteria.

13.3.3 GetDocumentByKey

The `GetDocumentByKey` method of the NotesView class has the same format as the `GetAllDocumentsByKey` method except that it returns only the first match in the sorted column and not a collection of all matches. So, line 2 from Example 13.6 could be changed to return only the first match.

```
Set doc = view.GetDocumentByKey("Barkley",True)
```

This would return the first document in the view that matches (if it exists). The return document can be checked for existence like this.

```
If Not (doc Is Nothing) Then. …
```

This executes the body of the `If … Then` condition if the doc is not nothing, so it exists.

13.4 Searching a database

The NotesDatabase class facilitates searching the whole database. It contains four methods: `FTSearch`, `Search`, `UnprocessedFTSearch`, and `UnprocessedSearch`. `FTSearch` and `UnprocessedFTSearch` are similar. Likewise for `Search` and `UnprocessedSearch`. The `Unprocessed` methods search only those documents considered unprocessed. An agent considers a document it has never processed as unprocessed.

13.4.1 FTSearch/UnprocessedFTSearch

`FTSearch/UnprocessedFTSearch` conduct a full-text search on the database. It *does* work if the database is not full-text indexed, but less efficiently. Both methods accept four possible parameters:

- search string
- maximum number of documents to return (`0` indicates all)
- sort options (Optional)
  - *`FT_SCORES`* The default value that sorts the collection by relevance scores
  - *`FT_DATE_DES`* Sorts the collection by creation data in descending order
  - *`FT_DATE_ASC`* Sorts the collection by creation data in ascending order
- other options (Optional)

- *FT_STEMS* Uses stem words as the basis for the search
- *FT_THESAURUS* Uses the thesaurus to search

Note These methods run only in agent or view action scripts, and only on the current database. That is, you must use the `CurrentDatabase` property of the NotesSession object to use these methods.

Example 13.7

```
  Sub Initialize
     Dim session As New NotesSession
     Dim db As NotesDatabase
     Dim dc As NotesDocumentCollection
     Dim searchString As String
1    seachString = |((FIELD FORM = "Sales") And (FIELD LastName =_
        "Cunningham"))|
     Set db = session.CurrentDatabase
2    Set dc = db.FTSearch(searchString,0,FT_DATE_ASC)
3    Print "The number of documents found :   " & dc.Count
  End Sub
```

Explanation

1 Sets the search string. We want all documents created with the Sales form and a last name of Cunningham.

2 The `search` method of the NotesDatabase object is called to form a collection of documents that match the criteria. The results will be sorted by creation data in acsending order.

3 Prints the number of documents returned.

The `UnprocessedFTSearch` method works the same way, but it returns only those documents not previously processed by the agent. The unprocessed flag can indicate a new document or one modified since the last time the agent ran. This is helpful in keeping users up to date concerning new documents of interest to them.

Example 13.8

This example keeps a user up-to-date on new documents related to a certain person. The results are sent to their email, so they stay informed.

```
Sub Initialize
   Dim session As New NotesSession
   Dim db As NotesDatabase
   Dim dc As NotesDocumentCollection
   Dim searchString As String
   Dim news As NotesNewsLetter
   Dim newsDoc As NotesDocument
   seachString = |((FIELD FORM = "Sales") And (FIELD LastName =_
```

```
        "Cunningham"))|
    Set db = session.CurrentDatabase
1   Set dc = db.UnprocessedFTSearch(searchString,0,FT_DATE_ASC)
2   If (dc.Count > 0) Then
3     Set news = session.CreateNewsLetter(dc)
      Set doc = news.FormatMsgWithDoclinks(db)
      doc.SendTo = "Mr President"
      doc.DoSubject = False
      doc.DoScore = True
      doc.Form = "Memo"
      doc.Subject = "New docs for Cunningham"
      Call doc.Send(False)
    End If
4   Call dc.UpdateAll
  End Sub
```

Explanation

1 Creates a collection of documents by searching the unprocessed documents in the database.

2 Proceeds if the collection is not empty.

3 Creates a newsletter from the collection.

4 Marks all documents in the collection as processed by the agent. This guarantees the documents will not be processed repeatedly.

Note The `UpdateAll` method of the NotesDocumentCollection object must be used in agents that are set to run on new/modified documents, pasted documents, or any other variation. It must be used to ensure that the documents are not continually processed.

13.4.2 Search/UnprocessedSearch

Although the `FTSearch/UnprocessedFTSearch` methods can be used on databases without a full-text index, the `Search/UnprocessedSearch` methods are provided for databases without an index. The advantage with these methods is that they allow @functions to be included in the search string.

Note Care must be taken when using @functions in search strings. The search string must include only text values to be valid, so if functions like @date is used it must be converted to text using @text. If the search string does not contain all text, it will be invalid and the search will always return zero matches.

Both methods accept three parameters:

- *formula/search string*
- *cutoff date* Returns only those documents created/modified since the cutoff date
- *maximum number of docs* (zero indicates to return all)

Example 13.9

```
   Sub Initialize
      Dim s As New NotesSession
      Dim db As NotesDatabase
      Dim dc As NotesDocumentCollection
1     Dim dt As New NotesDateTime("01/01/97")
      Dim searchString As String
2     searchString = |FORM = "Sales" & !@IsResponseDoc|
      Set db = s.CurrentDatabase
3     Set dc = db.Search(searchString, dt, 0)
      ...
   End Sub
```

Explanation

1 Instantiates a new NotesDateTime object.

2 Constructs the search string. The string works according to @function rules so the & operator is the logical AND and not concatenation. The ! is the NOT operator. So, we want all documents created with the sales form that are not response documents.

3 Calls the `Search` method of the NotesDatabase object to return a NotesDocument-Collection of documents that match the search criteria (if any).

The `UnprocessedSearch` method functions exactly the same way, except it returns only those documents matching the search criteria and not previously processed by the document.

Note Actually, the `UnprocessedFTSearch` and `UnprocessedSearch` methods first search for documents not previously processed and then searches that collection for the search string.

13.4.3 Creating a full-text index

The `UpdateFTIndex` method of the NotesDatabase object can be used to update a database's full text index or create a new one if it does not currently exist. It accepts one parameter that is used to tell the system whether to create a new full text index (`True`) if it does not currently exist, or not to create (`False`). The only problem with this method is that it only works for local databases. An error is returned if you attempt to create an index on a database that is not local.

Example 13.10

```
   Dim s As New NotesSession
   Dim db As NotesDatabase
   Set db = s.CurrentDatabase
1  If (db.IsFTIndexed) Then
      MsgBox "Database already has a full text index."
   Else
2     Call db.UpdateFTIndex(True)
   End If
```

Explanation

1 Uses the `IsFTIndexed` method of the NotesDatabase object to check if the database has a full-text index or not.

2 Creates one if it is not full-text indexed.

13.5 Chapter summary

The searching capabilities of Domino are one of its strongest points, and LotusScript makes it available to the developer in many ways. Views, databases, and collections can be searched. A database does not have to have a full text index to be searched, but it is much more efficient if it does. Giving the users the power to perform their own searches expands the power of the application.

13.6 Chapter review

- Collections, databases, and views can be searched.
- Search strings can be contained within braces ({}), double quotes (""), and vertical bars (||).
- Logical operators like AND, NOT, and OR can be used to make more powerful searches.
- The `FTSearch` methods of the NotesDatabase and NotesDocumentCollection objects can be used on databases with full text indexes or not.
- The `UnprocessedFTSearch` and `UnprocessedSearch` methods of the NotesDatabase object searches only those documents not previously processed by the agent.
- The `search` method of the NotesDatabase object allows the use of @Functions as search arguments.
- The `IsFTIndexed` method of the NotesDatabase object returns `true` if the database is full-text indexed and `false` otherwise.
- A full-text index can be created through script with the `UpdateFTIndex` method, but this is only legal on local databases.

C H A P T E R 14

Reports

14.1 Chapter objectives 220
14.2 Reports as documents 220
14.3 Chapter summary 233
14.4 Chapter review 233

14.1 Chapter objectives

- With data comes the need for reports
- Views can serve as simple reports
- Create reports using arrays, lists, and user-defined data types
- Store reports in a database
- Send reports via email
- Create reports on a scheduled basis
- NotesNewsLetter class

Reporting is one area where users continually want more. Products like Crystal Reports, Microsoft Access, Lotus Approach, and Notes Reporter provide very powerful reporting capabilities. On the other hand, separate products require more time for installation, setup, and learning.

Views provide a rudimentary type of report with categorization, sorting, and total columns. As the number of documents in a database increases, so does the data. Consequently, it becomes more difficult to get a grasp on the data. Also, large views can take a long time to load. LotusScript can ease this burden.

The power provided by LotusScript allows the generation of custom reports within the Notes environment. Reports can be created from a view, button, or on a scheduled basis. Also, the format of the report may take the form of an email message, Notes document, or a simple message box.

Note This chapter is heavily dependent on concepts from the other chapters up to this point.

14.2 Reports as documents

We have a database that contains sales records for six divisions: One, Two, Three, Four, Five, and Six. The manager wants a monthly report that summarizes sales for the six divisions (figure 14.1).

Example 14.1

```
  Sub Initialize
     Dim s As New NotesSession
     Dim db As NotesDatabase
     Dim dc As NotesDocumentCollection
     Dim doc As NotesDocument
     Dim divisionItem As NotesItem, salesItem As NotesItem
1    Dim divisionTotals List As Currency
     Set db = s.CurrentDatabase
     Set dc = db.AllDocuments
2    Call dc.FTSearch(|FIELD FORM = "salesRecord"|,0)
     If (dc.Count > 0) Then
```

```
      For x = 1 To dc.Count
         Set doc = dc.GetNthDocument(x)
3        If ((doc.HasItem("divisionName")) And _
            (doc.HasItem("salesAmount"))) Then
            Set divisionItem = doc.GetFirstItem("divisionName")
            Set salesItem = doc.GetFirstItem("salesAmount")
4           If ((Cstr(divisionItem.Values(0)) <> "") And _
               (Cstr(salesItem.Values(0)) <> "")) Then
5              If (Iselement(divisionTotals(divisionItem.Values(0)))) Then
6                 divisionTotals(divisionItem.Values(0)) = _
                     divisionTotals(divisionItem.Values(0))_
                     + salesItem.Values(0)
               Else
7                 divisionTotals(divisionItem.Values(0)) = salesItem.Values(0)
               End If
            End If
         End If
      Next x
   End If
8  If Not (Isempty(divisionTotals)) Then
      Dim reportDoc As NotesDocument
      Set reportDoc = db.CreateDocument
      reportDoc.Form = "divisionReport"
9     reportTitle = Inputbox$("Please enter a title for the report")
10    Forall v In divisionTotals
         valueString = valueString + Cstr(v) + Chr(10)
         titleString = titleString + Listtag(v) + Chr(10)
         total = total + v
      End Forall
11    Set valueItem = New NotesItem(reportDoc, "values", valueString)
      Set labelItem = New NotesItem(reportDoc, "labels", titleString)
      Set titleItem = New NotesItem(reportDoc, "title", reportTitle)
12    titleItem.IsSummary = True
      Set total = New NotesItem(reportDoc, "total", total)
      Call reportDoc.Save(True,True)
   End If
End Sub
```

Explanation

1 Declares a list of currency values that will be used to track divisions and their corresponding total sales.

2 Sets, initially, the collection to all documents in the database. This is reduced by searching for only those documents that are sales records.

3 Processes the document only if it has the proper fields.

4 Checks the contents of the fields before proceeding. If the contents are empty, skips the document.

5 The `IsElement` method of the list object signals `true` if an item is in the list or `false` otherwise. The first time through the loop, it will evaluate to `true`.

6 If the item is in the list, increments the sales amount for the item with the value from the current document.

7 If the item is not in the list, adds it.

8 Generates the report once the processing of the documents is complete. The report is created only if the list is not empty.

9 Prompts the user to enter a title for the report.

10 Uses a `Forall` loop to access all elements in the list. Strings containing the values from the lists are created: one string for the division names, and another for the sales totals. The strings contain newline characters that separate the values. The fields on the report allow multivalues and separate the entries with carriage returns. Also, a total variable adds all of the sales amounts for the divisions.

11 NotesItem objects are created for the fields on the report.

12 The `IsSummary` property allows a field to be used in a view when it set to `true`.

Output

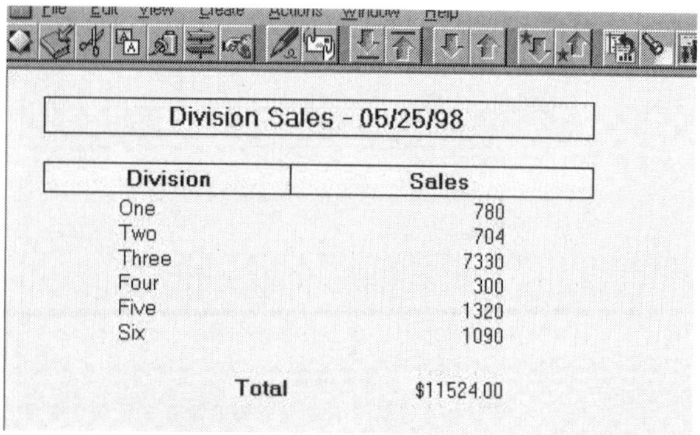

Figure 14.1
Example 14.1 sample output

14.2.1 Email

Example 14.1 stored the reports in the database where a special view could be created to view them. On the other hand, the reports could have been emailed to the appropriate person(s). The report form in the database must be included with the document so the recipients can read it. The first parameter of the `Send` method of the NotesDocument object allows this to be set. A `true` indicates to send the form with the document. Also, fields that are needed for emailing are added. This includes a SendTo and Subject field at a minimum. We will add a CopyTo field to ours as well. Also, a SaveOptions field is added to the report form so the document will not be saved since we are mailing it (it will be set to `0`).

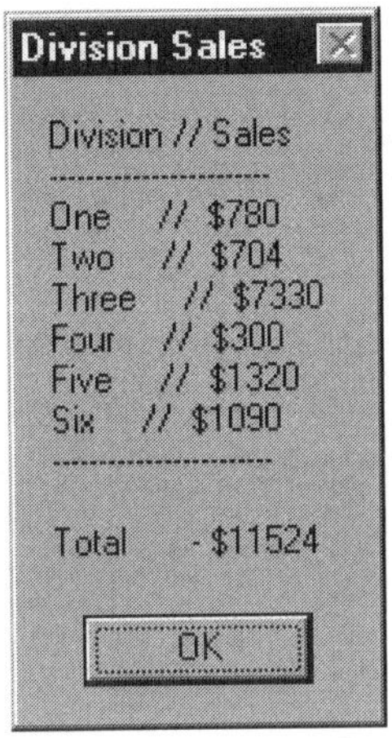

Figure 14.2 Notes 4.6 Form options box

Example 14.2

The following lines of code replace the Save method from example 14.1.

```
reportDoc.SendTo = "Tony Patton"
reportDoc.CopyTo = "Manager"
reportDoc.Subject = "Division Sales Report"
Call reportDoc.Send(True)
```

Note The Send method of the NotesDocument class accepts recipients' names as a second optional parameter. It can be a String or array of Strings. If it is used, the SendTo and CopyTo fields are not needed.

14.2.2 Scheduled

The report from Example 14.1 could be scheduled to be created on a set basis. One line of code from the script must be changed. Line 9 from the example needs to be removed and replaced with a set string. The `InputBox` function cannot be used in the back end, it requires user interaction. The line could be changed to this:

```
reportTitle = "Division Sales Report"
```

Once that is changed, the script can be placed into a scheduled agent to run as defined. This allows reports to be generated and saved or mailed without any user interaction.

14.2.3 Selective/custom reports

The script from Example 14.1 processes all documents in the database, but this could be easily changed to allow the user to select which documents are processed. The line just before line 2 would be changed from

```
Set dc = db.AllDocuments
```

to

```
Set dc = db.UnProcessedDocuments
```

This forms a collection of all documents selected, but we still keep line 2 to make sure we process the proper documents. This code could be placed in an action button in a view or run from the Actions drop down menu.

14.2.4 *MessageBox*

If there is no need for documents to be saved or emailed, a message box can be used to display the results to the user. The code from example 14.1 would be the same up until line 8. Starting with line 8 the code would look like this:

```
   If Not (Isempty(divisionTotals)) Then
     reportTitle = Inputbox$("Please enter report title.")
1    msgString = msgString & "Division // Sales" & Chr(10)
     msgString = msgString & "-----------------------" & Chr(10)
     Forall v In divisionTotals
2      msgString = msgString & Listtag(v) & Space$(5) & "//  $" & v & Chr(10)
       total = total + v
     End Forall
     msgString = msgString & "-----------------------" & Chr(10)
3    msgString = msgString & Chr(10) & "Total " & Space$(5) & " - $" & total
4    Msgbox msgString, 0,reportTitle
   End If
```

Explanation

1 Sets the heading of the report.

2 Adds each division's numbers.

3 Adds the totals line.

4 Displays the message box.

14.2.5 *Form as a Front-End*

If your reporting needs require a lot of user input, thus creating a number of custom reports, then a Notes form can be used as a reporting front end. This involves creating a Notes form that contains fields for the user to enter report criteria. The form will have a SaveOptions field set to false (zero) so that it is never saved. It is never saved, because it is only used to create reports. The user enters his/her criteria and selects a button to trigger report generation. The script attached to the button gets the values from the form and creates the report (figure 14.3).

The next example allows the user to select the divisions to include in the report via a Notes form and a keyword list. The frontend form looks like figure 14.3.

The example takes advantage of arrays, classes, functions, and script libraries to name a few.

Example 14.3

The script library is listed first with an explanation. The code for the hot spot button follows it.

```
[Declarations]
```

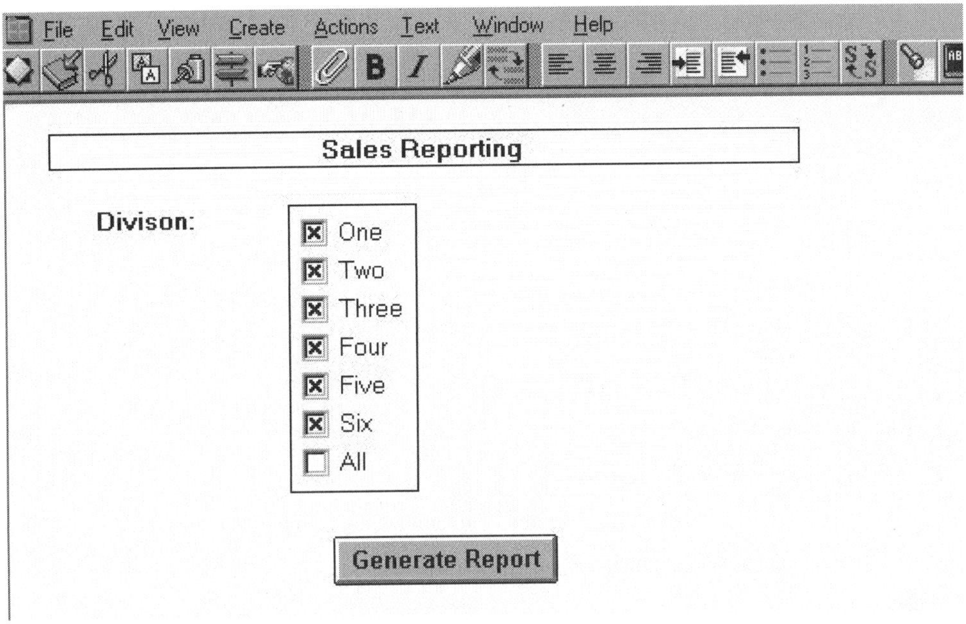

Figure 14.3 Report frontend form

```
    Public Class Sales
1   Private DivisionName As String
2   Private SalesAmount As Currency
3   Private ReturnsAmount As Currency
4   Private totalCount As Long
5   Property Set Division As String
      DivisionName = Division
    End Property
6   Property Get Division As String
      Division = DivisionName
    End Property
    Property Set Sales As Currency
      SalesAmount = SalesAmount + Sales
    End Property
    Property Get Sales As Currency
      Sales = SalesAmount
    End Property
    Property Set Returns As Currency
      ReturnsAmount = ReturnsAmount + Returns
    End Property
    Property Get Returns As Currency
      Returns = ReturnsAmount
    End Property
    Property Get Count As Long
      Count = totalCount
    End Property
    Property Set Count As Long
```

```
      totalCount = totalCount + Count
    End Property
  End Class

Public oneFlag As Variant
Public twoFlag As Variant
Public threeFlag As Variant
Public fourFlag As Variant
Public fiveFlag As Variant
Public sixFlag As Variant
Public allFlag As Variant
```

Explanation

1 `Private` class variable stores the division name.

2 `Private` variable tracks sales.

3 `Private` variable tracks returns.

4 `Private` variable counts the number of items for the division.

5 `Property Set` sets the contents for all variables.

6 `Property Get` retrieves the contents of all variables.

The next subroutine sets flags according to the option(s) selected by the user.

```
  Sub setFlags(passedDoc As NotesDocument)
1    oneFlag = False
     twoFlag = False
     threeFlag = False
     fourFlag = False
     fiveFlag = False
     sixFlag = False
     allFlag = False
2    Forall v In passedDoc.division
3       Select Case v
           Case "One" : oneFlag = True
           Case "Two" : twoFlag = True
           Case "Three" : threeFlag = True
           Case "Four" : fourFlag = True
           Case "Five" : fiveFlag = True
           Case "Six" : sixFlag = True
           Case "All" : allFlag = True
        End Select
     End Forall
  End Sub
```

Explanation

1 Initializes flag variables to `false`. These flags signal the options (divisions) selected by the user.

2 Uses a `Forall` loop to access the values from the division keyword list.

3 Uses a select case statement to set the flags according to what the user selected.

The next function assembles the search string used to assemble the document collection to create the report.

```
1  Function setSearchString As String
2    Dim oneString As String, twoString As String, threeString As String
     Dim fourString As String, fiveString As String, sixString As String
     Dim orString As String
3    oneString = | (FIELD divisionName = "One") |
     twoString = | (FIELD divisionName = "Two") |
     threeString = | (FIELD divisionName = "Three") |
     fourString = | (FIELD divisionName = "Four") |
     fiveString = | (FIELD divisionName = "Five") |
     sixString = | (FIELD divisionName = "Six") |
4    orString = " OR "
     Dim FirstTime
5    If (allFlag) Then
       setSearchString = oneString & orString & twoString & orString & _
         threeString & orString_
         & FourString & orString & fiveString & orString & sixString
     Else
6      FirstTime = True
7      If (oneFlag) Then
         setSearchString = oneString
8        FirstTime = False
       End If
       If (twoFlag) Then
         If (FirstTime) Then
           setSearchString = twoString
           FirstTime = False
         End If
9        setSearchString = setSearchString & orString & twoString
       End If
       If (threeFlag) Then
         If (FirstTime) Then
           setSearchString = threeString
           FirstTime = False
         End If
         setSearchString = setSearchString & orString & threeString
       End If
       If (fourFlag) Then
         If (FirstTime) Then
           setSearchString = fourString
           FirstTime = False
         End If
         setSearchString = setSearchString & orString & fourString
       End If
       If (fiveFlag) Then
         If (FirstTime) Then
           setSearchString = fiveString
           FirstTime = False
         End If
         setSearchString = setSearchString & orString & fiveString
       End If
       If (sixFlag) Then
```

```
            If (FirstTime) Then
               setSearchString = sixString
               FirstTime = False
            End If
            setSearchString = setSearchString & orString & sixString
         End If
      End If
   End Function
```

Explanation

1 Function declaration. Returns a string value.

2 Declares the strings to be used in the function. These strings assemble the search string.

3 Sets the search string for division one. A string for each division is set, and they are pieced together according to the divisions selected by the user.

4 Places the OR logic in the search string.

5 If the allFlag is set, the user wants all divisions, so set the search string accordingly.

6 Signals whether or not we are processing the first item in the search string. This is significant because the OR is placed before all elements in the search string except the first one.

7 Checks each flag named for the divisions and sets the search string.

8 Processes the first element in the string, then sets the FirstTime flag to `false` so everything else will be properly assembled with an OR clause.

9 Sets the search string. This is the return value of the function.

The next section is the code behind the button on the form.

```
   Sub Click(Source As Button)
      Dim uiw As New NotesUIWorkspace
      Dim uidoc As NotesUIDocument
      Dim doc As NotesDocument, fedoc As NotesDocument
      Set uidoc = uiw.CurrentDocument
      Set fedoc = uidoc.Document
      Dim dc As NotesDocumentCollection
      Dim s As New NotesSession
      Dim db As NotesDatabase
      Set db = s.CurrentDatabase
      Set dc = db.AllDocuments
      Dim searchString As String
      If (fedoc.HasItem("division")) Then
1        Call setFlags(fedoc)
2        searchString = setSearchString
3        Call dc.FTSearch(|FIELD FORM = "salesRecord"|,0)
4        Call dc.FTSearch(searchString,0)
            If (dc.Count > 0) Then
5              Dim salesArray() As Sales
```

```
      For x = 1 To dc.Count
         Set doc = dc.GetNthDocument(x)
         If ((doc.HasItem("divisionName")) And_
            (doc.HasItem("salesAmount"))) Then
6           If (x = 1) Then
7              Redim salesArray(0) As Sales
8              Set salesArray(0) = New Sales
9              salesArray(0).division = doc.divisionName(0)
10             salesArray(0).sales = doc.salesAmount(0)
11             salesArray(0).returns = doc.returnAmount(0)
12             salesArray(0).count = 1
            Else
13             Found = False
14             For y = 1 To Ubound(salesArray)
15                If (salesArray(y).division = doc.divisionName(0)) Then
                     salesArray(y).sales = doc.salesAmount(0)
                     salesArray(y).returns = doc.returnAmount(0)
                     salesArray(0).count = 1
                     Found = True
                  End If
               Next y
               If (Found = False) Then
16                Redim Preserve salesArray(Ubound(salesArray) + 1)_
                     As Sales
17                Set salesArray(Ubound(salesArray)) = New Sales
                  salesArray(Ubound(salesArray)).division = _
                     doc.divisionName(0)
                  salesArray(Ubound(salesArray)).sales = _
                     doc.salesAmount(0)
                  salesArray(Ubound(salesArray)).returns = _
                     doc.returnAmount(0)
                  salesArray(Ubound(salesArray)).count = 1
               End If
            End If
         End If
      Next x
   End If
18 If (Isarray(salesArray)) Then
      Dim reportDoc As NotesDocument
      Set reportDoc = db.CreateDocument
      reportDoc.Form = "divisionReport"
      reportTitle = Inputbox$("Please enter a title for the report")
19    For z = 1 To Ubound(salesArray)
         valueString = valueString + Cstr(salesArray(z).sales) + Chr(10)
         titleString = titleString + Cstr(salesArray(z).division) +_
            Chr(10)
         returnString = returnString + Cstr(salesArray(z).returns) +_
            Chr(10)
      Next z
      Set valueItem = New NotesItem(reportDoc, "values", valueString)
      Set labelItem = New NotesItem(reportDoc, "labels", titleString)
      Set titleItem = New NotesItem(reportDoc, "title", reportTitle)
      Set returnItem = New NotesItem(reportDoc, "returns", _
         returnString)
```

```
            titleItem.IsSummary = True
            Call reportDoc.Save(True,True)
        End If
    End If
End Sub
```

Explanation

1 Calls the `setFlags` subroutine to set the division flag variables.

2 Calls the setSearchString function.

3 Reduces the document collection to only those sales record documents.

4 Trims the document collection further to only those meeting the search string criteria.

5 Declares an array of Sales objects (from the Sales class declaration).

6 A value of `1` for `x` signals the first time through the loop. This requires the array be initialized.

7 Uses the `Redim` and `Preserve` commands to initialize the array with one element.

8 Uses the `Set` and `New` keywords to instantiate the sales object.

9 Sets the `divisionName` property of the sales object.

10 Sets the `salesAmount` property of the sales object.

11 Sets the `returnAmount` property of the sales object.

12 Sets the `totalCount` property of the sales object.

13 The found Boolean variable signals whether an item has been found in the current array. It is set to `false` before the search begins.

14 The `For` loop allows access to every sales object in the array.

15 Checks whether the current item from the array matches the item from the document in the collection.

16 If a match is found, increments the amounts and the found variable is set to `false`.

17 Adds a new element to the array, if the item is not found.

18 Creates the report document only if the array exists.

19 Loops through the values in the array to assemble the field values for the report document.

The last example was very extensive. It allows the user to select what divisions they wanted, and it creates the reports from the selection(s). The extra code is required because the user choices are a big unknown, so everything has to be checked.

14.2.6 Newsletter

Another way to keep users informed about data is to send a newsletter to their Notes mailbox. The NotesNewsLetter class facilitates this. The Notes 4.6 discussion template uses the newsletter class to notifiy users of documents posted pertaining to their user profile. The NotesNewsLetter class takes a document collection and mails a document with details about the documents in the collection.

The NotesNewsLetter class contains only three properties:

1. `DoScore` `True` or `false` signaling whether the relevance score should be included. The relevance score applies to collections formed by searching. These collections are sorted according to their relevance to the search criteria. Applicable to the FormatMsgWithDoclinks method only.
2. `DoSubject` `True` or `false` signaling whether or not to include a subject line next to each doclink. The field used for the subject is set with the `SubjectItemName` property. Applicable to the `FormatMsgWithDoclinks` method only.
3. `SubjectItemName` Used in conjunction with the `DoSubject` property. It sets which field will be used as the subject tag next to the doclinks.

The two methods, `FormatMsgWithDocLinks` and `FormatDocument`, are shown in the examples.

Example 14.4

```
   Sub Initialize
      Dim s As New NotesSession
      Dim db As NotesDatabase
      Dim dc As NotesDocumentCollection
1     Dim news As NotesNewsLetter
      Dim doc As NotesDocument
      Set db = s.CurrentDatabase
      Set dc = db.AllDocuments
      Call dc.FTSearch(|(FIELD FORM = "salesRecord") OR _
         (FIELD divisionName = "One")|,0)
      If (dc.Count > 0) then
2        Set news = New NotesNewsLetter(dc)
3        Set doc =   news.FormatMsgWithDoclinks(db)
4        doc.SendTo = "DivisionOne"
         doc.CopyTo = "Ben Hur"
5        doc.DoSubject = True
6        doc.DoScore = False
7        doc.SubjectItemName = "salesAmount"
8        doc.Form = "Memo"
         doc.Subject = "Division One Sales Report"
9        Call doc.Send(False)
      End If
```

Explanation

1 Declares a NotesNewsLetter object.

2 Instantiates the NotesNewsLetter object with the document collection.

3 Assigns notes document to the newsletter. The `FormatMsgWithDocLinks` method tells the system to insert `doclinks` to the documents in the collection in the email.

4 Sets the SendTo field to signal who receives the newsletter. A group named DivisionOne is used.

5 Sets the `DoSubject` property to `true`. The field salesAmount will be the subject as defined in step 8.

6 Sets the `DoScore` property to `false`, so no relevance scores will be in the memo.

7 The `SubjectItemName` property specifies the field to use as the subject next to the doclinks.

8 Sets the form to memo, so it can be read in the mail database.

9 Sets the memo with no form attached. The form is not needed since every email database has the basic memo form.

The `CreateNewsLetter` method of the NotesSession object can be used to create newsletters as well. The next example shows how it is used, and it utilizes the `FormatDocument` method of the NotesNewsLetter class. This method mails a document from a collection—the whole document, not a doclink.

```
  Sub Initialize
     Dim s As New NotesSession
     Dim db As NotesDatabase
     Dim dc As NotesDatabase
     Dim newsDoc As NotesDocument
     Dim dc As NotesDocumentCollection
     Dim news As NotesNewsLetter
     Set dc = db.FTSearch("|(FIELD FORM = "salesRecord") OR _
        (FIELD divisionName = "One")|,0)
     If (dc.Count > 0) Then
1       Set news = s.CreateNewsLetter(dc)
        For x = 1 to dc.Count
2          Set doc = news.FormatDocument(db,x)
           doc.SendTo = "DivisionOne"
           doc.Subject = "Division One"
3          Call doc.Send(False)
        Next x
     End If
  End Sub
```

Explanation

1 Uses the `CreateNewsLetter` method of the NotesSession object to create a newsletter with the document collection.object.

2 Prepares the current document in the loop to be mailed.

3 Mails the document. This is similar to forwarding a document, the document from the collection will appear in the body of the email message.

14.3 Chapter summary

Many Lotus Notes/Domino users complain about its lack of reporting capabilities. Although add-on or third party products are available for reporting, the LotusScript language puts the power in the developer's hands to give the users the capability to generate the desired reports. Whether it is a quick pop-up message box, a detailed table in a document, or a newsletter, Notes does offer reporting solutions.

14.4 Chapter review

- There is a great need for reports from Domino/Notes data. Reports can give a high level or quick overview of a large sum of data.
- Notes views provide basic report functionality. Sorting, categorization, and column totals are crucial elements.
- Views break down when there is a large amount of data.
- Document collections and searching provide an easy way to assemble a group of data for a report.
- Arrays, lists, and user-defined data types help group or sort the data.
- Report data can be saved in a database using a separate form/view, or it can be emailed to the appropriate persons.
- A form can be set up as a front end for users to create custom reports. The form is never saved.
- The NotesNewsLetter class provides a means to send users a list of doclinks to documents that may interest them, or it can mimic the activity of forwarding by mailing a document.

CHAPTER 15

LotusScript data objects

15.1 Chapter objectives 236
15.2 Domino.Connect 236
15.3 SQL 238
15.4 ODBCConnection 239
15.5 ODBCQuery 241
15.6 ODBCResultSet 241
15.7 Handling errors 242
15.8 Accessing data in a result set 244
15.9 Adding/deleting records 246
15.10 Domino.Connect 248
15.11 NotesSQL 248
15.12 Chapter summary 249
15.13 Chapter review 249

15.1 Chapter objectives

- LS:DO
- ODBC
- SQL
- ODBCConnection class
- ODBCQuery class
- ODBCResultSet class
- Handling ODBC errors
- Working with data
- Adding new records
- Deleting records
- Domino.Connect
- NotesSQL

The Notes database is great for numerous applications, but it is not a relational database. In addition, it was not designed to hold the amount of data stored in enterprise databases. An *enterprise database* stores information for the whole organization, and applications that need to access it. This provides a central location for data thus reducing redundant data.

Database vendors such as Oracle, Sybase, and IBM have products that were built to house with ease an unlimited amount of data, and there are times when a Lotus Notes/ Domino application will need to access this information. For example, an order entry application used on the Web via a Domino server needs up-to-date quantity information for products. This information may only be available in an Oracle database, so Domino needs to access the proper Oracle table(s) and execute the necessary Structured Query Language (SQL) statement(s).

15.2 Domino.Connect

For this reason, Lotus introduced the Domino.Connect product. Domino.Connect includes everything you need to hook Lotus Notes/Domino to another database product. It includes LotusScript Extensions (LSXs) for use with Oracle and other popular database products. Also, it includes information on using Open DataBase Connectivity (ODBC) and the LotusScript Data Object (LS:DO).

This chapter will concentrate on the use of the LS:DO. Additional information is included for using the Domino.Connect and NotesSQL products.

15.2.1 LS:DO

LS:DO facilitates Lotus Notes/Domino applications accessing data in other applications via ODBC. The data can be accessed directly from Domino, or imported into it. LS:DO consists of three classes: ODBCConnection, ODBCQuery, and ODBCResultSet. Before we dive into using the classes, let's take a brief look at ODBC and SQL.

15.2.2 ODBC

ODBC is a uniform interface standard that can be used to access databases. It is a database access library that enables applications to work with data in a database. The great thing about ODBC is that it can be used to access just about any type of database: Access, Oracle, Sybase, DB2, Btrieve, spreadsheets, and text files.

ODBC consists of a driver and driver manager. The driver is specific to a database vendor's product. For instance, Sybase provides a driver for accessing Sybase databases through ODBC. The driver manager is used to install drivers and set up data sources to be used in applications.

Figure 15.1 shows the ODBC driver manager from my Windows 95 workstation. I have set up a data source to be used in the examples in this book. It is called LSSBookTest, and it accesses a Microsoft Access database.

One limitation of ODBC is that it must be installed on every computer that will be using ODBC calls, but the client/server structure of Domino allows the ODBC driver to be set up on the server. All ODBC access is handled on the server. An advantage of ODBC is that it offers independence through the use of drivers. For example, if the database you are accessing changes to Oracle from Sybase, you only need to change the driver and your code/scripts will continue to perform as designed. Another positive is

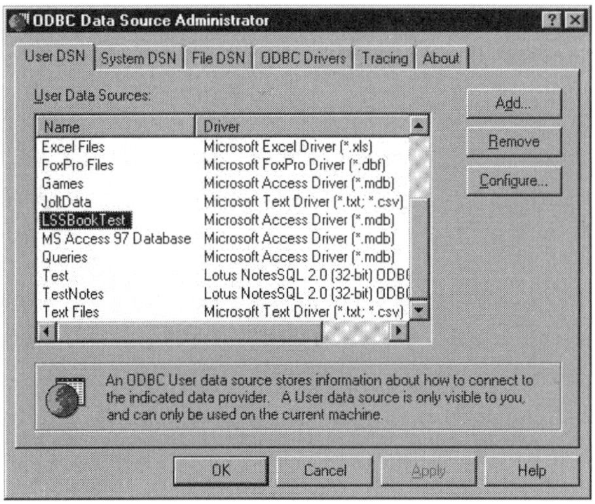

Figure 15.1
An ODBC driver manager

that the process of learning a new product is avoided, because all ODBC drivers support a core set of SQL.

15.3 SQL

SQL is a language for managing relational databases and is the standard when it comes to relational databases. The core functionality provided in SQL is platform, operating system, and vendor independence. Database vendors may add their own special functions for use with their products, but this is not a concern when working with ODBC. The best thing about SQL is it is easy to learn.

The intention of this book or chapter is not teaching SQL, but here are three commonly used SQL statements:

15.3.1 SELECT

`SELECT` is the most heavily used statement in SQL. It returns the chosen contents of one or more tables as a result table. It can be used to select all columns from a table or tables, or only certain columns that are specified. An asterisk (*) signals that all columns are returned.

15.3.2 FROM

`FROM` must immediately follow a `SELECT` statement. It lists the one or more tables from which the result table will be assembled.

Example 15.1

```
SELECT * FROM myTable
```

Explanation

Returns every row and column of data from the table specified: myTable.

Example 15.2

```
SELECT col2, col3 FROM myTable
```

Explanation

Returns every row, but only the columns labeled col2 and col3 from the table called myTable.

15.3.3 WHERE

The `WHERE` keyword lets you filter the results of a `SELECT` statement. It can be very simple or very complex, but we will cover only simple uses. When working with data from a Domino database and a relational database like Access, `WHERE` can be used to tell the system to return only those records where a field in a Notes document is equal to a column value in the relational database.

Example 15.3

```
SELECT * FROM externalTable WHERE (columnValue = NotesField)
```

Explanation

This may be used on a certain Notes document. It returns all columns for only those records in the table named externalTable whose column value in columnValue is equal to a field from the Notes document (NotesField).

That concludes a quick overview of three basic SQL statements. They are basic but very powerful. If you want/need to learn more about SQL there are a number of books that cover it in great depth.

Note The LSX that provides access to ODBC data in LotusScript: LSXODBC must be referenced in the Options section of a script before any of the ODBC-related classes can be used. The following line is placed in the Options section:

```
Uselsx "*LSXODBC"
```

The asterisk (*) before its name tells the system to search the registry for its location on the system.

15.4 ODBCConnection

The ODBCConnection class is used to establish a connection to an ODBC data source. The data source can already be registered, or the class can be used to register it. Also, properties and methods are available to test the connection, close a connection, and list available data sources, tables (figure 15.2), fields, and store procedures.

Example 15.4

```
    (Options)
1   Uselsx "*LSXODBC"

    Sub Initialize
2   Dim con As New ODBCConnection
    Dim tableList As Variant
    Dim msgTL As String
3   con.ConnectTo("LSSBookTest")
4   tableList = con.ListTables("LSSBookTest")
    Forall tables in tableList
       msgTL = msgTL + tables + Chr(10)
    End Forall
    MsgBox msgTL,0,"List of available tables"
5   Call con.Disconnect
    End Sub
```

Output

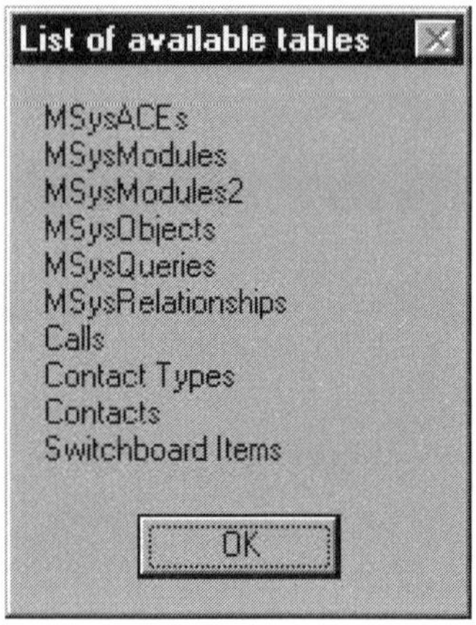

Figure 15.2
Example 15.4 output

Explanation

1 This line is required. Tells the system to allow access to all classes in the LSX. A compile error is generated if this line is omitted.

2 Declares a new ODBCConnection object.

3 Sets the object to the ODBC connection registered as LSSBookTest on the system via the ODBC Driver Manager.

4 Retrieves the list of tables from the ODBC data source named LSSBookTest. This method returns an array of values, so a variant object is used.

5 Closes the connection.

`ListDataSources`, `ListFields`, and `ListProcedures` all perform the same type of function; each one returns an array of values.

Example 15.5

```
    Dim newCon As New ODBCConnection
    newCon.ConnectTo(LSSBookTest)
1   If (newCon.IsConnected) then
      MsgBox "Connected"
    Else
      MsgBox "No Connection established."
    End If
    newCon.Disconnect
```

Explanation

1 Tests the connection to see if it was established.

The previous example could have used the `ConnectTo` method as well. The connect method returns a Boolean (`True` or `False`) value signaling whether or not the connection was established. The `IsConnected` property can be used later in a script to make sure that a connection is still active. This line shows its use.

```
If (newCon.ConnectTo("LSSBookTest")) Then ...
```

Basically, the ODBCConnection class is used to manage ODBC connections in your script(s). The `ConnectTo` method can accept a `userid` and password (if required) as well. Your data source may require `userid`/password access. The next example shows how this is used.

Example 15.6

```
   Dim conn As New ODBCConnection
1  If (conn.ConnectTo("datasourceName","userid","secretPassword")) Then
     MsgBox "Userid and password accepted......connected.")
   Else
     MsgBox "Connection could not be established."
   End If
```

Explanation

1 Establishes a connection with an ODBC data source, and a userid and password are included.

15.5 ODBCQuery

The ODBCQuery class is the next class used after ODBCConnection. It specifies the SQL to be used. It has three properties: `SQL`, `Connection`, and `QueryExecuteTimeOut`. The `SQL` property is used to set up the SQL to be used. The `Connection` property links it to an ODBCConnection object. `QueryExecuteTimeOut` allows you to specify the maximum amount of time (in seconds) to wait for a query to execute. A ODBCQuery object cannot be instantiated without an ODBCConnection object.

Example 15.7

```
   Dim newCon As New ODBCConnection
   If (newCon.ConnectTo("LSSBookTest")) Then
1    Dim newQry As New ODBCQuery
2    Set newQry.Connection = newCon
3    newQry.SQL = "SELECT * FROM Contacts"
   End If
```

Explanation

1 Declares an ODBCQuery object if the connection is successful.

2 Sets the `Connection` property of the ODBCQuery object to the ODBCConnection object.

3 Sets the `SQL` property of the ODBCQuery object. This will be used to get data from the data source.

15.6 ODBCResultSet

The last, and the most often used, of the ODBC-related classes is ODBCResultSet. It holds the values returned by the SQL property of the ODBCQuery object. The `Query` property is set to an ODBCQuery object and its `Execute` method is called to assemble an ODBCResultSet.

Example 15.8

```
   Dim newCon As New ODBCConnection
   If (newCon.ConnectTo("LSSBookTest")) Then
   Dim newQry As New ODBCQuery
1  Dim newRes As New ODBCResultSet
2  Set newQry.Connection = newCon
3  newQry.SQL = "SELECT * FROM Contacts"
4  Set newRes.Query = newQry
5  Call newRes.Execute
   End If
   newCon.Disconnect
```

Explanation

1 Declares a new ODBCResultSet object.

2 Sets the `Connection` property of the ODBCQuery object to the current connection object.

3 Sets the `SQL` property of the ODBCQuery object. We want everything from the contacts table.

4 Sets the `Query` property of the ODBCResultSet object to the ODBCQuery object.

5 Executes the `SQL`; assembles a result set containing all data returned by the `SQL` statement.

Note You will notice that `SET` is used for the `Query` property of the ODBCResultSet class and the `Connection` property of the ODBCQuery class, but not the `SQL` property. This is because the first two are using objects, the latter is only setting text.

15.7 Handling errors

The ODBCConnection, ODBCQuery, and ODBCResultSet classes all contain three methods for working with errors: `GetError`, `GetErrorMessage`, and `GetExtendedErrorMessage`. The `GetError` method returns an error code as an integer. `GetErrorMessage` returns a short description of an error, and `GetExtendedErrorMessage` returns a long description of an error. Table 15.1 shows a list of error constants (that can be used in your code) and their respective error descriptions. The first item in the list is one that you may use most often (DBstsSUCCESS). It allows you to test if there were no errors.

Table 15.1 ODBC Error constants and messages

Named constant	Description of the error
DBstsSUCCESS	Not an error, SUCCESS (cannot be trapped by ON ERROR)
DBstsACCS	Unable to get user ID and password

Table 15.1 ODBC Error constants and messages (continued)

Named constant	Description of the error
DBstsAHVR	The previous added row has not been updated
DBstsBADP	Bad parameter
DBstsCANF	Cannot find named data source
DBstsCARR	Cannot access requested row
DBstsCCON	Unable to connect
DBstsCNVD	String length exceeded
DBstsCNVR	Cannot convert data from native to expected or requested datatype
DBstsCOAR	Operation not allowed on AddRow workspace
DBstsCPAR	Cannot position at AddRow
DBstsCXIN	Could not execute insert or update
DBstsENTR	Entry missing
DBstsEOFD	End of data has been reached
DBstsFAIL	The operation failed for unspecified reasons
DBstsHSTMT	ODBC could not allocate a new statement handle
DBstsILLG	Unrecognized or illegal data type
DBstsINTR	Internal buffer limit reached when creating a string
DBstsINVC	Field ID is out of range
DBstsINVR	Invalid row number
DBstsMEMF	Out of memory
DBstsNAFI	Cannot insert new row before AddRow
DBstsNCOJ	No valid connection object
DBstsNCOL	Table did not return any columns
DBstsNCON	Not connected to a data source
DBstsNODA	The result contains no data
DBstsNOEX	Never executed successfully or result set closed
DBstsNQOJ	No valid query object
DBstsNUNQ	Update or Delete cannot locate a unique data row
DBstsODBC	ODBC could not complete the requested operation
DBstsPMIS	Missing parameter in query
DBstsRCHG	Original row data changed. Cannot be updated or deleted
DBstsRDON	Read Only. Data cannot be updated or deleted
DBstsROWD	The row has previously been deleted
DBstsRUNC	No changes in row
DBstsSNFD	A resource string could not be found in the resource file
DBstsUBLE	Column not updateable
DBstsUNIM	Unimplemented feature

Example 15.9

```
  (Options)
  Uselsx "*LSXODBC"

  Sub Initialize
  Dim newCon As New ODBCConnection
  If (newCon.ConnectTo("LSSBookTestBAD")) Then
     Dim newQry As New ODBCQuery
     Dim newRes As New ODBCResultSet
     Set newQry.Connection = newCon
     newQry.SQL = "SELECT * FROM Contacts"
     Set newRes.Query = newQry
     Call newRes.Execute
  End If
1 If (newCon.GetError = DBstsSUCCESS) Then
2    If (newCon.GetError = DBstsNCON) Then
        Msgbox "ODBC Connection could not be established",64, _
           "ODBC Connection Error!"
     Else
        Msgbox newCon.GetErrorMessage,64,"ODBC Error!"
     End If
  Else
     Call newCon.Disconnect
  End If
  End Sub
```

Explanation

1 The `GetError` method of the ODBCConnection class is used to check if there were any errors. A return value of `DBstsSuccess` signals no errors; otherwise, there were problems.

2 The `GetError` method is used to check for a certain value. One message is displayed if there is a match; otherwise, another message is displayed.

15.7.1 On Error

The On Error Goto <label name> can be used with the ODBC classes as well. Refer to chapter 7 for more information on this technique.

15.8 Accessing data in a result set

At this point we have covered every aspect of working with data in Non-Domino databases: establish a connection, set up the SQL, execute the SQL, and handle errors. The result of all of those steps is an ODBCResultSet object that contains the results of the SQL.

Example 15.10

```
(Options)
Uselsx "*LSXODBC"
```

```
Sub Initialize
  Dim ocon As New ODBCConnection
  Dim oqry As New ODBCQuery
  Dim ores As New ODBCResultSet
  Dim fname As String, lname As String, msgText As String
  If (ocon.ConnectTo("LSSBookTest")) Then
    Set oqry.Connection = ocon
    oqry.SQL = "SELECT FirstName,LastName,Title From Contacts"
    Set ores.Query = oqry
    Call ores.Execute
1   If (ores.NumRows <> 0) Then
      Do
2       ores.NextRow
3       If (ores.GetError = DBstsSUCCESS) Then
4         fname = ores.GetValue("FirstName")
          lname = ores.GetValue("LastName")
          msgText = msgText + lname + ", " + fname + Chr(10)
        End If
5       Loop Until ores.IsEndOfData
        ocon.Disconnect
        MsgBox msgText,,"Contacts"
    End If
    Else
      MsgBox ocon.GetErrorMessage,0,"ODBC Error!"
    End If
End Sub
```

Explanation

1 The `NumRows` property of the ODBCResultSet class does not return the total number of rows in a result set until after all rows have been retrieved. On the other hand, it will return zero if there are not rows in the result set.

2 The `NextRow` method retrieves the next row in the result set. The first time it is called after executing a query, it returns the first row in the result set.

3 Gets column values if there were no errors.

4 Uses the `GetValue` method of the ODBCResultSet class to get a value from a column in the result set. The column name is specified.

5 The `Do` loop continues until the Boolean property of the ODBCResultSet class returns `True`, signaling that the end of the data in the result set has been reached.

Note Line 1 from the previous example could have been replaced with a line using the `IsResultSetAvailable` property:

```
If (ores.IsResultSetAvailable) Then
```

15.9 Adding/deleting records

The LS:DO classes can be used to synchronize data in a Notes/Domino database with its counterpart in a non-Notes database, or vice versa. An import of data could easily be performed as well. The next few examples work with these issues. They were developed with Microsoft Access as the non-Notes database.

Example 15.11

This bit of code creates documents in a Domino database for every record in an Access database.

```
  (Options)
  Uselsx "*LSXODBC"

  Sub Initialize
  Dim s As New NotesSession
  Dim db As NotesDatabase
  Dim doc As NotesDocument
  Dim fnameItem As NotesItem, lnameItem As NotesItem
  Dim titleItem As NotesItem
  Dim lname As String, fname As String, title As String
  Dim dbcon As New ODBCConnection
  Dim dbqry As New ODBCQuery
  Dim dbset As New ODBCResultSet
  Set db = s.CurrentDatabase
  If (dbcon.ConnectTo("LSSBookTest")) Then
     Set dbqry.Connection = dbcon
1    dbqry.SQL = "SELECT * FROM Contacts"
     Set dbset.Query = dbqry
     Call dbset.Execute
     If (dbset.NumRows <> 0) Then
        Do
           dbset.NextRow
           If (dbset.GetError = DBstsSUCCESS) Then
2             lname = dbset.GetValue("LastName")
              fname = dbset.GetValue("FirstName")
              title = dbset.GetValue("Title")
3                   Set doc = db.CreateDocument
              doc.Form = "Contact"
              Set fnameItem = New NotesItem(doc,"FirstName",fname)
              fnameItem.IsSummary = True
              Set lnameItem = New NotesItem(doc,"LastName",lname)
              lnameItem.IsSummary = True
              Set titleItem = New NotesItem(doc, "Title", title)
4                titleItem.IsSummary = True
              Call doc.Save(True, True)
           End If
        Loop Until dbset.IsEndOfData
     End If
     dbcon.Disconnect
     End If
  End If
  End Sub
```

Explanation

1 Sets the `SQL` to retrieve all records from the contacts table in the data source.

2 Retrieves the last name, first name, and title from columns from the contacts table.

3 Creates a new document in Notes to store the contact information.

4 The `IsSummary` property of the NotesItem class signals whether an item's value can be used in a view column (`true`) or not (`false`).

The next example is useful for the one-way transfer of data. The next code demonstrates synchronizing the data in a Notes/Domino database with data in an Access table. First, the Notes database is checked for the existence of the records in an Access table. If a record is not found, it is added to the Notes database. If no match is found, the record is added to Access.

Example 15.12

```
(Options)
Uselsx "*LSXODBC"

Sub Initialize
   Dim s As New NotesSession
   Dim db As NotesDatabase
   Dim view As NotesView
   Dim doc As NotesDocument
   Dim fname As String, lname As String, title As String
   Dim address As String, city As String, state As String
   Dim postalcode As String, phone As String, company As String
   Dim dbcon As ODBCConnection
   Dim dbqry As ODBCQuery
   Dim dbset As ODBCResultSet
   Set db = s.CurrentDatabase
   Set view = db.GetView("Contacts")
   Set doc = view.GetFirstDocument
   If (dbcon.ConnectTo("LSSBookTest")) Then
      Set dbqry.Connection = dbcon
1     While Not (doc Is Nothing)
2        sqlString = "SELECT * FROM Contacts WHERE FirstName = " &_
            doc.fname(0) & " AND LastName  = " & doc.lname(0)
         dbqry.SQL = sqlString
         dbset.Query = dbqry
         dbset.Execute
3        If (dbset.NumRows = 0) Then
4           addStatus = dbset.AddRow
5           addStatus = dbset.SetValue("FirstName",doc.fname(0))
            addStatus = dbset.SetValue("LastName",doc.lname(0))
            addStatus = dbset.SetValue("Address",doc.address(0))
            addStatus = dbset.SetValue("City",doc.city(0))
            addStatus = dbset.SetValue("StateOrProvince",doc.state(0))
            addStatus = dbset.SetValue("Title",doc.title(0))
            addStatus = dbset.SetValue("PostalCode",doc.zipcode(0))
            addStatus = dbset.SetValue("Company",doc.company(0))
```

```
6           addStatus = dbset.SetValue("WorkPhone",doc.phone(0))
            addStatus = dbset.UpdateRow
7           If (addStatus <> True) Then
               Print "Error adding " & doc.lname(0) & ", " & doc.fname(0) &_
                  "to the Access database."
            End If
8           dbset.Close(DB_Close)
         End If
      Wend
   End If
End Sub
```

Explanation

1 Processes every document in the view.

2 This `SQL` statement searches the Access database for records that match the record in Notes. It selects all records `WHERE` the last and first names equal their counterparts in the Notes document.

3 Continues only if no matches were found.

4 The `AddRow` method of the ODBCResultSet class creates a record in the external data source. It returns a value of `False` if errors are encountered.

5 The `SetValue` method of the ODBCResultSet class adds a new column value. The first parameter is the column name in the data source, and the second column is the data to store in it. This method cannot be called without an `AddRow` being used first. It returns a value of `False` if errors are encountered.

6 The `UpdateRow` method of the ODBCResultSet class saves the new record to the data source. It returns a value of `False` if errors are encountered.

7 Checks the return value to make sure the new record was saved.

8 Closes the dataset.

15.10 Domino.Connect

The ODBC LSX is included with the Domino.Connect product. Domino.Connect allows relational databases and transaction systems to be easily integrated into a Domino application. This could be used to present data to users via a web browser or Notes client. In addition, LSXs are included for accessing Oracle, SAP, and MQSeries among others. The product-specific tools like the SAP R3 LSX differ from the ODBC LSX in that they allow Notes/Domino to access data via its native driver.

15.11 NotesSQL

The NotesSQL tool is provided in the Domino.Connect package as well. It works the opposite way as the LS:DO. It gives external database tools access to data in Domino databases. Install the NotesSQL driver in your ODBC driver manager and set up an ODBC connection. Once this is done, data from Notes can be accessed.

15.12 Chapter summary

The tools available in the Domino.Connect product expand the power available in Domino. Domino is not a relational database, and it is not suited to store relational-type data. On the other hand, data from a relational database can be incorporated in a Domino application through ODBC or native drivers and the appropriate LSX. The reverse is possible with the NotesSQL ODBC driver. This driver allows external databases to access data stored in a Notes/Domino database.

15.13 Chapter review

- LS:DO stands for LotusScript: Data Object.
- LS:DO allows Domino applications to access non-Domino data through ODBC.
- ODBC stands for Open DataBase Connectivity.
- ODBC was originally developed by Microsoft Corporation. It allows access to almost any type of database.
- One of ODBC's strong points is that it is driver independent. If your source changes from Oracle to Sybase, change the driver and the application will continue to work as planned.
- SQL stands for Structured Query Language.
- SQL is the universal language for working with relational databases.
- ODBC supports a core set of SQL statements.
- The LotusScript ODBCConnection class establishes a connection in Notes to an external data source via ODBC.
- The LotusScript ODBCQuery class specifies the SQL to be used.
- The LotusScript ODBCResultSet holds values returned (if any) by an SQL query.
- Data can transfer both ways in Notes. That is, data can be retrieved from a non-Notes database or it can be written to a non-Notes database. You do have to make sure that your ODBC driver allows data to be written to the external data source.
- Domino.Connect is a commercial product available from Lotus Corporation. It includes the LS:DO and many other native LSXs for access non-Notes databases.
- NotesSQL is the ODBC driver for non-Notes databases to access Lotus Notes/Domino data.

CHAPTER 16

Working with date/time values

16.1 Chapter objectives 252

16.2 LotusScript 252

16.3 Extracting portions of time/date values 253

16.4 NotesDateTime class 255

16.5 Methods 256

16.6 Chapter summary 266

16.7 Chapter review 267

16.1 Chapter objectives

- NotesDateTime class
- LotusScript date/time values
- The differences between NotesDateTime and LotusScript date/time values
- Adjusting date/time values
- Extracting the day from a date/time value
- Extracting the weekday from a date/time value
- Extracting the month from a date/time value
- Extracting the year from a date/time value
- Finding the difference between two time/date values
- Searching using date/time values
- NotesDateRange
- NotesInternational
- Y2K

There are two ways to work with date and/or time values in Lotus Notes: the NotesDateTime class or core LotusScript commands. The NotesDateTime class is much more thorough in its storage of date/time values.

16.2 LotusScript

The core LotusScript language contains numerous commands that make it easy to work with dates.

Now This function returns the current date and time.

Today This function returns the current date.

Time This function returns the current time.

```
Print "The current date/time is:  " & Cstr(Now)
Print "The current date is:  " & Cstr(Today)
Print "The current time is:  " & Cstr(Time)
```

In addition to built-in functions, you can set date/time values with string representations or numbers using the following functions:

`DateValue("String Value")` This function allows a date value to be initialized with the string passed into it.

```
Dim dt As Variant
dt = DateValue("01/01/1999")
```

CDat("String Value") Converts a string value into a date value.

```
Dim dt As Variant
dt = CDat("01/01/1999")
```

DateNumber(yyyy, mm, dd) Converts the integer values into a date value. The first parameter is the year, second is the month, and the last is the day.

```
Dim dt As Variant
dt = DateNumber(1999, 01, 01)
```

TimeNumber(hour, minute, second) Converts the integer values into a time value. The first parameter is the hour, the second is the minute, and lastly is the seconds.

```
Dim dt As Variant
dt = TimeNumber(10, 30, 00)
```

TimeValue("String Value") The `TimeValue` function coverts a string value into its time representation.

```
Dim dt As Variant
dt = TimeValue("10:30:00")
```

16.3 Extracting portions of time/date values

Once a date and/or time value is initialized, certain portions of it can be extracted. This includes the date, day, hour, minute, year, month, or weekday. Each function is presented next.

Day(date) The `Day` function returns only the day portion of a date as an Integer.

```
Dim dt As Variant, day As Integer
dt = DateValue("10/10/1999")
theday = Day(dt)
```

Month(date) The `Month` function returns only the month portion of a date as an integer. An integer value between one and twelve is returned. The list below shows the mapping of the integer value to its month.

```
1 - January
2 - February
3 - March
4 - April
5 - May
6 - June
7 - July
8 - August
9 - September
10 - October
```

```
11 - November
12 - December

theMonth As String
Select Case (Month(Today))
   Case 1:   theMonth = "January"
   Case 2:   theMonth = "February"
   Case 3:   theMonth = "March"
   Case 4:   theMonth = "April"
   Case 5:   theMonth = "May"
   Case 6:   theMonth = "June"
   Case 7:   theMonth = "July"
   Case 8:   theMonth = "August"
   Case 9:   theMonth = "September"
   Case 10: theMonth = "October"
   Case 11: theMonth = "November"
   Case 12: theMonth = "December"
End Select
```

`Year(date)` The `Year` function returns only the year portion of a date as an integer.

```
Dim theYear As Integer
theYear = Year(Today)
```

`WeekDay(date)` The `Weekday` function returns an integer between one and seven representing the day of the week. The list below shows the mapping of the integer value to the days of the week.

```
1 - Sunday
2 - Monday
3 - Tuesday
4 - Wednesday
5 - Thursday
6 - Friday
7 - Saturday

Dim theWeekday As String
Select Case (Weekday(Today))
  Case 1:  theWeekday = "Sunday"
  Case 2:  theWeekday = "Monday"
  Case 3:  theWeekday = "Tuesday"
  Case 4:  theWeekday = "Wednesday"
  Case 5:  theWeekday = "Thursday"
  Case 6:  theWeekday = "Friday"
  Case 7:  theWeekday = "Saturday"
End Select
```

`Minute(date/time value)` The `Minute` function returns the minute portion of a date/time value.

```
Dim theMinutes As Integer
```

```
theMinutes = Minute(Now)
```

Hour(date/time value) The Hour function returns the hour portion of a date/time value.

```
Dim theHour As Integer
theHour = Hour(Now)
```

Second(time/date value) The Second function returns the seconds portion of a date/time value.

```
Dim theSeconds As Integer
theSeconds = Second(Now)
```

The many LotusScript date/time statements give developers a lot of flexibility when working with date/time values. On the other hand, the NotesDateTime class provides more power by allowing various useful attributes.

16.4 NotesDateTime class

The NotesDateTime class is used to represent a date and time in the Lotus Notes format. It provides a vehicle for converting a LotusScript date/time to the proper Notes format.

The properties of the NotesDateTime class:

- *Dateonly* A string representation of the date portion of the date/time value.
- *Gmttime* A string representation of the date/time value converted to Greenwich Mean Time.
- *IsDST* Signals True/False whether or not a time value reflects daylight savings time.
- *Localtime* A string representation of the date/time in the local time zone.
- *Lsgmttime* A variant representation of the date/time value converted to Greenwich Mean Time.
- *LSLocalTime* A variant representation of the date/time value in the local time zone.
- *Timeonly* A string representation of the time portion of a date/time value in the local time zone.
- *Timezone* An integer representing the time zone of a date/time. The Help file states that this value *usually* represents what value must be added to a time value to adjust it to Greenwich Mean Time (positive or negative).
- *Zonetime* String representation of the time portion of the date/time value adjusted for the TimeZone and IsDST properties.

Because that is a lot to keep track of, a graphic (figure 16.1) may be easier to handle. The following code instantiates a NotesDateTime object using the current date/time. The `SetNow` method is used to set the time/date value to the current date/time.

```
Dim dt As New NotesDateTime("")
Call dt.SetNow
```

The code is executed and figure 16.1 shows the properties of the NotesDateTime object when it is run.

16.5 Methods

In addition to the properties, there are plenty of methods at your disposal.

First, there are a number of functions that can be used to alter portions of a date/time value. Each accepts two parameters: the first is an integer signaling the number to increment (positive) or decrement (negative) and the second is a Boolean value signaling whether daylight savings time adjustments should be made.

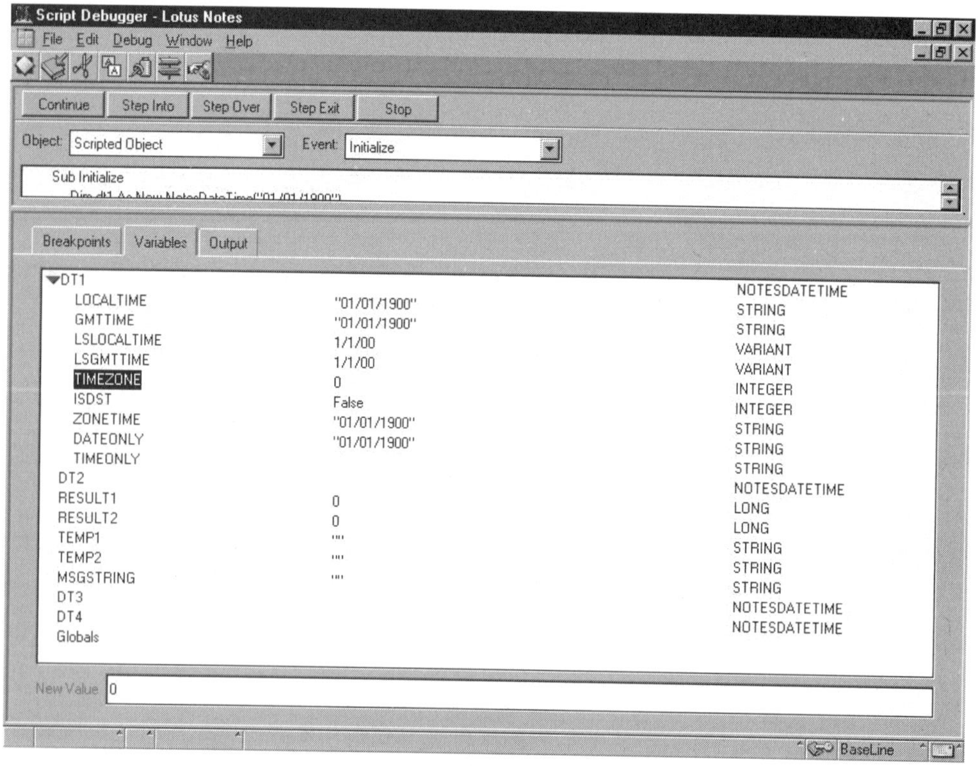

Figure 16.1 NotesDateTime class properties in action

`AdjustDay` Adjusts the day portion of a date/time value.

```
Dim dt As New NotesDateTime("01/01/1999")
Call dt.AdjustDay(-2,True)
```

`AdjustHour` Adjusts the hour portion of a date/time value.

```
Dim dt As New NotesDateTime("01/01/1999 10:10:00 AM")
Call dt.AdjustHour(-2,True)
```

`AdjustMinute` Adjusts the minutes portion of a date/time value.

```
Dim dt As New NotesDateTime("01/01/1999 10:10:00 AM")
Call dt.AdjustHour(-2,True)
```

`AdjustMonth` Adjusts the month portion of a date/time value.

```
Dim dt As New NotesDateTime("01/01/1999 10:10:00 AM")
Call dt.AdjustMinute(90,True)
```

`AdjustSecond` Adjusts the seconds portion of a date/time value.

```
Dim dt As New NotesDateTime("01/01/1999 10:10:00 AM")
Call dt.AdjustSecond(45,True)
```

`AdjustYear` Adjusts the year portion of a date/time value.

```
Dim dt As New NotesDateTime("01/01/1999 10:10:00 AM")
Call dt.AdjustYear(1,True)
```

`ConvertToZone` Allows the time zone to be changed and the daylight savings time setting to be altered. The first parameter is the new time zone setting (`0-15`), and the second parameter signals `True/False` whether or not daylight savings time is in effect.

```
Dim dt As New NotesDateTime("")
Call dt.SetNow
Call dt.ConvertTimeZone(3, True)
```

`SetAnyDate` Sets the date portion of a time/date value to a wildcard value. This means it will match any date when compared.

```
Dim dt As New NotesDateTime("")
Call dt.SetNow
Call dt.SetAnyDate
```

`SetAnyTime` Sets the time portion of a time/date value to a wildcard value. This means it will match any time when compared.

```
Dim dt As New NotesDateTime("")
Call dt.SetNow
Call dt.SetAnyTime
```

`SetNow` Sets the time/date value to the current date and time. We have seen this method used often.

```
Dim dt As New NotesDateTime("")
Call dt.SetNow
```

`TimeDifference` Finds the difference between two date/time values in seconds. The method is called on one NotesDateTime object with another NotesDateTime object passed in.

Example 16.1

```
1   Dim dt1 As New NotesDateTime("01/01/2000 12:00:00")
2   Dim dt2 As New NotesDateTime("")
    Dim diff As Long, msgString As String
3   Call dt2.SetNow
4   diff = dt1.TimeDifference(dt2)
5   msgString = "There are " & Cstr(diff) & " seconds until doomsday."
6   msgString = msgString & Chr(10) & "There are " & Cstr(diff/60) &_
       " minutes until doomsday."
7   msgString = msgString & Chr(10) & "There are " & Cstr(diff/3600) &_
       " hours until doomsday."
8   msgString = msgString & Chr(10) & "There are " & Cstr(diff/86400) &_
       " days until doomsday."
9   MsgBox msgString, 0, "Doomsday Countdown!!"
```

Explanation

1 Declares/instantiates a new NotesDateTime object with the value of noon on January 1, 2000.

2 Declares another NotesDateTime object.

3 Sets the date/time of the dt2 NotesDateTime object to the current date and time.

4 Calculates the difference (in seconds) between the first date/time object (1/1/2000) and the second object that contains the current date/time. The result is stored in a variable of type `Long`.

5 Begins assembling a string that will be used in a MessageBox for display (figure 16.2). This line shows the difference in seconds. Each line is separated by a carriage return.

6 The second line uses the difference, in seconds, to calculate and display the difference in minutes.

7 The third line uses the difference to calculate and display the difference in hours.

8 The fourth line uses the difference to calculate and display the difference in days.

9 The results are displayed in a message box.

The previous bit of code shows how many days, hours, minutes, and seconds until the year 2000.

Output

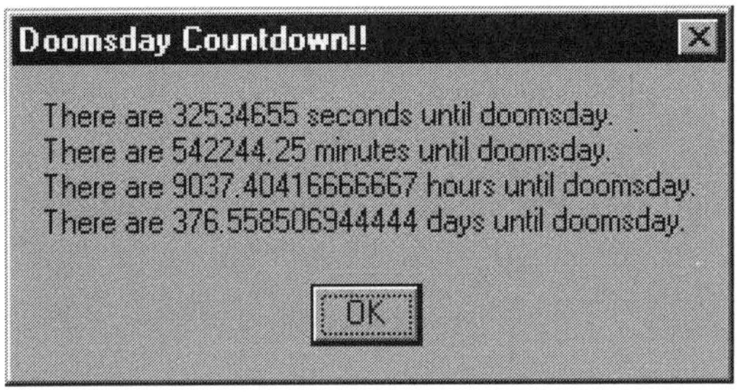

Figure 16.2 TimeDifference example – the countdown to doomsday

16.5.1 Creating a NotesDateTime object

There are three ways to create/instantiate a NotesDateTime object.

- `Dim dt As New NotesDataTime("")`
- `Set dt = New NotesDateTime("")`
- `Dim session As New NotesSession`
  `Set dt = session.CreateDateTime("")`

Example 16.2

```
  Sub Initialize
1    Dim currentDT As New NotesDateTime("")
     Dim currentMonth As String, currentDay As String
     Dim theYear As Integer, theDay As Integer, msgString As String
2    Call currentDT.SetNow
3    Select Case Weekday(currentDT.LSLocalTime)
        Case 1 : currentDay = "Sunday"
        Case 2 : currentDay = "Monday"
        Case 3 : currentDay = "Tuesday"
        Case 4 : currentDay = "Wednesday"
        Case 5 : currentDay = "Thursday"
        Case 6 : currentDay = "Friday"
        Case 7 : currentDay = "Saturday"
     End Select
4    Select Case Month(currentDT.LSLocalTime)
        Case 1 : currentMonth = "January"
        Case 2 : currentMonth = "February"
        Case 3 : currentMonth = "March"
        Case 4 : currentMonth = "April"
        Case 5 : currentMonth = "May"
        Case 6 : currentMonth = "June"
        Case 7 : currentMonth = "July"
        Case 8 : currentMonth = "August"
```

```
        Case 9 : currentMonth = "September"
        Case 10 : currentMonth = "October"
        Case 11 : currentMonth = "November"
        Case 12 : currentMonth = "December"
     End Select
5    theDay = Day(currentDT.LSLocalTime)
6    theYear = Year(currentDT.LSLocalTime)
7    msgString = "Today is  " & currentDay & " "& currentMonth & " " &_
        Cstr(theDay) & ", " & Cstr(theYear)
8    MsgBox msgString, 0, "Current date/time"
  End Sub
```

Explanation

1 Declares new NotesDateTime object.

2 Sets the date/time of the NotesDateTime object to the current date/time.

3 Uses the weekday function to set the `currentDay` variable to the proper day of the week for the date. The `LSLocalTime` property of the NotesDateTime object is used. This gives you the localized LotusScript date/time.

4 Uses the month function to set the `currentMonth` variable to the proper month for the date.

5 Uses the day function to get the day portion of the date/time value.

6 Uses the year function to get the year portion of the date/time value.

7 Assembles the results into the format: weekday, month, day, year.

8 Presents the results in a message box (figure 16.3).

Output

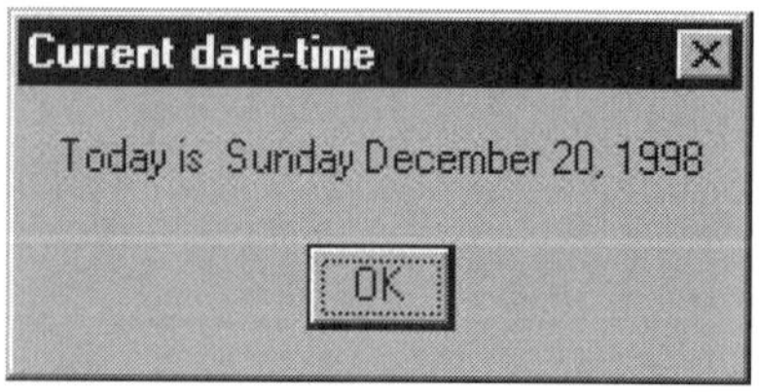

Figure 16.3 Output of example 16.2

The keywords `Yesterday`, `Today`, and `Tomorrow` can be used to instantiate NotesDateTime objects as well.

```
Dim dt1 As New NotesDateTime("Yesterday")
Dim dt2 As New NotesDateTime("Today")
Dim dt3 As New NotesDateTime("Tomorrow")
```

16.5.2 NotesDateRange class

The NotesDateRange class is another time/date related LotusScript Notes class. This class is used to represent a range of dates and times.

A NotesDateRange object has only three properties:

- *`StartDateTime`* Starting date of a date/time range
- *`EndDateTime`* Ending date of a date/time range
- *`Text`* Text associated with a range (start date/time—end date/time)

Creating a New NotesDateRange object involves the NotesSession class and its `CreateDateRange` method.

```
Dim s As New NotesSession
Dim dateRange As New NotesDateRange
Set dateRange = s.CreateDateRange
```

Example 16.3

```
    Dim s As New NotesSession
1   Dim dt1 As New NotesDateTime("12/1/1999")
2   Dim dt2 As New NotesDateTime("4/1/1999")
3   Dim dateRange As NotesDateRange
4   Set dateRange = s.CreateDateRange
5   Set dateRange.StartDateTime = dt1
6   Set dateRange.EndDateTime = dt2
7   Print dateRange.Text
```

Explanation

1 Creates/instantiates NotesDateTime object.

2 Creates/instantiates NotesDateTime object.

3 Creates NotesDateRange object.

4 Instantiates the NotesDateRange object via the `CreateRange` method of the NotesSession class.

5 Sets the starting date/time of the date range.

6 Sets the ending date/time of the date range.

7 Displays the date/time range.

Output

12/1/99 – 4/1/99

The NotesDateRange class is used extensively when working with schedules in a application that involves a calendar.

16.5.3 Year 2000 issues

Example 16.1 provides a short routine for calculating the time until 2000 is upon us. Many have predicted this day as doomsday, because older computer systems used two-digit dates. The two-digit dates will play havoc with any date-related calculations since the year 2000 will be represented as 00. Computers will see 00 as 1900, so you can imagine the problems.

Lotus Notes has been year 2000-compliant since version 2. The year portion of date values is displayed as two digits until the year 2000 when four digits are used. Actually, internally all dates are stored with four-digit years. Version 5.0 will allow the displaying of all dates as four digits.

The core Lotus Notes/Domino architecture is Year 2000-compliant (including LotusScript), but developers can still design applications that are not 2000-compliant. Generally, dates can be displayed in views and the columns may not be wide enough to display four digits (adjusting the column size fixes this).

The one possible big area of concern within Notes is situations where time/date values are translated to text. The text representation will/may contain only two-digit years. If you try to convert this text value back to its time/date representation, it may not translate correctly.

The next example illustrates where problems can occur. Two dates are initialized: one is Jan. 1, 1900, and the other is Jan. 1, 2000. The difference between the two is calculated, and each is converted to the format `d/m/yy` using the `Format` function. After the formatting, they are converted back to time/date values and the difference is calculated once again. Watch the results and notice what LotusScript does to a date with 00 as the year.

Example 16.4

```
  Sub Initialize
1    Dim dt1 As New NotesDateTime("01/01/1900")
2    Dim dt2 As New NotesDateTime("01/01/2000")
     Dim result1 As Long, result2 As Long
     Dim temp1 As String, temp2 As String, msgString As String
3    result1 = dt1.TimeDifference(dt2)
4    temp1 = Format(Cstr(dt1.DateOnly),"m/d/yy")
     temp2 = Format(Cstr(dt2.DateOnly),"m/d/yy")
5    Dim dt3 As New NotesDateTime(temp1)
6    Dim dt4 As New NotesDateTime(temp2)
7    result2 = dt3.TimeDifference(dt4)
8    msgString = "Initial Dates:  " & temp1 & " - " & temp2 & Chr(10)
     msgString = msgString & "Initial Difference:  " & Cstr(result1) & Chr(10)
     msgString = msgString & "Changed Dates:  " & Cstr(dt3.DateONly) & _
        " - " & Cstr(dt4.DateOnly) & Chr(10)
     msgString = msgString & "Changed Difference:  " & Cstr(result2)
9    Msgbox msgString, 0 , "Y2K"
  End Sub
```

Explanation

1 Declares/instantiates NotesDateTime object to Jan. 1, 1900.

2 Declares/instantiates NotesDateTime object to Jan. 1, 2000.

3 Calculates the difference between the two date/times in seconds.

4 Formats the dates using the `Format` function.

5 Declares/instantiates NotesDateTime object using the formatted time/date: 1/1/00.

6 Declares/instantiates NotesDateTime object using the formatted time/date: 1/1/00.

7 Calculates the difference between the two date/times in seconds.

8 Assembles the message string to display via `MessageBox` statement.

9 Presents the results (figure 16.4).

Output

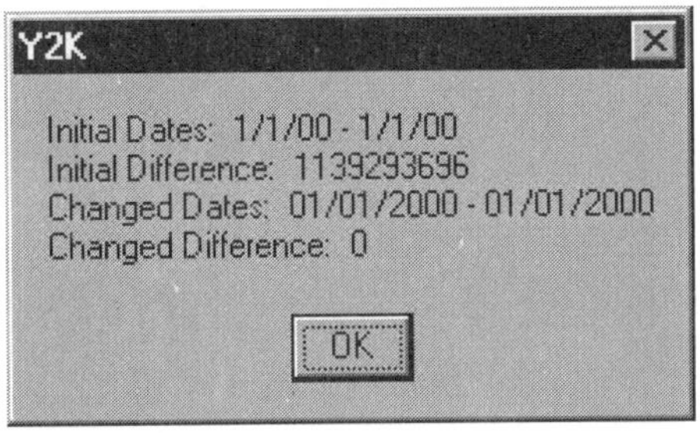

Figure 16.4 Y2K issues—example 16.4

For two-digit date values from 00 to 49, LotusScript recognizes them as 2000 to 2049. Two-digit date values from 50 to 99 are seen as 1950 to 1999. Problems can occur whenever two-digit dates are used. The next example is a repeat of example 16.4 except the values 1950 and 2050 are used.

Example 16.5

```
Sub Initialize
  Dim dt1 As New NotesDateTime("01/01/1950")
  Dim dt2 As New NotesDateTime("01/01/2050")
  Dim result1 As Long, result2 As Long
  Dim temp1 As String, temp2 As String, msgString As String
  result1 = dt1.TimeDifference(dt2)
  temp1 = Format(Cstr(dt1.DateOnly),"m/d/yy")
  temp2 = Format(Cstr(dt2.DateOnly),"m/d/yy")
  Dim dt3 As New NotesDateTime(temp1)
  Dim dt4 As New NotesDateTime(temp2)
  result2 = dt3.TimeDifference(dt4)
  msgString = "Initial Dates:  " & temp1 & " - " & temp2 & Chr(10)
  msgString = msgString & "Initial Difference:  " & Cstr(result1) & Chr(10)
  msgString = msgString & "Changed Dates:  " & Cstr(dt3.DateONly) & _
    " - " & Cstr(dt4.DateOnly) & Chr(10)
  msgString = msgString & "Changed Difference:  " & Cstr(result2)
  Msgbox msgString, 0 , "Y2K"
End Sub
```

Output

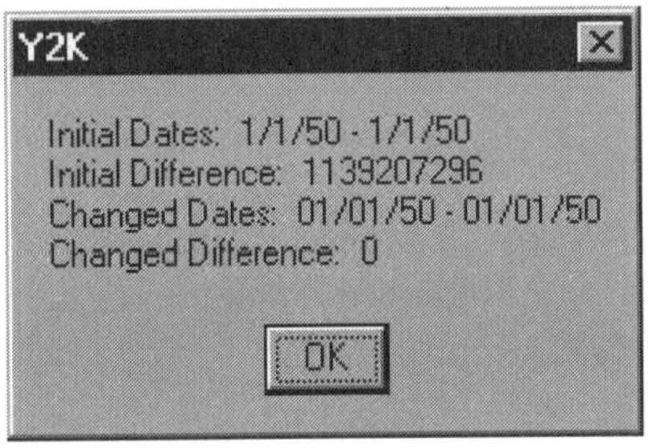

Figure 16.5 Example 16.4

Notice the results from example 16.5 in the same way as example 16.4, so you must be very careful with time/date values. Never convert date values to text with two-digit years. If, for some reason, you must convert a date value to text do so with four digit dates. The next example alters example 16.4 ever so slightly, but it produces the correct results.

Example 16.6

```
  Sub Initialize
     Dim dt1 As New NotesDateTime("01/01/1900")
     Dim dt2 As New NotesDateTime("01/01/2000")
     Dim result1 As Long, result2 As Long
     Dim temp1 As String, temp2 As String, msgString As String
     result1 = dt1.TimeDifference(dt2)
1    temp1 = Format(Cstr(dt1.DateOnly),"m/d/yyyy")
2    temp2 = Format(Cstr(dt2.DateOnly),"m/d/yyyy")
     Dim dt3 As New NotesDateTime(temp1)
     Dim dt4 As New NotesDateTime(temp2)
     result2 = dt3.TimeDifference(dt4)
     msgString = "Initial Dates:  " & temp1 & " - " & temp2 & Chr(10)
     msgString = msgString & "Initial Difference:  " & Cstr(result1) & Chr(10)
     msgString = msgString & "Changed Dates:  " & Cstr(dt3.DateONly) & _
        " - " & Cstr(dt4.DateOnly) & Chr(10)
     msgString = msgString & "Changed Difference:  " & Cstr(result2)
     Msgbox msgString, 0 , "Y2K"
  End Sub
```

Explanation

1 Formats the first date using the format function. This time the year is set to four digits.

2 Formats the second date using the format function. This time the year is set to four digits (figure 16.6).

Output

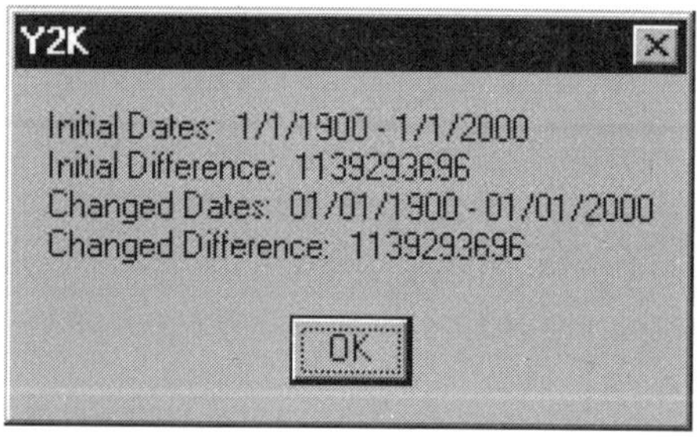

Figure 16.6 Example 16.5 output

The results are now what we want, expect, and need. Year 2000 has made four-digit years a necessity instead of a luxury.

16.5.4 NotesInternational class

With the new global economy upon us, we have to keep in mind that our applications may be used outside of the country in which they were designed. The NotesInternational class provides a way to work with some of the date/time issues (as well as others). It represents the international settings for the operating system. These settings can be found via the Control Panel in Microsoft Windows.

16.5.5 Properties

`AMString` The string used to denote *AM* time. For English, this will be "*AM*".

`CurrencyDigits` The number of decimal digits in numbers.

`DateSep` The character used to separate months, days, and years.

`DecimalSep` The character used as the decimal separator in numbers.

`IsCurrencySpace` Boolean flag that signals if currency numbers have a space between the currency symbol.

`IsCurrencySuffix` Boolean flag that signals if the currency symbol follows the number.

`IsCurrencyZero` Boolean flag that signals if fractional numbers have zero before the decimal separator.

`IsDateDMY` Boolean flag that signals if the date format is day-month-year.

`IsDateMDY` Boolean flag that signals if the date format is month-day-year.

`IsDateYMD` Boolean flag that signals if the date format is year-month-day.

`IsDST` Boolean flag signals if the time format indicates daylight savings time.

`IsTime24Hour` Boolean flag signals if the time format is 24 hours.

`PMString` The string used to denote *PM* time. For English, this will be "*PM*".

`ThousandsSep` The character used to separate thousands in numbers. A comma is commonly used.

`TimeSep` The character used to separate hours, minutes, and seconds in a time value.

`TimeZone` An integer denoting the time zone. Lotus Help states that this number represents the number of hours that must be added (positive or negative value) to get the Greenwich Mean Time for a time value.

`Today` The string that means "Today" in a time/date specification. Remember, this string can be used to instantiate NotesDateTime objects to the current date/time.

`Tomorrow` The string that means "Tomorrow" in a time/date specification. Remember, this string can be used to instantiate NotesDateTime objects to the next day's time/date.

`Yesterday` The string that means "Yesterday" in a time/date specification. Remember, this string can be used to instantiate NotesDateTime objects to the previous day's time/date.

Creating/instantiating a NotesInternational object A NotesInternational object can be declared using the international setting of the NotesSession class.

```
Dim s As New NotesSession
Dim international As NotesInternational
Set international = s.International
```

Example 16.7

```
Sub Initialize
Dim LF As String
LF = Chr(10)
Dim session As New NotesSession
Dim intl As NotesInternational
Dim msgString As String
Set intl = session.International
msgString = LF & "date/time Settings" & LF
msgString = msgString & "AM String:  " & intl.AMString & LF
msgString = msgString & "PM String:  " & intl.PMString & LF
msgString = msgString & "Date Separator:  " & intl.DateSep & LF
```

```
msgString = msgString & "Date format DMY?  " & intl.IsDateDMY & LF
msgString = msgString & "Date format MDY?  " & intl.IsDateMDY & LF
msgString = msgString & "Date format YMD?  " & intl.IsDateYMD & LF
msgString = msgString & "Daylight Savings?  " & intl.IsDST & LF
msgString = msgString & "24 Hour Clock?  " & intl.IsTime24Hour & LF
msgString = msgString & "Time separator:  " & intl.TimeSep & LF
msgString = msgString & "Time zone:  " & intl.TimeZone & LF
msgString = msgString & "Today denoted by:  " & intl.Today & LF
msgString = msgString & "Tomorrow denoted by:  " & intl.Tomorrow & LF
msgString = msgString & "Yesterday denoted by:  " & intl.Yesterday & LF
msgString = msgString & LF & "Currency Settings" & LF
msgString = msgString & "Currency Digits:  " & intl.CurrencyDigits & LF
msgString = msgString & "Currency Symbol:  " & intl.CurrencySymbol & LF
msgString = msgString & "Decimal Separator:  " & intl.DecimalSep & LF
msgString = msgString & "Currency Space?  " & intl.IsCurrencySpace & LF
msgString = msgString & "Currency Suffix?  " & intl.IsCurrencySuffix & LF
msgString = msgString & "Currency Zero?  " & intl.IsCurrencyZero & LF
msgString = msgString & "Thousands separator:  " & intl.ThousandsSep & LF
MsgBox msgString, 0, "International Settings"
End Sub
```

Output

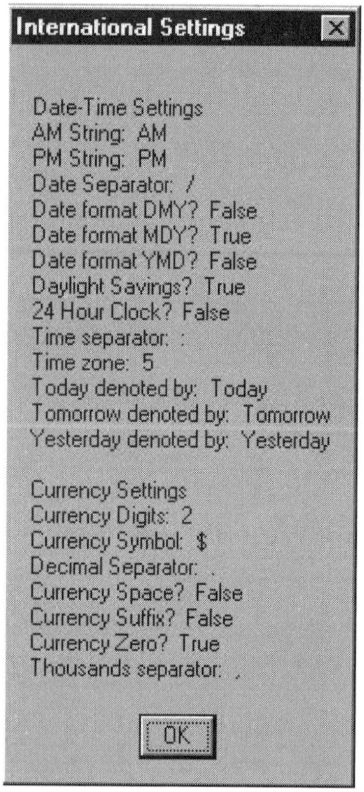

Figure 16.7
Example of 16.6 output

The NotesInternational class provides a means of checking local time/date and currency settings when working with these types of data.

16.6 Chapter summary

The way LotusScript and Lotus Notes store date/time values differs in precision. Lotus Notes stores many more details concerning a time/date value. The Lotus-DateTime class provides a way to convert between the formats. In addition, the NotesDateRange class allows a range of dates to be stored. This class is most useful when working with calendar applications. The core Lotus Notes system is Year 2000 compliant, but developers can design applications that are not. The main source of Y2K problems is formatting dates as two digits rather than four. Four-digit dates should always be used. Also, the NotesInternational class provides easy access to the operating system settings for time/date and currency values.

16.7 Chapter review

- The core LotusScript language includes numerous functions for working with date/time values.
- The Month function returns the month value of a date represented as an integer.
- The Weekday function returns the weekday value of a date represented as an integer.
- The Year function returns only the year portion of a date value.
- The Day function returns only the day portion of a date value.
- The `CDat` function can be used to convert a string value to a time/date value.
- The NotesDateTime class allows you to work with time/date values using the Lotus Notes format.
- The NotesDateTime class provides many properties such as the time zone, date only, and time only.
- The `LSLocalTime` property of the NotesDateTime class provides the LotusScript format of the date/time value.
- The NotesDateRange class stores a range of time/date values. It includes a starting date/time and an ending date/time.
- Lotus Notes has been Year 2000-compliant since version 2.0, but developers can develop noncompliant applications when formatting dates with two-digit years.

The NotesInternational class provides easy access to the operating system's international settings for time/date and currency values.

C H A P T E R 1 7

Working outside the Domino/ Notes environment

17.1 Chapter objectives 270
17.2 Shell 270
17.3 Chapter summary 277
17.4 Chapter review 277

17.1 Chapter objectives

- Activating other applications that open others
- Kicking off external applications
- How LotusScript handles the Shell command
- Using @Functions with Evaluate

The need to execute an external application arises sooner than later. Whether it is a batch file, self-extracting zipped file, Notepad, or FTP, LotusScript allows you to do it. A whole set of commands is reserved for these tasks. Another necessity is utilizing @Functions in your scripts. All of these topics are covered in detail in this chapter.

17.2 Shell

Simply, the Shell function starts another program. It accepts the program name (including path) and an optional parameter that signals what type of window to use to open the application. The window style parameter can be an integer from 1 to 9.

Table 17.1

Style	Description	**Constant that can be used
1,5,9	Normal with focus.	SHELL_NORMAL_FOCUS
2	*Minimized with focus (default).	SHELL_MIN_FOCUS
3	*Maximized with focus.	SHELL_MAX_FOCUS
4,8	Normal without focus.	SHELL_NORMAL_NO_FOCUS
6,7	*Minimized without focus.	SHELL_MIN_NO_FOCUS

* Minimized and Maximized are terms describing window behavior on Windows platforms.
** Constants defined in the file LSCONST.LSS. This file must be included in your script to use the constants.

Note The application that is currently in the foreground or selected is said to have focus.

Example 17.1

```
   Sub Click(Source As Button)
      Dim returnValue As Long
1        returnValue = Shell("C:\Program Files\Accessories\WORDPAD.EXE",1)
2        If (returnValue <> 33) Then
            Msgbox "I am sorry, wordpad could not be started.",64,"Error"
         End If
3        Activateapp("Document - WORDPAD")
   End Sub
```

Explanation

1 A new instance of the wordpad application is started. Wordpad is a text editor for the Windows 95 platform. It is opened as a normal window (platform settings define normal) with focus. (Figure 17.1.)

2 On Windows 95 systems the shell command will return `33` if the Shell function executes with no problems. Otherwise an error is returned.

3 The `ActivateApp` statement activates a program window giving it focus. It accepts one parameter which is the name of the window.

Output

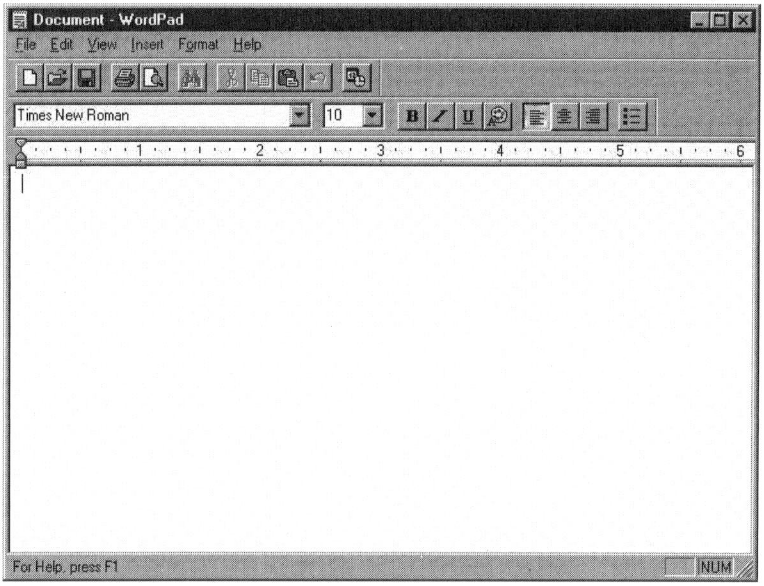

Figure 17.1 Example 17.1 results—Notice title of window is used in ActivateApp function

At first glance the `Shell` function seems like a powerful feature that can be exploited in various ways, but problems arise with the way it executes. When your script reaches a line with the `Shell` function, it executes and continues with the rest of the script. That's right, the remainder of your script is processed while the external application called by the `Shell` function is running. This creates a huge problem if the remainder of the code following the `Shell` line depends on the external application being finished.

The LotusScript manual shows how to implement functions from the Windows 3.1 application programming interface (API), but working with an operating system API can get tricky. Both the Windows 3.1 and 95 APIs are written in C or C++, so this adds to the complexity. On the other hand, it does provide a means to an end.

17.2.1 Declare

The `Declare` statement can be used to set up calls to API routines. A LotusScript function or subroutine is declared that calls the API routine. This allows your script to access API routines. The next `Declare` statement is taken from the LotusScript manual (it is specific to the Windows 3.1 platform).

```
(Declarations)
Declare Function GetModuleUsage Lib "Kernel" (ByVal taskID As Integer) _
  As Integer
```

This makes the `GetModuleUsage` function from the Windows 3.1 API accessible to the LotusScript program. The function accepts the task ID as an integer and returns an integer value. The `Shell` function returns the task ID of the program on the Windows 3.1 platform. The next bit of code takes advantage of the `GetModuleUsage` declaration.

Example 17.2

```
  Sub RunNotepad
      Dim taskID As Integer
1     taskID = Shell("notepad.exe")
2     Do While GetModuleUsage(taskID) > 0
3        Yield
      Loop
  End Sub

  Sub Initialize
4     Call RunNotepad
5     MsgBox "The application has finished."
  End Sub
```

Explanation

1 Starts the Windows program notepad program.

2 Uses the `GetModuleUsage` routine to wait for the notepad application to finish before continuing the script. `GetModuleUsage` returns `0` when an application is no longer active.

3 The LotusScript `Yield` statement transfers control to Windows if the notepad program is still running. Control is passed from the LotusScript code to the operating system. Thus, the script does not complete until notepad is closed.

4 Calls the subroutine from the `Initialize` subroutine.

5 Display the messagebox only after the notepad application is shut down.

17.2.2 Windows 95/NT

This is not a book on programming with the Windows API, but the Windows 95 API is considerably different than the 3.1 version. The next example shows how the Windows 95 API can be used so your script waits for the external application started by the `Shell` function to finish before continuing.

```
(Declarations)
Type STARTUPINFO
  cb As Long
  lpReserved As String
  lpDesktop As String
  lpTitle As String
  dwX As Long
  dwY As Long
  dwXSize As Long
  dwYSize As Long
  dwXCountChars As Long
  dwYCountChars As Long
  dwFillAttribute As Long
  dwFlags As Long
  wShowWindow As Integer
  cbReserved2 As Integer
  lpReserved2 As Long
  hStdInput As Long
  hStdOutput As Long
  hStdError As Long
End Type

Type PROCESS_INFORMATION
hProcess As Long
hThread As Long
dwProcessID As Long
dwThreadID As Long
End Type

Declare Function WaitForSingleObject Lib "kernel32" (Byval hHandle As Long,
Byval dwMilliseconds As Long) As Long
Declare Function CreateProcessA Lib "kernel32" (Byval lpApplicationName As
Long, Byval lpCommandLine As String, Byval lpProcessAttributes As Long, Byval
lpThreadAttributes As Long, Byval bInheritHandles As Long, Byval dwCreation-
Flags As Long, Byval lpEnvironment As Long, Byval lpCurrentDirectory As Long,
lpStartupInfo As STARTUPINFO, lpProcessInformation As PROCESS_INFORMATION) As
Long
Declare Function CloseHandle Lib "kernel32" (Byval hObject As Long) As Long
Declare Function TerminateProcess Lib "kernel32" Alias "TerminateProcess"
(Byval hObject As Long, Byval ExitCode As Long) As Long

Private Const NORMAL_PRIORITY_CLASS = &H20&
Private Const INFINITE = -1&

Public Sub RunApp (program$)
  Dim proc As PROCESS_INFORMATION
```

```
  Dim start As STARTUPINFO
  structure:
  start.cb = Len(start)
  ret& = CreateProcessA(0&, program$, 0&, 0&, 1&, NORMAL_PRIORITY_CLASS, 0&,_
     0&, start, proc)
  ret& = WaitForSingleObject(proc.hProcess, INFINITE)
  ret& = CloseHandle(proc.hProcess)
End Sub
```

I am not going to begin explaining the Windows 95 API, but the three critical functions in the previous declarations are `CreateProcessA`, `WaitForSingleObject`, and `CloseHandle`. `CreateProcessA` starts a new instance of an application; `WaitForSingleObject` waits for the application started with `CreateProcessA` to finish; and `CloseHandle` closes the application. The next bit of code uses the functions.

Example 17.3

```
  Sub Click(Source As Button)
1      RunApp("C:\Program Files\Accessories\wordpad.exe")
2      MsgBox "Wordpad has finished"
  End Sub
```

Explanation

1 Calls the `RunApp` subroutine (defined in Declarations) to run the wordpad application. Control remains in the `RunApp` subroutine until wordpad is closed.

2 Displays the messagebox once wordpad has been closed.

The next example takes advantage of the Windows API to close the current window in the Windows environment. This can be used to close Lotus Notes.

Example 17.4

The first few lines declare the Windows API routines making them available to LotusScript.

```
Const WinCLOSE = &H10
Declare Function GetForegroundWindow Lib "user32" Alias "GetForegroundWindow"
() As Long
Declare Function PostMessage Lib "user32" Alias "PostMessageA" (Byval hwnd As
Long, Byval wMsg As Long, Byval wParam As Long, Byval IParam As Long) As Long
```

Use the following line to use these functions in your code.

```
rValue = PostMessage(GetForegroundWindow, WinClose, 0, 0)
```

17.2.3 ActivateApp

Example 17.1 showed the `ActivateApp` statement in use. This statement makes a designated program window active.

```
Format:  ActivateApp <window name>
```

The window name must match the program name that appears in the title bar of the application. For example, example 17.1 activated the wordpad application by using `Document—WORDPAD` as the window name. This window name exactly matched the name that appears in the title bar of the wordpad application for a new document.

The following line would activate Microsoft Word (if it is open and running).

```
ActivateApp "Microsoft Word"
```

Note The window name parameter must not match the program title verbatim. Only the leftmost characters must be matched, so the window name "Workspace" would open Lotus Notes with the title Workspace at Home—Lotus Notes.

17.2.4 Evaluate

Evaluate allows the use of @Functions within your LotusScript. The @Functions are the predecessors to the modern LotusScript language. Development in release 3 of Lotus Notes required a certain cleverness with the use of @Functions to obtain the desired results. Nowadays, @Functions are still used in Notes/Domino, but not for the more complicated tasks. You may find yourself yearning for a certain @Function when creating a script. This is where `Evaluate` steps in.

The result of using the `Evaluate` statement is an array, `Variant` data type. If an operation returns only one value, access element zero to get the results. Certain functions like @DBColumn will return multiple values that will be accessed as separate values in the array.

Example 17.5

```
   Sub Click(Source As Button)
      Dim result
1     result = Evaluate(|@Begins("LotusScript is cool!";"LotusScript")|)
2     If (result(0) = 1) Then
         Msgbox "Yes, match found!"
      Else
         Msgbox "No match found!"
      End If
   End Sub
```

Explanation

1 The `Evaluate` function is used to take advantage of the @Begin @function. This @function determines if one string begins with another.

2 The result returns `1` for `true` if a match is found, otherwise `0` for `false`. Notice the result is returned as an array, so we access element zero.

The next example takes advantage of the @Name function.

Example 17.6

```
Sub Click(Source As Button)
   Dim username As Variant
   username = Evaluate(|@Name([CN];@UserName)|)
   MsgBox "Your common name is:  " & username(0),0,"Username"
End Sub
```

Output

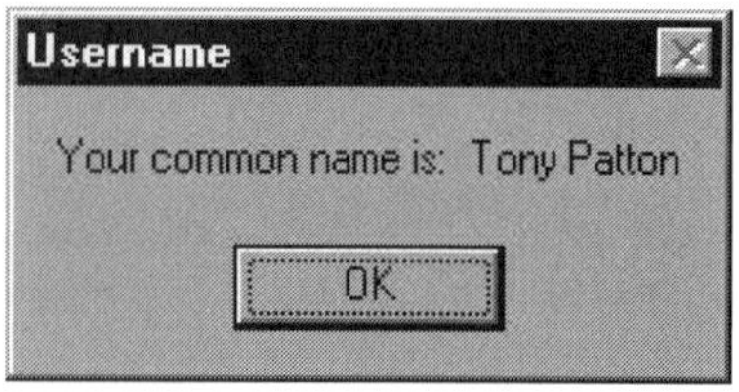

Figure 17.2 Example 17.6 output

There are numerous @Functions in Lotus Notes that provide functionality that is not readily available in LotusScript. One in particular is @ProperCase which formats a string by changing all characters in it to lowercase with the exception of the first character in each word in the string. The next bit of code demonstrates how it is used.

```
string := @ProperCase("TONY pATton")
```

The result returned in string is `"Tony Patton"`. This is a wonderful and quick solution for formatting names, among many other values. The next example uses the `Evaluate` statement to utilize the `@ProperCase` function in LotusScript.

Note Notes versions prior to 4.6.1 did not accept dynamic arguments in the Evaluate statement. That is, the `Evaluate` parameters had to be known at compile time. For this reason, example 17.7 (figure 17.3) will work only with Notes version 4.6.1 or later. Example 17.5 will work with prior versions of Lotus Notes.

Example 17.7

```
Dim rValue As Variant
Dim par1 As String, par2 As String
par1 = "wHatEVER whenEVER"
par2 = |@ProperCase("| & par1 & |")|
rValue = Evaluate(par2)
MsgBox rValue(0)
```

Output

Figure 17.3 ProperCase example

Another excellent use of the `Evaluate` command is the `@UserRoles` function. This function gives you quick and easy access to the roles for a user. This functionality is not easily available in the Lotus Notes LotusScript classes. The next example shows how `@UserRoles` may be used in script.

Example 17.8

```
Dim listOfRoles as Variant
Dim msgString As String
listOfRoles = Evaluate("@UserRoles")
Forall roles In listOfRoles
msgString = roles & Chr(10)
End Forall
MsgBox msgString
```

17.3 Chapter summary

External applications can be launched in LotusScript through the use of the `Shell` command. This allows MS-DOS or other Windows programs to be launched. Also, Windows API routines can be incorporated into LotusScript code via the `Declare` statement. Finally, the `Evaluate` statement broadens the functionality of LotusScript by making @Functions and @Commands available to LotusScript programmers.

17.4 Chapter review

- The `Shell` function allows external applications to be launched from LotusScript.
- The `ActivateApp` statement brings a window to the front by making it the active window.
- The `Declare` statement allows external C functions (such as the Windows API) to be used within LotusScript.
- `Evaluate` allows many useful @Function/@Commands to be incorporated into LotusScript code.

CHAPTER 18

LotusScript and the Web

18.1 Chapter objectives 280
18.2 Print 280
18.3 Browsers 280
18.4 Environment variables 281
18.5 Query_String 283
18.6 Chapter summary 288
18.7 Chapter review 288

18.1 Chapter objectives

- How LotusScript interacts with web browsers
- What are environment variables?
- What is Query_String?
- Running agents from a browser client
- WebQuerySave event
- WebQueryOpen event
- DocumentContext

There are a variety of scripting languages available to work within the web browser environment. JavaScript is the most popular. Microsoft has their version, Jscript, and another language derived from Visual Basic: VBScript. Unfortunately, LotusScript is not supported by *any* browser on the market. It is a proprietary language used within the Lotus family of products, period. On the other hand, Lotus Notes/Domino does allow a certain level of interaction with a browser client. This chapter focuses on this interaction.

18.2 Print

One of the most used LotusScript commands, when working with web clients, is the `Print` statement. In the Notes client environment, all print output is sent to the status bar, but it is sent to the browser window when used with a browser. This allows HTML to be sent to the browser.

Example 18.1

```
Print "<HTML><HEAD><TITLE>LotusScript Test</TITLE></HTML>"
Print "<H1>LotusScript Test</H1>"
Print "</HTML>"
```

Explanation

This outputs a standard web page with "LotusScript Test" displayed. Now, this has to be accessed by a web client to work and that involves a little more understanding of how it works.

18.3 Browsers

The connection made between a web browser client, such as Netscape Navigator, and a web server is not permanent. It is *stateless*. That is, information is sent to and from the browser and the connection is closed. For this reason, you must keep track of everything or maintain state. There are a number of techniques for achieving this type of *tracking*; one of the most popular is cookies. Basically, a cookie is a file stored on the client PC that stores information (whatever information is deemed relevant). Another method is passing hidden fields from web page to page. The technique we will work with in this chapter is using the document ID that is unique to the Domino environment.

Every document in a Notes/Domino database has its own unique document ID and we can use this to our advantage when working with browser-based clients. Before we move into utilizing it, let's look at other information that is readily available.

18.4 Environment variables

There are a number of invaluable pieces of information that are made available about the web client. This information takes the form of environment variables. These variables include information about the client, server, user, or form data. Form data is data that is entered by the user and sent to the web server.

Table 18.1

Domino environment variable	Description
AUTH_TYPE	The authentication method used to validate the user (if any).
CONTENT_LENGTH	The length of the data in bytes.
CONTENT_TYPE	The MIME type of the data.
GATEWAY_INTERFACE	The revision of the Common Gateway Interface that the server uses.
HTTP_ACCEPT	A list of the MIME types that the client can accept.
HTTP_REFERER	The URL of the document that the client accessed before accessing the current page.
HTTPS	Signals whether or not Secure Sockets Layer (SSL) is enabled on the server.
HTTP_USER_AGENT	The browser used by the client.
PATH_INFO	Extra path information.
PATH_TRANSLATED	The translated version of the path given by the `PATH_INFO` variable.
QUERY_STRING	The query information submitted; it is appended to a question mark ('?') in the URL.
REMOTE_ADDR	The IP address of the client.
REMOTE_HOST	The hostname of the client.
REMOTE_IDENT	The user making the request; not supported by most browsers.
REMOTE_USER	The authenticated name of the user. This contains a value only if the site/page has security enabled so that the user must enter a valid name/password pair to enter/view.
REQUEST_METHOD	The method with which the the request was made (POST/GET).
SCRIPT_NAME	The virtual path of the script being executed.
SERVER_NAME	The server's hostname or IP address.

Table 18.1 (continued)

Domino environment variable (continued)	Description
SERVER_PORT	The port number of the host on which the server is running; usually 80.
SERVER_PROTOCOL	The name and revision of the information protocol the request came in with.
SERVER_SOFTWARE	The name and version of the server software that is answering the client's request.
SERVER_URL_GATEWAY_INTERFACE	Version of the CGI specification to which the server adheres.

The `Environment` variables can be accessed just like any other field on a Notes form when submitted via a browser. The DocumentContext object gives a handle on a document submitted from a browser.

18.4.1 DocumentContext

One of the biggest complaints or problems when dealing with browsers is the fact that the LotusScript UI classes (NotesUIDocument, NotesUIView, etc.) are not available. The DocumentContext property of the NotesSession class fills the void. `DocumentContext` is a read-only property that allows access to documents created through the Notes API. The Domino web server creates documents through the Notes API.

The `DocumentContext` property returns a NotesDocument object. When used with the web, the NotesDocument object will represent the document submitted by a web browser. The `DocumentContext` property is used in conjuction with a Notes agent. The document is created by Domino and then runs an agent. The agent takes advantage of the `DocumentContext` property to access the newly created document in memory.

Example 18.2

```
  Sub Initialize
    Dim browser As String, referer As String
    Dim s As New NotesSession
    Dim webDoc As NotesDocument
1   Set webDoc = s.DocumentContext
2   browser = "Browser:  " & webDoc.HTTP_USER_AGENT(0)
3   referer = "Previous page:  " & webDoc.HTTP_REFERER(0)
4   Print "<HTML><HEAD><TITLE>LotusScript Example</TITLE></HEAD>"
5   Print browser
    Print referer
6   Print "</HTML>"
  End Sub
```

Explanation

1 Instantiates the NotesDocument object to the current documents.

2 Accesses the `HTTP_USER_AGENT` environment variable and stores it in a string variable.

3 Accesses the `HTTP_REFERER` environment variable and stores it in a string variable.

4 Outputs HTML header tags.

5 Prints the browser variable to the web browser.

6 Prints closing HTML tags.

The previous example demonstrates that environment variables appear as fields on the NotesDocument object returned by the `DocumentContext` property.

18.5 Query_String

A brief overview of the `Query_String` variable is in order before we move forward to techniques for utilizing it with Domino.

When information is submitted via a browser to a Domino server it is placed into the `Query_String` environment variable. This variable can be accessed via the `DocumentContext` property, but a few wrinkles are added. `Query_String` will contain all fields and their values as pairs unless otherwise specified. The pairs are connected with an equal sign. Also, all spaces are converted to pluses (+) and other nonstandard characters are converted to their hexadecimal equivalent. The field pairs are separated by ampersands.

An example of `Query_String` of a form submitted with two fields: LastName and FirstName with the values Tony and Patton:

```
http://www.myserver.com/test.nsf?OpenAgent&LastName=Patton&FirstName=Tony
```

The `Query_String` variable can be overridden with your own values, if you so desire. This is very useful for submitting a pointer to the document just submitted to your Domino server. We append the unique document ID, as the `Query_String`, when we call our agent. The following code (@functions) are included in a button formula. When the button is pressed (from a browser), the agent is executed with the unique document ID submitted in the `Query_String` environment variable.

Note Utilizing the power of LotusScript when interacting with web users requires the use of agents. The agents must be set to "Run Once ..." as the trigger option; "Manually from the actions menu" for the documents on which it acts; and it must be a shared agent.

Button formula

```
dbPath := "/" + @ReplaceSubstring(@Subset(@DbName;-1);"\\";"/");
@URLOpen(dbPath + "/WebAgent?OpenAgent&UNID=" +_
   @Text(@DocumentUniqueID))
```

Explanation

1 Sets the dbPath variable to the path of the current database.

2 The `?OpenAgent` command is used to execute an agent and pass the Unique Document ID as the `Query_String`.

Once the button is selected, the agent is executed. The agent parses the `Query_String` variable to retrieve the Document ID. The Document ID is used to locate the document in the database. The code follows:

Example 18.3

```
   Sub Initialize
      Dim session As New NotesSession
      Dim db As NotesDatabase
      Dim doc As NotesDocument, webDoc As NotesDocument
      Set db = session.CurrentDatabase
1     Set webDoc = session.DocumentContext
2     If Not (webDoc Is Nothing) Then
         Dim qsItem As NotesItem
         Dim serverItem As NotesItem
3        Set qsItem = webDoc.GetFirstItem("QUERY_STRING")
4        Set serverItem = webDoc.GetFirstItem("SERVER_NAME")
5        Print "<HTML><HEAD><TITLE>Web Agent Results</TITLE></HEAD>"
6        If ((Isnull(qsItem)) Or (Isempty(qsItem))) Then
            Print "No Query_String found.</HTML>"
            Exit Sub
         End If
7        pos = Instr(qsItem.Text,"=")
8        qsLength = Len(qsItem.Text) - pos
9        qs = Right(qsItem.Text, qsLength)
10       Set doc = db.Getdocumentbyunid(qs)
11       Call doc.Send(False,ApproversGroup)
12       Print "<CENTER>"
         Print "<H1>Results </H1>"
13       nsfPosition = Instr(webDoc.HTTP_REFERER(0),"nsf")
14       homeAddress = Left(webDoc.HTTP_REFERER(0),nsfPosition+2)
         Print "[ "
15       Print |<A HREF="| & homeAddress & |">Home Page</A> - |
16       Print |<A HREF="| & webDoc.HTTP_REFERER(0) & |">Back</A>| & Chr(13) &_
            Chr(10)
         Print " ]"
         Print "</CENTER>"
         Print "</HTML>"
      End If
   End Sub
```

Explanation

1 Sets the NotesDocument to the document created in memory by Domino.

2 Continues only if the document exists.

3 Retrieves the `QUERY_STRING` variable.

4 Retrieves the `SERVER_NAME` environment variable.

5 Sends HTML header tags to the browser.

6 Exits the agent if the environment variables are empty or null.

7 Locates the equal sign in the `Query_String`. The document ID was passed as UNID=#####, so everything to the right of the equal sign is the document ID.

8 The length of the `Query_String` variable will be everything to the right of the equal sign, so the position from the previous line is used to get its length.

9 Once we have the length from line 8, we can get the `Query_String` contents with the `Right` function.

10 Since the `Query_String` is a unique document ID, it uses the `GetDocument-ByUnid` method of NotesDatabase object to get a handle on it.

11 Mails the new document to a group of users.

12 Sends more HTML tags to the browser.

13 Searches the `HTTP_REFERER` environment variable for the substring "`nsf`". The `nsf` signals a Domino database.

14 Uses the position of the `nsf` substring from line 13 to retrieve the base URL for the database. This is the home page for the site.

15 Creates a link to the home page using the variable from line 14.

16 Sends more HTML to the browser. Creates a link to the previous page using the `HTTP_REFERER` environment variable.

Here is another agent that has no need for the `Query_String`. It prints the values of all of the environment variables.

Example 18.4

```
   Sub Initialize
     Dim s As New NotesSession
     Dim db As NotesDatabase
     Dim doc As NotesDocument
1    Dim envVariables List As String
     Set db = s.CurrentDatabase
2    Set doc = s.DocumentContext
3    envVariables("Auth_Type") = doc.Auth_Type(0)
     envVariables("Content_Length") = doc.Content_Length(0)
     envVariables("Content_Type") = doc.Content_Type(0)
     envVariables("Gateway_Interface") = doc.Gateway_Interface(0)
     envVariables("HTTP_Accept") = doc.HTTP_Accept(0)
     envVariables("HTTP_Referer") = doc.HTTP_Referer(0)
     envVariables("HTTPS") = doc.HTTPS(0)
     envVariables("HTTP_User_Agent") = doc.HTTP_User_Agent(0)
```

```
    envVariables("Path_Info") = doc.Path_Info(0)
    envVariables("Path_Translated") = doc.Path_Translated(0)
    envVariables("Query_String") = doc.Query_String(0)
    envVariables("Remote_Addr") = doc.Remote_Addr(0)
    envVariables("Remote_Host") = doc.Remote_Host(0)
    envVariables("Remote_Ident") = doc.Remote_Ident(0)
    envVariables("Remote_User") = doc.Remote_User(0)
    envVariables("Request_Method") = doc.Request_Method(0)
    envVariables("Script_Name") = doc.Script_Name(0)
    envVariables("Server_Name") = doc.Server_Name(0)
    envVariables("Server_Port") = doc.Server_Port(0)
    envVariables("Server_Protocol") = doc.Server_Protocol(0)
    envVariables("Server_Software") = doc.Server_Software(0)
    envVariables("Server_URL_Gateway_Interface") =_
      doc.Server_URL_Gateway_Interface(0)
4   print "<HTML><HEAD><TITLE>Environment Variables</TITLE></HEAD>"
    print "<BR><BR>"
5   Forall v in envVariables
6     print ListTag(v) & " - " & v & "<BR>"
    End Forall
    Print "<BR><BR>"
7   Print "</HTML>"
End Sub
```

Explanation

1 Declares List of strings to store environment variables and labels.

2 Gets the document submitted by the browser.

3 Adds the environment variables to the list. Their name is the list index value.

4 Sends HTML header tags to the browser window.

5 Loops through all elements in the list.

6 Sends the element index value (listtag) and its contents to the browser with an HTML break appended.

7 Ends HTML tag.

18.5.1 Events

There are two events that you need to be concerned with when dealing with web-based clients. Both events are new to version 4.6 of Notes/Domino.

The format for both events is as follows.

```
@Command([ToolsRunMacro]; "<Your agent goes here>")
```

This is the default setting of the events, so the name of the agent to run is inserted in the quotation marks.

18.5.2 *WebQueryOpen*

This event is triggered before the page is presented to the user; that is, before the Domino server converts it to HTML for viewing by the browser. The document data cannot be accessed and/or modified. Also, any output (such as print statements) are ignored.

Example 18.4 could have taken advantage of this event.

Note This event can be similated on a 4.5 server through the use of a hidden field, $$QueryOpenAgent.

18.5.3 *WebQuerySave*

This event is triggered just before a document is sent to the Domino server. The document data can be accessed or modifed. Output can be sent to the browser window with the print statement.

Example 18.3 could have used this event instead of a button.

Note This event can be simulated on a 4.5 server through the use of a hidden field, $$QuerySaveAgent.

18.5.4 *Executing agents*

There are four ways to execute LotusScript agents from a browser.

1 *`?OpenAgent`* The name of the agent to run proceeds the `?OpenAgent` command. Any values to pass into the agent (in the `Query_String`) immediately follow the command.

   Ex: `http://www.myserver.com/test.nsf/agentName?OpenAgent`

2 *`?CreateDocument`* The use of the `?CreateDocument` command takes advantage of the `WebQueryOpen` event. When this command is used, the Domino server creates a document and executes the agent specified, if any, in the `WebQueryOpen` event (or QueryOpenAgent field in release 4.5).

   Ex: `http://www.myserver.com/test.nsf/formname?CreateDocument`

3 *`?OpenDocument`* The use of the `?OpenDocument` command takes advantage of the `WebQueryOpen` event as well. When this command is used, the Domino server opens the specified document and executes the agent specified, if any, in the `WebQueryOpen` event (or QueryOpenAgent field in release 4.5).

4 *Submit button* When a document is saved/submitted on a Domino server, any agent specified in the `WebQuerySave` (or QuerySaveAgent field in release 4.5) will be executed.

18.5.5 *Web Navigator database(s)*

The Notes client and Domino server include Web Navigator database templates that can be used to access data on the Internet. The Server Web Navigator resides on the server; it allows web pages to be cached and shared via Notes clients. The users can use the Personal Web Navigator database to view pages from the server database or straight from the Internet. There are a few LotusScript methods that are specifically designed for use with these databases.

The `getDocumentByURL` method in the NotesDatabase class instantiates a document in the web navigator database and returns a NotesDocument object for it.

Example 18.5

```
    Dim s As New NotesSession
    Dim db As NotesDatabase
    Dim doc As NotesDocument
    Set db = s.CurrentDatabase
1   Set doc = db.GetDocumentByURL("http://www.BaseLineInc.com",1)
```

Explanation

1 Instantiates the NotesDocument object to the specified web page. The `1` parameter tells the system to reload the page from the Internet.

Note There are numerous optional parameters for the `GetDocument-ByURL` method. Check the Notes Help database for more details.

Example 18.6

```
  Sub Initialize
1    Set w = New NotesUIWorkspace
2    w.URLOpen("http://www.lotus.com")
  End Sub
```

Explanation

1 Instantiates a new NotesUIWorkspace object to the current workspace.

2 The `URLOpen` method of the NotesUIWorkspace object to opens a web page in the Web Navigator database defined in the Location document on the Notes Client.

18.6 Chapter summary

Your investment in the LotusScript language does not lose its value when dealing with browser-based clients. An understanding of the interaction between the browser and the Domino server is very important for the creation of proper LotusScript. When dealing with browsers, LotusScript agents are the only form of LotusScript that can be used. This stems from the fact that the only player in the interaction that will support LotusScript will be the Domino server (on which the agents will run). The agents can be triggered (kicked off) any number of ways, and the agents can perform all necessary operations through the use of the CGI environment variables.

18.7 Chapter review

- `HTTP environment` variables can be easily accessed in LotusScript.
- The `WebQueryOpen` and `WebQuerySave` events are triggered by browser clients.

- The `DocumentContext` property allows documents submitted by a browser (such as Opera) to be easily accessed in LotusScript.
- Document IDs can be passed into an agent via the `Query_String` environment variable. This allows the document to be easily accessed using its unique id.
- The Web Navigator database (local or on server) can be used to retrieve pages from the Internet.

CHAPTER 19

Input validation, NotesAgent class, and script libraries

19.1 Chapter objectives 292
19.2 Validation 292
19.3 NotesAgent class 296
19.4 RunOnServer 298
19.5 Script libraries 299
19.6 Chapter summary 300
19.7 Chapter review 301

19.1 *Chapter objectives*

- Using LotusScript for validating fields
- Working with the NotesAgent class
- Working with Script libraries

19.2 *Validation*

Data validation is a critical aspect of good application design. You have to make sure that users enter values into fields, and take it a step further by checking for appropriate values.

19.2.1 *Input validation*

Every editable field contains an Input Validation event. Unfortunately, only @Functions can be used with them. Another drawback to this approach is that a separate dialog box is presented for every field that takes advantage of Input Validation. For example, if you have ten fields then the user would be presented with ten separate message boxes if they failed the Input Validation formula. This is a bit too much.

19.2.2 *QuerySave event*

One solution is to take advantage of the `QuerySave` event of a form or subform. This gives you the power to check multiple fields and present one message box telling the user which fields need to be checked.

Example 19.1

```
Sub QuerySave(Source As Notesuidocument, Continue As Variant)
     Dim fieldCheck1 As String, fieldCheck2 As String, fieldCheck3 As String
     Dim msgBody As String, msgTitle As String
     Dim flag
1    fieldCheck1 = "name"
     fieldName1 = "Name"
     fieldCheck2 = "address"
2    fieldName2 = "Address"
     fieldCheck3 = "phone"
     fieldName3 = "Phone Number
3    If (Source.FieldGetText(fieldCheck1) = "") Then
4       msgBody = msgBody & "  - " & fieldName1 & Chr(10)
5       flag = True
     End If
     If (Source.FieldGetText(fieldCheck2) = "") Then
        msgBody = msgBody & "  - " & fieldName2 & Chr(10)
        flag = True
     End If
     If (Source.FieldGetText(fieldCheck3) = "") Then
        msgBody = msgBody & "  - " & fieldName3 & Chr(10)
        flag = True
     End If
```

```
6     If (flag) Then
7        msgTitle = "Please fill in the following fields before saving:"
8        MsgBox msgTitle & Chr(10) & msgBody,64,"Input Error"
9        Continue = False
      End If
   End Sub
```

Explanation

1 Sets the name of the field(s) to check.

2 Sets the label name of the field(s) to check. They will be used to tell the user which fields need to be corrected.

3 The `FieldGetText` method of the NotesUIDocument class checks for missing values in the field.

4 If the field is blank, assembles the message to display to the user.

5 Sets the flag to `true` to signal that fields were missing.

6 A `true` value in the flag variable signals that there was at least one field missing.

7 Assembles the title for the message box.

8 Tells the user which fields he/she needs to correct.

9 Sets the Continue flag to false to abort the saving of the document. The variable continue is passed into the `QuerySave` event.

19.2.3 Field exit event

Fields on a Notes form have `Entering` and `Exiting` events. The `Entering` event is triggered when the field gets focus (mouse click, tab key, or arrow keys), and the `Exiting` event triggers when the field loses focus (mouse click, tab key, or arrow keys). The `Exiting` event can be used to validate a field's contents. The value will be verified when the user attempts to leave the field.

Example 19.2

```
1     Sub Exiting(Source As Field)
      Dim uiw As New NotesUIWorkspace
      Dim uidoc As NotesUIDocument
2     Set uidoc = uiw.CurrentDocument
      Dim company As String
3     company = uidoc.FieldGetText("company")
4     If (company = "") Then
         Print "Please enter company name."
5        Call uidoc.GotoField("company")
      End If
   End Sub
```

> *Warning* One field's `Exiting` event is another's `Entering` event. Be forewarned that weird behavior may appear when both are used in different fields on the same form.

Explanation

1 The beginning of the `Exiting` event sub for the company field.

2 Sets the NotesUIDocument object to the currently open document.

3 Retrieves the value entered in the company field.

4 Notifies the user if the company is blank/empty.

5 Places the cursor in the company field until a value is entered.

19.2.4 Unique values

In addition to checking field values, there are times when an item entered needs to be confirmed as unique or it has not been previously entered. For example, you wouldn't want the same work order entered twice. The next example shows the use of script for checking for existing documents with the same work order number.

Example 19.3

```
1   Function CheckForExistingTasks(passedKey As String) As NotesDocument
      Dim s As New NotesSession
      Dim db As NotesDatabase
      Dim view As NotesView
      Set db = s.CurrentDatabase
2     Set view = db.GetView("(WorkOrders)")
3     Set CheckForExistingTasks = view.GetDocumentByKey(passedKey,True)
    End Function

4   Sub CreateWorkOrder(pUI As NotesUIWorkspace, pUIDoc as NotesUIDocument,_
      pJobName As String)
      Dim doc As NotesDocument
      Dim searchString As String
      Dim woDoc As NotesUIDocument
      Set reqDoc = pUIDoc.Document
5     searchString = Trim$(reqDoc.JobNumber(0)) & Trim$(pJobName)
6     Set doc = CheckForExistingTasks(searchString)
7     If (doc Is Nothing) Then
8        Set woDoc =  passedUIW.ComposeDocument("","","WorkOrder")
         Call woDoc.FieldSetText("JobName",pJobName)
         Call woDoc.FieldSetText("WorkStatus","Open")
      Else
         Messagebox "I'm sorry that work order already exists for this" & _
         "Job.",64,"Work Order exists"
      End If

9   Sub Click(Source As Button)
      Dim uiw As New NotesUIWorkspace
      Dim uidoc As NotesUIDocument
      Set uidoc = uiw.CurrentDocument
10    Call CreateWorkOrder(uiw,uidoc,"WorkOrder")
    End Sub
```

Explanation

1 This function is used later, but it searches for an existing document. If the search returns nothing, a new document is created.

2 Uses a hidden view to conduct the search.

3 Uses the `GetDocumentByKey` method of the NotesView class to search for an existing document.

4 Creates a work order. It checks for an existing order, and creates one if nothing is found. It accepts a NotesUIWorkspace object, NotesUIDocument object, and the job name.

5 Creates the search string.

6 Calls the function from step 1 to check for an existing document.

7 Creates a document if one is not found.

8 Composes a new document.

9 The script for an Action button. Fires the click event when the button is clicked.

10 Calls the sub from step 4 to start the process of creating a work order.

19.2.5 ComputeWithForm

The `ComputeWithForm` method of the NotesDocument class allows a document to be validated through the backend (the document is not open/visible). The method executes default value, input translation, and input validation formulas. Also, fields that obtain their values from @DBLookup/@DBColumn formulas are refreshed as well.

`ComputeWithForm` accepts two Boolean parameters: the first is ignored so specify either `True` or `False`, the second signals whether an error is raised if an input validation formula fails. A return value of `False` is returned if any errors are raised (and second parameter is `True`).

Example 19.4

```
  Sub Initialize
     Dim s As New NotesSession
     Dim db As NotesDatabase
     Dim view As NotesView
     Dim doc As NotesDocument
     Set db = s.CurrentDatabase
     Set view = db.GetView("New Docs")
     Set doc = view.GetFirstDocument
1    While Not (doc Is Nothing)
2       returnFlag = doc.ComputeWithForm(False,True)
3       If (returnFlag) Then
           Call doc.Save(True,False)
        End If
        Set doc = view.GetNextDocument(doc)
     Wend
  End Sub
```

Explanation

1 Processes all documents in the view.

2 Calls the `ComputeWithForm` method. The second parameter (`True`) tells the system to return a value of `False` if, and only if, any input validation formulas fail on the form.

3 Saves the document if `True` is returned by the `ComputeWithForm` method (no input validation errors).

LotusScript offers more power and flexibility when it comes to data validation, but the Input Validation formula is very powerful as well. The choice of the two comes down to the needs of the application and preference of the developer.

19.3 NotesAgent class

Agents allow tasks to be automated within the Notes/Domino environment. The NotesAgent class provides a means to work with agents within scripts. There are various properties that provide valuable information and methods to work with agents (figure 19.1).

Example 19.5

```
   Sub Initialize
      Dim s As New NotesSession
      Dim db As NotesDatabase, pDB As NotesDatabase
1     Dim agent As NotesAgent
      Set db = s.CurrentDatabase
2     Forall agents In db.Agents
         msg = ""
3        msg = msg & "Common Owner:  " & agents.CommonOwner & Chr(10)
4        msg = msg & "Enabled:  " & agents.IsEnabled & Chr(10)
5        msg = msg & "Public:  " & agents.IsPublic & Chr(10)
6        msg = msg & "Last ran:  " & agents.LastRun & Chr(10)
7        msg = msg & "Query:  " & agents.Query & Chr(10)
8        If (agents.ServerName = "") Then
            msg = msg & "Server Name:  " & "<Local>" & Chr(10)
         Else
            msg = msg & "Server Name:  " & agents.ServerName & Chr(10)
         End If
9        msg = msg & "Comments:  " & agents.Comment & Chr(10)
10       Set pDB = agents.Parent
11       msg = msg & "Database:  " & pDB.Title & Chr(10)
12       MsgBox msg,64,"Agent:  " & agents.Name
      End Forall
   End Sub
```

Explanation

1 Declares a new NotesAgent object.

2 Uses a `Forall` loop to access all agents in the database. The Agents property of the NotesDatabase class returns an array of NotesAgent objects.

3 Uses the String variable `msg` to assemble agent information for displaying in a message box. The `CommonOwner` property returns the common name of the user who last saved the agent.

4 The `IsEnabled` property returns `True` or `False` whether or not the agent is set to run.

5 The `IsPublic` property returns `True` or `False` whether or not the agent is shared (public).

6 The `LastRun` property returns the date and time the agent last ran.

7 The `Query` property returns any additional search criteria added via the Search button in the agent.

8 The `ServerName` property returns the name of the server on which the agent runs/lives. It returns an empty string if it is local.

9 The `Comment` property returns any comments entered by the agent developer.

10 The `Parent` property returns a NotesDatabase object pointing to the database container of the agent.

11 Retrieves the database title from the parent database object.

12 Displays the results of the agent.

Output:

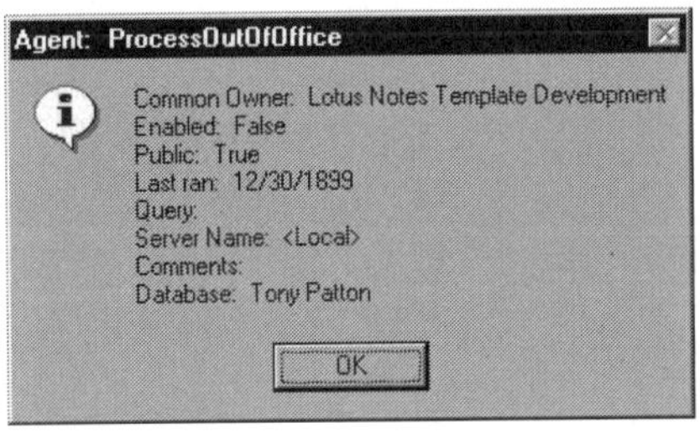

Figure 19.1
Agent in Notes Mail template

In addition to the information that can be retrieved about agents, a few actions can be performed on them. Agents can be deleted from a database via the `Remove` method. The `Save` method writes any modifications to an agent to disk. The Run method allows agents to be executed by another agent. Agents cannot call the `Run` method on themselves, and the debugger will not step into an agent that is called via that method.

Example 19.6

```
  Sub Initialize
    Dim db As New NotesDatabase("ServerName","test.nsf")
    Dim agent As NotesAgent
1   Set agent = db.GetAgent("Test")
2   If Not (agent Is Nothing) Then
3     Call agent.Run
```

```
    End If
End Sub
```

Explanation

1. Sets the NotesAgent object to the agent named `Test`. The `GetAgent` method of the NotesDatabase class is used; it accepts the agent name as its only parameter.
2. Continues only if the agent does exist.
3. Runs the agent. The agent will be run by the workstation on which the script is executed.

Example 19.7

```
  Sub Initialize
     Dim db As New NotesDatabase("ServerName","test.nsf")
     Dim agent As NotesAgent
1    aName = InputBox("Please enter name of agent to delete.")
     If (Len(aName) > 1) Then
2       Set agent = db.GetAgent(aName)
        If Not (agent Is Nothing) Then
3          Call agent.Remove
        Else
           MsgBox "The agent named " & aName & "does not exist.",33,_
              "Agent not found.")
        End If
     End If
  End Sub
```

Explanation

1. The name of the agent to delete.
2. Sets the NotesAgent object to the agent specified by the user. The `GetAgent` method of the NotesDatabase class is used.
3. Deletes the agent from the database.

19.4 RunOnServer

Many agents are written to specifically run on a Domino server and problems arise when attempting to test such an agent. The developer does not always have access to the server to test the agent by running it from the server workstation. For this reason, the `RunOnServer` method was introduced. `RunOnServer` allows an agent to be specifically run on a server. The method returns an error if it is referenced for a local agent.

> *Note* `RunOnServer` cannot be called from within its own script. Also, it is not a Boolean property that can be set to true or false to signal whether to run on server or not.

Example 19.8

```
  Sub Initialize
1    Dim db As New NotesDatabase("server name","test.nsf")
     Dim theAgent As NotesAgent
2    Set theAgent = db.GetAgent("TestAgent")
     If Not (theAgent Is Nothing) Then
3       Call theAgent.RunOnServer
     End If
  End Sub
```

Explanation

1 Sets up the database object that contains the agent to run.

2 Gets a handle on the agent to run.

3 Uses the `RunOnServer` method to run the agent on the server.

Note The `RunOnServer` method returns True if the agent ran successfully and `False` otherwise.

The `RunOnServer` method is a blessing for all Notes/Domino developers. Finally, there is an easy way to test server-based agents.

19.5 Script libraries

Common routines/functions are used extensively in many applications. Other programming languages such as C (#include) and Java (import) provide a mechanism for code sharing/reuse. Code is placed in one location and accessed by many different scripts. This reduces the likelihood of errors; there is only one place where the code must be edited if changes are needed or bugs are found.

The Notes/Domino development environment has provided the Script Library. Script libraries allow code to be shared among many elements in a database and across different databases (if properly configured). Script libraries can be used across several databases by copying the script library from one database to another, and selecting yes to the question of whether the script library design should be inherited.

Script libraries are listed under the Design twistie for a database just below Navigators. A new script library can be created using Create | Design | Script Library.

I love to use script libraries to define constants that are used throughout an application. This allows the constants to be updated in one and only one location, reducing maintenance time.

Example 19.9

```
[Options]

Option Public
Const "path" = "C:\test"
Const "name" = "test"
```

Explanation

The Script Library defines two constants named *path* and *name* that can be used in scripts that use the library.

19.5.1 Using script libraries

The `Use` command makes the contents of a script library available in another script.

Format:

```
Use "library name"
```

The `Use` command is placed in the Options section of the script. Once added, all aspects of a script library are made available to the other script. If we save the script library from example 19.9 as *Test,* we would use it like this:

```
[Options}
Use "Test"
```

Note The contents of a script library are seen as part of a script, so no functions, subs, or variables in the two can have the same name. The system will not allow the script to be saved if there are conflicts.

19.6 Chapter summary

This chapter covered a few topics that individually would not merit a complete chapter, but are very important taken together. Form validation can be streamlined with Lotus-

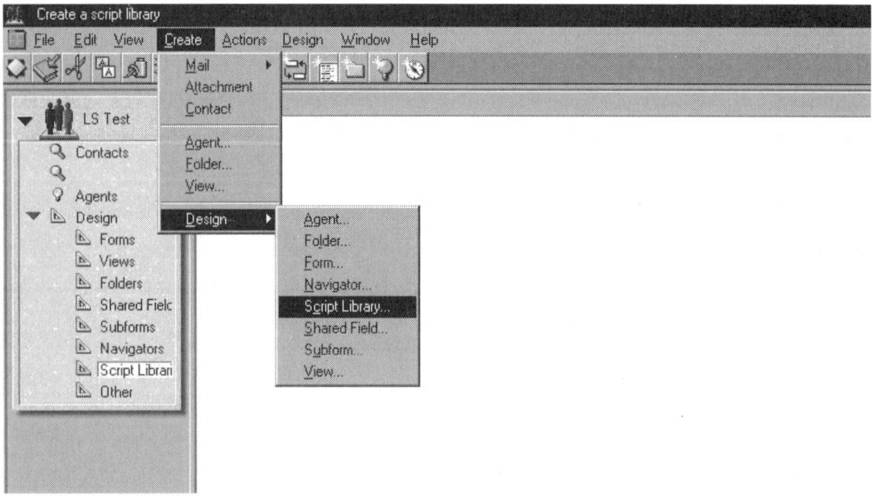

Figure 19.2 Creating a script library

Script, thus reducing the number of dialog boxes displayed. The NotesAgent class allows agents to be accessed through script, and script libraries are a wonderful design feature that facilitates code reuse and can cut develoment and maintenance times.

19.7 Chapter review

- Field `Exiting` events can be used for field validation, but the user must enter the field for it to be triggered.
- The `ComputeWithForm` method of the NotesDocument class recalculates field values on a document.
- The `QuerySave` event of NotesDocuments facilitates field validation.
- The NotesAgent class allows access to agents in script.
- The `RunOnServer` method of the NotesAgent class allows agents to be run on a server from a workstation.
- Script libraries allow code to be reused/shared.

CHAPTER 20

Notes 5.0

20.1 Chapter objectives 304
20.2 Integrated development environment 305
20.3 Other enhancements 327
20.4 Chapter summary 327
20.5 Chapter review 328

20.1 Chapter objectives

- IDE enhancements
- Performance enhancements
- New variable types
- Threads
- NotesOutline class
- NotesOutlineEntry class
- NotesUIWorkspace class enhancements
- FileOpenDialog, PickList, Prompt
- Spelling checker
- NotesDocumentCollection class enhancements
- Generating HTML
- NotesReplication class
- NotesRichTextParagraphStyle class
- NotesViewEntryCollection class
- NotesViewEntry class
- NotesUIView class enhancements
- NotesUIDatabase class enhancements
- NotesAgent class enhancements
- NotesACL/ACLEntry class enhancements
- Events
- Other enhancements

The rise of Java and its introduction into the Notes/Domino development environment has led many to predict the demise of LotusScript. Java was introduced into Notes with release 4.6, and the evolution continues with 5.0. The development environment for 5.0 allows Java to be used for coding everything from events to agents, and the code can be entered directly into the IDE.

On the other hand, LotusScript continues to evolve. Notes 5.0 has introduced LotusScript 4.0 with many new classes, and various methods and properties have been added to existing classes, and the IDE has been enhanced. LotusScript is not dead.

20.2 *Integrated development environment*

The browser checkbox (see chapter 1) has been replaced with a window on the left side of the IDE (figure 20.1) with two tabs: ObjectView and InfoView. The ObjectView tab shows all events/subroutines for the currently selected object. The InfoView tab serves the same purpose as the browser from version 4.6 (figure 20.2).

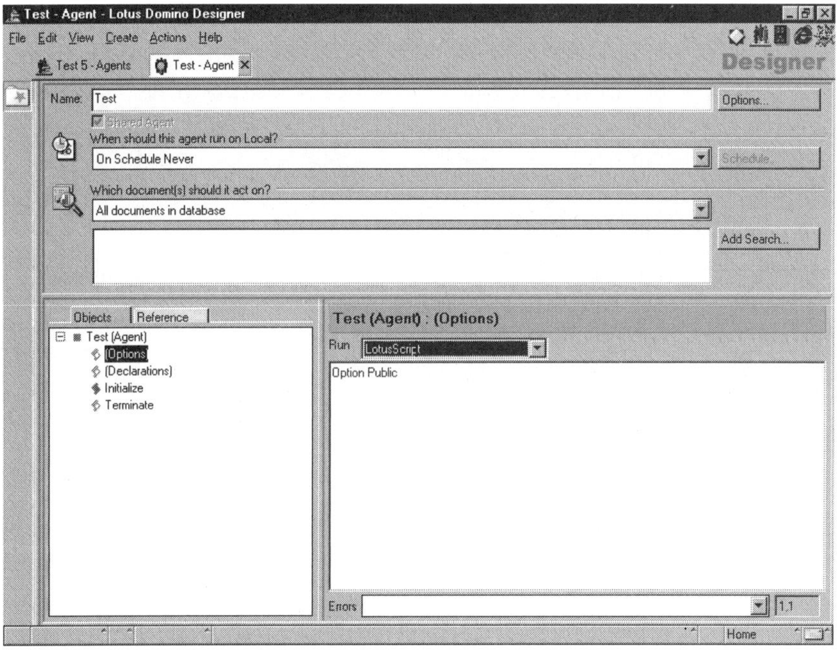

Figure 20.1 Notes 5.0 IDE - ObjectView

Figures 20.1 and 20.2 showcase one of the enhancements to Notes with version 5.0. All current windows on the workspace are listed as tabs just below the toolbar and above the ObjectView/InfoView tabs from Figure 20.2. Also, it allows LotusScript to be indented or not. Indenting is turned on/off through the properties dialog box for the design pane (figure 20.3).

Note The @Function and @Command buttons have been removed from the IDE. They are now listed in the InfoView tab.

Notes 4.x made printing scripts a real pain. The script had to be exported and opened with an editor or word processor for printing. Version 5.0 allows scripts to be printed directly from the IDE. Right-click in the designing pane (figure 20.4) and print (print is a selection) the code from the window.

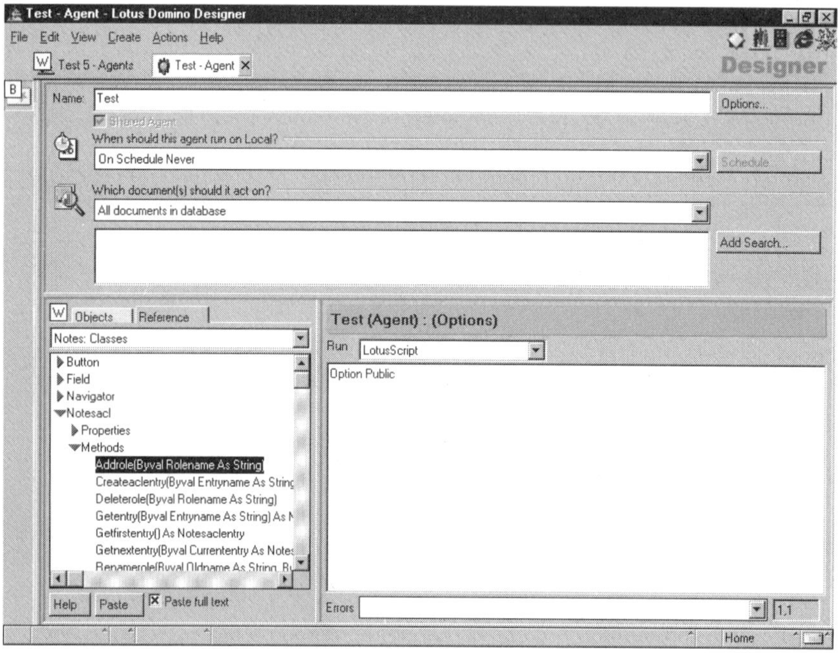

Figure 20.2 Notes 5.0 IDE - InfoView

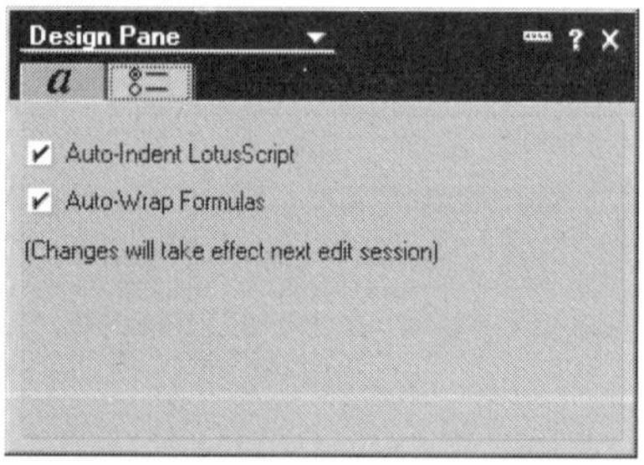

Figure 20.3 Design pane properties

Another great feature added to the 5.0 IDE is the inclusion of the row and column number of the current cursor position. This is displayed in the lower right portion of the IDE. Figure 20.5 shows that the cursor is currently on row nineteen and column seven. This is most useful when errors are encountered. The errors box will show you the line in which errors occur and the position box can help you find them quickly.

New design elements such as script libraries and agents are now created via buttons in their respective locations in the IDE. Figure 20.6 shows the button to create a script library.

20.2.1 Performance

LotusScript 4.0 is used in Notes/Domino 5.0 and it is backward compatible to LotusScript 3 code developed in Notes 4.x. Also there have been several performance enhancements:

- Script libraries load much faster.

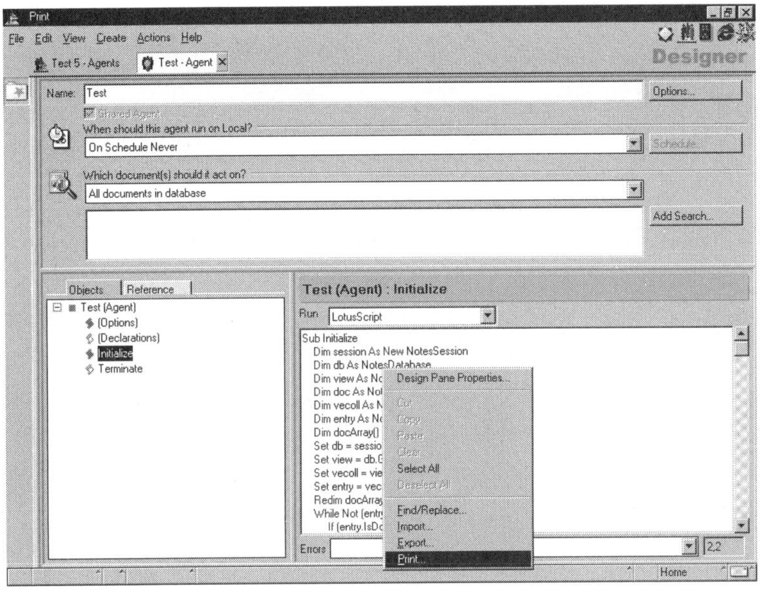

Figure 20.4 Printing a script

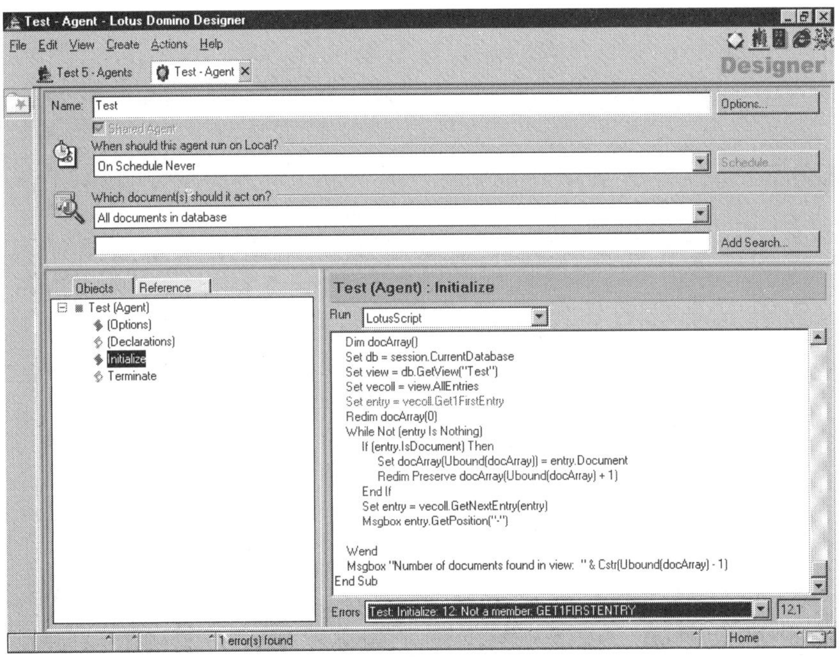

Figure 20.5 The position box (bottom right) shows the current postion of cursor (row, column)

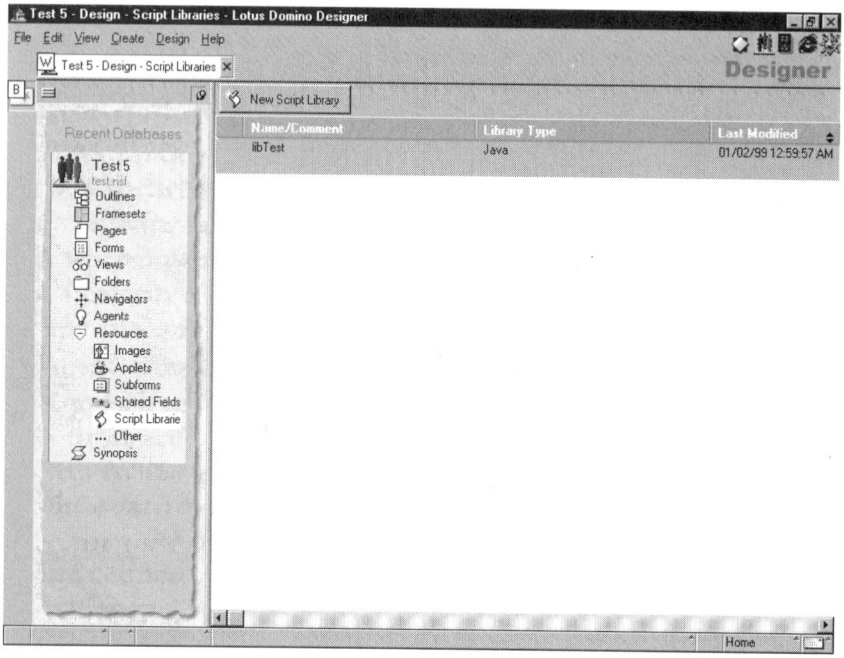

Figure 20.6 New script library button

- Total size of compiled code is now limited to 2GB up from 64K.
- Array size increased from 64K to 8 dimensions with dimensions from -32768 to 32768.
- String limit increased to 2GB from 64K.
- Stack size has been increased.

The new 2GB ceiling for scripts is by far my favorite. It allows a script's size to increase without the usual never-ending worries about size.

20.2.2 Forward references

LotusScript 4.0 allows functions and methods to be referenced/called before they have been defined. This is available in most other languages. It is called forward referencing.

```
Class ForwardRef
   Sub sub1()
      Call sub2()   ' This is a forward reference
   End Sub
   Sub sub2()
      Call sub1()
   End Sub
End Class
```

20.2.3 *Variable types*

Two new variable types have been added to LotusScript 4.0: `byte` and `Object`.

- *`byte`* Integer value from 0 to 255.

  ```
  Dim variable As byte
  ```

- *`Object`* Reference to a Notes/Domino or OLE object.

  ```
  Dim generic As Object
  ```

20.2.4 *Threads*

LotusScript is multithreaded. A thread is a thread of control in a script. A script or section of a script can run independently of other threads within the script/application. This allows more than one process to start/run simultaneously. The following commands will be used to work with threads:

- `Sleep`
- `CreateLock`
- `CodeLock`
- `CodeUnlock`
- `CodeLockCheck`
- `DestroyLock`
- `GetThreadInfo`

20.2.5 *Classes*

Note The new classes, methods, and properties (Notes 5.0 Developer Test Build 2) are listed in appendix B and denoted as such.

20.2.6 *NotesOutline*

There is a new design component called an outline. An outline provides a site map of a database, and it is presented in the left pane (folders in version 4.6) when a database is opened. Links to URLs, databases, views, documents, and so forth. can be included in the outline. The outline gives much more control over the appearance of items in the folder pane. Outlines are created and entries are added in the development environment. Figure 20.7 shows the creation of an outline. Buttons are provided to add entries, indent entries, outdent entries, generate the default outline, and save the outline.

Each of the entries added to an outline (from figure 20.7) appear when the database is opened (figure 20.8).

The NotesOutline and NotesOutlineEntry classes are provided to work with this new design element.

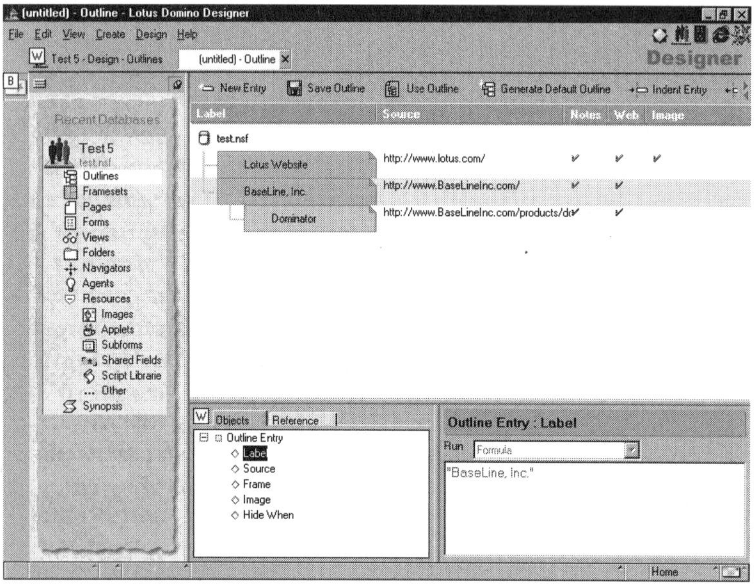

Figure 20.7 Creating an outline

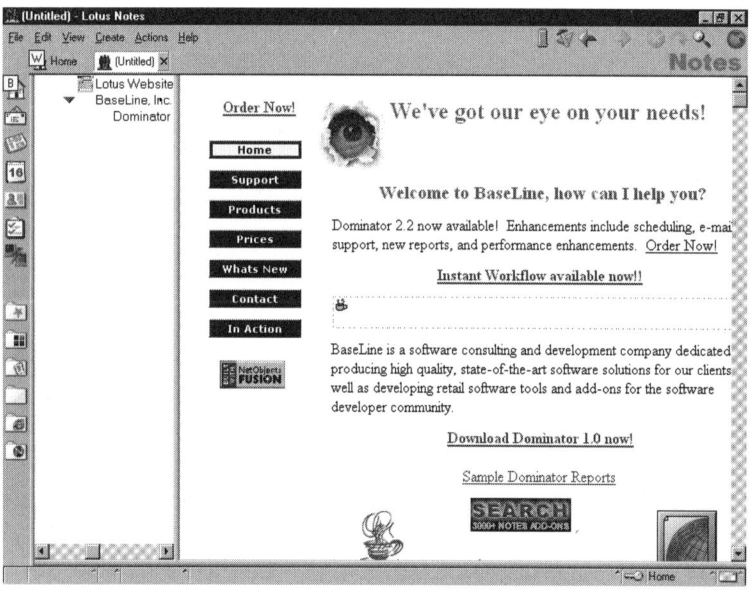

Figure 20.8 Outline presented when database opens

20.2.7 NotesOutlineEntry

The NotesOutlineEntry class enables you to access individual entries in an outline. The next example accesses the outline for the current database and scrolls through every entry in it.

Example 20.1

```
    Sub Initialize
      Dim s As New NotesSession
      Dim db As NotesDatabase
      Set db = s.CurrentDatabase
1     Dim out As New NotesOutline(db)
2     Dim outent As NotesOutlineEntry
3     Set outent = out.GetFirst
4     While Not (outent Is Nothing)
5       If (outent.IsInThisDB) Then
6         MsgBox "(Outline entry:  " & outent.TitleText &_
            " is in this database."
        Else
          MsgBox "(Outline entry:  " & outent.TitleText &_
            " is not in this database."
        End If
7       Set outent = out.GetNext(outent)
      Wend
    End Sub
```

Explanation

1 Declares a new NotesOutline object. It accepts the name of the database for the outline.

2 Declares a new NotesOutlineEntry object. It will be used to access individual entries from the previous step.

3 Sets the NotesOutlineEntry object to the first entry in the NotesOutline object through the use of the `GetFirst` method.

4 Loops through the entries until no more are found (`Nothing`).

5 Uses the `IsInThisDB` property to check if the entry is in the current database. An entry to an element in the database such as a view or document would return `True`. Entries that contain URLs would return `False`.

6 Displays message stating that the entry is not in the database with its title. The `TitleText` property returns the title assigned to an entry during creation.

7 Uses the `GetNextEntry` method of the NotesOutline class to access the next entry from the outline (if it exists). The current entry is passed as the position to use for retrieving the next entry.

Working with an outline is similar to working with document collections and views. All have methods for accessing the first item, next item, last item, previous item, and so forth. The following list shows more methods of the NotesOutline class.

20.2.8 NotesOutline class methods

```
1   AddEntry(NotesOutlineEntry)
2   Clear
3   GetFirst
4   GetLast
5   GetLevel(NotesOutlineEntry)
6   GetNext(NotesOutlineEntry)
7   GetNextSibling(NotesOutlineEntry)
8   GetParent(NotesOutlineEntry)
9   GetPrev(NotesOutlineEntry)
10  GetPrevSibling(NotesOutlineEntry)
11  MoveEntries(NotesOutlineEntry, NotesOutlineEntry,NotesOutLineEntry)
12  MoveEntry(NotesOutlineEntry, NotesOutlineEntry)
13  New(NotesDatabase)
14  RemoveEntry(NotesOutlineEntry)
```

Explanation

1 Adds the NotesOutlineEntry passed into it to the outline.

2 Clears all entries from the outline.

3 Retrieves the first entry from the outline.

4 Retrieves the last entry from the outline.

5 Retrieves the level number (position) of the entry in the outline.

6 Retrieves the next entry from the outline, using an entry as a reference point.

7 Retrieves the next entry at the same level of the entry passed into it.

8 Retrieves the parent entry for an entry.

9 Retrieves the previous entry from the outline, using an entry as a reference point.

10 Retrieves the previous entry at the same level of the entry passed into it.

11 Moves entries starting at the first entry passed and ending with the last entry passed into it to the location specified by the last entry.

12 Moves one entry.

13 Declares a new NotesOutline object.

14 Removes the designated entry from the outline.

The NotesOutlineEntry class has properties that signal the type of entry, where it is located, its title, and so forth.

20.2.9 NotesOutlineEntry class properties

- `HasChildren` Signals whether or not the entry has children.
- `IsAutoSorted` signals whether or not the entry is sorted.
- `IsExpandable` signals whether or not the entry is expandable (has children).
- `IsHidden` signals whether or not it is a hidden entry.
- `IsInThisDB` signals whether or not the entry points to an element in the current database.
- `IsTemporary` signals whether or not the entry is temporary.
- `Level` returns an entry's position within an outline.
- `TitleText` the title of the entry.
- `Type` the type of entry.

20.2.10 NotesUIWorkspace

Two valuable properties have been added to the NotesUIWorkspace class: `CurrentDatabase` and `CurrentView`. These properties allow you to access the currently open database and/or view. NotesSession, NotesView, and NotesDatabase objects had to be used with earlier versions to obtain a handle on these elements. The next example, a variation from example 20.1, takes advantage of the `CurrentDatabase` property.

Example 20.2

```
    Sub Initialize
1       Dim uiw As New NotesUIWorkspace
2       Dim uidb As NotesUIDatabase
3       Set uidb = uiw.CurrentDatabase
4       Dim out As New NotesOutline(uidb.Database)
        Dim outent As NotesOutlineEntry
        Set outent = out.GetFirst
        While Not (outent Is Nothing)
          If (outent.IsInThisDB) Then
            MsgBox "(Outline entry:  " & outent.TitleText &_
              " is in this database."
          Else
            MsgBox "(Outline entry:  " & outent.TitleText &_
              " is not in this database."
          End If
          Set outent = out.GetNext(outent)
        Wend
5       Call uiw.SetCurrentLocation("Home")
    End Sub
```

Explanation

1 Declares a new NotesUIWorkspace object to set up our environment.

2 Declares a new NotesUIDatabase object.

3 Obtains a handle on the current database through the `CurrentDatabase` property of the NotesUIWorkspace class. The property returns a NotesUIDatabase object.

4 Passes a NotesDatabase object to create a NotesOutline object through the use of the `Database` property of the NotesUIDataBase class. It returns a NotesDatabase object.

5 SetCurrentLocation, a new method allows the current location to be changed through script or user interaction. If the location name parameter is omitted (empty string ""), the change location dialog box is presented to the user.

20.2.11 User interaction

The NotesUIWorkspace contains a few new methods that allow more interaction with the user. `OpenFileDialog` displays the Open File dialog box, and allows the user to specify files to open. It returns the names of the file selected or empty if no selections are made.

20.2.12 File open

Example 20.3

```
  Sub Initialize
       Dim uiw As New NotesUIWorkspace
       Dim filesSelected As Variant
1      filesSelected = uiw.OpenFileDialog(False, _
          "Select files to open.", "|Text Files|*.txt","C:\")
2      If (filesSelected(0) = "") Then
          Print "You selected no files to open."
       End If
    < code to open the file >
  End Sub
```

Explanation

1 Calls the `OpenFileDialog` method of the NotesUIWorkspace class. The first parameter signals whether multiple files can be selected (`True/False`). The second parameter defines a title for the dialog box; the third defines filters for files that are listed. This example shows only text files. The fourth parameter defines the initial directory to list. A fifth parameter (not used) can be used to specify the initial file to list.

2 Returns an empty string if the user does not choose any files or selects cancel.

20.2.13 PickLists

Picklists can now be assembled and displayed in LotusScript. Picklists display a dialog box with documents listed for users to select. The `@PickList` function was available in release 4.5 and later. The user selections can be returned in two formats: NotesDocumentCollection or an array of string values.

Example 20.4

```
  Sub Initialize
    Dim uiw As New NotesUIWorkspace
    Dim dc As NotesDocumentCollection
    Dim doc As NotesDocument
1   Set dc = uiw.PickListCollection(PICKLIST_CUSTOM, True, "Server",_
      "database/filename","view","title","prompt","key value or blank")
2   If (dc.Count > 0) Then
      Set doc = dc.GetNthDocument(x)
3     <code to process the documents>
    End If
  End Sub
```

Explanation

1 Uses the `PickListCollection` method of the NotesUIWorkspace class to assemble a collection of documents selected by the user. The first parameter has only one possible value (shown). The second parameter signals whether multiple documents can be selected. The third parameter is the server name on which the view to use in the pick list is located; this is empty for the current or a local database. The path to the database containing the view is the fourth parameter, and it is empty for the current database. The fifth parameter designates the view to use. The sixth parameter sets the title for the dialog box, and the seventh parameter sets the text for the prompt string. The last possible parameter (not shown) signals which column is used as the return value.

2 Continues only if there were documents selected.

3 Processes all documents selected by the user.

The return value could have been set up as an array of string values instead of a NotesDocumentCollection using the `PickListStrings` method of the NotesUIWorkspace class. Here is how line 1 from the previous example could have looked:

```
returnValues = PickListSrings(PICKLIST_CUSTOM, True, "Server", "database",_
  "view", "title", "prompt")
```

It has the same parameters as the `PickListCollection` method, but the first parameter can be `PICKLIST_NAMES` (names lookup dialog box), `PICKLIST_RESOURCES` (resources dialog), or `PICKLIST_ROOMS` (rooms dialog) as well.

20.2.14 Prompt

Another excellent addition is the `Prompt` method of the NotesUIWorkspace class. It facilitates the usage of a prompt box for data entry, the same as the prompt @Function.

Format

```
Variant = NotesUIWorkspace.Prompt(prompt_type, title, prompt, default_value,_
  possible_values)
```

- `prompt_type` can be `PROMPT_OK`, `PROMPT_YESNO`, `PROMPT_YESNOCANCEL`, `PROMPT_EDIT`, `PROMPT_LIST`, `PROMPT_COMBO`, `PROMPT_EDITCOMBO`, `PROMPT_LISTMULT`, or `PROMPT_PASSWORD`.
- `possible_values` is a variant array of string values that contains all posssible selections for those prompts that have predefined selection (`LIST`, `COMBO`, `MULT`).

The `Prompt` method of the NotesUIWorkspace class has the same behavior as the prompt @Function.

20.2.15 Spelling checker

The new `SpellCheck` method of the NotesUIDocument object allows spelling in a document to be checked from script. In addition, `FindString`, `FindFreeTimeDialogEx`, and `GetSelectedText` methods have been added. The `FindString` method allows an open document to be searched for a specific string. The `FindFreeTimeDialogEx` opens the find free time dialog box, and `GetSelectedText` copies selected text on an open document to the clipboard.

Example 20.5

```
Sub Initialize
   Dim uiw As New NotesUIWorkspace
   Dim uidoc As NotesUIDocument
```

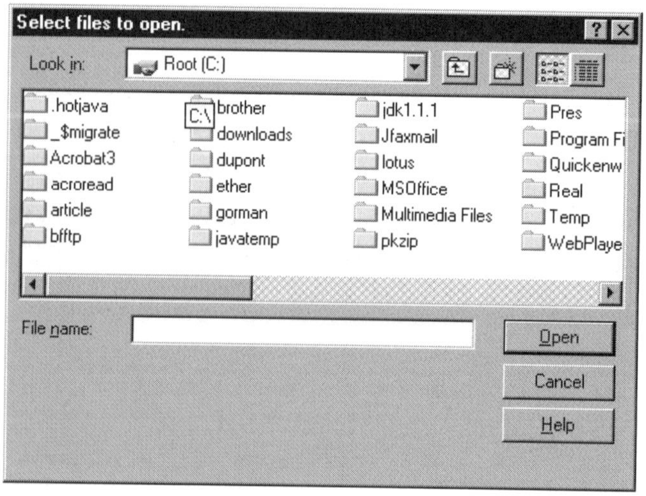

Figure 20.9 Example 20.3 output

```
    Set uidoc = uiw.CurrentDocument
1   Call uidoc.SpellCheck
    fString = InputBox$("Enter string to find.")
2   Call uidoc.FindString(fString)
3   mString = uidoc.GetSelectedText
  End Sub
```

Explanation

1 Checks the spelling in the current open document.

2 Searches the current document for the string entered by the user.

3 Copies text selected in the current document to the clipboard.

20.2.16 NotesDocumentCollection

One of the most significant enhancements to the Notes/Domino classes is the ability to add and/or remove entries from a document collection. This is functionality that has been requested since the first release of LotusScript in the Notes environment.

Example 20.6

```
  Sub Initialize
     Dim x As Integer
     Dim s As New NotesSession
     Dim db As NotesDatabase
     Dim dc1 As NotesDocumentCollection
     Dim dc2 As NotesDocumentCollection
     Dim doc As NotesDocument
     Set db = s.CurrentDatabase
     Set dc1 = db.AllDocuments
     Set dc2 = db.FTSearch(|FIELD FORM = "Defaule"|,0)
     Set doc = dc1.GetFirstDocument
     While Not (doc Is Nothing)
        If (doc.Created < Now) Then
1          Call dc2.AddDocument(doc)
        Set doc2 = dc1.GetNExtDocument(doc)
        Else
           Set doc2 = dc1.GetNextDocument(doc)
2          Call dc1.DeleteDocument(doc)
           Set doc = doc2
        End If
     Wend
  End Sub
```

Explanation

1 Uses the `AddDocument` method of the NotesDocumentCollection class to add a document to the second collection from the first.

2 Uses the `DeleteDocument` method of the NotesDocumentCollection class to remove a document from the first collection.

20.2.17 Generating HTML

The NotesDocument, NotesItem, and NotesRichTextItem classes now contain methods called `GenerateHTML` and `GenerateHTMLString`. These methods create HTML documents or a string containing the HTML for their respective objects. `GenerateHTML` accepts an optional paramater that signals the complete path to save the new file; The Notes data directory path is used if not specified. `GenerateHTMLString` returns a string value containing the HTML generated for the object's text contents. The next example shows how they might be used on a NotesDocument object.

Example 20.7

```
Sub Initialize
  Dim s As New NotesSession
  Dim db As NotesDatabase
  Dim doc As NotesDocument
  Dim dc As NotesDocumentCollection
  Dim htmlString AsString
  Set db = s.CurrentDatabase
  Set dc = db.AllDocuments
  For x = 1 to dc.Count
    Set doc = dc.GetNthDocument(x)
    html = doc.GenerateHTML
    htmlString = doc.GenerateHTMLString
  Next x
  End Sub
```

20.2.18 NotesReplication

Another great feature added to 5.0 is the ability to access a database's replication settings. The NotesReplication class provides access to various properties and methods that work with database replication settings.

Example 20.8

```
     Sub Initialize
       Dim s As New NotesSession
       Dim db As NotesDatabase
1      Dim rep As NotesReplication
       Set db = s.CurrentDatabase
2      Set rep = db.ReplicationInfo
3      With rep
4        Print .Abstract
5        Print "Replication cutoff delete date:  " & .CutOffDelete
6        Print "Replication cutoff interval:  " & .CutOffInterval
7        Print "Replication disabled?  " & .Disabled
8        Print "Catalog replication or not?  " & .DoNotCatalog
9        Print "Design is hidden?  " & .HideDesign
10       Print "Ignore deletes during replication?  " & .IgnoreDeletes
11       Print "Ignore deletes in the destination database during replication?_
           " & .IgnoreDestDeletes
12       Print "Never replicate?  " & .NeverReplicate
```

```
13      Print "Replication priority:  " & .Priority
      End With
14    Call rep.Reset()
15    Call rep.Save()
   End Sub
```

Explanation

1 Declares a new NotesReplication object.

2 Instantiates the NotesReplication object using the `ReplicationInfo` property of the NotesDatabase class.

3 Uses a `With/End With` block to work with the NotesReplication object.

4 Prints the abstract property.

5 The `CutOffDelete` property contains a date signaling the cut-off date for deletions.

6 The `CutOffInterval` contains the replication cut off interval (long value).

7 The `Disabled` property signals whether replication is disabled or not.

8 The `DoNotCatalog` property signals whether the database containing the replication settings is cataloged or not.

9 The `HideDesign` property signals whether or not the design of the database is hidden.

10 The `IgnoreDeletes` property signals whether deletes in the current database are ignored during replication.

11 The `IgnoreDestDeletes` property signals if deletes in the destination database are ignored during replication.

12 The `NeverReplicate` property signals whether replication is allowed.

13 The `Priority` property contains the replication priority.

14 The `Reset` method resets the replication settings for the database.

15 The `Save` method saves all replication settings in the database.

Most of the properties can be set as well.

Example 20.9

```
Sub Initialize
   Dim s As New NotesSession
   Dim db As NotesDatabase
   Dim rep As NotesReplication
   Set db = s.CurrentDatabase
   Set rep = db.ReplicationInfo
   rep.Abstract = "Replication Info"
   rep.CutOffDelete = "11/1/98"
   rep.CutOffInterval = 0
   rep.Disabled = False
```

```
   rep.DoNotBrowse = False
   rep.HideDesign = True
   rep.DoNotCatalog = True
   rep.IgnoreDeletes = False
   rep.IgnoreDestDeletes = True
   rep.MultiDBIndex = False
   rep.NeverReplicate = False
   rep.NoChronos = True
   rep.Priority = "1"
   Call rap.Save()
End Sub
```

Explanation

The various properties of the NotesReplication object are set and the save method is called to save the changes to disk.

20.2.19 Replicating a database

`Replicate` has been added to the NotesDatabase class. It returns a Boolean value signaling whether or not replication was successful. There are two ways to use the new method:

```
Call NotesDatabase.Replicate("Server Name")
    -or-
Boolean = NotesDatabase.Replicate("Server Name")
```

The `Replicate` method accepts one string parameter that signals the server with which the database will replicate.

Example 20.10

```
     Dim uiw As New NotesUIWorkspace
     Dim uid As NotesUIDatabase
     Dim db As NotesDatabase
1    Set uid = uiw.CurrentDatabase
2    Set db = uid.Database
     Dim flag As Variant
3    If (db.Replicate("Server Name")) Then
        Print "Replication was successful."
     Else
        Print "Replication was not successful."
     End If
```

Explanation

1 Sets the NotesUIDatabase object to the currently open database.

2 Sets the NotesDatabase object.

3 Replicates the database and displays the results. The calling of the replication method returns `True` if successful, and `False` otherwise.

20.2.20 *NotesRichTextTab*

Add tabs to a Rich Text item.

20.2.21 *NotesRichTextParagraphStyle*

NotesRichTextParagraphStyle class allows spacing and tabs to be set for paragraphs within a Rich Text item. The new `AppendParagraphStyle` method applies the style to the Rich Text item. The next example shows how it and other new features may be used.

Example 20.11

```
   Sub QuerySave(Source As NotesUIDocument, Continue As Variant)
     Dim rtItem As NotesRichTextItem
     Dim doc As NotesDocument
     Set doc = Source.Document
     If (doc.HasItem("Body")) Then
       Set rtItem = doc.GetFirstItem("Body")
1      Call rtItem.AddPageBreak
       Dim s As New NotesSession
       Dim rtStyle As NotesRichTextStyle
2      rtStyle.PassThruHTML = True
3      Dim rtParStyle As NotesRichTextParagraphStyle
       Set rtStyle = s.CreateRichTextStyle
4      rtParStyle.LeftMargin = 10
5      rtParStyle.RightMargin = 70
6      rtParStyle.SpacingAbove = 10
7      rtParStyle.SpacingBelow = 10
8      rtParStyle.FirstLineLeftMargin = 11
9      rtParStyle.InterLineSpacing = 0
10     Print rtParStyle.tabs
11     Call rtParStyle.ClearAllTabs()
12     Call rtParStyle.SetTab(10, 5)
13     Call rtParStyle.SetTabs(5, 10, 70)
14     Call rtItem.AppendParagraphStyle(rtParStyle)
15     Call rtItem.AddPageBreak(rtParStyle)
16     Dim rtTab As NotesRichTextTab
17     rtTab.Position = 5
18     Call rtItem.GenerateHTML("C:\")
19     htmlValue = rtItem.GenerateHTMLString
     End If
   End Sub
```

Explanation

1. Uses `AddPageBreak` to add a page break to the Rich Text item.
2. Uses `PassThruHTML` of the NotesRichTextStyle which can be used to set the style to Pass thru HTML.
3. Declares a new NotesRichTextParagraphStyle object. The `CreateRichTextParagraphStyle()` method of the NotesSession class could have been used as well (Set `NotesRichTextParagraphStyle = NotesSession.CreateRichTextParagraphStyle`).

4 The `LeftMargin` property of the NotesRichTextParagraphStyle class sets the left margin.

5 The `RightMargin` property of the NotesRichTextParagraphStyle class set the right margin.

6 The `SpacingAbove` property of the NotesRichTextParagraphStyle class sets the spacing above the paragraph.

7 The `SpacingBelow` property of the NotesRichTextParagraphStyle class sets the spacing below the paragraph.

8 The `FirstLineLeftMargin` property of the NotesRichTextParagraphStyle class sets the first line of the left margin in the paragraph.

9 The `InterLineSpacing` property of the NotesRichTextParagraphStyle class sets the spacing between lines in the paragraph.

10 The `Tabs` property of the NotesRichTextParagraphStyle is read only, but it shows the current tab settings in the paragraph.

11 The `ClearAllTabs` method of the NotesRichTextParagraphStyle class clears all tabs from the paragraph.

12 The `SetTab` method of the NotesRichTextParagraphStyle class sets an individual tab in the paragraph.

13 The `SetTabs` method of the NotesRichTextParagraphStyle class sets tabs with a width equal to the first parameter, starting position is the second parameter, and the third parameter signals the ending position of the tabs.

14 Uses the `AppendParagraphStyle` method of the NotesRichText item class to apply a paragraph style to the Rich Text item. It accepts a NotesRichTextParagraph-Style object as a parameter.

15 Another page break is added to the Rich Text item with a NotesRichTextItemPara-graphStyle as a parameter which is applied to the new paragraph after the new break.

16 Declares a new NotesRichTextTab object.

17 The `position` property of the NotesRichTextTab class sets the position of the tab.

18 The `GenerateHTML` method of the NotesRichTex-tItem class generates an HTML file containing the contents of the Rich Text item. The parameter tells it to save it in the root of drive C.

> *Note* The NotesRichTextTab class was not fully incorporated in the prerelease version of 5.0 used for this chapter, so it could not be fully tested/utilized.

19 The `GenerateHTMLString` method of the NotesRichTextItem generates a string variable that contains an HTML representation of the Rich Text field's contents.

20.2.22 NotesViewEntryCollection

Another new class in Notes/Domino 5.0 is the NotesViewEntryCollection class. This class operates the same as a NotesDocumentCollection except that it forms collections of all entries in views. The entries may be categories, totals, or actual documents. The NotesViewEntry class is used to access individual elements in the collection.

Example 20.12

```
   Sub Initialize
      Dim s As New NotesSession
      Dim db As NotesDatabase
1     Dim view As NotesView
2     Dim vec As NotesViewEntryCollection
3     Dim ve As NotesViewEntry
      Dim doc As NotesDocument
      Set db = s.CurrentDatabase
4     Set view = db.GetView("Default")
5     Set vec = view.AllEntries
6     Set ve = vec.GetFirstEntry
7     While Not (ve Is Nothing)
8        Print "Number of children:  " & ve.ChildCount
9        Print "Number of descendants:  " & ve.DescendantCount
10       Print "Full text search score:  " & ve.FtSearchScore
11       Print "Indent level:  " & ve.IndentLevel
12       Print "Entry is a category?  " & ve.IsCategory
13       Print "Entry is a document?  " & ve.IsDocument
14       Print "Entry is totals?  " & ve.IsTotals
15       Print "Entry is unread?  " & ve.IsUnRead
16       Print "Entry is valid?  " & ve.IsValid
17       Print "Note ID:  " & ve.NoteID
18       Print "Number of siblings:  " & ve.SiblingCount
19       Print "Universal ID:  " & ve.UniversalID
20       If (ve.isDocument) Then
            Set doc = ve.Document
         End If
21       Set ve = vec.GetNextEntry(ve)
      Wend
   End Sub
```

Explanation

1 Declares the NotesView object that will be used to set up the collection.

2 Declares a NotesViewEntryCollection object.

3 Declares a NotesViewEntry object.

4 Sets the NotesView object to the view named Default.

5 Instantiates the NotesViewEntryCollection object using the `AllEntries` property of the NotesView object.

6 Sets the NotesViewEntry object to the first entry in the collection using the `GetFirstEntry` method of the NotesViewEntryCollection class.

7 Continues until all entries have been processed.

8 The `ChildCount` property of the NotesViewEntry class returns the number of entries that are children of the entry.

9 The `DescendantCount` property returns the number of entries under the current entry.

10 If the entry was returned via a full text search, this returns its score in the search. Otherwise it is blank.

11 The `IndentLevel` property signals how many levels the current entry is indented.

12 The `IsCategory` property signals whether or not the current entry is a category.

13 The `IsDocument` property signals whether or not the current entry is a document.

14 The `IsTotals` property signals whether or not the current entry contains totals.

15 The `IsUnRead` property signals whether or not the current entry has been read.

16 The `IsValid` property signals whether or not the current entry is valid.

17 The `NoteID` property returns the NoteID for the entry, if it is a document.

18 The `SiblingCount` property returns the number of entries at the same level of the current entry.

19 The `UniversalID` property returns the Universal ID for the entry, if it is a document.

20 The `IsDocument` property signals whether an entry is a document. If it is a document, the NotesDocument object is set to it by accessing the `Document` property of the NotesViewEntry class.

21 The `GetNextEntry` method of the NotesViewEntryCollection class is used to access the next entry in the collection. The current entry is passed into it to act as a reference point for next.

20.2.23 NotesUIView

A print method has been added to the NotesUIView class. This allows the printing of the currently open view.

Example 20.13

```
  Sub Initialize
     Dim uiw As New NotesUIWorkspace
     Dim uiv As NotesUIView
1    Set uiv = uiw.CurrentView
2    Call uiv.Print
  End Sub
```

Explanation

1 Sets the NotesUIView object to the currently open view.

2 Prints the currently open view.

20.2.24 NotesUIDatabase

`OpenNavigator`, a new method that allows navigators to be opened has been added.

Example 20.14

```
  Sub Initialize
     Dim uiw As New NotesWorkspace
     Dim uid As NotesUIDatabase
     Set uid = uiw.CurrentDatabase
1    Call uid.OpenNavigator("Navigator Name",True)
2    Call uid.OpenView("View Name", "Key", True)
  End Sub
```

Explanation

1 Uses the new `OpenNavigator` method to open a navigator. The first parameter is the name of the navigator and the second paramater is a Boolean value (`True`/`False`) signaling whether a new instance (if already open) should be opened (go to existing open window if it exists).

2 The `OpenView` method has two new parameters. One is a key string variable that can open the view to a specific place in the view. It is similar to the OpenView @Command. The other signals whether a new instance (`True`/`False`) should be opened.

20.2.25 NotesAgent

An agent can be tested to see if it is a Notes agent (IsNotesAgent) or Web agent (IsWebAgent). Also, the target of an agent and its trigger can be viewed.

```
  Sub Initialize
     Dim s As New NotesSession
     Dim db As NotesDatabase
     Set db = s.CurrentDatabase
     Dim agent As NotesAgent
     Set agent = db.GetAgent("Test")
1    If (agent.IsNotesAgent) Then
        MsgBox "This agent is for Notes."
     End If
2    If (agent.IsWebAgent) Then
        MsgBox "This agent is for the Web."
     End If
3    Print NotesAgent.Target
4    Print NotesAgent.Trigger
  End Sub
```

Explanation

1 The `IsNotesAgent` property signals whether or not the agent is for Notes.

2 The `IsWebAgent` property signals whether or not the agent is for the web.

3 Prints the target setting for the agent.
Possible values: TARGET_ALL_DOCS, TARGET_NEW_DOCS, TARGET_NEW_OR_MODIFIED_DOCS, TARGET_ALL_DOCS_IN_VIEW, TARGET_UNREAD_DOCS_IN_VIEW, TARGET_PROMPT_USER, TARGET_UI_SELECTABLE_OBJECT, TARGET_NONE.

4 Prints the trigger setting for the agent.
Possible values: TRIGGER_SCHEDULED, TRIGGER_NEW_MAIL, TRIGGER_DOC_PASTED, TRIGGER_MANUAL, TRIGGER_DOC_UPDATE, TRIGGER_SYNCHRONOUS_NEW_MAIL, TRIGGER_NONE.

20.2.26 NotesACL/NotesACLEntry

One new property has been added to the NotesACL class: `InternetLevel`. This sets the maximum Internet level for a database. Corresponds to the last tab on the database ACL dialog box.

```
NotesACL.InternetLevel = ACLLEVEL_MANAGER
```

The NotesACLEntry class has numerous new properties, they are all Boolean values (`True`/`False`)

- *`CanCreateLSOrJavaAgent`* Signals whether or not an entry can create LotusScript or Java agents in the database.
- *`CanCreateSharedFolder`* Signals whether or not an entry can create shared folders in the database.
- *`IsAdminReaderAuthor`* Signals whether or not an entry is allowed to administer, read, and author documents.
- *`IsAdminServer`* Signals whether an entry is allowed to administer the server.
- *`IsGroup`* Signals whether or not an entry is a group.
- *`IsPerson`* Signals whether or not an entry is a person.
- *`IsServer`* Signals whether or not an entry is a server.

20.2.27 Events

New events have been added to various objects in the Notes environment.

20.2.28 View

- *`QueryDragDrop`* Triggered after an item has been selected (right mouse button) and before it is dropped (moved).

- `PostDragDrop` Triggered after an item has been moved with a mouse.

20.2.29 Document

- `OnHelpRequest` Contains only @Formulas, not LotusScript.
- `PostSave` Triggered after a document has been saved, so it is after the `QuerySave` event.

In addition, there have been numerous methods/properties added to existing classes. Appendix B lists all 5.0 properties/methods for each class.

20.3 Other enhancements

- Date fields can now be displayed using four-digit years.
- Field controls that were only available in layout regions are now available anywhere on forms.
- A password display type is now supported that displays data in the field as asterisks.
- Frames are fully supported for viewing by browser clients as well as the Notes client. A tool called the frameset designer facilitates the designing of framesets.
- Security for Java applets can be specified.
- Embedded objects for views and outlines can be displayed as Java applets to browser clients.
- The ability to test your web designs in multiple browsers.
- Support nested tables.
- Support tabbed tables.
- Better information provided on @Formula errors; it will now tell you the field that failed an input validation test.

20.4 Chapter summary

There have been numerous modifications to the development environment. The new features make working with Internet/intranet applications much simpler. The IDE is much more intuitive and user friendly. The many methods added to the NotesUIWorkspace class allow much more user interaction, and views are more accessible with the additions to the NotesView class and the new NotesViewEntry and NotesViewEntryCollection classes. Combine this with the performance enhancements and they will lead to more robust, full-featured applications.

20.5 Chapter review

- The Notes IDE has improved greatly.
- The object browser has been moved to a permanent position on the left.
- Formula and command buttons have been removed.
- The NotesUIWorkspace contains many new methods such as `prompt` and `filedialog` that allow more user interaction through script.
- The NotesOutline class allows access to the new outline design element.
- The NotesView class has numerous methods to work with individual elements in a view.
- The NotesViewEntry and NotesViewEntryCollection classes allow easy access to individual entries in a view, even if they are not documents.
- Currently open views can now be printed with the `print` method in the NotesUIView class.
- The NotesUIView class now allows navigators to be opened, and views to be opened to specific entries.
- Replication can now be automated with the NotesReplication class and `replicate` method in the NotesDatabase class.

CHAPTER 21

Working with NotesPump

21.1 Chapter objectives 330
21.2 NotesPump classes 330
21.3 NPFieldList 333
21.4 NPField 336
21.5 Data types 341
21.6 Conclusion 341

21.1 *Chapter objectives*

- How to use the NotesPump LotusScript classes
- NPActivity
- NPConnect
- NPFieldList
- NPField
- NotesPump data types

Lotus NotesPump is an add-on tool for moving data between data sources. It allows data to be moved between almost any DBMS (Oracle, Sybase, DB/2, etc.) and Lotus Notes/ Domino. The product name describes the movement of data as pumping. The pumping of data can be on command or based on a schedule. It is comprised of the NotesPump server engine and its management application.

The focus of this chapter is using LotusScript to work with NotesPump. It does not serve as an introduction or overview of NotesPump (more information can be found on its website http://www.lotus.com/notespump/).

NotesPump includes its own set of LotusScript classes which extend the core classes that are available for working with Lotus Notes. The NotesPump documentation lists the following situations where scripting may be needed:

- Data needs to be manipulated.
- Data needs to be updated at the source database after the record is synchronized.
- Multiple tables need to be accessed during each transfer cycle, for each record of the transfer activity.
- Relational data needs to be conglomerated into one record or document as summary information.
- Multiple rows of data need to be summarized into one record or document.
- Many links must be used simultaneously in the applicaton.

21.2 *NotesPump classes*

The NotesPump classes are made available by including the NotesPump LSX in your script. This is achieved by the USE command in the Options section of your script. It will look like this:

Note NotesPump must be installed (or at least the LSX installed) on the machine that runs the script.

```
Uselsx "*lnplsx"
```

21.2.1 NPActivity

Each Activity has global state information which is managed by NotesPump. This state is used to manage Link libraries and connections, allocated objects, error and event information, count logs, and communications with the NotesPump Server.

Properties

- `RaiseExceptionsBoolean` `True/False` value signaling whether or not NotesPump raises errors as exceptions in LotusScript.

Methods

- `ClearStatus` Clears the activity status.
- `GetStatus` Gets the current activity status.
- `GetStatusStream` Gets error message text for an error.
- `GetCommand` Obtains command from the NotesPump server.
- `Log` Logs an error or event.
- `LogEx` Logs a parameterized error or event.
- `LogStream` Logs an externally generated error or event.
- `LogStreamEx` Logs an externally generated parameterized error or event.
- `GetLogLast` Gets information on the last log call.
- `AddProperty` Adds a new property to an activity.
- `ListProperty` Lists properties available to the current activity.
- `GetProperty` Gets a property value.
- `SetProperty` Sets a property value.
- `ListLink` Lists available links.
- `LookupLink` Gets information on a specific link.
- `Print` Prints a message to the console.
- `RunActivity` Runs one or more other activities.

21.2.2 Creating an NPActivtiy

A new NPActivity object is initialized using the `New` keyword:

```
Dim newAct As New NPActivity(0, "Name of Activity")
```

It accepts two parameters: the first is not used and the second assigns a user-defined name to the activity.

21.2.3 *Deleting an NPActivity object*

Delete `newAct`

Example 21.1

```
    Option Public
1   Uselsx "*lnplsx"

    Sub Initialize
2     Dim newAct As New NPActivity(0, "Name of Activity")
      <....more code here...>
3     Delete newAct
    End Sub
```

Explanation

1 Makes the NotesPump classes available to the script.

2 Declares a new NPActivity object with the name specified.

3 Discards the NPActivity object.

21.2.4 *NPConnect*

The NPConnect class is used to manage individual link connections within an activity object. It enforces link state and requirements, and it is required when working with Links. One NPConnect object should be used for each and every data connection through a link used in an Activity object.

21.2.5 *Methods*

- *`ListProperty`* Lists properties available for the current NPConnect object.
- *`GetProperty`* Gets a property's value.
- *`SetProperty`* Sets a property's value.
- *`Connect`* Establishes a connection to a data source.
- *`Disconnect`* Disconnects from a data source.
- *`Execute`* Executes a statement against a data source.
- *`Select`* Performs a link-independent selection controlled by various link properties.
- *`Catalog`* Produces a result set containing a metadata catalog.
- *`Fetch`* Gets records from the current result set.
- *`Insert`* Inserts a new record into the data source.
- *`Update`* Updates records in the data source. Key and update values are provided.
- *`Remove`* Removes records from the data source. Key values are provided.
- *`Create`* Creates a metadata object.

- `Drop` Drops an existing metadata object.
- `Action` Executes one of a set of predefined actions.

21.2.6 Creating an NPConnect object

The `New` constructor is used to instantiate a new NPConnect object.

```
Dim connect As New NPConnect(0, "Name of Link")
```

Note For activities defined in the NotesPump administration database, the second parameter must correspond to a link name in the administration database.

21.2.7 Deleting an NPConnect object

Delete connect.

Example 21.2

```
Option Public
Uselsx "*lnplsx"

Sub Initialize
   Dim newAct As New NPActivity(0, "Activity")
   Dim connect As New NPConnect(0, "Connection")
   Call Source.Connect
   <...more code here...>
   Delete connect
   Delete newAct
End Sub
```

21.3 NPFieldList

An NPFieldList object represents metadata for a record. It may contain data for one or more record values. That is, it is a list of fields and field names for a record. The fields in the list can be added, modified, retrieved, or listed in multiple ways.

21.3.1 Properties

Fields within an NPFieldList object can be accessed using dot notation and their names. So, if you have a field called address it could be accessed this way.

21.3.2 Methods

- `Copy` Create a new NPFieldList object using the existing object. The field data is copied as well.
- `CopyRef` Creates a new NPFieldList object using the existing object, but the field data is not copied.
- `GetCount` Get the number of fields in the current NPFieldList object.

- `GetRecordCount` Get the record count specified when the NPFieldList item was initialized.
- `GetSequence` Get sequence number for fieldlist.
- `GetField` Get a field from a fieldlist using its field index value.
- `GetName` Get a copy of the field name from a field list using its field index value.
- `GetNameLength` Get total length of all field names, in bytes, from a fieldlist.
- `Lookup` Get a field from a fieldlist by its name.
- `ListSetup` Prepare a fieldlist for iteration.
- `List` Iterate through all fields in a fieldlist. The listSetup method must be called first.
- `Append` Add a new field to a fieldlist.
- `Insert` Insert a new field in the fieldlist.
- `Replace` Replace a field in a field list with another field.
- `Remove` Remove a field from a fieldlist.
- `SetName` Rename a field in the fieldlist.
- `Merge` Merge a name fieldlist with a data fieldlist to produce a mapped fieldlist.
- `MergeVirtual` Merges a name fieldlist and data fieldlist to produce a mapped fieldlist. Fields with matching virtual codes are added to a new virtual fieldlist.

21.3.3 Creating an NPFieldList object

```
Dim Record As New NPFieldlist (1,0)
```

Two parameters: the first signals the number of records the field list can hold and the second parameter default field flags defined to each new field as it is created.

21.3.4 Deleting an NPFieldList object

Delete `Record`.

Example 21.3

```
    Option Public
    Uselsx "*lnplsx"

    Sub Initialize
1     Dim newAct As New NPActivity (0, "Activity")
2     Dim conn As New NPConnect (0, "Test Connection")
3       Dim rec As New NPFieldlist (1,0)
4       Dim fld As New NPField (NPTYPE_TEXT, 1)
5       Dim txt As New NPStream
        Dim count As Long
6       conn.Connect
```

```
7       Call conn.Catalog (NPOBJECT_METADATA, rec, count)
8       If (count = 0) Then
           txt.AsLsString = "No Data Found."
           Call newAct.LogStream (0, txt, 0)
        Else
9          txt.DataFree
10         Call conn.Fetch (rec, 1, 1, count)
11         While (count > 0)
12            rec.GetField 1, NPSTREAMFMT_NATIVE, fld, NPNULLHANDLE
13            If (txt.DataGetLength = 0) Then
                 txt.AsLsString = "The table names are:"
              End If
14            txt.AsLsString = txt.AsLsString & "|" & fld.AsLsString
15            Call conn.Fetch (rec, 1, 1, count)
           Wend
16         Call newAct.LogStream (NPLOGSTREAMF_EVENT, Text, 0)
        End If
17      Delete txt
        Delete fld
        Delete rec
        Delete conn
        Delete newAct
     End Sub
```

Explanation

1 Creates NPActivity object.

2 Creates an NPConnect object. We are using a link defined in the NotesPump administration database named Test Connection.

3 Creates an NPFieldList object.

4 Creates an NPField object. This is used to access specific fields in the field list object.

5 Creates an NPStream object. NPStream represents two of the seven datatypes in NotesPump: text and binary. We are reading text.

6 Connects to the data source using the defined link.

7 Retrieves field list object.

8 Sends message to log if no records returned in the field list.

9 Frees up the data stream.

10 Retrieves first record from the result set.

11 Loops through all documents in the result set.

12 Gets the first field from the field list for the current record.

13 Sets the contents if the text of the first field is empty.

14 Sets the text of the field to the data and the field name.

15 Gets next record from the result set.

16 Logs event.

17 Deletes objects.

21.4 NPField

NPField is a data object containing one or more data values of a designated data type. The previous example used it to access a text field.

21.4.1 Methods

- `Compare` Compares two fields, returns `0` if they are equal.
- `Convert` Converts data value to the type of a destination field.
- `Copy` Creates a field with the settings and value of the current field.
- `GetBuffer` Gets data for a field.
- `GetFlags` Gets field flags for a field.
- `GetFormatDateTime` Gets date/time format for a date/time field.
- `GetFormatNumber` Gets number format for a number field.
- `GetFormatStream` Gets flags, maximum length, and format for a stream field.
- `GetType` Gets the data type for a field.
- `GetTypeSize` Gets size of data in a field.
- `GetValueCount` Gets number of data values in a field.
- `GetVirtualCode` Gets the virtual code for a field.
- `IsNull` Boolean signaling whether or not a field is null.
- `SetFlags` Assigns the field flags for a field.
- `SetFormatDateTime` Sets date/time format for a field.
- `SetFormatNumber` Set the number format for a field.
- `SetFormatStream` Sets the stream format for a field.
- `SetNull` Sets the field value to null.
- `SetVirtualCode` Sets the virtual code for a field.

21.4.2 Creating an NPField object

```
Dim fieldName As New NPField (<fieldtype>, 1)
```

Parameters The first parameter signals the data type for the field (see list of data types below); the second signals the number of values in the field.

Legal field types:

```
NPTYPE_INT
NPTYPE_FLOAT
NPTYPE_CURRENCY
NPTYPE_NUMERIC
NPTYPE_DATETIME
NPTYPE_TEXT
NPTYPE_BYTE
```

21.4.3 Deleting an NPField object

Delete `fieldName`

The next example is taken from the NotesPump documentation.

Example 21.4

```
   Uselsx "*lnplsx"
   Dim State As NPActivity
   Sub Initialize
     Set State = New NPActivity (0, "The Test Activity")
1    Dim IntField As New NPField (NPTYPE_INT, 1)
2    Dim FloatField As New NPField (NPTYPE_FLOAT, 1)
3    Dim CurrencyField As New NPField (NPTYPE_CURRENCY, 1)
4    Dim NumericField As New NPField (NPTYPE_NUMERIC, 1)
5    Dim DatetimeField As New NPField (NPTYPE_DATETIME, 1)
6    Dim TextField As New NPField (NPTYPE_TEXT, 1)
     Dim IntValue As Long
     Dim FloatValue As Double
7    Dim CurrencyValue As New NPCurrency
8    Dim NumericValue As New NPNumeric
9    Dim DatetimeValue As New NPDatetime
10   Dim TextValue As New NPStream
     Dim OldFlags As Long
     Dim NewFlags As Long
     Dim OldFormat As Long
     Dim NewFormat As Long
11   TextValue.Create 0, 0, NPSTREAMFMT_UNICODE
12   NumericValue.create NPMAX_NUMERIC_PREC, NPMIN_NUMERIC_SCALE +_
       NPMAX_NUMERIC_PREC
     IntValue = -123
     FloatValue = 1234456.789
13   CurrencyValue.AsLsString = "922337203685477.5807"
14   NumericValue.AsLsString =
       "9.99999999999999999999999999999999999999999999999999999999999
       999999999999999999999999999e126" ' maximum value for a numeric
15   DatetimeValue.SetCurrent
16   TextValue.AsLsString = "A Single licence is all you need for both &
       developing new applications as well as deploying existing
       applications"
17   LogMessage "The fields have the following values before _
       assignment:|IntField=" & IntField.AsLsString & "|FloatField=" &_
       FloatField.AsLsString & "|CurrencyField=" &_
       CurrencyField.AsLsString & "|DatetimeField=" &_
       DatetimeField.AsLsString & "|NumericField=" &_
       NumericField.AsLsString & "|TextField=" & TextField.AsLsString
18   IntField.SetInt 1, IntValue
```

```
19   FloatField.SetFloat 1, FloatValue
20   CurrencyField.SetCurrency 1, CurrencyValue
21   DatetimeField.SetDatetime 1, DatetimeValue
22   NumericField.SetNumeric 1, NumericValue
23   TextField.SetStream 1, TextValue
     LogMessage "The fields have the following values after_
       assignment:|IntField=" & IntField.AsLsString & "|FloatField=" &_
       FloatField.AsLsString & "|CurrencyField=" &_
       CurrencyField.AsLsString & "|DatetimeField=" &_
       DatetimeField.AsLsString & "|NumericField=" &_
       NumericField.AsLsString & "|TextField=" & TextField.AsLsString
24   IntField.GetInt 1, IntValue, 0
25   FloatField.GetFloat 1, FloatValue, 0
26   CurrencyField.GetCurrency 1, CurrencyValue, 0
27   DatetimeField.GetDatetime 1, DatetimeValue, 0
28   NumericField.GetNumeric 1, NumericValue, 0
29   TextField.GetStream 1, NPSTREAMFMT_UNICODE, TextValue, 0
     OldFlags = CurrencyField.GetFlags()
30   CurrencyField.SetFlags NPFIELDF_NO_INSERT
     NewFlags = CurrencyField.GetFlags()
     LogMessage "Currency Field old flags = " & OldFlags &_
       "    new flags = " & NewFlags
     LogMessage "The Text field is NotesPump type #" & TextField.GetType()
     LogMessage "The Text field requires " & TextField.GetTypeSize() &_
       " byte(s)"
     TextField.GetBuffer 1, 0, OldFlags
     If (OldFlags) Then
       LogMessage "The text field is (null)"
     Else
       LogMessage "The text field is *NOT* (null)"
     End If
     LogMessage "The Text field has " & TextField.GetValueCount() &_
       " value(s)"
     LogMessage "The Text field has the virtual code " &_
       TextField.GetVirtualCode()
     TextField.SetVirtualCode 2
     LogMessage "The Text field now has the virtual code " &_
       TextField.GetVirtualCode()
31   DatetimeField.GetFormatDatetime OldFormat, 0
32   DatetimeField.SetFormatDatetime NPDATETIMEF_NO_DATE, 0
     DatetimeField.GetFormatDatetime NewFormat, 0
     LogMessage "Datetime Field old format = " & OldFormat &_
     "    new format = " & NewFormat
33   IntField.GetFormatNumber OldFormat, 0, 0, 0
34   IntField.SetFormatNumber NPNUMBERF_UNSIGNED, 0, 0, 0
     IntField.GetFormatNumber NewFormat, 0, 0, 0
     LogMessage "Numeric Field old format = " & OldFormat &_
       "    new format = " & NewFormat
35   TextField.GetFormatStream OldFormat, 0, 0
36   TextField.SetFormatStream NPSTREAMF_NO_CASE, 0, 0
     TextField.GetFormatStream NewFormat, 0, 0
     LogMessage "Text Field old format = " & OldFormat & "    new format = " &_
       NewFormat
     Dim Different As Long
```

```
37    FloatField.Compare 1, IntField, 1, 1, NPCOMPAREF_LOW_PREC, Different
      If (Different) Then
38      LogMessage "in a low precision comparison, " &_
          FloatField.AsLsString & " does *NOT* equal "  &_
          IntField.AsLsString
      Else
        LogMessage "in a low precision comparison, " &_
          FloatField.AsLsString & " equals " & IntField.AsLsString
      End If
      LogMessage "The Int field = " & IntField.AsLsString
39    IntField.Convert 1, FloatField, 1, 1
      LogMessage "After converting from Float field, the Int field = " &_
        IntField.AsLsString
      LogMessage "The Int field = " & IntField.AsLsString
40    IntField.Copy FloatField
      LogMessage "After copy from Float field, the Int field = " &_
        IntField.AsLsString
41    TextField.AsLsString = "HopScotch"
42    If (TextField.IsNull (1)) Then
        LogMessage "The text field is (null)"
      Else
        LogMessage "The text field is *NOT* (null)"
      End If
43    TextField.SetNull 1, True
44    If (TextField.IsNull (1)) Then
        LogMessage "The text field is (null)"
      Else
        LogMessage "The text field is *NOT* (null)"
      End If
    End Sub
    Sub LogMessage (Message As String)
45    Dim Text As New NPStream
46    Text.AsLsString = Message
47    State.LogStream NPLOGSTREAMF_EVENT, Text, 0
    End Sub
```

Explanation

1 Declares an NPField object of type Integer.

2 Declares an NPField object of type Float.

3 Declares an NPField object of type Currency.

4 Declares an NPField object of type Numeric.

5 Declares an NPField object of type DateTime.

6 Declares an NPField object of type Text.

7 Declares an NPCurrency object. Use to handle Currency fields.

8 Declares an NPNumeric object. Use to handle Numeric fields.

9 Declares an NPDateTime object. Use to handle date/time fields.

10 Declares an NPStream object. Use to handle text or byte fields.

11 Sets Stream object to hold unicode (byte) value.

12 Creates numeric value.

13 Sets maximum currency value.

14 Sets maximum numeric value.

15 Sets date/time value to current system date/time.

16 Sets text value.

17 Sends message to log. The `Log` subroutine is used.

18 Sets Integer field value.

19 Sets Float field value.

20 Sets Currency field value.

21 Sets DateTime field value.

22 Sets Numeric field value.

23 Sets Stream field value.

24 Gets value from Integer field.

25 Gets value from Float field.

26 Gets value from Currency field.

27 Gets value from Numeric field.

28 Gets value from DateTime field.

29 Gets value from Stream field.

30 Sets flags for Currency field.

31 Gets format for DateTime field.

32 Sets format for the DateTime field.

33 Gets format for Integer field.

34 Sets format for Integer field.

35 Gets format for Stream field.

36 Sets format for Stream field.

37 Compares Float field with Integer field.

38 Sends message to log if two values compared were not the same.

39 Converts Integer field to Float field.

40 Copies Integer field to the Float field.

41 Sets text of Text field.

42 Determines if the Text field is null or not.

43 Sets the Text field contents to null.

44 Determines if the Text field is null. Sends message to log accordingly.

45 Declares a new NPStream object. This will be used to send message to log.

46 Sets text of NPStream object to the message passed into the subroutine.

47 Sends message to the log.

21.5 Data types

The NotesPump LotusScript classes support seven data types: Integer, Float, Numeric, Text, DateTime, Currency, and Stream. Each as its own class which are subclasses of the NPField class.

The classes are:

- NPInt
- NPFloat
- NPCurrency
- NPDateTime
- NPNumeric
- NPStream

Note NPStream is used to work with text and byte values.

21.6 Conclusion

This chapter provides only an introduction to programming NotesPump in LotusScript. Release 5.0 of Notes/Domino will include NotesPump (and its classes) as standard components of the Notes/Domino development environment.

appendix A

Notes/Domino constants

LSCONST.LSS

This file is located in the root notes directory. It contains LotusScript constants. These constants can be used in your scripts via the `USELSX` command:

```
USELSX "LSCONST.LSS"
```

```
FILE:
```

```
'------------------------------------------------------------------
' File:        LSCONST.LSS
' Copyright (c) 1993 Lotus Development Corporation
'
' Description: LotusScript Global Constants.
'
'------------------------------------------------------------------
' Variant DataType Values
'------------------------------------------------------------------
Public Const V_EMPTY = 0' Empty variant
Public Const V_NULL = 1' Variant containing Null
Public Const V_INTEGER = 2' Integer
Public Const V_LONG = 3' Long integer (4 bytes)
Public Const V_SINGLE = 4' Single
Public Const V_DOUBLE = 5' Double
```

```
Public Const V_CURRENCY = 6' Currency
Public Const V_DATE = 7' Date value
Public Const V_STRING = 8' String
Public Const V_DISPATCH = 9' OLE object
Public Const V_ERROR = 10' ERROR (from OLE only)
Public Const V_BOOLEAN = 11' BOOLEAN (from OLE only)
Public Const V_VARIANT = 12' VARIANT array or list
Public Const V_IUNKNOWN = 13' OLE unknown object
Public Const V_UNISTR = 14' OLE unicode string
Public Const V_CLIENTHDL = 32' LotusScript client adt handle
Public Const V_TYPEINST = 33' LotusScript TYPE instance
Public Const V_LSOBJ = 34' LotusScript object
Public Const V_PRODOBJ = 35' Product object
Public Const V_BYREF   = &h4000' By Refrence
Public Const V_ARRAY   = &h2000' Array
Public Const V_LIST    = &h0800' List
Public Const V_DYNAMIC = &h0200' Dynamic (with V_ARRAY)
'-------------------------------------------------------------------
' MsgBox parameters
'-------------------------------------------------------------------
Public Const MB_OK = 0 ' OK button only
Public Const MB_OKCANCEL = 1' OK and Cancel buttons
Public Const MB_ABORTRETRYIGNORE = 2' Abort, Retry, and Ignore buttons
Public Const MB_YESNOCANCEL = 3' Yes, No, and Cancel buttons
Public Const MB_YESNO = 4' Yes and No buttons
Public Const MB_RETRYCANCEL = 5' Retry and Cancel buttons
Public Const MB_ICONSTOP = 16' Critical message
Public Const MB_ICONQUESTION = 32' Warning query
Public Const MB_ICONEXCLAMATION = 48' Warning message
Public Const MB_ICONINFORMATION = 64' Information message

Public Const MB_APPLMODAL = 0' Application Modal Message Box
Public Const MB_DEFBUTTON1 = 0' First button is default
Public Const MB_DEFBUTTON2 = 256' Second button is default
Public Const MB_DEFBUTTON3 = 512' Third button is default
Public Const MB_SYSTEMMODAL = 4096' System Modal
'-------------------------------------------------------------------
' MsgBox return values
'-------------------------------------------------------------------
Public Const IDOK = 1' OK button pressed
Public Const IDCANCEL = 2' Cancel button pressed
Public Const IDABORT = 3' Abort button pressed
Public Const IDRETRY = 4' Retry button pressed
Public Const IDIGNORE = 5' Ignore button pressed
Public Const IDYES = 6' Yes button pressed
Public Const IDNO = 7' No button pressed
'-------------------------------------------------------------------
' SetAttr, Dir, GetAttr functions
'-------------------------------------------------------------------
Public Const ATTR_NORMAL = 0' Normal files
Public Const ATTR_READONLY = 1' Read-only files
Public Const ATTR_HIDDEN = 2' Hidden files
Public Const ATTR_SYSTEM = 4' System-attribute set
Public Const ATTR_VOLUME = 8' Volume label
```

```
Public Const ATTR_DIRECTORY = 16' Directory
Public Const ATTR_ARCHIVE = 32' Archive bit set
'---------------------------------------------------------------------
' FileAttr function
'---------------------------------------------------------------------
Public Const ATTR_MODE = 1' Return mode of file (below)
Public Const ATTR_HANDLE = 2' Return OS handle for file
Public Const ATTR_INPUT = 1' File opened for Input mode
Public Const ATTR_OUTPUT = 2' File opened for Output mode
Public Const ATTR_RANDOM = 4' File opened for Random mode
Public Const ATTR_APPEND = 8' File opened for Append mode
Public Const ATTR_BINARY = 32' File opened for Binary mode
'---------------------------------------------------------------------
' Shell Window Style
'---------------------------------------------------------------------
Public Const SHELL_NORMAL_FOCUS = 1' Normal, with focus
Public Const SHELL_MIN_FOCUS = 2' Minimized, with focus (default)
Public Const SHELL_MAX_FOCUS = 3' Maximized, with focus
Public Const SHELL_NORMAL_NO_FOCUS=4' Normal, no focus
Public Const SHELL_MIN_NO_FOCUS = 6' Minimized, no focus
'---------------------------------------------------------------------
' IMEStatus values
'---------------------------------------------------------------------
Public Const IME_NOT_INSTALLED = 0 ' value for all non-Asian countries
Public Const IME_ON = 1' Asia
Public Const IME_OFF = 2' Asia
Public Const IME_HIRAGANA = 4' Japan
Public Const IME_KATAKANA_DBCS = 5' Japan
Public Const IME_KATAKANA_SBCS = 6' Japan
Public Const IME_HANGEUL = 4' Korea
Public Const IME_HANJACONVERT= 5' Korea
Public Const IME_ALPHA_DBCS = 7' Asia
Public Const IME_ALPHA_SBCS = 8' Asia
'---------------------------------------------------------------------
' StrConv values
'---------------------------------------------------------------------
Public Const SC_UPPERCASE = 1' convert to uppercase
Public Const SC_LOWERCASE = 2' convert to lowercase
Public Const SC_PROPERCASE = 3' convert to propercase
Public Const SC_WIDE = 4' convert narrow to wide
Public Const SC_NARROW = 8' convert wide to narrow
Public Const SC_KATAKANA = 16' convert Hiragana to Katakana
Public Const SC_HIRAGANA = 32' convert Katakana to Hiragana
```

LSERR.LSS

This file is located in the root Notes directory. It contains error message constants. These constants can be used in your scripts via the USELSX command:

```
USELSX "LSERR.LSS"

FILE:
```

```
' lserr.lssCopyright (c) 1994 Lotus Development Corporation
Public Const APISUCCESS=  0
Public Const APIErrRETRY=  1
Public Const APIErrYIELD=  2
Public Const APIErrBREAK =  3
Public Const APIErrSTOP=  4
Public Const APIErrUSER_BREAK =  5
'  Api Error Severity Codes
Public Const SevWARNING=  1
Public Const SevERROR=  2
Public Const SevFATAL=  3
'  Client Errors
Public Const APIErrEND= 10
Public Const APIErrUSER_ABORT= 11
Public Const APIErrABORT= 12
Public Const APIErrRETURN= 13
Public Const APIErrMEMORY= 14
Public Const APIErrRESOURCE = 15
Public Const APIErrACCESS= 16
Public Const APIErrEXISTS= 17
Public Const APIErrUNAVAIL= 18
Public Const APIErrSYNTAX= 19
Public Const APIErrIOERR= 20
Public Const APIErrOVERRUN= 21
Public Const APIErrSYMREL= 22
Public Const APIErrINVALADT= 23
Public Const APIErrFILEINVAL= 24
Public Const APIErrFILEREV= 25
Public Const APIErrCLIENTIO= 26
Public Const APIErrOPENERROR= 27
Public Const APIErrMODEXISTS= 28
Public Const APIErrNOSYMBOL= 29
Public Const APIErrLINE = 30
Public Const APIErrMODINUSE= 31
Public Const APIErrAPIBADARG= 32
Public Const APIErrCURSOREND= 33
Public Const APIErrCURSORBAD= 34
Public Const APIErrCURSOROBJNOTSET= 35
Public Const APIErrCURSORARRAYNOTDIMED= 36
Public Const APIErrRUN_BADARG= 37
Public Const APIErrRUN_ARGCNT= 38
Public Const APIErrRUN_PARAMTYPE= 39
Public Const APIErrREG_First= 40
Public Const APIErrREG_INVALIDPARENT= 41
Public Const APIErrREG_FORWARDCLASS= 42
Public Const APIErrREG_INVALIDCOLLECTION= 43
Public Const APIErrREG_INVALIDNAME= 44
Public Const APIErrREG_BADATTRIB= 45
Public Const APIErrREG_CONTROLPROC= 46
Public Const APIErrREG_RET_INVALID= 47
Public Const APIErrREG_ARG_INVALID= 48
Public Const APIErrREG_ARG_INVALIDFIXED= 49
Public Const APIErrREG_ARG_INVALIDSTRING= 50
Public Const APIErrREG_ARG_INVALIDFORWARD= 51
```

```
Public Const APIErrREG_ARG_INVALIDCLASS= 52
Public Const APIErrREG_ARG_INVALIDOPTIONAL= 53
Public Const APIErrREG_ARG_INVALIDBYVALCONT= 54
Public Const APIErrREG_ARG_INVALIDVOID= 55
Public Const APIErrREG_Last= 56
Public Const APIErrENUM_DONE= 57
Public Const APIErrDROPPED= 58
Public Const APIErrNOQUEUE= 59
Public Const APIErrADT_VERSION = 60
Public Const APIErrREG2_First= 61
Public Const APIErrREG_ARG_COUNT= 62
Public Const APIErrREG_Reserved1= 63
Public Const APIErrREG_Reserved2= 64
Public Const APIErrREG_Reserved3= 65
Public Const APIErrREG_Reserved4= 66
Public Const APIErrREG_Reserved5= 67
Public Const APIErrREG_Reserved6= 68
Public Const APIErrREG_Reserved7= 69
Public Const APIErrREG_Reserved8= 70
Public Const APIErrREG_Reserved9= 71
Public Const APIErrREG2_Last= 72
Public Const APIErrLAST= 72
' Run Time LOI Errors
' The following adjust MAC Resource Grouping
Public Const ErrLoiFIRST= 13000
Public Const ErrLoiArgOutofRange= 13001
Public Const ErrLoiBadPropertyName= 13002
Public Const ErrLoiBadMethodName= 13003
Public Const ErrLoiInvalidObject= 13004
Public Const ErrLoiTypeMismatch= 13005
Public Const ErrLoiInvalidArgument= 13006
Public Const ErrLoiPrintFailed= 13007
Public Const ErrLoiCouldNotLaunch= 13008
Public Const ErrLoiBadCoordinates= 13009
Public Const ErrLoiFileNotCreated= 13010
Public Const ErrLoiCouldNotSave= 13011
Public Const ErrLoiBadExecutable= 13012
Public Const ErrLoiClipboardEmpty= 13013
Public Const ErrLoiDocumentReadOnly= 13014
Public Const ErrLoiBadClipboardFormat= 13015
Public Const ErrLoiInvocationError= 13017
Public Const ErrLoiUnknownUnit= 13018
Public Const ErrLoiInvalidPropertyValue= 13019
Public Const ErrLoiLAST= 13019
' The following adjust MAC Resource Grouping
' Run Time Errors
Public Const ErrUSER= 1
Public Const ErrReturnWithoutGoSub= 3
Public Const ErrIllegalFunctionCall= 5
Public Const ErrOverflow= 6
Public Const ErrOutOfMemory= 7
Public Const ErrSubscriptOutOfRange= 9
Public Const ErrDivisionByZero=  11
Public Const ErrTypeMismatch=  13
```

```
Public Const ErrOutOfStringSpace=  14
Public Const ErrCantContinue=  17
Public Const ErrNoResume=  19
Public Const ErrResumeWithoutError=  20
Public Const ErrOutOfStackSpace=  28
Public Const ErrSubOrFunctionNotDefined=  35
Public Const ErrErrorInLoadingDLL=  48
Public Const ErrBadDLLCallingConvention=  49
Public Const ErrInternalError=  51
Public Const ErrBadFileNameOrNumber=  52
Public Const ErrFileNotFound=  53
Public Const ErrBadFileMode=  54
Public Const ErrFileAlreadyOpen=  55
Public Const ErrDeviceIOError=  57
Public Const ErrFileAlreadyExists=  58
Public Const ErrBadRecordLength=  59
Public Const ErrDiskFull=  61
Public Const ErrInputPastEndOfFile=  62
Public Const ErrBadRecordNumber=  63
Public Const ErrBadFileName=  64
Public Const ErrTooManyFiles=  67
Public Const ErrDeviceUnavailable=  68
Public Const ErrPermissionDenied=  70
Public Const ErrDiskNotReady=  71
Public Const ErrCantRenameWithDifferent=  74
Public Const ErrPathFileAccessError=  75
Public Const ErrPathNotFound=  76
Public Const ErrObjectVariableNotSet=  91
Public Const ErrForLoopNotInitialized=  92
Public Const ErrInvalidPatternString=  93
Public Const ErrInvalidUseOfNull=  94
Public Const ErrCannotDestroyActiveInst=  95
Public Const ErrFileNotWritable=  96
Public Const ErrFileNotReadable=  97
Public Const ErrBadFileNumber=  98
Public Const ErrFileNotOpen =  99
Public Const ErrConflictingFileModes= 100
Public Const ErrOpenFailed= 101
Public Const ErrIllegalOperation= 102
Public Const ErrDataTooBig= 103
Public Const ErrBadAttribute= 104
Public Const ErrCouldNotSetAttribute= 105
Public Const ErrListItemDoesNotExist= 120
Public Const ErrLinkNoModule= 150
Public Const ErrLinkNoSymbol= 151
Public Const ErrLinkBadSymbol= 152
Public Const ErrModule_Exist= 153
Public Const ErrModule_Not_Exist= 154
Public Const ErrModule_Bad= 155
Public Const ErrCompile= 156
Public Const ErrAdtCtrlFuncNotPresent= 158
Public Const ErrAdtNamedObjectNonExist= 159
Public Const ErrAdtUnknownClass= 160
Public Const ErrAdtHandleChanged= 161
```

```
Public Const ErrCCallBadArg= 162
Public Const ErrCCallUnsupportedArgType= 163
Public Const ErrCCallUnsupportedRetType= 164
Public Const ErrCCallSubUnavail= 165
Public Const ErrEventNotHooked= 166
Public Const ErrModuleInUse= 167
Public Const ErrModuleOverRun= 168
Public Const ErrNotAListTag= 169
Public Const ErrRedimFixedArray= 170
Public Const ErrArraySizeTooBig= 171
Public Const ErrIllegalLikePattern= 172
Public Const ErrArgOutOfRange= 173
Public Const ErrCircularUse= 174
Public Const ErrDuplicatePublic= 175
Public Const ErrExprRange= 176
Public Const ErrInvalidPowerOprand= 177
Public Const ErrLinkNoUseModule= 178
' Last Of V2 Error Messages ; V3 Error Messages Start
Public Const ErrUnderflow= 179
Public Const ErrNoPlatSupport= 180
Public Const ErrSuffixTypeMismatch= 181
Public Const ErrNamedMemberNonExist= 182
Public Const ErrNotAnObject= 183
Public Const ErrNotAContainer= 184
Public Const ErrWrongNumberOfArgs= 185
Public Const ErrNotAMethod = 186
Public Const ErrIllegalUseOfSub= 187
Public Const ErrIllegalUseOfFunction= 188
Public Const ErrIllegalUseOfProp= 189
Public Const ErrReadOnlyProp= 190
Public Const ErrInvalidListIndex= 191
Public Const ErrInvalidIsElemArg= 192
Public Const ErrIllegalDelete= 193
Public Const ErrNotAProductObject= 194
Public Const ErrNamedEventNonExist= 195
Public Const ErrEventHandlerArgType= 196
Public Const ErrEventHandlerArgCnt= 197
Public Const ErrNotaPublicMember= 198
Public Const ErrMissingArgument= 199
Public Const ErrUninitDynArray= 200
Public Const ErrDisallowed= 201
Public Const ErrNeedSetAssign= 202
Public Const ErrCollectItemError= 203
Public Const ErrCollectionIndex= 204
Public Const ErrNotACollection= 205
Public Const ErrCollectionItemNotFound= 206
Public Const ErrOLEError= 207
Public Const ErrOLECantCreate= 208
Public Const ErrOLEFileName= 209
Public Const ErrOLEMemberNotFound= 210
Public Const ErrOLEArgumentCount= 211
Public Const ErrOLEArgumentType= 212
Public Const ErrOLEException= 213
Public Const ErrForallSource= 214
```

```
Public Const ErrOutOfSysStack= 215
Public Const ErrIllegalRedim= 216
Public Const ErrAdtCreateError= 217
Public Const ErrAdtPropertyError= 218
Public Const ErrAdtMethodError= 219
Public Const ErrAdtError= 220
Public Const ErrEvaluateError= 221
Public Const ErrEventHandlerRetType= 222
Public Const ErrEventHandlerProcType= 223
Public Const ErrWrongNumberOfArgsProp= 224
Public Const ErrIllegalUseOfMember= 225
Public Const ErrPropSetNotDefined= 226
Public Const ErrPropGetNotDefined= 227
Public Const ErrStringTooLarge= 228
Public Const ErrReadOnlyVariable= 229
Public Const ErrUnknownClassId= 230
Public Const ErrCollectItemAssign= 231
Public Const ErrWrongNumDims= 232
Public Const ErrLAST= 232
```

LSXBEERR.LSS

This file is located in the Notes root directory. It contains error message constants. These constants can be used in your scripts via the `USELSX` command:

```
USELSX "LSERR.LSS"

FILE:

Public Const lsERR_NOTES_ERROR =  4000
Public Const lsERR_SYS_OUT_OF_MEMORY=  4001
Public Const lsERR_SYS_LOAD_OUT_OF_MEM=  4002
Public Const lsERR_SYS_FILE_NOT_FOUND =  4003
Public Const lsERR_SYS_DICT_NOT_ON_PATH =  4004
Public Const lsERR_NOTES_ERROR2 =  4005
Public Const lsERR_SYS_RESOURCE_NOT_FOUND =  4008
Public Const lsERR_SYS_LOADING_RESOURCE =  4009
Public Const lsERR_SYS_LOCKING_RESOURCE =  4010
Public Const lsERR_SYS_FREEING_RESOURCE =  4011
Public Const lsERR_SYS_NOSUCH_RESOURCE =  4012
Public Const lsERR_SYS_WARNING_TITLE =  4016
Public Const lsERR_MAIL_COPEN_FAILED =  4026
Public Const lsERR_MAIL_PAOPEN_FAILED =  4027
Public Const lsERR_MAIL_LAOPEN_FAILED =  4028
Public Const lsERR_MAIL_VIM_MESSAGE =  4029
Public Const lsERR_MAIL_CANT_CREATE =  4030
Public Const lsERR_MAIL_UNKNOWN_PROP =  4031
Public Const lsERR_MAIL_INVALID_MSG =  4032
Public Const lsERR_MAIL_NOPUBLIC_GRP =  4033
Public Const lsERR_MAIL_NOPRIVATE_GRP =  4034
Public Const lsERR_MAIL_GRPCREATE_FAILED =  4035
Public Const lsERR_MAIL_GROUP_DELETED =  4036
Public Const lsERR_MAIL_NAME_REQUIRED =  4037
```

```
Public Const lsERR_NOTES_FAILURE = 4038
Public Const lsERR_NOTES_NOSUCH_VIEW = 4039
Public Const lsERR_NOTES_NOFTINDEX = 4040
Public Const lsERR_NOTES_DBCREATE_FAILED = 4041
Public Const lsERR_NOTES_DBDELETE_FAILED = 4042
Public Const lsERR_NOTES_DBOPEN_FAILED = 4043
Public Const lsERR_NOTES_INVALID_FORMULA = 4044
Public Const lsERR_NOTES_INVALID_DATE = 4045
Public Const lsERR_NOTES_COPY_FAILED = 4046
Public Const lsERR_NOTES_VIEWOPEN_FAILED = 4047
Public Const lsERR_NOTES_NOTEDEL_FAILED = 4048
Public Const lsERR_NOTES_NEXTITEM_FAILED = 4049
Public Const lsERR_NOTES_FINDITEM_FAILED = 4050
Public Const lsERR_NOTES_MODLOAD_FAILED = 4051
Public Const lsERR_NOTES_PROCFIND_FAILED = 4052
Public Const lsERR_NOTES_RTWRITE_FAILED = 4053
Public Const lsERR_NOTES_RTCONVERT_FAILED = 4054
Public Const lsERR_NOTES_FTSRCH_FAILED = 4055
Public Const lsERR_NOTES_QUERY_FAILED = 4056
Public Const lsERR_NOTES_DOCSEARCH_FAILED = 4057
Public Const lsERR_NOTES_ITEMCOPY_FAILED = 4058
Public Const lsERR_NOTES_CREATENOTE_FAILED = 4059
Public Const lsERR_NOTES_DBNOACCESS = 4060
Public Const lsERR_NOTES_UNAME_LOOKUP = 4061
Public Const lsERR_NOTES_SESOPEN_FAILED = 4062
Public Const lsERR_NOTES_DATABASE_NOTOPEN = 4063
Public Const lsERR_NOTES_SESSION_DATECONV = 4064
Public Const lsERR_NOTES_SESSION_VALNOTSUPP = 4065
Public Const lsERR_NOTES_CANT_GETNTH = 4066
Public Const lsERR_NOTES_ATTACH_FAILED = 4067
Public Const lsERR_NOTES_DETACH_FAILED = 4068
Public Const lsERR_NOTES_EXTRACT_FAILED = 4069
Public Const lsERR_NOTES_DIRSEARCH_FAILED = 4070
Public Const lsERR_NOTES_BAD_INDEX = 4071
Public Const lsERR_NOTES_NOSUCH_DIRECTORY = 4072
Public Const lsERR_CDTEXTCREATE_FAILED = 4073
Public Const lsERR_CDASSIM_FAILED = 4074
Public Const lsERR_NOT_RT_ITEM = 4075
Public Const lsERR_NOTES_FORMCOMP_FAILED = 4076
Public Const lsERR_NOTES_FORMEVAL_FAILED = 4077
Public Const lsERR_NOTES_ITEMCREATE_FAILED = 4078
Public Const lsERR_NOTES_DECRYPT_FAILED = 4079
Public Const lsERR_NOTES_NOTLOCAL_IDX = 4080
Public Const lsERR_NOTES_FTIDX_FAILED = 4081
Public Const lsERR_NOTES_NOTEOPEN_FAILED = 4082
Public Const lsERR_NOTES_RENDER_FAILED = 4083
Public Const lsERR_NOTES_FILENOTFOUND = 4084
Public Const lsERR_NOTES_UNKNOWN_TYPE = 4085
Public Const lsERR_NOTES_FILEOPEN_FAILED = 4086
Public Const lsERR_NOTES_FILEWRITE_FAILED = 4087
Public Const lsERR_NOTES_DATE_NOTSET = 4088
Public Const lsERR_NOTES_NODBNAME = 4089
Public Const lsERR_NOTES_TEMPLCOPY_FAILED = 4090
Public Const lsERR_NOTES_BAD_UNID = 4091
```

```
Public Const lsERR_NOTES_UNAME_REQ =  4092
Public Const lsERR_NOTES_GETACL_FAILED =  4093
Public Const lsERR_NOTES_ACLENTRY_FAILED =  4094
Public Const lsERR_NOTES_ACL_INVALID =  4095
Public Const lsERR_NOTES_QUERYACL_FAILED =  4096
Public Const lsERR_NOTES_REFRESH_FAILED =  4097
Public Const lsERR_NOTES_OLEPKG_FAILED =  4098
Public Const lsERR_NOTES_TMPFILE_FAILED =  4099
Public Const lsERR_NOTES_READFILE_FAILED =  4100
Public Const lsERR_NOTES_RTRENDER_FAILED =  4101
Public Const lsERR_NOTES_WRONG_CLASS =  4102
Public Const lsERR_NOTES_INVALID_ID =  4103
Public Const lsERR_NOTES_INVALID_AGENT =  4104
Public Const lsERR_NOTES_VIEWCLONE_FAILED =  4105
Public Const lsERR_NOTES_NOVIEWNAME =  4106
Public Const lsERR_NOTES_NEWSGROUPDB_FAILED =  4107
Public Const lsERR_NOTES_NONEWSGROUPNAME =  4108
Public Const lsERR_LOG_DBOPEN_FAILED =  4135
Public Const lsERR_LOG_FOPEN_FAILED =  4136
Public Const lsERR_LOG_CDCREATE_FAILED =  4137
Public Const lsERR_LOG_MAILLOG_FAILED =  4138
Public Const lsERR_MEM_HVPOOLFULL =  4139
Public Const lsERR_NOTES_COPYACL_FAILED =  4150
Public Const lsERR_NOTES_DOC_NOTINVIEW =  4151
Public Const lsERR_NOTES_NOFTQUERY =  4152
Public Const lsERR_NOTES_NOITEMNAME =  4153
Public Const lsERR_NOTES_NOTEUPDATE_FAILED =  4154
Public Const lsERR_NOTES_NOTELOCATE_FAILED =  4155
Public Const lsERR_NOTES_VIEWDEL_FAILED =  4156
Public Const lsERR_LOG_CONSTRUCT_FAILED =  4157
Public Const lsERR_SEM_ALLOC_FAILED =  4158
Public Const lsERR_NOTES_LOOKUP_FAILED =  4159
Public Const lsERR_NOTES_SEND_FAILED =  4160
Public Const lsERR_NOTES_NCREATE_FAILED =  4161
Public Const lsERR_MACRO_IDTBL_FAILED =  4162
Public Const lsERR_MACRO_RUN_FAILED =  4163
Public Const lsERR_NOTES_DBOPEN_NOTLOCAL =  4164
Public Const lsERR_NOTES_SIGN_NOPERM =  4165
Public Const lsERR_NOTES_ENCRYPT_NOPERM =  4166
Public Const lsERR_NOTES_ENCRYPT_FAILED =  4167
Public Const lsERR_NOTES_NOSENDTO =  4168
Public Const lsERR_LOG_EVENTPUT_FAILED =  4169
Public Const lsERR_LOG_INVALID_EVTYPE =  4170
Public Const lsERR_LOG_INVALID_SEVERITY =  4171
Public Const lsERR_NOTES_NO_NEWSLETTERDOCS =  4172
Public Const lsERR_NOTES_MAILDBOPEN_FAILED =  4173
Public Const lsERR_NOTES_NEWSLETTER_FAILED =  4174
Public Const lsERR_NOTES_DFLT_VID_FAILED =  4175
Public Const lsERR_NOTES_KEYFIND_FAILED =  4176
Public Const lsERR_NOTES_RTTEXT_FAILED =  4177
Public Const lsERR_NOTES_RTDOCLINK_FAILED =  4178
Public Const lsERR_NOTES_NOPERM_DISKIO =  4179
Public Const lsERR_NOTES_NOPERM_SIGN =  4180
Public Const lsERR_NOTES_NOPERM_ENCRYPT =  4181
```

```
Public Const lsERR_NOTES_NOPERM_ENVIRON =  4182
Public Const lsERR_NOTES_NOPERM_ANY =  4183
Public Const lsERR_NOTES_NOSERV_DB =  4184
Public Const lsERR_NOTES_INVALID_DB =  4185
Public Const lsERR_NOTES_INVALID_CREDEL =  4186
Public Const lsERR_NOTES_INVALID_DOC =  4187
Public Const lsERR_NOTES_DBS_MUST_MATCH =  4188
Public Const lsERR_NOTES_RESPONSE_FAILED =  4189
Public Const lsERR_NOTES_NOLISTS =  4190
Public Const lsERR_NOTES_CONTAINS_FAILED =  4191
Public Const lsERR_NOTES_MUSTBE_STRING =  4192
Public Const lsERR_NOTES_DESVIEW_FAILED =  4193
Public Const lsERR_NOTES_ITEMARR_FAILED =  4194
Public Const lsERR_NOTES_SRVSEARCH_FAILED =  4195
Public Const lsERR_NOTES_UNKNOWN_SRCHTYPE =  4196
Public Const lsERR_NOTES_MUSTCALL_FIRSTDB =  4197
Public Const lsERR_NOTES_ALLDOCS_FAILED =  4198
Public Const lsERR_NOTES_ITYPENOT_TEXT =  4199
Public Const lsERR_NOTES_INVALID_ITYPE =  4200
Public Const lsERR_NOTES_NOSUCH_FOLDER =  4201
Public Const lsERR_NOTES_ADDRBOOK_FAILED =  4202
Public Const lsERR_NOTES_NOTCONTEXT_DB =  4203
Public Const lsERR_NOTES_LTDACCESS_FAILED =  4204
Public Const lsERR_NOTES_LTDUPDATE_FAILED =  4205
Public Const lsERR_NOTES_BADVIEW_VERSION =  4206
Public Const lsERR_NOTES_NEED_ADT =  4207
Public Const lsERR_NOTES_ACLWRITE_FAILED =  4208
Public Const lsERR_NOTES_RENAME_FAILED =  4209
Public Const lsERR_NOTES_NOSUCH_ROLENAME =  4210
Public Const lsERR_NOTES_PRIVNAME_FAILED =  4211
Public Const lsERR_NOTES_READPRIV_FAILED =  4212
Public Const lsERR_NOTES_DELPRIV_FAILED =  4213
Public Const lsERR_NOTES_DELENTRY_FAILED =  4214
Public Const lsERR_NOTES_NOSERV_EVENTS =  4215
Public Const lsERR_NOTES_INVALID_ACLENTRYNAME =  4216
Public Const lsERR_NOTES_ENTRYNAME_FAILED =  4217
Public Const lsERR_NOTES_NOTLOCAL_REPL =  4218
Public Const lsERR_NOTES_REPL_FAILED =  4219
Public Const lsERR_NOTES_NOTLOCAL_COMPACT =  4220
Public Const lsERR_NOTES_COMPACT_FAILED =  4221
Public Const lsERR_NOTES_TIMEADJUST_FAILED  =  4222
Public Const lsERR_NOTES_NOSUCH_EMBED  =  4223
Public Const lsERR_NOTES_NOSUCH_EOFILE  =  4224
Public Const lsERR_NOTES_NOSUCH_PATH  =  4225
Public Const lsERR_NOTES_EMBEDARR_FAILED  =  4226
Public Const lsERR_NOTES_NOADDRS_FOUND  =  4227
Public Const lsERR_NOTES_DUP_ROLENAME  =  4228
Public Const lsERR_NOTES_CANTCREATE_FOLDER  =  4229
Public Const lsERR_NOTERENDER_FAILED  =  4230
Public Const lsERR_NOFROMFIELD  =  4231
Public Const lsERR_TEXTLIST_FAILED  =  4232
Public Const lsERR_NOTES_NOTA_DOCUMENT  =  4233
Public Const lsERR_NOTES_VALIDATE_FAILED  =  4234
Public Const lsERR_NOTES_ABSTRACT_BUFFER  =  4235
```

```
Public Const lsERR_NOTES_ABSTRACTING_TEXT  =  4236
Public Const lsERR_NOTES_DESAGENT_FAILED  =  4237
Public Const lsERR_NOTES_MIXED_ARRAY  =  4238
Public Const lsERR_NOTES_INVALID_DOCLINK  =  4239
Public Const lsERR_TEXTLIST_BAD_INPUT  =  4240
Public Const lsERR_NOTES_CANTREMOVE  =  4241
Public Const lsERR_NOTES_CANTENCRYPT  =  4242
Public Const lsERR_NOTES_CANTCLOSEDB  =  4243
Public Const lsERR_NOTES_CANTRUN_OLEOBJ  =  4244
Public Const lsERR_NOTES_CANTSHOW_OLEOBJ  =  4245
Public Const lsERR_NOTES_NOEMBEDDED_OBJ  =  4246
Public Const lsERR_NOTES_NOSUCH_EMBEDCLASS  =  4247
Public Const lsERR_NOTES_CANTGET_DBSUMMARY  =  4248
Public Const lsERR_NOTES_CANTCOPY_ITEMTYPE  =  4249
Public Const lsERR_NOTES_NEED_DB  =  4250
Public Const lsERR_NOTES_NEED_NOTE  =  4251
Public Const lsERR_NOTES_CANT_LINK_OLE1  =  4252
Public Const lsERR_NOTES_ROLENAME_TOOBIG  =  4253
Public Const lsERR_NOTES_EOARRAY_FAILED  =  4254
Public Const lsERR_NOTES_ATTACHINFO_FAILED  =  4255
Public Const lsERR_NOTES_QUOTAINFO_FAILED  =  4256
Public Const lsERR_NOTES_DOCNOTSAVED  =  4257
Public Const lsERR_NOTES_ACLNEXT_INVALID  =  4258
Public Const lsERR_NOTES_NOTAFILE  =  4259
Public Const lsERR_NOTES_CANTFIND_ATTACHMENT  =  4260
Public Const lsERR_NOTES_NOSUCH_VERB  =  4261
Public Const lsERR_NOTES_DOVERB_FAILED  =  4262
Public Const lsERR_NOTES_INVALID_ADTTYPE  =  4263
Public Const lsERR_NOTES_FTQUERY_FAILED  =  4264
Public Const lsERR_NOTES_NOSUCH_DBID  =  4265
Public Const lsERR_NOTES_OPENBYRID_FAILED  =  4266
Public Const lsERR_NOTES_BAD_UNPROCFT  =  4267
Public Const lsERR_AGENT_NO_RECURSION  =  4268
Public Const lsERR_NOTES_CANTGET_MAILSERVER  =  4269
Public Const lsERR_NOTES_BAD_NOTEID  =  4270
Public Const lsERR_NOTES_DBSECURITY  =  4271
Public Const lsERR_NOTES_DELETE_AGENT  =  4272
Public Const lsERR_NOTES_RUN_AGENT  =  4273
Public Const lsERR_NOTES_NOSUCH_DOCINDEX  =  4274
Public Const lsERR_NOTES_BAD_SOURCE_CLASS  =  4275
Public Const lsERR_NOTES_CANT_CHANGE_DEFACL  =  4276
Public Const lsERR_NOTES_LINKNOCLASS =  4277
Public Const lsERR_NOTES_CANTDO_ARRAYOFARRAY  =  4278
Public Const lsERR_NOTES_SESSION_CLOSED  =  4279
Public Const lsERR_NOTES_CANTOPEN_URLDB  =  4280
Public Const lsERR_NOTES_NEED_URL  =  4281
Public Const lsERR_NOTES_INVALID_URL  =  4282
Public Const lsERR_NOTES_INVALID_URLHEADER  =  4283
Public Const lsERR_NOTES_NOSUCH_URLHEADER  =  4284
Public Const lsERR_NOTES_NOUNPROC_DOCS  =  4285
Public Const lsERR_NOTES_EMBED_FAILED  =  4286
Public Const lsERR_NOTES_NODEL_CURRENTDB  =  4287
Public Const lsERR_NOTES_INVALID_TIMEEXPR  =  4288
Public Const lsERR_NOTES_RECURSIVE_RENDER  =  4289
```

```
Public Const lsERR_NOTES_INVALID_ITEM  =  4290
Public Const lsERR_NOTES_NOMOVETO_PRIV1STUSE  =  4291
Public Const lsERR_NOTES_SAMESRV_REPLICA  =  4292
Public Const lsERR_NOTES_CANT_SIGN  =  4293
Public Const lsERR_NOTES_NO_MATCH  =  4294
Public Const lsERR_NOTES_AMBIGUOUS_MATCH  =  4295
Public Const lsERR_NOTES_DBALREADY_OPEN  =  4296
Public Const lsERR_NOTES_OLE_NOTAVAIL  =  4297
Public Const lsERR_NOTES_ARRAY_NOGOOD  =  4298
Public Const lsERR_NOTES_REGARG_NOTGIVEN  =  4299
Public Const lsERR_NOTES_MISSING_CERTID  =  4300
Public Const lsERR_NOTES_NOCERT_CTX  =  4301
Public Const lsERR_NOTES_REGFAILED  =  4302
Public Const lsERR_NOTES_SRVREGFAILED  =  4303
Public Const lsERR_NOTES_CERTREGFAILED  =  4304
Public Const lsERR_NOTES_XCERTFAILED  =  4305
Public Const lsERR_NOTES_RECERTFAILED  =  4306
Public Const lsERR_NOTES_NOSUCH_BOOL  =  4307
Public Const lsERR_NOTES_CANTSWITCH_ID  =  4308
Public Const lsERR_NOTES_NOSUCH_MAILPATH  =  4309
Public Const lsERR_NOTES_BAD_IDFILE  =  4310
Public Const lsERR_NOTES_CANTADD_USER  =  4311
Public Const lsERR_NOTES_CANTADD_SERV  =  4312
Public Const lsERR_NOTES_CANTADD_CERT  =  4313
Public Const lsERR_NOTES_NOCURRENT_AGENT  =  4314
Public Const lsERR_NOTES_AGENTLOG_FAILED  =  4315
Public Const lsERR_NOTES_NOSUCH_CERTIDTYPE  =  4316
Public Const lsERR_NOTES_NOCURRENT_FTRESULT  =  4317
Public Const lsERR_NOTES_IDTBL_FAILED  =  4318
Public Const lsERR_NOTES_PROF_ARG_MISSING  =  4319
Public Const lsERR_NOTES_NOSUCH_PROFILE  =  4320
Public Const lsERR_NOTES_PROFUPDATE_FAILED  =  4321
Public Const lsERR_NOTES_PROFDELETE_FAILED  =  4322
Public Const lsERR_NOTES_NOSUCH_ARG  =  4323
Public Const lsERR_NOTES_WRONG_UNID_LEN  =  4324
Public Const lsERR_NOTES_DESFORM_FAILED  =  4325
Public Const lsERR_NOTES_FORMDEL_FAILED  =  4326
Public Const lsERR_NOTES_NOCLOSE_CURRDB  =  4327
Public Const lsERR_NOTES_FREETIME_FAILED  =  4328
Public Const lsERR_NOTES_UNIFORM_FAILED  =  4329
Public Const lsERR_NOTES_GETOPTION_FAILED  =  4330
Public Const lsERR_NOTES_MARKREAD_FAILED  =  4331
Public Const lsERR_NOTES_MARKUNREAD_FAILED  =  4332
Public Const lsERR_NOTES_MULTIDB_FAILED  =  4333
Public Const lsERR_NOTES_ADDPROF_FAILED  =  4334
Public Const lsERR_NOTES_ULOOKUP_FAILED  =  4335
Public Const lsERR_NOTES_INVALID_OBJECT  =  4336
Public Const lsERR_NOTES_STAMP_FAILED  =  4337
Public Const lsERR_NOTES_BAD_ORGUNIT  =  4338
Public Const lsERR_NOTES_BAD_FTSORT  =  4339
Public Const lsERR_NOTES_NOTCONTEXT_COLLEC  =  4340
Public Const lsERR_NOTES_ECLACCESS_FAILED  =  4341
Public Const lsERR_NOTES_W32DOM_FAILED  =  4342
Public Const lsERR_NOTES_W32DOM_NOFIRSTUSER  =  4343
```

```
Public Const lsERR_NOTES_W32DOM_BADPLATFORM  =  4344
Public Const lsERR_NOTES_W32DOM_BADNETAPI32  =  4345
Public Const lsERR_NOTES_W32DOM_DOMAIN_CONTROLLER  =  4346
Public Const lsERR_NOTES_TOOMANY_SORT_KEYS  =  4347
Public Const lsERR_NOTES_BAD_KEYTYPE  =  4348
Public Const lsERR_NOTES_CANT_SELF_ASSIMILATE  =  4349
Public Const lsERR_NOTES_CANT_SELF_COPY  =  4350
Public Const lsERR_NOTES_POP3_FAILED  =  4351
Public Const lsERR_NOTES_ARRCREATE_FAILED  =  4352
Public Const lsERR_NOTES_AGSAVE_FAILED  =  4353
Public Const lsERR_NOTES_CANTREMOVE_AGC  =  4354
Public Const lsERR_NOTES_CANTENCRYPT_AGC  =  4355
Public Const lsERR_NOTES_RTSTYLE_CREATEFAILED  =  4356
Public Const lsERR_NOTES_RTSTYLE_APPENDFAILED  =  4357
Public Const lsERR_NOTES_RTSTYLE_BADFONT  =  4358
Public Const lsERR_NOTES_NO_CONTEXTDB =  4359
Public Const lsERR_NOTES_NULL_APPENDLIST  =  4360
Public Const lsERR_NOTES_NOSUCH_JAVA_TYPE  =  4361
Public Const lsERR_NOTES_INVALID_JARRAY  =  4362
Public Const lsERR_NOTES_RTSTYLE_BADBOOL  =  4363
Public Const lsERR_NOTES_RTSTYLE_BADFONTSIZE  =  4364
Public Const lsERR_NOTES_RTSTYLE_BADCOLOR  =  4365
Public Const lsERR_NOTES_RTSTYLE_BADEFFECT  =  4366
Public Const lsERR_NOTES_NOTREMOTE_DB  =  4367
Public Const lsERR_NOTES_RTITEM_EXISTS  =  4368
Public Const lsERR_NOTES_NOFORM  =  4369
Public Const lsERR_NOTES_NOTA_VECTOR  =  4370
Public Const lsERR_NOTES_SERVER_SWITCH  =  4371
Public Const lsERR_NOTES_DBDIR_THREAD  =  4372
```

LSXUIERR.LSS

This file is located in the Notes root directory. It contains user interface error message constants. These constants can be used in your scripts via the USELSX command:

```
USELSX "LSXUIERR.LSS"

FILE:

Public Const lsERR_LSXUI_UNKNOWN_PROP =  4400
Public Const lsERR_LSXUI_INVALID_ARGS  =  4401
Public Const lsERR_LSXUI_NO_WORKSPACE_WND  =  4402
Public Const lsERR_LSXUI_NO_DATABASE_WND  =  4403
Public Const lsERR_LSXUI_LSBE_DB_CREATE  =  4404
Public Const lsERR_LSXUI_NO_DOCUMENT_WND  =  4405
Public Const lsERR_LSXUI_LSBE_DOC_CREATE  =  4406
Public Const lsERR_LSXUI_DOC_CMD_NOT_AVAILABLE  =  4407
Public Const lsERR_LSXUI_FIELD_CMD_NOT_AVAILABLE  =  4408
Public Const lsERR_LSXUI_CMD_NOT_AVAILABLE  =  4409
Public Const lsERR_LSXUI_DOC_OBJ_NOT_VALID  =  4410
Public Const lsERR_LSXUI_DOC_SAVE_CANCELLED  =  4411
Public Const lsERR_LSXUI_NOTES_ERROR  =  4412
Public Const lsERR_LSXUI_INVALID_LSX  =  4413
```

```
Public Const lsERR_LSXUI_INVALID_STR_ARG  =  4414
Public Const lsERR_LSXUI_INVALID_NULL_ARG  =  4415
Public Const lsERR_LSXUI_NO_NOTE  =  4416
Public Const lsERR_LSXUI_MODALEDIT_DIALOGUP. =  4417
Public Const lsERR_LSXUI_QUERY_OPEN  =  4418
Public Const lsERR_LSXUI_INVALID_OBJ_ARG  =  4419
```

appendix B

Notes/Domino classes

NotesACL class

The NotesDataRange class can be used to represent a range of dates and times. The `CreateDateRange` method in the NotesSession class can be used to create an instance.

Properties

Parent

Description	The database that contains the ACL.
Format	Sets NotesDatabase = NotesACL.Parent
Type	NotesDatabase
Access	Read

Roles

Description	Retrieves a list of the roles defined in an ACL.
Format	Array = NotesACL.Roles
Type	Array of String values
Access	Read

UniformAccess

Description	Signals whether or not uniform access is set on the ACL. This setting is located in the advanced section of the ACL dialog box.
Format	Boolean = NotesACL.UniformAccess NotesACL.UniformAccess = Boolean
Type	Boolean
Access	Read/Write

InternetLevel (Notes 5.0 or higher)

Description	Sets the maximum Internet name and password access. Located on the Advanced tab of the ACL dialog box.
Format	Integer = NotesACL.InternetLevel NotesACL.InternetLevel = Integer
Type	Integer
Access	Read/Write

Methods

AddRole

Description	Adds a new role to the ACL.
Parameters	String - name of the role to add.
Format	Calls NotesACL.AddRole(String)
Return	None

CreateACLEntry

Description	Adds a new entry to the ACL.
Parameters	String - name of the user/group/server. Integer - access level (ACLLEVEL_NOACCESS,ACLLEVEL_MANAGER,ACLLEVEL_DESIGNER,ACLLEVE L_EDITOR,ACLLEVEL_AUTHOR,ACLLEVEL_READER,ACLLEVEL_DEPOSITOR)
Format	Sets NotesACLEntry = NotesACL.CreateACLEntry(String,Integer)
Return	NotesACLEntry object

DeleteRole

Description	Removes a role from an ACL.
Parameters	String - name of the role to remove.
Format	Calls NotesACL.DeleteRole(String)
Return	None

GetEntry

Description	Obtains handle on entry in the ACL.
Parameters	String - name of the entry to retrieve.
Format	Sets NotesACLEntry = NotesACL.GetEntry(String)
Return	NotesACLEntry object or NOTHING if no match is found.

GetFirstEntry

Description	Returns the first entry from an ACL. Use with GetNextEntry method to traverse all entries in the ACL.
Parameters	None
Format	Sets NotesACLEntry = NotesACL.GetFirstEntry
Return	NotesACLEntry

GetNextEntry

Description	Retrieves the next entry from an ACL given a NotesACLEntry object as the reference point.
Parameters	NotesACLEntry - the entry to use as reference point for retrieving the next entry.
Format	Sets NotesACLEntry = NotesACL.GetNextEntry(NotesACLEntry)
Return	NotesACLEntry object or NOTHING if there are no more entries.

RenameRole

Description	Renames a role in the ACL.
Parameters	String - the current role name. String - the new role name.
Format	Calls NotesACL.RenameRole(String, String)
Return	None

Save

Description	Writes modifications to the ACL to disk.
Parameters	None
Format	Calls NotesACL.Save
Return	None

NotesACLEntry class

The NotesACLEntry class.

Properties

CanCreateDocuments

Description	Signals whether or not an ACL entry can create documents.
Format	Boolean = NotesACLEntry.CanCreateDocuments NotesACLEntry.CanCreateDocuments = Boolean
Type	Boolean
Access	Read/Write

CanCreateLSOrJavaAgent (Notes 5.0 or higher)

Description	Signals whether or not an ACL entry can create LS/Java agents. This is a new selection on the Basics tab in the ACL dialog box.
Format	Boolean = NotesACLEntry.CanCreateLSOrJavaAgent NotesACLEntry.CanCreateLSOrJavaAgent = Boolean

Type	Boolean
Access	Read/Write

CanCreatePersonalAgent

Description	Signals whether or not an ACL entry can create personal agents.
Format	Boolean = NotesACLEntry.CanCreatePersonalAgent NotesACLEntry.CanCreatePersonalAgent = Boolean
Type	Boolean
Access	Read/Write

CanCreatePersonalFolder

Description	Signals whether or not an ACL entry can create personal folders.
Format	Boolean = NotesACLEntry.CanCreatePersonalFolder NotesACLEntry.CanCreatePersonalFolder = Boolean
Type	Boolean
Access	Read/Write

CanDeleteDocuments

Description	Signals whether or not an ACL entry can delete documents.
Format	Boolean = NotesACLEntry.CanDeleteDocuments NotesACLEntry.CanDeleteDocuments = Boolean
Type	Boolean
Access	Read/Write

IsAdminReaderAuthor (Notes 5.0 or higher)

Description	Signals whether an ACL entry is an admin reader/author.
Format	Boolean = NotesACLEntry.IsAdminReaderAuthor NotesACLEntry.IsAdminReaderAuthor = Boolean
Type	Boolean
Access	Read/Write

IsAdminServer (Notes 5.0 or higher)

Description	Signals whether or not an entry is adminstration server.
Format	Boolean = NotesACLEntry.IsAdminServer NotesACLEntry.IsAdminServerr = Boolean
Type	Boolean
Access	Read/Write

IsGroup (Notes 5.0 or higher)

Description	Signals whether or not an entry is a group.
Format	Boolean = NotesACLEntry.IsGroup NotesACLEntry.IsGroup = Boolean
Type	Boolean
Access	Read/Write

IsPerson (Notes 5.0 or higher)

Description	Signals whether or not an entry is a person.

Format	Boolean = NotesACLEntry.IsPerson NotesACLEntry.IsPerson = Boolean
Type	Boolean
Access	Read/Write

IsPublicReader

Description	Signals whether or not an ACL entry is a public reader.
Format	Boolean = NotesACLEntry.IsPublicReader NotesACLEntry.IsPublicReader = Boolean
Type	Boolean
Access	Read/Write

IsPublicWriter

Description	Signals whether or not an ACL entry is a public writer.
Format	Boolean = NotesACLEntry.IsPublicWriter NotesACLEntry.IsPublicWriter = Boolean
Type	Boolean
Access	Read/Write

IsServer (Notes 5.0 or higher)

Description	Signals whether or not an entry is a server.
Format	Boolean = NotesACLEntry.IsServer NotesACLEntry.IsServer = Boolean
Type	Boolean
Access	Read/Write

Level

Description	The access level for the entry.
Format	Integer = NotesACLEntry.Level NotesACLEntry.Level = Integer
Type	Integer
Access	Read/Write

Name

Description	The name (username, group, server) of an entry.
Format	String = NotesACLEntry.Name NotesACLEntry.Name = String
Type	String
Access	Read/Write

Parent

Description	The NotesACL that contains the entry.
Format	NotesACL = NotesACLEntry.Parent
Type	NotesACL
Access	Read

Roles

Description	The list of roles, if any, enabled for an entry.

Format	Array = NotesACLEntry.Roles
Type	Array of string values.
Access	Read

Methods

DisableRole	
Description	Disables a role for an entry.
Parameters	String - name of the role
Format	Calls NotesACLEntry.DisableRole(String)
Return	None
EnableRole	
Description	Enables a role for an entry.
Parameters	String - name of the role to enable.
Format	Calls NotesACLEntry.EnableRole(String)
Return	None
IsRoleEnabled	
Description	Signals whether or not an entry has a role enabled.
Parameters	String - name of the role to check.
Format	Boolean = NotesACLEntry.IsRoleEnabled(String)
Return	Boolean
New	
Description	Creates an entry in the ACL.
Parameters	NotesACL - the ACL in which the entry will be created String - Name of the new entry Integer - Access level of the new entry.
Format	Dim EntryName As New NotesACLEntry(NotesACL, String, Integer)
Return	None
Remove	
Description	Removes an entry from an ACL.
Parameters	None
Format	Call NotesACLEntry.Remove
Retrun	None

NotesAgent class

The NotesAgent class.

Properties

Comment

Description	Any comments associated with an agent.
Format	String = NotesAgent.Comment NotesAgent.Comment = String
Type	String
Access	Read/Write

CommonOwner

Description	The common name of the user that last modified and saved the agent.
Format	String = NotesAgent.CommonOwner
Type	String
Access	Read

IsEnabled

Description	Signals whether or not an agent is enabled.
Format	Boolean = NotesAgent.IsEnabled
Type	Boolean
Access	Read

IsNotesAgent (Notes 5.0 or higher)

Description	Signals whether or not an agent is a Notes agent (True) (web).
Format	Boolean = NotesAgent.IsNotesAgent
Type	Boolean
Access	Read

IsPublic

Description	Signals whether an agent is public or private.
Format	Boolean = NotesAgent.IsPublic
Type	Boolean
Access	Read

IsWebAgent (Notes 5.0 or higher)

Description	Signals whether an agent is a web agent (True) or Notes (False)
Format	Boolean = NotesAgent.IsWebAgent
Type	Boolean
Access	Read

LastRun

Description	The data an agent ran last.
Format	Variant = NotesAgent.LastRun
Type	Variant
Access	Read

Name

Description	The name of the agent.
Format	String = NotesAgent.Name
Type	String
Access	Read

Owner

Description	The fully distinguished name of the user that last modified and saved the agent.
Format	String = NotesACL.Owner
Type	String
Access	Read

Parent

Description	The NotesDatabase that contains the agent.
Format	NotesDatabase = NotesAgent.Parent
Type	NotesDatabase
Access	Read

Query

Description	The text, if any, of the query added via the Add Search button when creating/editing an agent.
Format	String = NotesAgent.Query
Type	String
Access	Read

ServerName

Description	The name of the server on which the agent resides.
Format	String = NotesAgent.ServerName
Type	String
Access	Read

Target (Notes 5.0 or higher)

Description	The target server for an agent.
Format	Integer = NotesAgent.Target
Type	Integer
Access	

Trigger (Notes 5.0 or higher)

Description	Starts a scheduled agent, such as New Mail or Newly Created and/or Modified documents.

Format	Integer = NotesAgent.Trigger
Type	Integer
Access	

Methods

Remove

Description	Deletes an agent from a database.
Parameters	None
Format	Calls NotesAgent.Remove
Return	None

Run

Description	Executes an agent; an agent cannot call this method on itself.
Parameters	None
Format	Call NotesAgent.Run
Return	None

NotesDatabase class

The NotesDatabase class

Properties

ACL

Description	The ACL of the database
Format	Set NotesACL = NotesDatabase.ACL
Type	NotesACL object
Access	Read

Agents

Description	The list of agents in a database.
Format	Array = NotesDatabase.Agents
Type	Array of NotesAgent objects
Access	Read

AllDocuments

Description	All documents from the database assembled in a collection.
Format	NotesDocumentCollection = NotesDatabase.AllDocuments
Type	NotesDocumentCollection object
Access	Read

Categories

Description	The categories assigned to the database in the Database Library database.
Format	String = NotesDatabase.Categories NotesDatabase.Categories = String
Type	String
Access	Read/Write

Created

Description	The date the database was created.
Format	Variant = NotesDatabase.Created
Type	Variant
Access	Read

CurrentAccessLevel

Description	The current user's access level in the database.
Format	Integer = NotesDatabase.CurrentAccessLevel
Type	Integer
Access	Read

DelayUpdates

Description	Signals whether updates to a server database are delayed.
Format	Boolean = NotesDatabase.DelayUpdates NotesDatabase.DelayUpdates = Boolean
Type	Boolean
Access	Read/Write

DesignTemplateName

Description	The template name, if any, from which the database inherits its design.
Format	String = NotesDatabase.DesignTemplateName
Type	String
Access	Read

FileName

Description	The file name of the database. It does not include the file extension or path.
Format	String = NotesDatabase.FileName
Type	String
Access	Read

FilePath

Description	The path and file name (including extension) of the database.
Format	String = NotesDatabase.FilePath
Type	String
Access	Read

FolderReferencesEnabled (Notes 5.0 or higher)

Description	Signals whether or not folder references are enabled.
Format	Boolean = NotesDatabase.FolderReferencesEnabled
Type	Boolean
Access	Read

Forms

Description	All forms in a database.
Format	Variant = NotesDatabase.Forms
Type	Array of NotesForm objects
Access	Read

IsFTIndexed

Description	Signals whether or not a database has a Full Text Index.
Format	Boolean = NotesDatabase.IsFTIndexed
Type	Boolean
Access	Read

IsMultiDBSearch

Description	Signals whether or not a database represents a multidatabase search index.
Format	Boolean = NotesDatabase.IsMultiDBSearch
Type	Boolean
Access	Read

IsOpen

Description	Signals whether or not a database is open.
Format	Boolean = NotesDatabase.IsOpen
Type	Boolean
Access	Read

IsPrivateAddressBook

Description	Signals whether or not a database is a private address book.
Format	Boolean = NotesDatabase.IsPrivateAddressBook
Type	Boolean
Access	Read

IsPublicAddressBook

Description	Signals whether or not a database is a public address book.
Format	Boolean = NotesDatabase.IsPublicAddressBook
Type	Boolean
Access	Read

LastFTIndexed

Description	The date the full text index, if exists, was last updated.
Format	Variant = NotesDatabase.LastFTIndexed

Type	Variant
Access	Read

LastModified

Description	The date the database was last modified.
Format	Variant = NotesDatabase.LastModified
Type	Variant
Access	Read

Managers

Description	The list of ACL entries that have Manager access to the database.
Format	Array = NotesDatabase.Managers
Type	Array of String values
Access	Read

Parent

Description	The NotesSession object that contains the database.
Format	Set NotesSession = NotesDatabase.Parent
Type	NotesSession object
Access	Read

PercentUsed

Description	The percent of a database that is taken by data.
Format	Double = NotesDatabase.PercentUsed
Type	Double
Access	Read

ReplicaID

Description	The ReplicaID of the database.
Format	String = NotesDatabase.ReplicaID
Type	String
Access	Read

ReplicationInfo (Notes 5.0 or higher)

Description	Returns a NotesReplication object representing the replication settings for a database.
Format	Set NotesReplication = NotesDatabase.ReplicationInfo
Type	NotesReplication object
Access	

Server

Description	The server on which the database resides.
Format	String = NotesDatabase.Server
Type	String
Access	Read

Size

Description	The size of the database is bytes.
Format	Double = NotesDatabase.Size
Type	Double
Access	Read

SizeQuota

Description	The size quote of a database.
Format	Long = NotesDatabase.SizeQuota
Type	Long
Access	Read

TemplateName

Description	The template name of the database, if it is a design template.
Format	String = NotesDatabase.TemplateName
Type	String
Access	Read

Title

Description	The database title.
Format	String = NotesDatabase.Title NotesDatabase.Title = String
Type	String
Access	Read/Write

UnprocessedDocuments

Description	Collection of documents that have not been processed previously. This is used by agents to retrieve only those documents not previously processed by them.
Format	NotesDocumentCollection = NotesDatabase.Unprocessed-Documents
Type	NotesDocumentCollection
Access	Read

Views

Description	List of views in the database.
Format	Variant = NotesDatabase.Views
Type	Array of NotesView objects
Access	Read

Methods

Compact

Description	Compacts the database; returns the difference in size from before and after compacting.
Parameters	None
Format	Long = NotesDatabase.Compact
Return	Long

Create

Description	Creates a database.
Parameters	String1 - server name for new database (blank if local). String2 - file name for new database, including path. Boolean - Signals to open the database after creating or not.
Format	Call NotesDatabase.Create(String1, String2, Boolean)
Return	None

CreateCopy

Description	Creates a copy of the database.
Parameters	String1 - server name for new database (blank if local). String2 - file name for new database.
Format	Sets NotesDatabase = NotesDatabase.CreateCopy(String1,String2)
Return	NotesDatabase object (the new copy)

CreateDocument

Description	Creates a document in the database. The new document is empty, so field values will have to be assigned and the document will need to be saved.
Parameters	None
Format	Sets NotesDocument = NotesDatabase.CreateDocument
Return	NotesDocument - the new document.

CreateFromTemplate

Description	If the current database is a template, it creates a new database using the current database as the template.
Parameters	String1 - server name for new database. String2 - file name for new database Boolean - Signals whether or not future design should be inherited.
Format	Sets NotesDatabase = NotesDatabase.CreateFromTemplate(String1, String2, Boolean)

Return	NotesDatabase - the new database

CreateReplica

Description	Creates a replica of the database.
Parameters	String1 - server name for new replica String2 - file name for new replica
Format	Sets NotesDatabase = NotesDatabase.CreateReplica(String1, String2)
Return	NotesDatabase - new Replica

FTSearch

Description	Forms a collection of documents by conducting a full text search on the database. This method does work if the database does not have a full text index, but slower.
Parameters	String - the search/query string Integer1 - maximum number of documents to return (0 for all) Integer2 - sorting option (OPTIONAL) Integer3 - search options (OPTIONAL)
Format	Sets NotesDocumentCollection = NotesDatabase.FTSearch(String, Integer1, Integer2, Integer3)
Return	NotesDocumentCollection containing all documents returned from the search.

GetAgent

Description	Returns a handle to the specified agent in the database (if it exists).
Parameters	String - name of the agent
Format	Sets NotesAgent = NotesDatabase.GetAgent(String)
Return	NotesAgent object or Nothing if the agent was not found

GetDocumentByID

Description	Returns a NotesDocument from the database that has the specified NoteID.
Parameters	String - NoteID
Format	Set NotesDocument = NotesDatabase.GetDocumentByID(String)
Return	NotesDocument with the NoteID; Nothing if there was no match found.

GetDocumentByUNID

Description	Returns NotesDocument from the database that has the specified Universal ID.
Parameters	String - Universal ID
Format	Sets NotesDocument = NotesDatabase.GetDocumentByUNID(String)

Return	NotesDocument with the Universal ID, or Nothing if no match was found.

GetDocumentByURL

Description	Creates a document in the Web Navigator database (personal or server based) containing the contents of the specified URL.
Parameters	String1 - URL Integer1 - Reloads the page (1) or not (0) or conditionally reload (2). (OPTIONAL) Integer2 - Signals to save links on web page in a special field or not (OPTIONAL). String2 - MIME Character set to use (OPTIONAL). String3 - web username for the page (OPTIONAL). String4 - web password for the page (OPTIONAL) String5 - proxy username (OPTIONAL). String6 - proxy password (OPTIONAL).
Format	Sets NotesDocument = NotesDatabase.GetDocumentByURL(String1, Integer1, Integer2, String2, String3, String4, String5, String6)
Return	NotesDocument containing contents of URL

GetForm

Description	Retrieves a form from a database.
Parameters	String - name of the form
Format	Sets NotesForm = NotesDatabase.GetForm(String)
Return	NotesForm object or Nothing if not found

GetProfileDocument

Description	Retrieves a profile document from a database.
Parameters	String1 - name of the profile String2 - username associated with the profile (OPTIONAL)
Format	Sets NotesDocument = NotesDatabase.GetProfileDocument(String1, String2)
Return	NotesDocument or Nothing if profile not found.

GetURLHeaderInfo

Description	Retrieves HTTP header information for a given URL.
Parameters	String1 - URL String2 - header string to retrieve (OPTIONAL). String3 - web username (OPTIONAL). String4 - web password (OPTIONAL). String5 - proxy username (OPTIONAL) String6 - proxy password (OPTIONAL)
Format	String = NotesDatabase.GetURLHeaderInfo(String1, String2, String3, String4, String5, String6)
Return	String

GetView

Description	Retrieves a specified view from a database.
Parameters	String - view name
Format	Sets NotesView = NotesDatabase.GetView(string)
Return	NotesView object or Nothing if view not found.

GrantAccess

Description	Adds or updates an entry's access level in the ACL.
Parameters	String - entry name Integer - access level
Format	Calls NotesDatabase.GrantAccess(String, Integer)
Return	None

New

Description	Creates a NotesDatabase object.
Parameters	String1 - server name String2 - file name
Format	Sets NotesDatabase = New NotesDatabase(String1, String2) Dim NotesDatabase As New NotesDatabase(String1 ,String2)
Return	NotesDatabase object

Open

Description	Opens a database; a database has to be opened for a LotusScript script to access its properties and/or methods.
Parameters	String1 - server name String2 - file name
Format	Boolean = NotesDatabase.Open(String1, String2)
Return	Boolean signals whether it was successfully opened.

OpenByReplicaID

Description	Opens a database by server name and replica ID.
Parameters	String1 - server name String2 - replica id
Format	Boolean = NotesDatabase.OpenByReplicaID(String1, String2)
Return	Boolean signals whether it was successfully opened.

OpenIfModified

Description	Opens a database if it has been modifed since a certain date.
Parameters	String1 - server name String2 - file name NotesDateTime - cutoff date; open database if it has been modified since this date.

Format	Boolean = NotesDatabase.OpenIfModified(String1, String2, NotesDateTime)
Return	Boolean signals whether it was successfully opened.

OpenMail

Description	Opens the current user's mail database.
Parameters	None
Format	Calls NotesDatabase.OpenMail
Return	None

OpenURLDB

Description	Opens the default Web Navigator database (server or workstation).
Parameters	None
Format	Boolean = NotesDatabase.OpenURLDB
Return	Boolean signals whether the database was successfully opened.

OpenWithFailOver

Description	Opens a database and takes advantage of clustering if available and needed.
Parameters	String1 - primary server name String2 - file name
Format	Boolean = NotesDatabase.OpenWithFailover(String1, String2)
Return	Boolean signals whether the database was successfully opened.

QueryAccess

Description	The access level for a person/server/group.
Parameters	String - entry name
Format	Integer = NotesDatabase.QueryAccess(String)
Return	Integer Constant (ACLLEVEL_NOACCESS, ACLLEVEL_MANAGER, ACLLEVEL_DESIGNER, ACLLEVEL_EDITOR, ACLLEVEL_AUTHOR, ACLLEVEL_READER, ACLLEVEL_DEPOSITOR)

Remove

Description	Deletes a database
Parameters	None
Format	Calls NotesDatabase.Remove
Return	None

Replicate

Description	Replicates a database with its replicas on a given server.

Parameters	String - name of server to replicate with.
Format	Boolean = NotesDatabase.Replicate(String)
Return	Boolean signals whether replication was successful.

RevokeAccess

Description	Removes an entry from the database ACL.
Parameters	String - entry name to remove.
Format	Calls NotesDatabase.RevokeAccess(String)
Return	None

Search

Description	Creates a collection of documents from the database by searching. This method differs from the FTSearch method in that @Functions can be used.
Parameters	String - search formula NotesDateTime - cutoff date; no documents older than this date are returned. Integer - the maximum number of documents to return (0 is all).
Format	Sets NotesDocumentCollection = NotesDatabase.Search(String, NotesDateTime, Integer)
Return	NotesDocumentCollection containing all documents from the search.

UnProcessedFTSearch

Description	Forms a collection of documents by conducting a full text search on the database of all documents not previously processed by the agent. This method does work if the database does not have a full text index, but slower.
Parameters	String - the search/query string Integer1 - maximum number of documents to return (0 for all) Integer2 - sorting option (OPTIONAL) Integer3 - search options (OPTIONAL)
Format	Sets NotesDocumentCollection = NotesDatabase.UnProcessedFTSearch(String,Integer1, Integer2, Integer3)
Return	NotesDocumentCollection containing all documents returned from the search.

UnProcessedSearch

Description	Creates a collection of documents from the database by searching the database of all documents not previously processed by the agent. This method differs from the FTSearch method in that @Functions can be used.

Parameters	String - search formula NotesDateTime - cutoff date; no documents older than this date are returned. Integer - the maximum number of documents to return (0 is all).
Format	Sets NotesDocumentCollection = NotesDatabase.UnProcessedSearch(String, NotesDateTime, Integer)
Return	NotesDocumentCollection containing all documents from the search.
UpdateFTIndex	
Description	Updates the Full Text Index for the database; it can create an index if it does not currently exist.
Parameters	Boolean - signals whether an index should be created.
Format	Call NotesDatabase.UpdateFTIndex(Boolean)
Return	None

NotesDateRange class

The NotesDateRange class can be used to represent a range of dates and times. The `CreateDateRange` method in the NotesSession class can be used to create a new instance.

Properties

StartDateTime	
Description	The starting date/time of a range.
Format	NotesDateTime = NotesDateRange.StartDateTime NotesDateRange.StartDateTime = NotesDateTime
Type	NotesDateTime
Access	Read/Write
EndDateTime	
Description	The ending date/time of a range.
Format	NotesDateTime = NotesDateRange.EndDateTime NotesDateRange.EndDateTime = NotesDateTime
Type	NotesDateTime
Access	Read/Write
Text	
Description	The date range value(s) as text.
Format	string$ = NotesDateRange.Text NotesDateRange.Text = string$

Type	String
Access	Read/Write

NotesDateTime class

The NotesDateTime class represents date/time in Notes format. Notes format is not the same as the date/time format in LotusScript. The `CreateDateTime` method in the NotesSession class or the `New` method in the NotesDateTime class can be used to create new NotesDateTime objects.

Properties

DateOnly (Notes 5.0 or higher)	
Description	The date portion of a NotesDateTime object.
Format	String = NotesDateTime.DateOnly
Type	String
Access	Read
GMTTime	
Description	NotesDateTime converted to Greenwich Mean Time.
Format	String$ = NotesDateTime.GMTTime
Type	String
Access	Read
IsDST	
Description	True/False indicating whether or not the NotesDateTime reflects Daylight Savings Time.
Format	Boolean = NotesDateTime.IsDST
Type	Boolean
Access	Read
LocalTime	
Description	A string representation of a NotesDateTime in the local time zone.
Format	String$ = NotesDateTime.LocalDateTime NotesDateTime.LocalDateTime = string$
Type	String
Access	Read/Write
LSGMTTime	
Description	LotusScript variant representation of a NotesDateTime converted to Greenwich Mean Time.
Format	Gmt = NotesDateTime.LSGMTTime
Type	Variant

Access	Read

LSLocalTime

Description	LotusScript variant representation of a NotesDateTime in the local time zone.
Format	Variant = NotesDateTime.LSLocalTime NotesDateTime.LSLocalTime = variant
Type	Variant
Access	Read/Write

TimeZone

Description	The time zone of a NotesDateTime.
Format	Integer = NotesDateTime.TimeZone
Type	Integer
Access	Read

ZoneTime

Description	NotesDateTime as a string adjusted for the TimeZone and IsDST properties.
Format	String$ = NotesDateTime.ZoneTime
Type	String
Access	Read

Methods

AdjustDate

Description	Increments a NotesDateTime by a certain number of days.
Parameters	Integer - the number of days to increment by. Boolean - adjusts for daylight savings time or not.
Format	Calls NotesDateTime.AdjustDate(Integer, Boolean)

AdjustHour

Description	Increments a NotesDateTime by a certain number of hours.
Parameters	Integer - the number of hours to increment by. Boolean - adjusts for daylight savings time or not.
Format	Calls NotesDateTime.AdjustHour(Integer,Boolean)

AdjustMinute

Description	Increments a NotesDateTime by a certain number of minutes.
Parameters	Integer - the number of minutes to increment by. Boolean - adjusts for daylight savings time or not.
Format	Call NotesDateTime.AdjustMinute(Integer, Boolean)

AdjustMonth

Description	Increments a NotesDateTime by a certain number of months.
Parameters	Integer - the number of months to increment by. Boolean - adjusts for daylight savings time or not.
Format	Calls NotesDateTime.AdjustMonth(Integer, Boolean)

AdjustYear

Description	Increments a NotesDateTime by a certain number of years.
Parameters	Integer - the number of years to increment by. Boolean - adjusts for daylight savings time or not.
Format	Calls NotesDateTime.AdjustYear(Integer, Boolean)

ConvertToZone

Description	Converts a NotesDateTime to the TimeZone and IsDST specified.
Parameters	Integer - the time zone (0 - 15) Boolean - daylight savings time in effect or not.
Format	Calls NotesDateTime.ConvertToZone(Integer, Boolean)

SetAnyDate

Description	Sets the date portion of a NotesDateTime object to a wild-card date value.
Parameters	None
Format	Calls NotesDateTime.SetAnyDate

SetAnyTime

Description	Sets the time portion of a NotesDateTime object to a wild-card time value.
Parameters	None
Format	Calls NotesDateTime.SetAnyTime

SetNow

Description	Sets the date and time values to current date and time.
Parameters	None
Format	Calls NotesDateTime.SetNow

New

Description	Creates a NotesDateTime object.
Parameters	String - date/time value
Format	Sets variable_name = New NotesDateTime("date/time value")

TimeDifference

Description	Returns the difference in seconds of two date/time values.
Parameters	NotesDateTime
Format	Long = NotesDateTime.TimeDifference(NotesDateTime)
Return	Long

NotesDBDirectory class

The NotesDBDirectory class is used to access a list of databases either on your local machine or a server. Once a list has been assembled, you can use certain methods to scroll through the list. The `GetDBDirectory` method of the NotesSession class or the `New` method of the NotesDBDirectory class can be used to create new instances of the NotesDBDirectory class.

Properties

Name	
Description	The name of the server (blank if local) from which the list will be assembled.
Format	String$ = NotesDBDirectory.Name
Type	String
Access	Read

Methods

GetFirstDatabase	
Description	Retrieves the first database from the list/directory.
Parameters	Integer - file type to get from server (DATABASE, REPLICA, REPLICA_CANDIDATE, TEMPLATE_CANDIDATE)
Format	Sets NotesDatabase = NotesDBDirectory.GetFirstDatabase
Return	NotesDatabase
GetNextDatabase	
Description	Retrieves the next database from the list/directory.
Parameters	None
Format	Sets NotesDatabase = NotesDBDirectory.GetNextDatabase
Return	NotesDatabase
New	
Description	Creates a NoteDBDirectory object.
Parameters	String - server name, blank if local.
Format	Sets variable_name = New NotesDBDirectory("Server Name")
Return	NotesDBDirectory

NotesDocument class

The NotesDocument class represents a document in the Notes database environment. Documents can be retrieved from the following classes: NotesDatabase, NotesDocumentCollection, NotesView, NotesUIDocument, or NotesNewsLetter.

Properties

Authors

Description	The user names of those who've saved a document.
Format	Array = NotesDocument.Authors
Type	Array of Strings
Access	Read

ColumnValues

Description	An array whose values correspond to columns in the parent view of a document. The document must be accessed through a view in order for it to return values.
Format	Array = NotesDocument.ColumnValues
Type	Array of Variants
Access	Read

Created

Description	The date a document was created.
Format	Date = NotesDocument.Created
Type	Variant
Access	Read

EmbeddedObjects

Description	Array of OLE objects in a document.
Format	Array = NotesDocument.EmbeddedObjects
Type	Array of NotesEmbeddedObjects objects
Access	Read

EncryptionKeys

Description	The keys used (if any) to encrypt a document.
Format	Array = NotesDocument.EncryptionKeys NotesDocument.EncryptionKeys = array
Type	Array of string values
Access	Read/Write

EncryptOnSend

Description	Signals whether or not a document will be encrypted when saved.
Format	Boolean = NotesDocument.EncryptOnSend NotesDocument.EncryptOnSend = Boolean

Type	Boolean
Access	Read/Write

FolderReferences (Notes 5.0 or higher)

Description	Signals which folder(s) a document resides in, if any.
Format	Variant = NotesDocument.FolderReferences
Type	Variant
Access	Read

FTSearchScore

Description	If a document was retrieved via a full text search, this property returns its score.
Format	Integer = NotesDocument.FTSearchScore
Type	Integer
Access	Read

HasEmbedded

Description	Indicates whether or not a document contains embedded objects.
Format	Boolean = NotesDocument.HasEmbedded
Type	Boolean
Access	Read

IsDeleted (Notes 5.0 or higher)

Description	Signals whether a document has been deleted.
Format	Boolean = NotesDocument.IsDeleted
Type	Boolean
Access	Read

IsNewNote

Description	Indicates whether or not a document is new.
Format	Boolean = NotesDocument.IsNewNote
Type	Boolean
Access	Read

IsProfile

Description	Indicates whether or not a document is a profile document.
Format	Boolean = NotesDocument.IsProfile
Type	Boolean
Access	Read

IsResponse

Description	Indicates whether or not a document is a response document.
Format	Boolean = NotesDocument.IsResponse
Type	Boolean
Access	Read

IsSigned

Description	Indicates whether a document is signed.
Format	Boolean = NotesDocument.IsSigned
Type	Boolean
Access	Read

IsUIDocOpen

Description	Indicates whether a document is accessed through a NotesUIDocument object.
Format	Boolean = NotesDocument.IsUIDocOpen
Type	Boolean
Access	Read

IsValid (Notes 5.0 or higher)

Description	Signals whether a document is valid or not.
Format	Boolean = NotesDocument.IsValid
Type	Boolean
Access	Read

Items

Description	All items (fields) on a document.
Format	Array = NotesDocument.Items
Type	Array of NotesItem objects
Access	Read

Key

Description	If the document is a profile document (IsProfile), this property returns the key (username) of the profile.
Format	String = NotesDocument.Key
Type	String
Access	Read

LastAccessed

Description	The last date/time a document was accessed (read or modified).
Format	Variant = NotesDocument.LastAccessed
Type	Variant
Access	Read

LastModified

Description	The last date/time a document was modified (saved).
Format	Variant = NotesDocument.LastModified
Type	Variant
Access	Read

NameOfProfile

Description	Returns the name of the profile if the document is a profile document.
Format	String = NotesDocument.NameOfProfile
Type	String
Access	Read

NoteID

Description	Returns the unique identifier of a document. The ID is only unique within the database.
Format	String = NotesDocument.NoteID
Type	String
Access	Read

ParentDatabase

Description	The database that contains the document.
Format	NotesDatabase = NotesDocument.ParentDatabase
Type	NotesDatabase
Access	Read

ParentDocumentUNID

Description	If a document is a response document, this property returns the universal ID of its parent document.
Format	String = NotesDocument.ParentUNID
Type	String
Access	Read

ParentView

Description	If a document was retrieved using a NotesView object, this property returns a pointer to the NotesView.
Format	NotesView = NotesDocument.ParentView
Type	NotesView
Access	Read

References (Notes 5.0 or higher)

Description	
Format	Variant = NotesDocument.References
Type	Variant
Access	Read

Responses

Description	The collection of immediate response documents to the document (if any).
Format	NotesDocumentCollection = NotesDocument.Responses
Type	NotesDocumentCollection
Access	Read

SaveMessageOnSend

Description	Indicates whether a document should be saved when it is mailed. Only applies to new documents.
Format	Boolean = NotesDocument.SaveMessageOnSend NotesDocument.SaveMessageOnSend = Boolean
Type	Boolean
Access	Read/Write

SentByAgent

Description	Indicates whether a document was emailed by a Notes agent.
Format	Boolean = NotesDocument.SentByAgent
Type	Boolean
Access	Read

Signer

Description	If a document is signed, this returns the name of the person who signed it.
Format	String = NotesDocument.signer
Type	String
Access	Read

SignOnSend

Description	Indicates whether or not a document is signed when mailed.
Format	Boolean = NotesDocument.SignOnSend NotesDocument.SignOnSend = Boolean
Type	Boolean
Access	Read/Write

Size

Description	The size of a document in bytes.
Format	Long = NotesDocument.Size
Type	Long
Access	Read

UniversalID

Description	The universal ID of a document.
Format	String = NotesDocument.UniversalID
Type	String
Access	Read

Verifier

Description	If a document is signed, this returns the name of the certificate that verified the signature.
Format	String = NotesDocument.Verifier

Type	String
Access	Read

Methods

AppendItemValue

Description	Creates an item and populates it.
Parameters	String - name of the item. Variant - value to populate the item.
Format	Sets NotesItem = NotesDocument.AppendItemValue(string, variant)
Return	NotesItem object

ComputeWithForm

Description	When creating documents through the back end, this method validates a document by running all default, input translation, and input validation formulas.
Parameters	Boolean1 - ignored by the system. Boolean2 - signals whether an error is generated if an input validation fails.
Format	Boolean = NotesDocument.ComputeWithForm(Boolean1, Boolean2)
Return	Boolean (signals false if errors occurred and the second parameter is true, otherwise true).

CopyAllItems

Description	Copies all items from one document to another.
Parameters	NotesDocument - destination document Boolean - signals whether items on new document are over-written or appended.
Format	Call NotesDocument.CopyAllItems(NotesDocument, Boolean)
Return	None

CopyToDatabase

Description	Copies document into a database.
Parameters	NotesDatabase - destination database
Format	Sets NotesDocument = NotesDocument.CopyToData-base(NotesDatabase)
Return	NotesDocument (the new document in the destination database)

CreateReplyMessage

Description	A message is created as a reply to the current document.
Parameters	Boolean - signals whether the recipients of the new docu-ment are the same as the current document.

Format	Sets NotesDocument = NotesDocument.CreateReplyMessage(Boolean)
Return	NotesDocument (the new reply)

CreateRichTextItem

Description	A Rich Text item is created on the document.
Parameters	String - the field name of the new Rich Text item.
Format	Sets NotesRichTextItem = NotesDocument.CreateRichTextItem(string)
Return	NotesRichTextItem (the new field)

Encrypt

Description	Encrypts a document.
Parameters	None
Format	Calls NotesDocument.Encrypt
Return	None

GenerateHTML (Notes 5.0 and higher)

Description	Generates HTML file version of the document.
Parameters	String - path for new HTML file.
Format	Calls NotesDocument.GenerateHTML(String)
Return	None

GenerateHTMLString (Notes 5.0 and higher)

Description	Creates string containing HTML for the document.
Parameters	None
Format	String = NotesDocument.GenerateHTMLString
Return	String

GetAttachment

Description	Retrieves a file attachment in the form of a NotesEmbeddedObject object.
Parameters	String - name of the attachment.
Format	Sets NotesEmbeddedObject = NotesDocument.GetAttachment(string)
Return	NotesEmbeddedObject

GetIFirsttem

Description	Returns the first occurrence of an item from a document. A document can have more than one item with the same name.
Parameters	String - name of the item to retrieve from the document.
Format	Set NotesItem = NotesDocument.GetFirstItem(string)
Return	NotesItem

GetItemValue

Description	Returns the value(s) associated with an item on a document.
Parameters	String - name of the item.

Format	Array = NotesDocument.GetItemValue(string)
Return	Array of the type of value in the item.

HasItem

Description	Signals whether or not a document contains an item.
Parameters	String - the name of the item/field to find.
Format	Boolean = NotesDocument.HasItem(string)
Return	Boolean

MakeResponse

Description	Makes one document a response to another.
Paramaters	NotesDocument - the parent document for the new response.
Format	Calls NotesDocument.MakeResponse(NotesDocument)
Return	None

New

Description	Creates a NotesDocument
Parameters	NotesDatabase - database to contain the new document.
Format	Sets NotesDocument = New NotesDocument(NotesDatabase)
Return	NotesDocument

PutInFolder

Description	Moves a document to a folder.
Parameters	String - the name of the folder.
Format	Calls NotesDocument.PutInFolder(string)
Return	None

RenderToRTItem

Description	Allows you to create a picture of a document and place it into a Rich Text field. Pictures of parent documents are placed on response documents from time to time.
Parameters	NotesRichTextItem - where to place the picture.
Format	Boolean = NotesDocument.RenderToRTItem(NotesRichTextItem)
Return	Boolean whether successful or not.

Remove

Description	Deletes a document from a database.
Parameters	Boolean - signals whether to delete the document if someone has modified it since it was opened.
Format	Calls NotesDocument.Remove(Boolean)

RemoveFromFolder

Description	Removes the document from a folder.
Parameters	String - folder name.
Format	Calls NotesDocument.RemoveFromFolder(string)

Return	None

RemoveItem

Description	Removes an item from a document.
Parameters	String - name of the item to delete.
Format	Calls NotesDocument.RemoveItem(string)
Return	None

ReplaceItemValue

Description	Replaces the value of an item(s) with a new value. If the item does not exist, it is created.
Parameters	String - name of the item. Variant - New values, depends on their type.
Format	Sets NotesItem = NotesDocument>ReplaceItem-Value(String, Variant)
Return	NotesItem - the new item.

Save

Description	Saves the document to disk.
Parameters	Boolean1 - signals whether or not to save the document if it is edited by another. Boolean2 - signals whether to create response to original. Ignored if first is true. Boolean3 - signals whether to mark document as read.
Format	Boolean = NotesDocument.Save(Boolean1, Boolean2, Boolean3)
Return	Boolean (true if saved, otherwise false)

Send

Description	Mails a document.
Parameter	Boolean - stores form in document or not. Array of strings - mail recipient list.
Format	Calls NotesDocument.Send(Boolean, array)
Return	None

Sign

Description	Signs the document.
Parameters	None
Format	Calls NotesDocument.Sign
Return	None

NotesDocumentCollection class

The NotesDocumentCollection is used to work with a group of documents (a collection). The collection can be formed using numerous methods.

Properties

Count

Description	The number of documents in the collection.
Format	Long = NotesDocumentCollection.Count
Type	Long
Access	Read

IsSorted

Description	Signals whether a collection is sorted. A collection is sorted only when it is the result of a full text search.
Format	Boolean = NotesDocumentCollection.IsSorted
Type	Boolean
Access	Read

Parent

Description	The database that contains the collection.
Format	NotesDatabase = NotesDocumentCollection.Parent
Type	NotesDatabase
Access	Read

Query

Description	If the collection was formed by a search, this returns the query used to form the collection.
Format	String = NotesDocumentCollection.Query
Type	String
Access	Read

Methods

AddDocument (Notes 5.0 and higher)

Description	Adds a NotesDocument to the collection.
Parameters	NotesDocument - document to add.
Format	Calls NotesDocumentCollection.AddDocument(NotesDocument)
Return	None

DeleteDocument (Notes 5.0 and higher)

Description	Removes a NotesDocument from the collection.
Parameters	NotesDocument - document to remove.
Format	Calls NotesDocumentCollection.DeleteDocument(NotesDocument)
Return	None

FTSearch

Description	Performs a full text search on a collection. This is used to refine a document collection. After calling this method, the collection contains only those documents returned by the search.
Parameters	String - search query Integer - maximum number of documents to return (zero is all).
Format	Calls NotesDocumentCollection.FTSearch(String, Integer)
Return	None

GetFirstDocument

Description	Retrieves the first document in the collection.
Parameters	None
Format	Sets NotesDocument = NotesDocumentCollection.GetFirstDocument
Return	NotesDocument object

GetLastDocument

Description	Retrieves the last document from a collection.
Parameters	None
Format	Sets NotesDocument = NotesDocumentCollection.GetLastDocument
Return	NotesDocument object

GetNextDocument

Description	Retrieves the next document from a collection, using a Notes document as the reference point.
Parameters	NotesDocument - the reference point in the collection.
Format	Sets NotesDocument = NotesDocumentCollection.GetNextDocument(NotesDocument)
Return	NotesDocument object

GetNthDocument

Description	Retrieves a document from a collection using the index value of its location in the collection.
Parameters	Integer - the index value in the collection.
Format	Sets NotesDocument = NotesDocumentCollection.GetNthDocument(Integer)
Return	NotesDocument

GetPrevDocument

Description	Retrieves the previous document from a collection, using a Notes document as the reference point.
Parameters	NotesDocument - the reference point in the collection.
Format	Sets NotesDocument = NotesDocumentCollection.GetPrevDocument(NotesDocument)
Return	NotesDocument object

PutAllInFolder

Description	All documents in a collection are added to a folder, the folder is created if it does not exist.
Parameters	String - folder name
Format	Calls NotesDocumentCollection.PutAllInFolder(String)
Return	None

RemoveAll

Description	All documents in a collection are removed from the database.
Parameters	Boolean - signals whether a document is deleted if another user has modified it since the script opened it.
Format	Calls NotesDocumentCollection.RemoveAll(Boolean)
Return	None

RemoveAllFromFolder

Description	All documents in a collection are removed from a folder.
Parameters	String - folder name
Format	Calls NotesDocumentCollection.RemoveAllFromFolder(String)
Return	None

StampAll

Description	Replaces the value of an item for all documents in the collection.
Parameters	String - name of the item. Variant - value to assign to the item; type depends on the value.
Format	Calls NotesDocumentCollection.StampAll(String, Variant)
Return	None

UpdateAll

Description	All documents in the collection are flagged as processed by an agent. This is used with agents that are triggered by New Mail, Pasted Items, New/Modified Items, and so forth, so that the agents don't repeatedly process a document.
Parameters	None
Format	Call NotesDocumentCollection.UpdateAll
Return	None

NotesEmbeddedObject class

The NotesEmbeddedObject class is used to work with OLE, links, or file attachments within LotusScript. It is supported only on the Windows platforms.

Properties

Class

Description	Returns the name of the application used to create the object.
Format	String = NotesEmbeddedObject.Class
Type	String
Access	Read

FileSize

Description	The size of the embedded object in bytes.
Format	Long = NotesEmbeddedObject.FileSize
Type	Long
Access	Read

Name

Description	The name of the embedded object. A name is/can be assigned during creation.
Format	String = NotesEmbeddedObject.Name
Type	String
Access	Read

Object

Description	Returns the OLE handle to an object, if it exists.
Format	Sets Variant = NotesEmbeddedObject.Object
Type	Variant
Access	Read

Parent

Description	The NotesRichTextItem that contains the embedded object.
Format	Sets NotesRichTextItem = NotesEmbeddedObject.Parent
Type	NotesRichTextItem
Access	Read

Source

Description	Returns the name of the embedded object. It returns the file name if the object is an attachment, otherwise it returns the Notes internal name that is used by Notes.
Format	String = NotesEmbeddedObject.Source
Type	String
Access	Read

Type

Description	Returns what type of object it is.
Format	Integer = NotesEmbeddedObject.Type
Type	Integer (Values: EMBED_ATTACHMENT, EMBED_OBJECT, and EMBED_OBJECTLINK)

Access	Read
Verbs	
Description	If the object is an OLE object, it returns the verbs supported by it.
Format	Array = NotesEmbeddedObject.Verbs
Access	Read

Methods

Activate	
Description	Causes an OLE object or object link to be loaded by OLE.
Parameters	Boolean - signals whether host OLE application should display its interface.
Format	Sets Variant = NotesEmbeddedObject.Activate(Boolean)
Return	Variant
DoVerb	
Description	Executes a verb on an OLE object.
Parameters	String - verb
Format	Variant = NotesEmbeddedObject.DoVerb(String)
Return	Variant
ExtractFile	
Description	Makes a copy of a file attachment to the path specified. It is only legal for file attachments; anything else returns an error.
Parameters	String - path of drive to receive copy.
Format	Call NotesEmbeddedObject.Copy(String)
Return	None
Remove	
Description	Removes an object permanently.
Parameters	None
Format	Call NotesEmbeddedOjbect.Remove
Return	None

NotesForm class

The NotesFrom class is used to work with forms within Lotus Notes databases.

Properties

Aliases

Description	The aliases of a form.
Format	Array = NotesForm.Aliases
Type	Array of string values
Access	Read

Fields

Description	All fields on a form.
Format	Array = NotesForm.Fields
Type	Array of string values
Access	Read

FormUsers

Description	The contents of the $FormUsers field.
Format	Array = NotesForm.FormUsers NotesForm.FormUsers = array
Type	Array of string values
Access	Read/Write

IsSubForm

Description	Signals whether or not a NotesForm is a subform.
Format	Boolean = NotesForm.IsSubForm
Type	Boolean
Access	Read

Name

Description	The name of the form.
Format	String = NotesForm.Name
Type	String
Access	Read

ProtectReaders

Description	Signals whether or not the $Readers field is protected from being overwritten by replication.
Format	Boolean = NotesForm.ProtectReaders NotesForm.ProtectReaders = Boolean
Type	Boolean
Access	Read/Write

ProtectUsers

Description	Signals whether the $FormUsers field is protected from being overwritten by replication.
Format	Boolean = NotesForm.ProtectUsers
Type	Boolean

Access	Read/Write
Readers	
Description	The contents of the $Readers field.
Format	Array = NotesForm.Readers NotesForm.Readers = array
Type	Array of string values
Access	Read/Write

Methods

Remove	
Description	Deletes a form from a database.
Parameters	None
Format	Call NotesForm.Remove
Return	None

NotesInternational class

The NotesInternational class is used to work with the international settings of the operating system. A handle to a NotesInternational object can be obtained through the `International` property of the NotesSession class.

Properties

AMString	
Description	How AM time is represented. In English it is "AM".
Format	String = NotesInternational.AMString
Type	String
Access	Read
CurrencyDigits	
Description	The number of decimal digits for numbers.
Format	Integer = NotesInternational.CurrencyDigits
Type	Integer
Access	Read
CurencySymbol	
Description	How currency is denoted. In the US, it is the dollar ($) sign.
Format	String = NotesInternational.CurrencySymbol
Type	String

Access	Read

DateStep

Description	The date separator.
Format	String = NotesInternational.DateSetp
Type	String
Access	Read

DecimalStep

Description	The decimal number separator.
Format	String
Type	String = NotesInternational.DecimalStep
Access	Read

IsCurrencySpace

Description	Signals if a space exists between the currency symbol and number.
Format	Boolean
Type	Boolean = NotesInternational.IsCurrencySpace
Access	Read

IsCurrencySuffix

Description	Signals if the currency symbol follows the number.
Format	Boolean = NotesInternational.IsCurrencySuffix
Type	Boolean
Access	Read

IsCurrencyZero

Description	Signals whether a fractional currency value has a leading zero before the decimal separator.
Format	Boolean = NotesInternational.IsCurrencyZero
Type	Boolean
Access	Read

IsDateDMY

Description	Signals whether the date format is day-month-year.
Format	Boolean = NotesInternational.IsDateDMY
Type	Boolean
Access	Read

IsDateMDY

Description	Signals whether the date format is month-day-year.
Format	Boolean = NotesInternational.IsDateMDY
Type	Boolean
Access	Read

IsDateYMD

Description	Signals whether the date format is year-month-day.
Format	Boolean = NotesInternational.IsDateYMD
Type	Boolean
Access	Read

IsDST

Description	Signals whether the date reflects daylight savings time.
Format	Boolean = NotesInternational.IsDST
Type	Boolean
Access	Read

IsTime24

Description	Signals whether or not the time format is 24 hour.
Format	Boolean = NotesInternational.IsTime24
Type	Boolean
Access	Read

PMString

Description	How PM time is represented. In English it is "PM".
Format	String = NotesInternational.PMString
Type	String
Access	Read

ThousandsSep

Description	The thousands separator for numbers.
Format	String = NotesInternational.ThousandsSep
Type	String
Access	Read

TimeSep

Description	The separator for time values, separates hour, minutes, and seconds.
Format	String = NotesInternational.TimeSep
Type	String
Access	Read

TimeZone

Description	An integer representing the time zone.
Format	Integer = NotesInternational.TimeZone
Type	Integer
Access	Read

Today

Description	The string that stands for today in the time/date specification.

Format	String = NotesInternational.Today
Type	String
Access	Read
Tomorrow	
Description	The string that stands for tomorrow in the time/date specification.
Format	String = NotesInternational.Tomorrow
Type	String
Access	Read
Yesterday	
Description	The string that stands for yesterday in the time/date specification.
Format	String = NotesInternational.Yesterday
Type	String
Access	Read

NotesItem class

The NotesItem class is used to work with data on Notes documents (fields).

Properties

DateTimeValue	
Description	Returns a NotesDateTime object representing the item's value. If the item is not a Date/Time then it returns Nothing.
Format	Set NotesDateTime = NotesItem.DateTimeValue Set NotesItem.DateTimeValue = NotesDateTime
Type	NotesDateTime
Access	Read/Write
IsAuthors	
Description	Signals whether or not an item is of the type AUTHORS.
Format	Boolean = NotesItem.IsAuthors NotesItem.IsAuthors = Boolean
Type	Boolean
Access	Read/Write
IsEncrypted	
Description	Signals whether or not an item is encrypted.
Format	Boolean = NotesItem.IsEncrypted NotesItem.IsEncrypted = Boolean
Type	Boolean
Access	Read/Write

IsNames

Description	Signals whether or not an item is of the type Names.
Format	Boolean = NotesItem.IsNames NotesItem.IsNames = Boolean
Type	Boolean
Access	Read/Write

IsProtected

Description	Signals whether or not an item is protected. Protected means that a user needs at least editor access to edit its values.
Format	Boolean = NotesItem.IsProtected NotesItem.IsProtected = Boolean
Type	Boolean
Access	Read/Write

IsReaders

Description	Signals whether an item is of the type READERS or not.
Format	Boolean = NotesItem.IsReaders NotesItem.IsReaders = Boolean
Type	Boolean
Access	Read/Write

IsSigned

Description	Signals whether or not an item is signed.
Format	Boolean = NotesItem.IsSigned NotesItem.IsSigned = Boolean
Type	Boolean
Access	Read/Write

IsSummary

Description	Signals whether or not an item's values can appear in a view. This value must always be set to True when an item is created and it needs to appear in a view column.
Format	Boolean = NotesItem.IsSummary NotesItem.IsSumary = Boolean
Type	Boolean
Access	Read/Write

LastModified

Description	The date an item was last modified.
Format	Variant = NotesItem.LastModified
Type	Variant
Access	Read

Name

Description	The name of an item.
Format	String = NotesItem.Name

Type	String
Access	Read

Parent

Description	The NotesDocument that contains the item.
Format	Set NotesDocument = NotesItem.Parent
Type	NotesDocument object
Access	Read

References (Notes 5.0 and higher)

Description	
Format	Variant = NotesItem.References
Type	Variant
Access	Read

SaveToDisk

Description	Signals whether or not an item is saved to disk (when the document is saved).
Format	Boolean = NotesItem.SaveToDisk NotesItem.SaveToDisk = Boolean
Type	Boolean
Access	Read/Write

Text

Description	The NotesItem value represented as text.
Format	String = NotesItem.Text
Type	String
Access	Read

Type

Description	The type of data of an item.
Format	Integer = NotesItem.Type
Type	Integer (Possible values: ATTACHMENT, AUTHORS, DATETIMES, EMBEDDEDOBJECT, ERRORITEM, FORMULA, HTML, ICON, NAMES, NOTESLINKS, NOTEREFS, NUMBERS, OTHEROBJECT, READERS, RICHTEXT, SIGNATURE, TEXT, UNAVAILABLE, UNKNOWN, USERDATA, or USERID)
Access	Read

ValueLength

Description	The size of an item in bytes.
Format	Integer = NotesItem.ValueLength
Type	Integer
Access	Read

Values

Description	The values stored in an item. It is represented as an array.

Format	Variant = NotesItem.Values NotesItem.Values = Variant
Type	Variant (depends on data type in the item).
Access	Read/Write

Methods

Abstract

Description	The contents of a NotesItem abbreviated.
Parameters	Long - the maximum length of the abbreviated text. Boolean1 - signals whether or not vowels are dropped from words. Boolean2 - signals whether the NOTEABBR.TXT file is used for abbreviates.
Format	String = NotesItem.Abstract(Long, Boolean1, Boolean2)
Return	String

AppendToTextList

Description	A new text item is added to the values; works if the item contains text values only.
Parameters	String or Array of Strings - new value(s) to add.
Format	Call NotesItem.AppendToTextList(String)
Return	None

Contains

Description	Signals whether an item's values matches a value exactly.
Parameters	Variant - the value to search for
Format	Boolean = NotesItem.Contains(Variant)
Return	Boolean

GenerateHTML (Notes 5.0 and higher)

Description	Generates HTML file containing contents of the item.
Parameters	String - path for the newly generated HTML file.
Format	Call NotesItem.GenerateHTML(String)
Return	None

GenerateHTMLString (Notes 5.0 and higher)

Description	Generates HTML string containing contents of the item.
Parameters	None
Format	String = NotesItem.GenerateHTMLString
Return	String

CopyItemToDocument

Description	Copies a NotesItem to the designated NotesDocument.

Parameters	NotesDocument - the document where the item will be copied. String - the new name for the item, specify blank to keep original name.
Format	Set NotesItem = NotesItem.CopyItemToDocument(Notes-Document)
Return	Notesitem - the newly copied item.

New

Description	Creates a NotesItem object on a document.
Parameters	NotesDocument - container for the item String - the name of the item (field name) Variant - the value for the new item (this data type determines item's data type) Integer - (OPTIONAL) signal special type for field (values: READERS, AUTHORS, or NAMES)
Format	Dim NotesItem As New NotesItem(NotesDocument, String, Variant, Integer) Set NotesItem = New NotesItem(NotesDocument, String, Variant, Integer)
Return	NotesItem - the newly created item.

Remove

Description	Delete an item from a document.
Parameters	None
Format	Call NotesItem.Remove
Return	None

NotesLog class

The NotesLog class allows the recording of activity during script execution. The activity can be recorded in a numbers of ways.

Properties

LogActions

Description	Signals whether or not action logging is enabled.
Format	Boolean = NotesLog.LogActions NotesLog.LogActions = Boolean
Type	Boolean
Access	Read/Write

LogErrors

Description	Signals whether or not error logging is enabled.
Format	Boolean = NotesLog.LogErrors NotesLog.LogErrors = Boolean

Type	Boolean
Access	Read/Write

NumActions

Description	The number of actions logged.
Format	Integer = NotesLog.NumActions
Type	Integer
Access	Read

NumErrors

Description	The number of errors logged.
Format	Integer = NotesLog.NumErrors
Type	Integer
Access	Read

OverwriteFile

Description	Indicates whether a log file should be overwritten. Used only when logging to files.
Format	Boolean = NotesLog.OverwriteFile NotesLog.OverwriteFile = Booleaan
Type	Boolean
Access	Read/Write

ProgramName

Description	Name assigned to the logging activity. This name will be displayed in log entries, so it needs to be something meaningful.
Format	String = NotesLog.ProgramName NotesLog.ProgramName = String
Type	String
Access	Read/Write

Methods

Close

Description	Closes the log.
Parameters	None
Format	Calls NotesLog.Close
Return	None

LogAction

Description	Records an action in the log.
Parameters	String - description of the action; this will appear in the log so make it meaningful.
Format	Call NotesLog.LogAction(String)
Return	None

LogError

Description	Records an error in the log.
Parameters	String - description of the error; this will appear in the log so make it meaningful.
Format	Calls NotesLog.LogError(String)
Return	None

LogEvent

Description	Sends an event notification onto the network; only works on server agents.
Parameters	String1 - message String2 - name of queue; Notes will select it if you leave it blank Integer1 - Event type Integer2 - Event severity
Format	Call NotesLog.LogEvent(String1, String2, Integer1, Integer2)
Return	None

New

Description	Creates an instance of the NotesLog class.
Parameters	String - name given to the log.
Format	Dim NotesLog As New NotesLog(String) Set NotesLog = New NotesLog(String)
Return	A NotesLog object.

OpenAgentLog

Description	Opens the agent log for the current agent. This is the same as selecting an agent from the agent list and selecting Agent Log.
Parameters	None
Format	Call NotesLog.OpenAgentLog
Return	None

OpenFileLog

Description	Starts logging to a specified file.
Parameters	String - file name and path of the log file.
Format	Call NotesLog.OpenFileLog(String)
Return	None

OpenMailLog

Description	Creates a mail memo for logging; the memo is sent when the log is closed.
Parameters	Array - recipient list String - memo subject
Format	Call NotesLog.OpenMailLog(Variant, String)
Return	None

OpenNotesLog

Description	Opens a Notes database for logging. The database should be created using the Notes Log template (alog4.ntf).
Parameters	String1 - server on which log is located. String2 - log file name
Format	Call NotesLog.OpenNotesLog(String1, String2)
Return	None

NotesName class

The NotesName class can be used to represent a user or server name.

Properties

Abbreviated

Description	The abbreviated name of a hierarchical name.
Format	String = NotesName.Abbreviated
Type	String
Access	Read

ADMD

Description	The administrative domain for the name.
Format	String - NotesName.ADMD
Type	String
Access	Read

Addr821 (Notes 5.0 and higher)

Description

Format

Type

Access

Addr822comment1 (Notes 5.0 and higher)

Description

Format

Type

Access

Addr822comment2 (Notes 5.0 and higher)

Description

Format

Type

Access

Addr822comment3 (Notes 5.0 and higher)

Description	
Format	
Type	
Access	

Addr822comment4 (Notes 5.0 and higher)

Description	
Format	
Type	
Access	

Addr822localpart (Notes 5.0 and higher)

Description	
Format	
Type	
Access	

Addr822phrase (Notes 5.0 and higher)

Description	
Format	
Type	
Access	

Addr822route (Notes 5.0 and higher)

Description	
Format	
Type	
Access	

Canonical

Description	The canonical name.
Format	String = NotesName.Canonical
Type	String
Access	Read

Common

Description	The common name.
Format	String = NotesName.Common
Type	String
Access	Read

Country

Description	The country component of the hierarchical name.
Format	String = NotesName.Country

Type	String
Access	Read

Generation

Description	The generation portion of the name.
Format	String = NotesName.Generation
Type	String
Access	Read

Given

Description	The given portion of the name.
Format	String = NotesName.Given
Type	String
Access	Read

Initials

Description	The initials portion of a name.
Format	String = NotesName.Initials
Type	String
Access	Read

IsHeirarchical

Description	Signals whether or not a name is hierarchical.
Format	Boolean = NotesName.IsHierarchical
Type	Boolean
Access	Read

Keyword

Description	The components of a name shown this way: Country \ organization \ organizational unit 1\ organization unit 2 \ organizational unit 3 \ organizational unit 3
Format	String = NotesName.Keyword
Type	String
Access	Read

Organization

Description	The organization part of a hierarchical name.
Format	String = NotesName.Organization
Type	String
Access	Read

OrgUnit1

Description	The first organizational unit of a hierarchical name.
Format	String = NotesName.OrgUnit1
Type	String
Access	Read

OrgUnit2

Description	The second organizational unit of a hierarchical name.
Format	String = NotesName.OrgUnit2
Type	String
Access	Read

OrgUnit3

Description	The third organizational unit of a hierarchical name.
Format	String = NotesName.OrgUnit3
Type	String
Access	Read

OrgUnit4

Description	The fourth organizational unit of a hierarchical name.
Format	String = NotesName.OrgUnit4
Type	String
Access	Read

PRMD

Description	The private management domain for a name.
Format	String = NotesName.PRMD
Type	String
Access	Read

SurName

Description	The surname portion of a name.
Format	String = NotesName.SurName
Type	String
Access	Read

Methods

New

Description	Creates a NotesName object.
Parameters	String - user/server name.
Format	Dim variable As New NotesName(String) Set variable = New NotesName(String)
Return	NotesName object

NotesNewsLetter class

The NotesNewsLetter class can be used to create a summary type of document that contains information and/or links to numerous other documents. The newsletters can be sent via email or saved in a database.

Properties

DoScore

Description	Signals whether the relevance score is included for each document link in the newsletter. Must be used in conjunction with the FormatMsgWithDoclinks method.
Format	Boolean = NotesNewsLetter.DoScore NotesNewsLetter.DoScore = Boolean
Type	Boolean
Access	Read/Write

DoSubject

Description	Signals whether a description is included for each item in a newsletter. Must be used in conjunction with the FormatMsg-WithDoclinks method.
Format	Boolean = NotesNewsLetter.DoSubject NotesNewsLetter.DoSubject = Boolean
Type	Boolean
Access	Read/Write

SubjectItemName

Description	Signals which field on documents should be used as the subject line (DoScore property) for links in the newsletter created with the FormatMsgWithDoclinks method.
Format	String = NotesNewsLetter.SubjectItemName NotesNewsLetter.SubjectItemName = String
Type	String
Access	Read/Write

Methods

FormatDocument

Description	Creates a document in a database from a document in a newsletter.
Parameters	NotesDatabase - the database in which the document is created. Integer - The document number from the newsletter to use.

Format	Set NotesDocument = NotesNewsLetter.FormatDocument(NotesDatabase, Integer)
Return	NotesDocument (the newly created document

FormatMsgWithDoclinks

Description	Creates a newsletter document in a specified database. The newsletter will contain doclinks to each document in the collection.
Parameters	NotesDatabase - The database in which the newsletter is created.
Format	Set NotesDocument = NotesNewsLetter.FormatMsgWithDoclinks(NotesDatabase)
Return	NotesDocument - the newly created newsletter document.

New

Description	Creates a newsletter object.
Parameters	NotesDocumentCollection - collection of documents to use in the Newletter.
Format	Dim variable As New NotesNewsLetter(NotesDocumentCollection) Sets variable = New NotesNewsLetter(NotesDocumentCollection
Return	NotesNewsLetter (newly created object)

NotesOutline class (Notes 5.0 or later)

The NotesOutline class can be used to work with Outline objects.

Properties

HasChanged

Description	Signals whether or not an outline has changed.
Format	Boolean = NotesOutline.HasChanged
Type	Boolean
Access	Read

Methods

AddEntry

Description	Adds a new entry to the outline.

Parameters	NotesOutlineEntry - new entry NotesOutlineEntry - the entry that is after the new entry. (OPTIONAL) Integer - mark as modified. (OPTIONAL)
Format	Calls NotesOutline.AddEntry(NotesOutlineEntry, NotesOutlineEntry, Integer)
Return	None
Clear	
Description	Removes an entry
Parameters	None
Format	Calls NotesOutlineEntry.Clear
Return	Integer
GetFirst	
Description	Retrieves the first entry from the outline.
Parameters	None
Format	Sets NotesOutlineEntry = NotesOutline.GetFirstEntry
Return	NotesOutlineEntry object
GetLast	
Description	Retrieves the last entry from the outline.
Parameters	None
Format	Sets NotesOutlineEntry = NotesOutline.GetLastEntry
Return	NotesOutlineEntry object
GetLevel	
Description	Retrieves the level of an entry.
Parameters	NotesOutlineEntry - the entry to get level information about.
Format	Long - NotesOutline.GetLevel(NotesOutlineEntry)
Return	Long
GetNextSibling	
Description	Retrieves the next entry at the same level as an entry.
Parameters	NotesOutlineEntry - entry to use as reference point.
Format	Sets NotesOutlineEntry = NotesOutline.GetNextSibling(NotesOutlineEntry)
Return	NotesOutlineEntry object
GetParent	
Description	Retrieves the parent entry for an entry.
Parameters	NotesOutlineEntry - the child entry.
Format	Sets NotesOutlineEntry = NotesOutline.GetParent(NotesOutlineEntry)
Return	NotesOutlineEntry object

GetPrev

Description	Retrieves the previous entry from the view.
Parameters	NotesOutlineEntry - reference entry for previous.
Format	Sets NotesOutlineEntry = NotesOutline.GetPrev(NotesOutlineEntry)
Return	NotesOutlineEntry object

GetPrevSibling

Description	Retrieves the previous entry at the same level.
Parameters	NotesOutlineEntry - reference point for level information.
Format	Sets NotesOutlineEntry = NotesOutline.GetPrevSibling(NotesOutlineEntry)
Return	NotesOutlineEntry object

MoveEntries

Description	Moves group of entries to another point in the outline.
Parameters	NotesOutlineEntry1 - starting entry for group to move. NotesOutlineEntry2 - ending entry for group to move. NotesOutlineEntry3 - the point to which the group will be moved. Integer1 - move after or not (OPTIONAL). Integer2 - mark as modified or not (OPTIONAL).
Format	Calls NotesOutline.MoveEntries(NotesOutlineEntry1, NotesOutlineEntry2, NotesOutlineEntry3, Integer1, Integer2)
Return	None

MoveEntry

Description	Moves one entry to another point in the outline.
Parameters	NotesOutlineEntry1 - entry to move. NotesOutlineEntry2 - the point to which the entry will be moved. Integer1 - move after or not (OPTIONAL). Integer2 - mark as modified or not (OPTIONAL).
Format	Call NotesOutline.MoveEntry(NotesOutlineEntry1, NotesOutlineEntry2, Integer1, Integer2)
Return	None

New

Description	Creates an Outline object.
Parameters	NotesDatabase - database in which outline is created.
Format	Sets variable = New NotesOutline(NotesDatabase) Dim variable As New NotesOutline(NotesDatabase)
Return	New NotesOutline object.

RemoveEntry

Description	Deletes an entry from the outline.

Parameters	NotesOutlineEntry - entry to remove. Integer - recursive delete or not (OPTIONAL)
Format	Calls NotesOutline.RemoveEntry(NotesOutlineEntry, Integer)
Return	None

NotesOutlineEntry class (Notes 5.0 or later)

The NotesOutlineEntry class is used to work with entries in Outline objects.

Properties

FrameText

Description	Text in frame.
Format	String = NotesOutlineEntry.FrameText
Type	String
Access	Read

HasChildren

Description	Signals whether the entry has children.
Format	Boolean = NotesOutlineEntry.HasChildren
Type	Boolean
Access	Read

ImagesText

Description	Text associated with image.
Format	String = NotesOutlineEntry.ImagesText
Type	String
Access	Read

IsAutoSorted

Description	Auto sorted or not.
Format	Boolean = NotesOutlineEntry.IsAutoSorted
Type	Boolean
Access	Read

IsExpandable

Description	Is the entry expandable or not.
Format	Boolean = NotesOutlineEntry.IsExpandable
Type	Boolean
Access	Read

IsHidden

Description	Is the entry hidden.
Format	Boolean = NotesOutlineEntry.IsHidden

Type	Boolean
Access	Read

IsInThisDB

Description	Is the entry in the current database.
Format	Boolean = NotesOutlineEntry.IsInThisDB
Type	Boolean
Access	Read

IsPrivate

Description	Is the entry private or public.
Format	Boolean = NotesOutlineEntry.IsPrivate
Type	Boolean
Access	Read

IsTemporary

Description	Is the entry temporary or not.
Format	Boolean = NotesOutlineEntry.IsTemporary
Type	Boolean
Access	Read

Level

Description	The entry's level within the outline.
Format	Long = NotesOutlineEntry.Level
Type	Long
Access	Read

OnClickText

Description	The text that is selected by the user from the entry.
Format	String = NotesOutlineEntry.OnClickText
Type	String
Access	Read

TitleText

Description	The text in the title of the entry.
Format	String = NotesOutlineEntry.TitleText
Type	String
Access	Read

Type

Description	The type of data displayed in the entry.
Format	Long = NotesOutlineEntry.Type
Type	Long
Access	Read

Methods

Clear

Description	Removes the entry from the outline.
Parameters	None
Format	Calls NotesOutlineEntry.Remove
Return	Integer

New

Description	Creates an instance of the NotesOutlineEntry class.
Parameters	NotesDocument - will be the entry.
Format	Sets varaible = New NotesOutlineEntry(NotesDocument) Dim variable As New NotesOutlineEntry(NotesDocument)
Return	NotesOutlineEntry instance

NotesRegistration class

The NotesRegistration class can be used to administer or create Notes ID files.

Properties

CertifierIDFile

Description	The certifier ID file (complete path) to use when creating ID files.
Format	String = NotesRegistration.CertifierIDFile NotesRegistration.CertifierIDFile = String
Type	String
Access	Read/Write

CreateMailDB

Description	Signals whether or not a mail database will be created when the ID file is created.
Format	Boolean = NotesRegistration.CreateMailDB NotesRegistration.CreateMailDB = Boolean
Type	Boolean
Access	Read/Write

Expiration

Description	The expiration date for newly created ID files.
Format	NotesDateTime = NotesRegistration.Expiration NotesRegistration.Expiration = NotesDateTime
Type	NotesDateTime object

Access	Read/Write

IDType

Description	The type of ID file to create.
Format	Integer = NotesRegistration.IDType NotesRegistration.IDType = Integer
Type	Integer (Possible Values: ID_FLAT, ID_HEIRARCHICAL, ID_CERTIFIER)
Access	Read/Write

IsNorthAmerican

Description	Signals whether an ID file is North American (True) or International (False)
Format	Boolean = NotesRegistration.IsNorthAmerican NotesRegistration.IsNorthAmerican = Boolean
Type	Boolean
Access	Read/Write

MinPasswordLength

Description	The minimum number of characters required for a password.
Format	Integer = NotesRegistration.MinPasswordLength NotesRegistration.MinPasswordLength = Integer
Type	Integer
Access	Read/Write

OrgUnit

Description	The organizational unit used to create ID files.
Format	String = NotesRegistration.OrgUnit NotesRegistration.OrgUnit = String
Type	String
Access	Read/Write

RegistrationLog

Description	The log file to use when creating ID files.
Format	String = NotesRegistration.RegistrationLog NotesRegistration.RegistrationLog = String
Type	String
Access	Read/Write

RegistrationServer

Description	The server to use to create ID files. Valid only when ID file is stored in the PNAB or the mail database is created during ID file creation.
Format	NotesRegistration.RegistrationServer = String String = NotesRegistration.RegistrationServer
Type	String
Access	Read/Write

StoreIDToAddressBook

Description	Signals whether the newly created ID file will be stored in the PNAB.
Format	Boolean = NotesRegistration.StoreIDToAddressBook NotesRegistration.StoreIDToAddressBook = Boolean
Type	Boolean
Access	Read/Write

UpdateAddressBook

Description	Signals whether the PNAB is updated or not when the ID file is created.
Format	Boolean = NotesRegistration.UpdateAddressBook NotesRegistration.UpdateAddressBook = Boolean
Type	Boolean
Access	Read/Write

Methods

AddCertifierToAddressBook

Description	Adds a certifier ID to the address book.
Parameters	String1 - certifer ID file to add (complete path) String2 - password for certifier ID file. (OPTIONAL) String3 - location field in the address book record. (OPTIONAL) String4 - comments field in the address book record. (OPTIONAL)
Format	Call NotesRegistration.AddCertifierToAddressBook(String1, String2, String3, String4)
Return	None

AddServerToAddressBook

Description	Creates a server entry in the address book.
Parameters	String1 - server ID file (complete path) String2 - name of the server String3 - domain name String4 - password for the ID file (OPTIONAL) String5 - Notes Named Network (OPTIONAL) String6 - Administrator's name for the server. (OPTIONAL) String7 - server title (OPTIONAL) String8 - location field in the server document (OPTIONAL) String9 - comments field in the server document (OPTIONAL)
Format	Calls NotesRegistration.AddServerToAddressBook(String1, String2, String3, String4, String5, String6, String7, String8, String9)
Return	None

AddUserProfile

Description	Adds a profile document for an ID file.
Parameters	String1 - username String2 - profile name
Format	Calls NotesRegistration.AddUserProfile(String1, String2)
Return	None

AddUserToAddressBook

Description	Creates a user entry in the address book.
Parameters	String1 - user ID file (complete path) String2 - user's full name String3 - user's last name String4 - user's password (OPTIONAL) String5 - user's first name (OPTIONAL) String6 - user's middle initial (OPTIONAL) String7 - user's home server (OPTIONAL) String8 - path to the user's mail file (OPTIONAL) String9 - user's forwarding address (OPTIONAL) String10 - location field on the person document (OPTIONAL) String11 - comments field on the person document (OPTIONAL)
Format	Calls NotesRegistration.AddUserToAddressBook(String1, String2, String3, String4, String5, String6, String7, String8, String9, String10, String11)
Return	None

CrossCertifier

Description	Cross certifies an ID file.
Parameters	String1 - the path to the ID file to cross certify. String2 - password for the certifier ID. String3 - comments field in the address book record.
Format	Calls NotesRegistration(String1, String2, String3)
Return	None

DeleteIDOnServer

Description	Removes an ID file from the server.
Parameters	String - the username for the ID file. Boolean - signals whether or not the file is a server ID.
Format	Calls NotesRegistration.DeleteIDOnServer(String, Boolean)
Return	None

GetIDFromServer

Description	Retrieves an ID file from a server.
Parameters	String1 - the username for the ID file. String2 - full path to the ID file. Boolean - signals whether or not the file is a server ID.
Format	Calls NotesRegistration.GetIDFromServer(String1, String2, Boolean)

Return	None

GetUserInfoFromServer

Description	Retrieves information concerning a user from the address book.
Parameters	String1 - username to retrieve String2 - returns the user's mail server. String3 - returns the user's mail file. String4 - returns the user's mail domain. String5 - returns the user's mail system. String6 - returns the user's user profile document.
Format	Calls NotesRegistration.GetUserInfoFromServer(String1, String2, String3, String4, String5, String6)
Return	Returns string values from each parameter except the first.

New

Description	Creates an instance of the NotesRegistration class.
Parameters	None
Format	Dim variable As New NotesRegistration Sets variable = New NotesRegistration
Return	None

Recertify

Description	Recertifies an ID file.
Parameters	String1 - the ID file to recertify. String2 - the password for the certifier ID file. String3 - the comments field in the address book record.
Format	Call NotesRegistration.ReCertifier(String1, String2, String3)
Return	

RegisterNewCertifier

Description	Registers a new certifier ID file.
Parameters	String1 - organization for the new certifier. String2 - ID file to register. String3 - password for the certifier ID file. String4 - country field in the address book record.
Format	Calls NotesRegistration.RegisterNewCertifier(String1, String2, String3, String4)
Return	None

RegisterNewServer

Description	Registers a new Server ID file.
Parameters	String1 - the server ID file to register (complete path). String2 - domain for the new server. String3 - password for the server ID file. String4 - location field in the address book record. String5 - comments field in the address book record. String6 - Notes Named Network for the server. String7 - server adminstrator's name. String8 - title field in the address book record.

Format	Calls NotesRegistration.RegisterNewServer(String1, String2, String3, String4, String5, String6, String7, String8)
Return	None

RegisterNewUser

Description	Registers a new user ID file
Parameters	String1 - user's last name. String2 - ID file to be registered (complete path). String3 - password for the certifier ID file. String4 - user's first name. String5 - user's middle initial. String6 - location field in the address book record. String7 - comment field in the address book record. String8 - path of the user's mail database relative to the mail directory on the server. String9 - forwarding domain for the user. String10 - user's password.
Format	Calls NotesRegistration.RegisterNewUser(String1, String2, String3, String4, String5, String6, String7, String8, String9, String10)
Return	None

SwithToID

Description	Switches to a new ID file.
Parameters	String1 - the ID file to switch to (complete path). String2 - password for the new ID file.
Format	Calls NotesRegistration.SwitchToID(String1, String2)
Return	None

NotesReplication class (Notes 5.0 or later)

The NotesReplication class can be used to work with the replication settings for a database.

Properties

Abstract

Description	Details about the replication.
Format	Variant = NotesReplication.Abstract NotesReplication.Abstract = Variant
Type	Variant
Access	Read/Write

CutOffDate

Description	The cutoff date for replication.
Format	Variant = NotesReplication.CutOffDate

Type	Variant
Access	Read

CutOffDelete

Description	The cutoff date for purging documents.
Format	Variant = NotesReplication.CutOffDelete NotesReplication.CutOffDelete = Variant
Type	Variant
Access	Read/Write

CutOffInterval

Description	The cutoff interval.
Format	Long = NotesReplication.CutOffInterval NotesReplication.CutOffInterval = Long
Type	Variant
Access	Read/Write

Disabled

Description	Signals whether or not replication is disabled.
Format	Boolean = NotesReplication.Disabled NotesReplication.Disabled = Boolean
Type	Boolean
Access	Read/Write

DoNotBrowse

Description	Signals whether or not browsing is disabled.
Format	Boolean = NotesReplication.DoNotBrowse NotesReplication.DoNotBrowse = Boolean
Type	Boolean
Access	Read/Write

DoNotCatalog

Description	Signals whether cataloging is disabled or not.
Format	Boolean = NotesReplication.DoNotCatalog NotesReplication.DoNotCatalog = Boolean
Type	Boolean
Access	Read/Write

HideDesign

Description	Signals whether or not design is hidden during replication.
Format	Boolean = NotesReplication.HideDesign NotesReplication.HideDesign = Boolean
Type	Boolean
Access	Read/Write

IgnoreDeletes

Description	Signals whether deletions are ignored during replication.

Format	Boolean = NotesReplication.IgnoreDeletes NotesReplication.IgnoreDeletes = Boolean
Type	Boolean
Access	Read/Write

IgnoreDestDeletes

Description	Signals whether deletions in the destination database are ignored.
Format	Boolean = NotesReplication.IgnoreDestDeletes NotesReplication.IgnoreDestDeletes = Boolean
Type	Boolean
Access	Read/Write

MultiDBIndex

Description	Signals whether the database is a multidatabase index or not.
Format	Boolean = NotesReplication.MultiDBIndex NotesReplication.MultiiDBIndex = Boolean
Type	Boolean
Access	Read/Write

NeverReplicate

Description	Signals whether replication can occur (False) or not (True).
Format	Boolean = NotesReplication.NeverReplicate NotesReplication.NeverReplicate = Boolean
Type	Boolean
Access	Read/Write

NoChronos

Description	Chronos disabled or not.
Format	Boolean = NotesReplication.NoChronos NotesReplication.NoChronos = Boolean
Type	Boolean
Access	Read/Write

Priority

Description	The replication priority.
Format	Long = NotesReplication.Priority NotesReplication.Priority = Long
Type	Long
Access	Read/Write

Methods

ClearHistory	
Description	Clear replication history.
Parameters	None
Format	Integer = NotesReplication.ClearHistory()
Return	Integer
Reset	
Description	Reset the replication.
Parameters	None
Format	Integer = NotesReplication.Reset()
Return	Integer
Save	
Description	Save the replication settings to disk.
Parameters	None
Format	Integer = NotesReplication.Save()
Return	Integer

NotesRichTextItem class

The NotesRichTextItem class is used to work with Rich Text items/fields.

Properties

EmbeddedObjects	
Description	All embedded objects (links, attachments, OLE objects, etc.) contained in a Rich Text item.
Format	Array = NotesRichTextItem.EmbeddedObjects
Type	Array of NotesEmbeddedObjects
Access	Read

Methods

AddNewLine	
Description	Appends carriage returns to the end of an item.
Parameters	Integer - the number of carriage returns to add. Boolean - signals whether or not a new paragraph is forced.
Format	Call NotesRichTextItem.AddNewLine(Integer, Boolean)

Return	None

AddTab

Description	Appends tabs to the end of an item.
Parameters	Integer - the number of tabs to add.
Format	Calls NotesRichTextItem.AddTab(Integer)
Return	None

AppendDocLink

Description	Adds a specified link to an item.
Parameters	Object (NotesDatabase, NotesView, or NotesDocument) - the link to insert. String - comments associated with a link.
Format	Calls NotesRichTextItem.AppendDocLink(Object, String)
Return	None

AppendRTItem

Description	The contents of one Rich Text item are appended to another.
Parameters	NotesRichTextItem - the item to append.
Format	Call NotesRichTextItem.AppendRTItem(NotesRich-TextItem)
Return	None

AppendStyle

Description	Applies a style to a Rich Text item.
Parameters	NotesRichTextStyle object - the style to apply.
Format	Calls NotesRichTextItem.AppendStyle(NotesRichText-Style)
Return	None

AppendText

Description	Appends text to the end of a Rich Text item.
Parameters	String - text to append.
Format	Call NotesRichTextItem.AppendText(String)
Return	None

EmbedObject

Description	Adds a link, OLE object, or file attachment to a Rich Text item.
Parameters	Integer - the type of link (Values: EMBED_ATTACHMENT, EMBED_OBJECT, EMBED_OBJECTLINK) String1 - name of application associated with OLE object; not used with other types. String2 - name of file to embed, attachment to add, or name of link. String3 - name to assign to object.

Format	Set NotesEmbeddedObject = NotesRichTextItem.EmbedObject(Integer, String1, String,2 String3)
Return	NotesEmbeddedObject or Nothing if not successful.

GenerateHTML (Notes 5.0 and higher)

Description	Generates HTML file containing contents of Rich Text item.
Parameters	String - path for the new file.
Format	Calls NotesRichTextItem.GenerateHTML(String)
Return	None

GenerateHTMLString (Notes 5.0 and higher)

Description	Generates HTML string containing contents of Rich Text item.
Parameters	None
Format	String = NotesRichTextItem.GenerateHTMLString
Return	String

GetEmbeddedObject

Description	Returns reference to an object from a Rich Text item.
Parameters	String - name of file attachment, OLE object, or link to retrieve.
Format	Set NotesEmbeddedObject = NotesRichTextItem.GetEmbeddedObject(String)
Return	NotesEmbeddedObject or Nothing if nothing found.

GetFormattedText

Description	Returns contents of Rich Text item as text; only text portion is returned. Embedded objects are not returned.
Parameters	Boolean - signals whether tabs are stripped out of the text or not. Integer - number of characters at which lines are wrapped (OPTIONAL).
Format	String = NotesRichTextItem.GetFormattedText(Boolean, Integer)
Return	String

NotesRichTextParagraphStyle class (Notes 5.0 or later)

The NotesRichTextParagraphStyle class can be used to apply styles to paragraphs in Rich Text items.

Properties

Alignment

Description	Alignment of the paragraph.
Format	Integer = NotesParagraphStyle.Alignment NotesParagraphStyle.Integer = Integer
Type	Integer
Access	Read/Write

FirstLineLeftMargin

Description	The line of the left margin.
Format	Long = NotesParagraphStyle.FirstLineLeftMargin NotesParagraphStyle.FirstLineLeftMargin = Long
Type	Long
Access	Read/Write

InterlineSpacing

Description	Interline setting for the paragraph.
Format	Integer = NotesParagraphStyle.InterlineSpacing NotesParagraphStyle.InterlineSpacing = Integer
Type	Integer
Access	Read/Write

LeftMargin

Description	The left margin for the paragraph.
Format	Long = NotesParagraphStyle.LeftMargin NotesParagraphStyle.Margin = Long
Type	Long
Access	Read/Write

RightMargin

Description	Right margin setting for the paragraph.
Format	Long = NotesParagraphStyle.RightMargin NotesParagraphStyle.RightMargin = Long
Type	Long
Access	Read/Write

SpacingAbove

Description	Spacing above the paragraph.
Format	Integer = NotesParagraphStyle.SpacingAbove NotesParagraphStyle.SpacingAbove = Integer
Type	Integer
Access	Read/Write

SpacingBelow

Description	Spacing below the paragraph.

Format	Integer = NotesParagraphStyle.SpacingBelow NotesParagraphStyle.SpacingBelow = Integer
Type	Integer
Access	Read/Write
Tabs	
Description	The tabs set for the paragraph.
Format	Variant = NotesParagraphStyle.Tabs NotesParagraphStyle.Tabs = Variant
Type	Variant
Access	Read/Write

Methods

ClearAllTabs	
Description	Clears the tabs set in the paragraph.
Parameters	None
Format	Calls NotesParagraphStyle.ClearAllTabs
Return	None
SetTab	
Description	Sets a tab in the paragraph.
Parameters	Long - tab position. Integer - type of tab.
Format	Calls NotesParagraphStyle.SetTab(Long, Integer)
Return	None
SetTabs	
Description	Sets numerous tabs in a paragraph.
Parameters	Integer1 - number of tabs to create. Long1 - starting tab. Long2 - tab interval. Integer2 - type of tabs. (OPTIONAL)
Format	Calls NotesParagraphStyle.SetTabs(Integer1, Long1, Long2, Integer2)
Return	None

NotesRichTextStyle class

The NotesRichTextStyle class is used to apply formatting to the data in Rich Text items/ fields. The `AppendStyle` method of the NotesRichTextItem class is used to apply a style to a Rich Text field.

Properties

Bold

Description	Creates bold text.
Format	Boolean = NotesRichTextStyle.Bold NotesRichTextStyle.Bold = Boolean
Type	Boolean
Access	Read/Write

Effects

Description	Applies various effects to text.
Format	Integer = NotesRichTextStyle.Effects NotesRichTextStyle.Effects = Integer (Values: EFFECTS_EMBOSS, EFFECTS_EXTRUDE, EFFECTS_NONE, EFFECTS_SHADOW, EFFECTS_SUBSCRIPT, EFFECTS_SUPERSCRIPT, STYLE_NO_CHANGE).
Type	Integers
Access	Read/Write

FontSize

Description	Sets the point size of the font.
Format	Integer = NotesRichTextStyle.FontSize NotesRichTextStyle.FontSize = Integer
Type	Integer
Access	Read/Write

Italic

Description	Italicizes the text.
Format	Boolean = NotesRichTextStyle.Italic NotesRichTextStyle.Italic = Boolean
Type	Boolean
Access	Read/Write

NotesColor

Description	Sets the color of the text.
Format	Integer = NotesRichTextStyle.NotesColor NotesRichTextStyle.NotesColor = Integer (Values: COLOR_BLACK, COLOR_BLUE, COLOR_CYAN, COLOR_DARK_BLUE, COLOR_DARK_CYAN, COLOR_DARK_GREEN, COLOR_DARK_MAGENTA, COLOR_DARK_RED, COLOR_DARK_YELLOW, COLOR_GRAY, COLOR_GREEN, COLOR_LIGHT_GRAY, COLOR_MAGENTA, COLOR_RED, COLOR_WHITE, COLOR_YELLOW, STYLE_NO_CHANGE)
Type	Integer

Access	Read/Write
NotesFont	
Description	Sets the font attribute of the text.
Format	Integer = NotesRichTextStyle.NotesFont NotesRichTextStyle.NotesFont = Integer (Values: FONT_COURIER, FONT_HELV, FONT_ROMAN, STYLE_NO_CHANGE)
Type	Integer
Access	Read/Write
PassthruHTML (Notes 5.0 and higher)	
Description	Sets the text of a Rich Text item to pass-thru HTML.
Format	Integer = NotesRichTextStyle.PassthruHTML NotesRichTextStyle.PassthruHTML = Integer
Type	Integer
Access	Read/Write
Strikethrough	
Description	Enables or disables strikethrough on the text.
Format	Boolean = NotesRichTextStyle.Strikethrough NotesRichTextStyle.Strikethrough = Boolean
Type	Boolean
Access	Read/Write
Underline	
Description	Enables/disables the underlining of text.
Format	Boolean = NotesRichTextStyle.Underline NotesRichTextStyle.Underline = Boolean
Type	Boolean
Access	Read/Write

NotesRichTextTab class (Notes 5.0 or later)

The NotesRichTextTab class can be used to work with tabs in Rich Text items.

Properties

Position	
Description	Tab position.
Format	Long = NotesRichTextTab.Position
Type	Long
Access	
Type	
Description	The type of tab.

Format	Integer = NotesRichTextTab.Type
Type	Integer
Access	

Methods

Clear

Description	Clear the tab.
Parameters	None
Format	Call NotesRichTextTab.Clear
Return	None

NotesSession class

The NotesSession class is used to set up the environment for back end scripts to work within.

Properties

AddressBooks

Description	The address books, both personal and public, that are known to the current script.
Format	Array = NotesSession.AddressBooks
Type	Array of NotesDatabase objects
Access	Read

AlternateLanguageTag (Notes 5.0 and higher)

Description	Alternate language(s) for the current user.
Format	String = NotesSession.AlternateLanguageTag
Type	String
Access	Read

AlternateUserName (Notes 5.0 and higher)

Description	Alternate username for the current user.
Format	String = NotesSession.AlternateUserName
Type	String
Access	Read

CommonUserName

Description	The common name of the current user. Same as the @Name([CN];@UserName) function.
Format	String = NotesSession.CommonUserName

Type	String
Access	Read

CurrentAgent

Description	The currently running agent.
Format	NotesAgent = NotesSession.CurrentAgent
Type	NotesAgent object
Access	Read

CurrentDatabase

Description	The database in which the session was declared.
Format	NotesDatabase = NotesSession.CurrentDatabase
Type	NotesDatabase object
Access	Read

DocumentContext

Description	An in-memory document created by an external application through the Notes API. This is commonly used to grab a document created through a web browser.
Format	Sets NotesDocument = NotesSession.DocumentContext
Type	NotesDocument object
Access	Read

EffectiveUserName

Description	The username that is currently running the script. It has the same result as CommonUserName except in cases where the script is running on a server, then EffectiveUserName returns the script owner.
Format	String = NotesSession.EffectiveUserName
Type	String
Access	Read

International

Description	The international settings for the environment.
Format	Sets NotesInternational = NotesSession.International
Type	NotesInternational object
Access	Read

IsOnServer

Description	Signals whether or not a script is running on a server.
Format	Boolean = NotesSession.IsOnServer
Type	Boolean
Access	Read

LastExitStatus

Description	The exit code returned by the agent manager the last time an agent ran.

Format	Integer = NotesSession.LastExitStatus
Type	Integer
Access	Read

LastRun

Description	The date the current agent was last run.
Format	Variant = NotesSession.LastRun
Type	Variant
Access	Read

NotesBuildVersion (Notes 5.0 and higher)

Description	The build number for the release of the Notes environment.
Format	String = NotesSession.NotesBuildVersion
Type	String
Access	Read

NotesVersion

Description	The release of the Notes environment.
Format	String = NotesSession.NotesVersion
Type	String
Access	Read

Platform

Description	The platform that the script is currently on.
Format	String = NotesSession.Platform (Values: Macintosh, MS-DOS, Netware, OS/2v1, OS/2v2, Windows/16, Windows/32, UNIX)
Type	String
Access	Read

SavedData

Description	The NotesDocument used by an agent in which to store data between runs.
Format	Sets NotesDocument = NotesSession.SavedData
Type	NotesDocument object
Access	Read

UserName

Description	The fully distinguished name of the current user.
Format	String = NotesSession.UserName
Type	String
Access	Read

Methods

CreateDateRange

Description	Creates a NotesDateRange object.
Parameters	None
Format	Sets NotesDateRange = NotesSession.CreateNotesDateRange()
Return	NotesDateRange object

CreateDateTime

Description	Creates a NotesDateTime object.
Parameters	String - the date/time that the NotesDateTime object will represent.
Format	Sets NotesDateTime = NotesSession.CreateDateTime(String)
Return	NotesDateTime object

CreateLog

Description	Creates a NotesLog object.
Parameters	String - name assigned to the log.
Format	Sets NotesLog = NotesSession.CreateLog(String)
Return	NotesLog object

CreateName

Description	Creates a NotesName object.
Parameters	String - the name of the user or server.
Format	Sets NotesName = NotesSession.CreateName(String)
Return	NotesName object

CreateNewsLetter

Description	Creates a NotesNewsLetter object.
Parameters	NotesDocumentCollection - collection of documents to include in newsletter.
Format	Sets NotesNewsLetter = NotesSession.CreateNewsLetter(Notes-DocumentCollection)
Return	NotesNewsLetter object

CreateRichTextParagraphStyle (Notes 5.0 and higher)

Description	Creates a NotesRichTextParagraphStyle object.
Parameters	None
Format	Sets NotesRichTextParagraphStyle = NotesSession.CreateRich-TextParagraphStyle()
Return	NotesRichTextParagraphStyle object

CreateRichTextStyle

Description	Creates a new NotesRichTextStyle object.
Parameters	None
Format	Sets NotesRichTextStyle = NotesSession.CreateRichTextStyle()

Return	NotesRichTextStyle object

CreateTimer

Description	Creates a NotesTimer object.
Parameters	None
Format	Sets NotesTimer = NotesSession.CreateTimer()
Return	NotesTimer object

FreeTimeSearch

Description	Finds free time slots for putting on a calendar and scheduling.
Parameters	NotesDateRange - starting and ending for the search. Integer - the length of the slot needed in minutes. Array of Strings - list of usernames to perform search for. Boolean - signals whether want the first matching date (True) or all (False).
Format	Sets NotesDateRange = NotesSession.FreeTimeSearch(Notes-DateRange, Integer, String array, Boolean)
Return	NotesDateRange of matching date(s) or Null if no matches.

GetDatabase

Description	Gets a handle on a NotesDatabase.
Parameters	String1 - server name String2 - database file name.
Format	Sets NotesDatabase = NotesSession.GetDatabase(String1, String2)
Return	NotesDatabase object

GetDbDirectory

Description	Gets a handle on a directory.
Parameters	String - server name
Format	Sets NotesDBDirectory = NotesSession.GetDbDirectory(String)
Return	NotesDBDirectory object

GetEnvironmentString

Description	Retrieves the value of an environment variable from the Notes.ini file.
Parameters	String - variable name Boolean - signals whether a dollar sign ($) is prepended to the variable name (False) or not (True).
Format	Variant = NotesSession.GetEnvironmentString(String, Boolean)
Return	Variant with type depending on data type in the variable.

GetEnvironmentValue

Description	Retrieves the value on a numeric environment variable.
Parameters	String - variable name Boolean - signals whether a dollar sign ($) is prepended to the variable name (False) or not (True).
Format	Variant = NotesSession.GetEnvironmentValue(String, Boolean)

Return	Variant

New

Description	Creates a NotesSession object
Parameters	None
Format	Dim variable As New NotesSession Sets NotesSession = New NotesSession
Return	NotesSession object

SetEnvironmentVar

Description	Sets the value of an environment variable in the Notes.ini.
Parameters	String - variable name Variant - value to store in the variable Boolean - if false, dollar sign ($) is prepended to the variable name; otherwise no.
Format	Calls NotesSession.SetEnvironmentVar(String, Variant, Boolean)
Return	None

UpdateProcessedDoc

Description	Marks a document as processed by an agent.
Parameters	NotesDocument - the document to mark as processed.
Format	Calls NotesSession.UpdateProcessedDoc(NotesDocument)
Return	None

NotesTimer class

The NotesTimer class can be used to schedule events within a script every so many seconds.

Properties

Comment

Description	Comments associated with the Timer.
Format	String = NotesTimer.Comment NotesTimer.Comment = String
Type	String
Access	Read/Write

Enabled

Description	Signals whether or not the NotesTimer object is enabled.
Format	Boolean = NotesTimer.Enabled NotesTimer.Enabled = Boolean
Type	Boolean
Access	Read/Write

Interval	
Description	The time interval for the timer to trigger an event in seconds.
Format	Integer = NotesTimer.Interval NotesTimer.Interval = Integer
Type	Integer
Access	Read/Write

Methods

New	
Description	Creates a NotesTimer object.
Parameters	Integer - the time interval in seconds. String - comments associated with the timer object.
Format	Dim variable As New NotesTimer(Integer, String) Sets NotesTimer = New NotesTimer(Integer, String)
Return	NotesTimer object

NotesUIDatabase class

The NotesUIDatabase class allows access to the currently open database in the workspace.

Properties

Database	
Description	The back end database object that corresponds to the front end database.
Format	Sets NotesDatabase = NotesUIDatabase.Database
Type	NotesDatabase object
Access	Read
Documents	
Description	All documents on which the current NotesUIDatabase is currently working.
Format	Sets NotesDocumentCollection = NotesUIDatabase.Documents
Type	NotesDocumentCollection object
Access	Read

Methods

OpenNavigator (Notes 5.0 and higher)

Description	Opens the specified navigator in the database.
Parameters	String - navigator name
Format	Calls NotesUIDatabase.OpenNavigator(String)
Return	None

OpenView

Description	Opens the specified view in the database.
Parameters	String - view name
Format	Calls NotesUIDatabase.OpenView(String)
Return	None

NotesUIDocument class

The NotesUIDocument class allows access to the currently open document in the workspace.

Properties

AutoReload

Description	Signals whether the document is automatically refreshed.
Format	Boolean = NotesUIDocument.AutoReload NotesUIDocument.AutoReload = Boolean
Type	Boolean
Access	Read/Write

CurrentField

Description	The name of the current field that has focus.
Format	String = NotesUIDocument.CurrentField
Type	String
Access	Read

DialogBoxCancelled

Description	Signals whether the user canceled a dialog box.
Format	Boolean = NotesUIDocument.DialogBoxCancelled
Type	Boolean
Access	Read

Document

Description	The back end document that corresponds to the currently open document.

Format	NotesDocument = NotesUIDocument.Document
Type	NotesDocument object
Access	Read

EditMode

Description	Signals whether or not a document is in edit mode.
Format	Boolean = NotesUIDocument.EditMode NotesUIDocument.EditMode = Boolean
Type	Boolean
Access	Read/Write

FieldHelp

Description	Signals whether field help is displayed or not.
Format	Boolean = NotesUIDocument.FieldHelp NotesUIDocument.FieldHelp = Boolean
Type	Boolean
Access	Read/Write

HiddenChars

Description	Signals whether or not hidden characters on a document (tabs, carriage returns, etc.) are displayed.
Format	Boolean = NotesUIDocument.HiddenChars NotesUIDocument.HiddenChars = Boolean
Type	Boolean
Access	Read/Write

HorzScrollBar

Description	Signals whether the horizontal scroll bar is displayed.
Format	Boolean = NotesUIDocument.HorzScrollBar NotesUIDocument.HorzScrollBar = Boolean
Type	Boolean
Access	Read/Write

InPreviewPane

Description	Signals whether or not the document is accessed in the preview pane.
Format	Boolean = NotesUIDocument.InPreviewPane
Type	Boolean
Access	Read

IsNewDoc

Description	Signals whether or not the document currently open is new (not previously saved).
Format	Boolean = NotesUIDocument.IsNewDoc
Type	Boolean
Access	Read

PreviewDocLink

Description	Signals whether a link's preview pane is displayed.
Format	Boolean = NotesUIDocument.PreviewDocLink NotesUIDocument.PreviewDocLink = Boolean
Type	Boolean
Access	Read/Write

PreviewParentDoc

Description	Signals whether or not the parent document's preview pane is displayed.
Format	Boolean = NotesUIDocument.PreviewParentDoc NotesUIDocument.PreviewParentDoc = Boolean
Type	Boolean
Access	Read/Write

Ruler

Description	Signals whether the ruler is displayed in the document window.
Format	Boolean = NotesUIDocument.Ruler NotesUIDocument.Ruler = Boolean
Type	Boolean
Access	Read/Write

WindowTitle

Description	Retrieves the window title for the current document.
Format	String = NotesUIDocument.WindowTitle
Type	String
Access	Read

Methods

Categorize

Description	Places a document in a category.
Parameters	String - name of the category
Format	Calls NotesUIDocument.Categorize(String)
Return	None

Clear

Description	Deletes the current selection (field values) from the document. This is only available in edit mode.
Parameters	None
Format	Calls NotesUIDocument.Clear
Return	None

Close

Description	Closes the current document window.
Parameters	None
Format	Calls NotesUIDocument.Close
Return	None

CollapseAllSections

Description	All sections on the document are collapsed.
Parameters	None
Format	Call NotesUIDocument.CollapseAllSections
Return	None

Copy

Description	The current document is copied to the clipboard.
Parameters	None
Format	Call NotesUIDocument.Copy
Return	None

CreateObject

Description	Creates an OLE object in the current Rich Text field. Only available in edit mode.
Parameters	String1 - the name to use to refer to the object. (OPTIONAL) String2 - the type of object to create. (OPTIONAL) String3 - path to the file to use to create the object. (OPTIONAL)
Format	Set Variant = NotesUIDocument.CreateObject(String1, String2, String3)
Return	Variant - handle to the newly created object.

Cut

Description	Removes the current selection from the document and places it in the clipboard.
Parameters	None
Format	Calls NotesUIDocument.Cut
Return	None

DeleteDocument

Description	Flags the document to be deleted. It is not deleted until the view is refreshed or the database is closed.
Parameters	None
Format	Calls NotesUIDocument.DeleteDocument
Return	None

DeselectAll

Description	Deselects all items selected from the document.
Parameters	None
Format	Calls NotesUIDocument.DeselectAll

Return	None

ExpandAllSections

Description	All sections on the document are expanded.
Parameters	None
Format	Calls NotesUIDocument.ExpandAllSections
Return	None

FieldAppendText

Description	Text values are appended to an item's values.
Parameters	String1 - field name String2 - test to append.
Format	Calls NotesUIDocument.FieldAppendText(String1, String2)
Return	None

FieldClear

Description	Clears the contents of the designated field.
Parameters	String - field name
Format	Calls NotesUIDocument.FieldClear(String)
Return	None

FieldContains

Description	Signals whether or not a field contains a specified value.
Parameters	String1 - field name String2 - string to find.
Format	Boolean = NotesUIDocument.FieldContains(String1, String2)
Return	Boolean

FieldGetText

Description	Retrieves the text value of a field.
Parameters	String - field name
Format	String = NotesUIDocument.GetFieldText(String)
Return	String

FieldSetText

Description	Sets the text value of a field. Only valid in edit mode.
Parameters	String1 - field name String2 - text value
Format	Call NotesUIDocument.FieldSetText(String1, String2)
Return	None

FindFreeTimeDialog (Notes 5.0 and higher)

Description	Find free time.

Parameters	String1 - list of required people. String2 - list of optional people. String3 - list of required rooms. String4 - list of optional rooms. String5 - list of required resources. String6 - list of optional resources. String7 - list of people to remove.
Format	Call NotesUIDocument.FindFreeTimeDialog(String1, String2, String3, String4, String5, String6, String7)
Return	None

FindString (Notes 5.0 and higher)

Description	Searches for a field name in the current document.
Parameters	String - fieldname
Format	Calls NotesUIDocument.FindString(String)
Return	None

Forward

Description	Forwards the document.
Parameters	None
Format	Calls NotesUIDocument.Forward
Return	None

GetObject

Description	Returns a handle to an OLE object on the document.
Parameters	String - name of OLE object to retrieve.
Format	Set Variant = NotesUIDocument.GetObject(String)
Return	Variant - handle on the OLE object or Nothing if not found.

GotoBottom

Description	Moves the cursor to the last editable field on the document. Only valid in edit mode.
Parameters	None
Format	Calls NotesUIDocument.GotoBottom
Return	None

GotoField

Description	Moves the cursor to the field specified. Only valid in edit mode.
Parameters	String - field name
Format	Calls NotesUIDocument.GotoField(String)
Return	None

GotoNextField

Description	Moves the cursor to the next editable field on the document. Only valid in edit mode.
Parameters	None
Format	Calls NotesUIDocument.GotoNextField

Return	None

GotoPrevField

Description	Moves the cursor to the previous editable field on the document. Only valid in edit mode.
Parameters	None
Format	Calls NotesUIDocument.GotoPrevField
Return	None

GotoTop

Description	Moves the cursor to the first editable field on the document. Only valid in edit mode.
Parameters	None
Format	Calls NotesUIDocument.GotoTop
Return	None

Import (Notes 5.0 and higher)

Description	Imports a file into the current selection.
Parameters	String1 - import type String2 - file name and path
Format	Calls NotesUIDocument.Import(String1, String2)
Return	None

InsertText

Description	Text is inserted at current position in the document. Only valid in edit mode.
Parameters	String - text to insert
Format	Calls NotesUIDocument.InsertText(String)
Return	None

NavBarSetText

Description	The text in the URL navigation bar in IE is set.
Parameters	String1 - the URL text String2 - window title (OPTIONAL)
Format	Calls NotesUIDocument.NavBarSetText(String1, String2)
Return	None

NavBarSpinnerStart

Description	Starts the navigation bar spinner in IE.
Parameters	None
Format	Calls NotesUIDocument.NavBarSpinnerStart()
Return	None

NavBarSpinnerStop

Description	Stops the navigation bar spinner in IE.
Parameters	None
Format	Calls NotesUIDocument.NavBarSpinnerStop

Return	None

Paste

Description	Pastes the contents of the clipboard into the current cursor position in the document. Only valid in edit mode.
Parameters	None
Format	Calls NotesUIDocument.Paste
Return	None

Print

Description	The current document is printed.
Parameters	Integer1 - number of copies to print (OPTIONAL) Integer2 - starting page; zero signals the beginning (OPTIONAL) Integer3 - ending page; zero signals the end (OPTIONAL) Boolean - signals whether it is a draft or not (OPTIONAL)
Format	Calls NotesUIDocument.Print Calls NotesUIDocument.Print(Integer1, Integer2, Integer3, Boolean)
Return	None

Refresh

Description	The contents of the document are refreshed. Just like hitting the F9 key.
Parameters	None
Format	Calls NotesUIDocument.Refresh
Return	None

RefreshHideFormulas

Description	The Hide-When formulas are refreshed for the document.
Parameters	None
Format	Calls NotesUIDocument.RefreshHideWhenFormulas
Return	None

Reload

Description	The current document is refreshed with any changes made to the backend document.
Parameters	None
Format	Calls NotesUIDocument.Reload
Return	None

Save

Description	Saves the document to disk. Only valid in edit mode.
Parameters	None
Format	Calls NotesUIDocument.Save
Return	None

SaveNewVersion

Description	Saves a copy of the document as a new version.

Parameters	None
Format	Calls NotesUIDocument.SaveNewVersion
Return	None
SelectAll	
Description	Selects the contents of the current field when in edit mode; otherwise the whole document contents are selected.
Parameters	None
Format	Calls NotesUIDocument.SelectAll
Return	None
Send	
Description	Mails a document.
Parameters	None
Format	Calls NotesUIDocument.Send
Return	None
SpellCheck (Notes 5.0 and higher)	
Description	Checks the spelling in the current document.
Parameters	None
Format	Calls NotesUIDocument.SpellCheck
Return	None

NotesUIView class

The NotesUIView class allows access to the currently open view in the workspace.

Properties

CalendarDateTime	
Description	The date and time of the current selection in a calendar view.
Format	Variant = NotesUIView.CalendarDateTime
Type	Variant
Access	Read
Documents	
Description	All documents currently being processed by the current view.
Format	Sets NotesDocumentCollection = NotesUIView.Documents
Type	NotesDocumentCollection object
Access	Read

View

Description	The back end NotesView object that corresponds to the current view.
Format	Sets NotesView = NotesUIView.View
Type	NotesView object
Access	Read

Methods

Print (Notes 5.0 and higher)

Description	Prints the current view.
Parameters	Integer1 - number of copies to print. (OPTIONAL) Integer2 - starting page. (OPTIONAL) Integer3 - top page. (OPTIONAL) Boolean - draft or not. (OPTIONAL) Integer4 - page separator. (OPTIONAL) String - form to use if form override. (OPTIONAL)
Format	Calls NotesUIView.Print(Integer1, Integer2, Integer3, Boolean, Integer4, String)
Return	None

SelectDocument

Description	Selects a document from the view.
Parameters	NotesDocument - document to select.
Format	Calls NotesUIView.SelectDocument(NotesDocument)
Return	None

NotesUIWorkspace class

The NotesUIWorkspace class allows access to the current workspace. This is used to set up the environment in which scripts running in the UI will work.

Properties

CurrentCalendarDateTime

Description	The date and time of the current selected region in a calendar view.
Format	Variant = NotesUIWorkspace.CurrentCalendarDateTime
Type	Variant
Access	Read

CurrentDatabase (Notes 5.0 and higher)

Description	The currently open database.
Format	Sets NotesUIDatabase = NotesUIWorkspace.CurrentDatabase
Type	NotesUIDatabase object
Access	Read

CurrentDocument

Description	The currently open document.
Format	Sets NotesUIDocument = NotesUIWorkspace.CurrentDocument
Type	NotesUIDocument object
Access	Read

CurrentView (Notes 5.0 and higher)

Description	The currently open view.
Format	Sets NotesUIView = NotesUIWorkspace.CurrentView
Type	NotesUIView object
Access	Read

Methods

AddDatabase

Description	Adds a database icon to the workspace (current page) and highlights the database icon. If the database icon already exists, the icon is highlighted.
Parameters	String1 - server name/location of the database String2 - database file name and path information
Format	Calls NotesUIWorkspace.AddDatabase(String1, String2)
Return	None

CheckAlarm

Description	Checks for new alarms in the mail file.
Parameters	None
Format	Calls NotesUIWorkspace.CheckAlarms()
Return	None

ComposeDocument

Description	A new document is created in the current workspace.
Parameters	String1 - server location of database in which new document will be created (OPTIONAL) String2 - file name of the database in which the new document will be created (OPTIONAL)

	String3 - name of form to use for new document (OPTIONAL) Double1 - window width of new document window (OPTIONAL) Double2 - window height of new document window (OPTIONAL)
Format	Sets NotesUIDocument = NotesUIWorkspace.ComposeDocument(String1, String2, String3, Double1, Double2)
Return	NotesUIDocument object representing the new document.

DialogBox

Description	Opens a dialog box with the current document, currently selected document, or specified document.
Parameters	String1 - form name Boolean1 - centers the dialog box horizontally. (OPTIONAL) Boolean2 - centers the dialog box vertically. (OPTIONAL) Boolean3- displays OK button only or both. (OPTIONAL) Boolean4 - new fields on dialog box form added to underlying form or not. (OPTIONAL) Boolean5 - don't pass edits to underlying document or not. (OPTIONAL) Boolean6 - prohibits writing to the document in the dialog box or not. (OPTIONAL) String2 - title for the dialog box. (OPTIONAL) NotesDocument - document to open in the dialog box. (OPTIONAL)
Format	Boolean = NotesUIWorkspace.DialogBox(String1, Boolean1, Boolean2, Boolean3, Boolean4, Boolean5, Boolean6, String2, NotesDocument)
Return	Boolean - signals if OK button was selected (TRUE) or the Cancel button (FALSE).

EditDocument

Description	Opens a document in edit mode. This may be the current document, specific document, or document selected in a view.
Parameters	Boolean1 - opens document in edit mode (TRUE) or in read mode or specified edit mode (FALSE). (OPTIONAL) NotesDocument - opens specific document. (OPTIONAL) Boolean2 - prohibits user from switching modes. (OPTIONAL)
Format	Sets NotesUIDocument = NotesUIWorkspace.EditDocument(Boolean1, NotesDocument, Boolean2)
Return	NotesUIDocument object representing the document being edited.

EditProfile

Description	Opens a new or existing profile in edit mode.
Parameters	String1 - profile name String2 - username associated with profile. (OPTIONAL)
Format	Calls NotesUIWorkspace.EditProfile(String1, String2)
Return	None

EnableAlarms

Description	Starts or stops alarm notifications.
Parameters	Boolean - enables or disables alarm notifications.
Format	Boolean = NotesUIWorkspace.EnableAlarms(Boolean)
Return	Boolean

Folder (Notes 5.0 and higher)

Description	Access folder
Parameters	String - folder name Variant - move or copy
Format	Variant = NotesUIWorkspace.Folder(String, Variant)
Return	Variant

GetListofTunes (Notes 5.0 and higher)

Description	Retrieves list of tunes for current environment.
Parameters	None
Format	Variant = NotesUIWorkspace.GetListofTunes()
Return	Variant

FindFreeTimeDialog

Description	Opens Find Free Time box to search for available times.
Parameters	String1 - field name that contains list of people in meeting. String2 - field name that contains list of people whose attendance is optional. (OPTIONAL) String3 - field name that contains required rooms. (OPTIONAL) String4- field name that contains optional rooms. (OPTONAL) String5 - field name that contains required resources. (OPTIONAL) String6- field name that contains optional resources. (OPTIONAL) String7 - field name that contains people to remove from meeting. (OPTIONAL) String8 - field name that contains the meeting start time. (OPTIONAL) String9 - field name that contains the meeting end time. (OPTIONAL) ** All fields are on the current document.
Format	Calls NotesUIWorkspace.FindFreeTimeDialog(String1, String2, String3, String4, String5, String6, String7, String8, String9)
Return	None

New

Description	Creates a NotesUIWorkspace object.
Parameters	None
Format	Dim variable As New NotesUIWorkspace
Return	NotesUIWorkspace object

OpenDatabase

Description — Open a database.

Parameters — String1 - server on which database resides.
String2 - file name and path to the database.
String3 - view to open in database; default view is opened if omitted. (OPTIONAL)
String4 - key value of document to highlight in view - first column. (OPTIONAL)
Boolean1 - opens new document window or not. (OPTIONAL)
Boolean2 - adds database to workspace, if doesn't exist, or not. (OPTIONAL)

Format — Calls NotesUIWorkspace.OpenDatabase(String1, String2, String3, String4, Boolean1, Boolean2)

Return — None

OpenFileDialog (Notes 5.0 and higher)

Description — Opens file dialog box.

Parameters — Variant - multiple selections or not.
String1 - title. (OPTIONAL)
String2 - file type filters. (OPTIONAL)
String3 - initial directory. (OPTIONAL)
String4 - intial file. (OPTIONAL)

Format — Variant = NotesUIWorkspace.OpenFileDialog(Variant, String1, String2, String3, String4)

Return — Variant

PickListCollection (Notes 5.0 and higher)

Description — Assembles pick list collection.

Parameters — Integer1 - type.
Integer2 - multiple selections or not. (OPTIONAL)
String1 - server name. (OPTIONAL)
String2 - database file name. (OPTIONAL)
String3 - view name. (OPTIONAL)
String4 - title. (OPTIONAL)
String5 - prompt type. (OPTIONAL)

Format — Variant = NotesUIWorkspace.PickListCollection(Integer1, Integer2, String1, String2, String3, String4, String5)

Return — Variant

PickListString (Notes 5.0 and higher)

Description — Assembles pick list string.

Parameters — Integer1 - type.
Integer2 - multiple selections or not. (OPTIONAL)
String1 - server name. (OPTIONAL)
String2 - database file name. (OPTIONAL)
String3 - view name. (OPTIONAL)
String4 - title. (OPTIONAL)
String5 - prompt type. (OPTIONAL)

Format — Variant = NotesUIWorkspace.PickListString(Integer1, Integer2, String1, String2, String3, String4, String5)

Return	Variant

PlayTune (Notes 5.0 and higher)

Description	Plays a tune.
Parameters	String - name of tune.
Format	Calls NotesUIWorkspace.PlayTune(String)
Return	None

Prompt (Notes 5.0 and higher)

Description	Displays prompt dialog box for data entry.
Parameters	Integer - prompt type. String1 - title for dialog box. String2 - prompt text. String3 - default choice. (OPTIONAL) Variant - possible values. (OPTIONAL)
Format	Variant = NotesUIWorkspace.Prompt(Integer, String1, String2, String3, Variant)
Return	Variant containing user entry.

RefreshParentNote (Notes 5.0 and higher)

Description	Refreshes parent document.
Parameters	None
Format	Calls NotesUIWorkspace.RefreshParentNote
Return	None

SaveFileDialog (Notes 5.0 and higher)

Description	Present save file dialog box.
Parameters	Boolean - multiple selections or not. String1 - dialog box title. (OPTIONAL) String2 - file type filters. (OPTIONAL) String3 - initial directory. (OPTIONAL) String4 - initial file. (OPITONAL)
Format	Calls NotesUIWorkspace.SaveFileDialogBox(Boolean, String1, String2, String3, String4)
Return	Variant

SetCurrentLocation (Notes 5.0 and higher)

Description	Sets current location document.
Parameters	String - location name.
Format	Calls NotesUIWorkspace.SetCurrentLocation(String)
Return	None

URLOpen

Description	Opens a web page.
Parameters	String1 - URL to open. (OPTIONAL) Integer1 - reloads from Internet (1) or not (0). (OPTIONAL) Integer2 - saves URL links on page in field or not. (OPTONAL) String2 - MIME character set to use. (OPTIONAL)

	String3 - web username. (OPTIONAL) String4 - web password. (OPTIONAL) String5 - proxy username. (OPTIONAL) String6 - proxy password. (OPTIONAL) Boolean - user web navigator database to open URL or not. (OPTIONAL)
Format	Calls NotesUIWorkspace.URLOpen(String1, Integer1, Integer2, String2, String3, String4, String5, String6, Boolean)
Return	None

UseLSX

Description	Loads a LotusScript extension file.
Parameters	String - LSX file name.
Format	Calls NotesUIWorkspace.UseLSX(String)
Return	None

ViewRefresh

Description	Refreshes the current view.
Parameters	None
Format	Calls NotesUIWorkspace.ViewRefresh
Return	None

NotesView class

The NotesView class allows access to a view in any database.

Properties

Aliases

Description	The aliases of a view.
Format	Array = NotesView.Aliases
Type	Array of Strings
Access	Read

AutoUpdate

Description	Signals whether or not the front end is updated automatically.
Format	Boolean = NotesView.AutoUpdate NotesView.AutoUpdate = Boolean
Type	Boolean
Access	Read/Write

BackgroundColor (Notes 5.0 and higher)

Description	The background color for the view.
Format	Integer = NotesView.BackgroundColor NotesView.BackgroundColor = Integer

Type	Integer
Access	Read/Write

ColumnCount (Notes 5.0 and higher)

Description	Count of columns in a view.
Format	Integer = NotesView.ColumnCount
Type	Integer
Access	Read

Columns

Description	All columns in a view.
Format	Array = NotesView.Columns
Type	Array of NotesViewColumn objects
Access	Read

Created

Description	The date the view was created.
Format	Variant = NotesView.Created
Type	Variant
Access	Read

GetAllEntries (Notes 5.0 and higher)

Description	All entries from a view returned in a NotesViewEntryCollection.
Format	NotesViewEntryCollection = NotesView.GetAllEntries
Type	NotesViewEntryCollection object
Access	Read

HeaderLines (Notes 5.0 and higher)

Description	Number of header lines in the view.
Format	Integer = NotesView.HeaderLines
Type	Integer
Access	Read

IsCalendar

Description	Signals whether or not the view is a calendar view.
Format	Boolean = NotesView.IsCalendar
Type	Boolean
Access	Read

IsConflict (Notes 5.0 and higher)

Description	Signals whether there is a conflict.
Format	Boolean = NoteView.IsConflict
Type	Boolean
Access	Read

IsDefaultView

Description	Signals whether or not the view is the default view for the database.
Format	Boolean = NotesView.IsDefaultView
Type	Boolean
Access	Read

IsFolder

Description	Signals whether the view is a folder.
Format	Boolean = NotesView.IsFolder
Type	Boolean
Access	Read

IsHierarchical (Notes 5.0 and higher)

Description	Signals whether or not the view is hierarchical.
Format	Boolean = NotesView.IsHierarchical
Type	Boolean
Access	Read

LastModified

Description	The last modified date of the view.
Format	Variant = NotesView.LastModified
Type	Variant
Access	Read

Name

Description	The name of the view
Format	String = NotesView.Name
Type	String
Access	Read

Parent

Description	The database that contains the view.
Format	Sets NotesDatabase = NotesView.Parent
Type	NotesDatabase object
Access	Read

ProtectReaders

Description	Signals whether the reader's fields in the view are overwritten by replication.
Format	Boolean = NotesView.ProtectReaders NotesView.ProtectReaders = Boolean
Type	Boolean
Access	Read/Write

Rowlines (Notes 5.0 and higher)

Description	The number of rows in a view.
Format	Integer = NotesView.Rowlines
Type	Integer
Access	Read

Spacing (Notes 5.0 and higher)

Description	Spacing in the view.
Format	Integer = NotesView.Spacing
Type	Integer
Access	Read

TopLevelEntryCount

Description	Count of the number of top level documents in the view.
Format	Integer = NotesView.TopLevelEntryCount
Type	Integer
Access	Read

Readers

Description	The readers field for the view.
Format	Array = NotesView.Readers NotesView.Readers = Array
Type	Array of Strings
Access	Read/Write

UniversalID

Description	The Universal ID of the view.
Format	String = NotesView.UniversalID
Type	String
Access	Read

Methods

Clear

Description	Clears the full text searching criteria on a view. Resets the view contents.
Parameters	None
Format	Call NotesView.Clear
Return	None

FTSearch

Description	Performs a full text search on a view, and the view contains only those documents that match the search.

Parameters	String - search string Integer - maximum number of documents to return (zero indicates all).
Format	Integer = NotesView.FTSearch(String, Integer)
Return	Integer - the number of documents returned in the view as a result of the search.

GetAllDocumentsByKey

Description	Assembles collection of documents that match key values. The keys are matched to columns in the view.
Parameters	Array of strings - Keys to search for. Boolean - exact match or not.
Format	Sets NotesDocumentCollection = NotesView.GetAllDocumentsByKey(Array, Boolean)
Return	NotesDocumentCollection containing the documents found.

GetChild

Description	Returns the first response document to a document in a view.
Parameters	NotesDocument - the parent document
Format	Sets NotesDocument = NotesView.GetChild(NotesDocument)
Return	NotesDocument object representing the child document.

GetDocumentByKey

Description	Locates a document in the view based on column values. Similar to the GetAllDocumentsByKey except this returns only one document.
Parameters	Array of strings - Keys to search for. Boolean - exact match or not.
Format	Sets NotesDocument = NotesView.GetDocumentByKey(Array, Boolean)
Return	NotesDocument or Nothing if no match.

GetFirstDocument

Description	Retrieves the first document from a view.
Parameters	None
Format	Sets NotesDocument = NotesView.GetFirstDocument
Return	NotesDocument object representing first document in the view or Nothing if the view is empty.

GetNextDocument

Description	Retrieves the next document from a view. A document to use as a point of reference for next is used.
Parameters	NotesDocument - reference point for next
Format	Sets NotesDocument = NotesView.GetNextDocument(NotesDocument)

Return	NotesDocument object representing the next document, or Nothing if no more documents.

GetNextSibling

Description	Retrieves the next document at the same level in the view of a document.
Parameters	NotesDocument - document to use as a reference point.
Format	Sets NotesDocument = NotesView.GetNextSibling(Notes-Document)
Return	NotesDocument object representing the next sibling document, or Nothing if no match found.

GetNthDocument

Description	Retrieves a document from a view based on its place in the view.
Parameters	Integer - document number to return
Format	Sets NotesDocument = NotesView.GetNthDocument(Integer)
Return	NotesDocument representing the document, or Nothing if no document found.

GetParentDocument

Description	Returns the parent document for a given document.
Parameters	NotesDocument representing document for which parent document will be found.
Format	Sets NotesDocument = NotesView.GetParentDocument(NotesDocument)
Return	NotesDocument object representing the parent document, or Nothing if not found.

GetPrevDocument

Description	Returns the previous document in a view; given a document as the point of reference.
Parameters	NotesDocument - the document that will act as the reference point for previous.
Format	Sets NotesDocument = NotesView.GetPrevDocument(NotesDocument)
Return	NotesDocument representing the previous document or Nothing if no match found.

GetPrevSibling

Description	Retrieves the previous document at the same level in the view of a document.
Parameters	NotesDocument - document to use as a reference point.
Format	Set NotesDocument = NotesView.GetPrevSibling(Notes-Document)
Return	NotesDocument object representing the previous sibling document, or Nothing if no match found.

Refresh

Description	Refreshs the view.
Parameters	None
Format	Calls NotesView.Refresh
Return	None

Remove

Description	Deletes a view from a database.
Parameters	None
Format	Calls NotesView.Remove
Return	None

NotesViewColumn class

The NotesViewColumn class allows access to specific columns in a NotesView.

Properties

Alignment (Notes 5.0 and higher)

Description	Text alignment.
Format	Integer = NotesViewColumn.Alignment
Type	Integer
Access	Read

Datatype (Notes 5.0 and higher)

Description	Data type displayed in column.
Format	Integer = NotesViewColumn.Datatype
Type	Integer
Access	Read

Datefmt (Notes 5.0 and higher)

Description	Date format for the column.
Format	Integer = NotesViewColumn.Datefmt
Type	Integer
Access	Read

FontColor (Notes 5.0 and higher)

Description	Color of the text in the column.
Format	Integer = NotesViewColumn.FontColor
Type	Integer
Access	Read

FontFace (Notes 5.0 and higher)

Description	Font face for the column.

Format	Integer = NotesViewColumn.FontFace
Type	Integer
Access	Read

FontPointSize (Notes 5.0 and higher)

Description	Text size in the column.
Format	Integer = NotesViewColumn.FontPointSize
Type	Integer
Access	Read

FontStyle (Notes 5.0 and higher)

Description	Styles applied to the text in the column.
Format	Integer = NotesViewColumn.FontStyle
Type	Integer
Access	Read

Formula

Description	The @Function formula for a column.
Format	String = NotesViewColumn.Formula
Type	String
Access	Read

HeaderAlignment (Notes 5.0 and higher)

Description	Text alignment for the column heading.
Format	Integer = NotesViewColumn.HeaderAlignment.
Type	Integer
Access	Read

IsCaseSensitiveSort (Notes 5.0 and higher)

Description	Signals whether or not the column is sorted by case.
Format	Boolean = NotesViewColumn.IsCaseSensitiveSort
Type	Boolean
Access	Read

IsCaseInsensitiveSort (Notes 5.0 and higher)

Description	Signals whether the column is not sorted by case.
Format	Boolean = NotesViewColumn.IsCaseInsensitiveSort
Type	Boolean
Access	Read

IsCategory

Description	Signals whether or not a column is categorized.
Format	Boolean = NotesViewColumn.IsCategory
Type	Boolean
Access	Read

IsField (Notes 5.0 and higher)

Description	Signals whether the column contains a field.
Format	Boolean = NotesViewColumn.IsField
Type	Boolean
Access	Read

IsFormula (Notes 5.0 and higher)

Description	Signals whether the column contains a formula.
Format	Boolean = NotesViewColumn.IsFormula
Type	Boolean
Access	Read

IsHidden

Description	Signals whether a column is hidden.
Format	Boolean = NotesViewColumn.IsHidden
Type	Boolean
Access	Read

IsHideDetail (Notes 5.0 and higher)

Description	Signals whether the details of the column are hidden.
Format	Boolean = NotesViewColumn.IsHideDetail
Type	Boolean
Access	Read

IsIcon (Notes 5.0 and higher)

Description	Signals whether the column contains an icon.
Format	Boolean = NotesViewColumn.IsIcon
Type	Boolean
Access	Read

IsResize (Notes 5.0 and higher)

Description	Signals whether the column can be resized.
Format	Boolean = NotesViewColumn.IsResize
Type	Boolean
Access	Read

IsResortAscending (Notes 5.0 and higher)

Description	Signals whether or not the column can be resorted ascending.
Format	Boolean = NotesViewColumn.IsResortAscending
Type	Boolean
Access	Read

IsResortDescending (Notes 5.0 and higher)

Description	Signals whether or not the column can be resorted descending.
Format	Boolean = NotesViewColumn.IsResortDescending

Type	Boolean
Access	Read

IsResortToView (Notes 5.0 and higher)

Description	
Format	Boolean = NotesViewColumn.IsResortToView
Type	Boolean
Access	Read

IsResponse

Description	Signals whether or not a column contains only response documents.
Format	Boolean = NotesViewColumn.IsResponse
Type	Boolean
Access	Read

IsSecondaryResort (Notes 5.0 and higher)

Description	Signals whether the column can be resorted with a secondary column as well.
Format	Boolean = NotesViewColumn.IsSecondaryResort
Type	Boolean
Access	Read

IsSecondaryResortDescending (Notes 5.0 and higher)

Description	Signals whether the column can be resorted with a secondary column in descending order as well.
Format	Boolean = NotesViewColumn.IsSecondaryResortDescending
Type	Boolean
Access	Read

IsShowTwistie (Notes 5.0 and higher)

Description	Signals whether a twistie is displayed for the column.
Format	Boolean = NotesViewColumn.IsShowTwistie
Type	Boolean
Access	Read

IsSortDescending (Notes 5.0 and higher)

Description	Signals whether the column is sorted in descending order.
Format	Boolean = NotesViewColumn.IsSortDescending
Type	Boolean
Access	Read

IsSorted

Description	Signals whether the column is sorted.
Format	Boolean = NotesViewColumn.IsSorted
Type	Boolean
Access	Read

ItemName

Description	Field name used in the column.
Format	String = NotesViewColumn.ItemName
Type	String
Access	Read

ListSep (Notes 5.0 and higher)

Description	List separator used in the column
Format	Integer = NotesViewColumn.ListSep
Type	Integer
Access	Read

NumberAttrib (Notes 5.0 and higher)

Description	The number attributes for a column.
Format	Integer = NotesViewColumn.NumberAttrib
Type	Integer
Access	Read

NumberDigits (Notes 5.0 and higher)

Description	The number of digits to display for numeric values.
Format	Integer = NotesViewColumn.NumberDigits
Type	Integer
Access	Read

NumberFormat (Notes 5.0 and higher)

Description	The format of numbers displayed in the column.
Format	Integer = NotesViewColumn.NumberFormat
Type	Integer
Access	Read

Position

Description	The position number of a column in the view. Numbers start at one.
Format	Integer = NotesViewColumn.Position
Type	Integer
Access	Read

TimeDateFormat (Notes 5.0 and higher)

Description	The format of date/time values displayed in the column.
Format	Integer = NotesViewColumn.TimeDateFormat
Type	Integer
Access	Read

TimeFormat (Notes 5.0 and higher)

Description	The format of time values displayed in the column.
Format	Integer = NotesViewColumn.TimeFormat

Type	Integer
Access	Read

TimeZoneFormat (Notes 5.0 and higher)

Description	The format of time zone for time values displayed in the column.
Format	Integer = NotesViewColumn.TimeZoneFormat
Type	Integer
Access	Read

Title

Description	The title of a column.
Format	String = NotesViewColumn.Title
Type	String
Access	Read

NotesViewEntry class (Notes 5.0 or later)

The NotesViewEntry class can be used to work with individual entries from a view.

Properties

ChildCount

Description	The number of child entries connected to an entry.
Format	Integer = NotesViewEntry.ChildCount
Type	Integer
Access	Read

ColumnValues

Description	List of columns in the entry.
Format	Variant = NotesViewEntry.ColumnValues
Type	Variant - array of column values.
Access	Read

DescendantCount

Description	The number of direct descendants for an entry.
Format	Integer = NotesViewEntry.DescendantCount
Type	Integer
Access	Read

Document

Description	The back-end document object associated with an entry.
Format	Set NotesDocument = NotesViewEntry.Document
Type	NotesDocument object

Access	Read

FTSearchScore

Description	The score for the document if returned from a full text search.
Format	Integer = NotesViewEntry.FTSearchScore
Type	Integer
Access	Read

IndentLevel

Description	The number of indents associated with an entry.
Format	Integer = NotesViewEntry.IndentLevel
Type	Integer
Access	Read

IsCategory

Description	Signals whether an entry is a category or not.
Format	Boolean = NotesViewEntry.IsCategory
Type	Boolean
Access	Read

IsConflict

Description	Signals whether or not an entry is a replication/save conflict.
Format	Boolean = NotesViewEntry.IsConflict
Type	Boolean
Access	Read

IsDocument

Description	Signals whether or not an entry is a NotesDocument.
Format	Boolean = NotesViewEntry.IsDocument
Type	Boolean
Access	Read

IsTotal

Description	Signals whether or not an entry represents column totals.
Format	Boolean = NotesViewEntry.IsTotal
Type	Boolean
Access	Read

IsUnread

Description	Signals whether or not an entry is unread.
Format	Boolean = NotesViewEntry.IsUnread
Type	Boolean
Access	Read

IsValid

Description	Signals whether or not the entry is valid.

Format	Boolean = NotesViewEntry.IsValid
Type	Boolean
Access	Read

NoteID

Description	The note ID associated with the entry.
Format	String = NotesViewEntry.NoteID
Type	String
Access	Read

Parent

Description	The NotesView that contains the entry.
Format	NotesView = NotesViewEntry.Parent
Type	NotesView object
Access	Read

SiblingCount

Description	Number of entries at the same level of the entry.
Format	Integer = NotesViewEntry.SiblingCount
Type	Integer
Access	Read

UniversalID

Description	The universal ID associated with the entry.
Format	String = NotesViewEntry.UniversalID
Type	String
Access	Read

Methods

GetPosition

Description	Retrieves the position of the entry.
Parameters	String - separator
Format	String = NotesViewEntry.GetPosition(String)
Return	String

NotesViewEntryCollection class (Notes 5.0 or later)

The NotesViewEntryCollection class can be used to work with the collection of entries from views.

Properties

Count

Description	Number of entries in the collection.
Format	Long = NotesViewEntryCollection.Count
Type	Long
Access	Read

Parent

Description	The NotesView object that contains the collection.
Format	Sets NotesView = NotesViewEntryCollectiion.Parent
Type	NotesView object
Access	Read

Query

Description	The search string associated with the collection, if any.
Format	String = NotesViewEntryCollection.Query
Type	String
Access	Read

Methods

AddEntry

Description	Adds an entry to the collection.
Parameters	NotesViewEntry object - entry to add.
Format	Calls NotesViewEntryCollection.AddEntry(NotesViewEntry)
Return	None

DeleteEntry

Description	Removes an entry from the collection.
Parameters	NotesViewEntry - object to delete.
Format	Calls NotesViewEntryCollection.DeleteEntry(NotesViewEntry)
Return	None

FTSearch

Description	Refines the collection using a full text search.
Parameters	String - search query Integer - maximum number of entries to return (zero is all).
Format	Calls NotesViewEntryCollection.FTSearch(String, Integer)
Return	None - collection is refined.

GetEntry

Description	Retrieves an entry from the collection.

Parameters	NotesViewEntry - object to get.
Format	Sets NotesViewEntry = NotesViewCollection(NotesViewEntry)
Return	NotesViewEntry object

GetFirstEntry

Description	Retrieves the first entry from the collection.
Parameters	None
Format	Sets NotesViewEntry = NotesViewEntryCollection.GetFirstEntry
Return	NotesViewEntry object

GetLastEntry

Description	Retrieves the last entry from the collection.
Parameters	None
Format	Sets NotesViewEntry = NotesViewEntryCollection.GetLastEntry
Return	NotesViewEntry object

GetNextEntry

Description	Retrieves the next entry from the collection.
Parameters	NotesViewEntry - reference point for next.
Format	Sets NotesViewEntry = NotesViewEntryCollection.GetNextEntry(NotesViewEntry)
Return	NotesViewEntry object

GetNthEntry

Description	Retrieves an entry from a collection using the location in the collection.
Parameters	Long - entry number
Format	Sets NotesViewEntry = NotesViewEntryCollection.GetNthEntry(Long)
Return	NotesViewEntry object

GetPrevEntry

Description	Retrieves the previous entry from the collection.
Parameters	NotesViewEntry - reference point for previous.
Format	Sets NotesViewEntry = NotesViewEntryCollection.GetPrevEntry(NotesViewEntry)
Return	NotesViewEntry object

PutAllInFolder

Description	Moves all entries in the collection into the folder.
Parameters	String - folder name
Format	Calls NotesViewEntryCollection.PutAllInFolder(String)
Return	None

RemoveAll

Description	Removes all entries in the collection from the database.
Parameters	None
Format	Calls NotesViewEntryCollection.RemoveAll
Return	None

RemoveAllFromFolder

Description	Removes all entries in the collection from a folder.
Parameters	String - folder name.
Format	Calls NotesViewEntryCollection.RemoveAllFromFolder(String)
Return	None

StampAll

Description	Marks field in all entries in the collection with a value.
Parameters	String - item name for values Variant - value for the item
Format	Calls NotesViewEntryCollection.StampAll(String, Variant)
Return	None

UpdateAll

Description	Marks all enties in the collection as processed.
Parameters	None
Format	Calls NotesViewEntryCollection.UpdateAll
Return	None

NotesViewNavigator class (Notes 5.0 or later)

The NotesViewNavigator class can be used to access entries in a view.

Properties

MaxLevel

Description	The maximum number of levels for a view.
Format	NotesViewNavigator.MaxLevel = Long
Type	Long
Access	Read

ParentViw

Description	The NotesView object associated with the NotesViewNavigator.
Format	Sets NotesView = NotesViewNavigator.ParentView
Type	NotesView object
Access	Read

Methods

GetChild

Description	Retrieves child entry associated with an entry.
Parameters	NotesViewEntry - parent entry
Format	Sets NotesViewEntry = NotesViewNavigator.GetChild(NotesViewEntry)
Return	NotesViewEntry object

GetEntry

Description	Retrieves an entry from the NotesViewNavigator.
Parameters	
Format	Sets NotesViewEntry = NotesViewNavigator.GetEntry
Return	NotesViewEntry object.

GetFirst

Description	Retrieves the first entry from the NotesViewNavigator.
Parameters	None
Format	Sets NotesViewEntry = NotesViewNavigator.GetFirst
Return	NotesViewEntry object

GetFirstDocument

Description	Retrieves first document from NotesViewNavigator.
Parameters	None
Format	Sets NotesViewEntry = NotesViewNavigator.GetFirstDocument
Return	NotesViewEntry object

GetLast

Description	Retrieves last entry from the NotesViewNavigator.
Parameters	None
Format	Sets NotesViewEntry = NotesViewNavigator.GetLast
Return	NotesViewEntry object

GetLastDocument

Description	Retrieves the last document from the NotesViewNavigator.
Parameters	None
Format	Sets NotesViewEntry = NotesViewNavigator.GetLastDocument
Return	NotesViewEntry object

GetNext

Description	Retrieves the next entry from the NotesViewNavigator.
Parameters	NotesViewEntry-object to use as reference point for next.
Format	Sets NotesViewEntry = NotesViewNavigator.GetNext(NotesViewEntry)

Return	NotesViewEntry object

GetNextCategory

Description	Retrieves the next category entry from the Notes-ViewNavigator.
Parameters	NotesViewEntry - used as reference point for next.
Format	Sets NotesViewEntry = NotesViewNavigator.GetNextCategory(NotesViewEntry)
Return	NotesViewEntry object

GetNextDocument

Description	Retrieves the next document from the NotesViewNavigator.
Parameters	NotesViewEntry - used as reference point for next.
Format	Sets NotesViewEntry = NotesViewNavigator.GetNextDocument(NotesViewEntry)
Return	NotesViewEntry object

GetNextSibling

Description	Retrieves the next entry at the same level as the entry passed into it.
Parameters	NotesViewEntry - used as reference point for next.
Format	Sets NotesViewEntry = NotesViewNavigator.GetNextSibling(NotesViewEntry)
Return	NotesViewEntry object

GetNth

Description	Retrieves an entry based on its location in the view.
Parameters	Long - position number.
Format	Sets NotesViewEntry = NotesViewNavigator.GetNth(Long)
Return	NotesViewEntry object

GetParent

Description	Retrieves the parent entry for an entry (if any).
Parameters	NotesViewEntry - reference point for parent.
Format	Set NotesViewEntry = NotesViewNavigator.GetParent(NotesViewEntry)
Return	NotesViewEntry object

GetPos

Description	Retrieves an entry based on its position.
Parameters	String1 - position String2 - separator
Format	Sets NotesViewEntry = NotesViewNavigator.GetPos(String1, String2)
Return	NotesViewEntry object

GetPrev

Description	Retrieves the previous entry.
Parameters	NotesViewEntry - reference point for previous.
Format	Sets NotesViewEntry = NotesViewNavigator.GetPrev(NotesViewEntry)
Return	NotesViewEntry object

GetPrevCategory

Description	Retrieves the previous category entry.
Parameters	NotesViewEntry - reference point for previous.
Format	Sets NotesViewEntry = NotesViewNavigator.GetPrevCategory(NotesViewEntry)
Return	NotesViewEntry object

GetPrevDocument

Description	Retrieves the previous document.
Parameters	NotesViewEntry - reference point for previous.
Format	Sets NotesViewEntry = NotesViewNavigator.GetPrevDocument(NotesViewEntry)
Return	NotesViewEntry object

GetPrevSibling

Description	Retrieves the previous sibling entry.
Parameters	NotesViewEntry - reference point for previous.
Format	Sets NotesViewEntry = NotesViewNavigator.GetPrevSibling(NotesViewEntry)
Return	NotesViewEntry object.

appendix C

LotusScript keywords

The following table lists most LotusScript 3.1 reserved words. For more information on their syntax please refer to online Help or the LotusScript Language Reference.

Note All items that have a dollar sign ($) appended return string values

Keyword	Description
Abs	Absolute value of a number.
ACos	ArcCosine function.
ActivateApp	Activate a window.
And	Logical AND.
Asc	ASCII value of a character.
ASin	ArcSine funciton.
ATn	ArcTangent function.

Keyword	Description
ATn2	Polar coordinate of a point.
Beep	Make a beep sound.
Bin/Bin$	Binary value of a number/string.
Call	Transfer control to a subroutine.
CCur	Convert value to currency.
CDat	Convert value to date.
CDbl	Convert value to double.
ChDir	Switch to a directory.
ChDrive	Switch to a drive.
Chr/Chr$	Character value of a code.
CInt	Convert value to an Integer.
Class	Class declaration.
CLng	Convert value to Long.
Close	Close a file.
Command	Command line arguments used to start program.
Command$	Same as Command, but returns a string value.
Const	Declare a constant.
Cos	Cosine function.
CreateObject	Create an OLE object.
CSng	Convert value to a Single.
CStr	Convert value to a String.
CurDir/CurDir$	The current directory.
CurDrive/CurDrive$	The current drive.
Currency	Declare a currency data type.
CVar	Convert a value to a Variant.
DataType	Return the data type of a variable.
Date/Date$	Return or set the current system date/time.
DateNumber	Date value for a day, month, and year.
DateValue	Date value represented by a String.
Day	Day of the month.
Declare	Declare function/sub that accesses API functions.
DefCur	Set range of values for currency.
DefDbl	Set range of values for doubles.
DefInt	Set range of values for integers.
DefLng	Set range of values for Long values.
DefSng	Set range of values for Singles.
DefStr	Set range of values for Strings.
DefVar	Set range of values for Variants.
Delete	Remove an object.
Dim	Declare a variable/object.

Keyword	Description
Dir/Dir$	Access files/directories/volumes.
Do	Do loop.
Double	Double number.
End	End a block of code.
Environ/Environ$	Retrieve information about system variables.
EOF	End of File.
Erase	Remove an array, list, or list element.
Erl	Line number at which an error occurred.
Err	Error number encountered.
Error/Error$	Error message.
Evaluate	Use @Functions in your scripts.
Execute	Compile and test a test expression as a temporary module.
Exit <block of code>	Exit a subroutine, loop, etc.
Exp	Returns exponential of a number.
FALSE	Constant for Boolean False.
FileAttr	File access type.
FileCopy	Copy a file.
FileDateTime	Date file was created.
FileLen	Length of file.
Fix	Integer portion of a number.
For	For/Next loop.
Forall	Access all elements in arrays, lists, etc.
Format/Format$	Customize the format of variables.
Fraction	Fractional portion of a number.
FreeFile	Obtain file handle from system.
Function	Function declaration.
Get	Read line from Random access file.
GetFileAttr	Get file attributes.
GetObject	Get handle on an OLE object.
Goto	Transfer script control to a label.
Hex/Hex$	Convert value to hexadecimal.
Hour	Hour portion of a date/time.
IMEStatus	Current input mode
If	Conditional if/then block.
%Include	Include external files in your script.
Input/Input$	Read line from file.
InputB/InputB$	Input sequence of bytes from a file.
InputBox/InputBox$	Retrieve user input.
InStr/InStrB	Search one string for another.
Int	Return nearest Integer value to a number.

Keyword	Description
IsA	Test if some object is of some type of object.
IsArray	Test if a variable is an array.
IsDate	Test if an item is a date.
IsElement	Test if an item is the member of a list.
IsEmpty	Test if a variable is empty.
IsList	Test if the item is a list.
IsNull	Test if the variable is NULL.
IsNumeric	Test if the item is numeric.
IsObject	Test if the item is an object.
IsScalar	Test if an item evaluates to a single value.
Kill	Delete a file.
Lbound	Lower bound of an array.
LCase/LCase$	Convert a string to all lower case.
Left/Left$	Return the specified number of characters from the left portion of a value.
LeftB	Return the specified bytes from the left portion of a value.
Len	Length of a string.
LenB	Length of a string in bytes.
Like	Compare one string to another to see if they are similar.
Line Input	Read in a line from a sequential file.
ListTag	Tag from a List.
LOC	Current position in a file.
Lock	Lock a file.
LOF	Length of a file in bytes.
Log	Natural logarithm.
Long	Long numerical value.
LSet	Assign a variable to a string; left-align it.
LTrim/LTrim$	Remove leading spaces from a value.
MessageBox	Display information to user in a dialog box.
Mid/Mid$	Retrieve a string from another string given certain parameters.
Minute	Minutes portion of a date/time.
Mkdir	Create a new directory.
Mod	Remainder of a division operation.
Month	Month portion of a date/time.
Name	Rename a file or directory.
New	Create a new instance of a class.
Not	Logical NOT.
NOTHING	Built -in constant for uninitialized/empty objects.
Now	The current date/time.
NULL	Built- in constant for NULL values.

Keyword	Description
Oct/Oct$	Octal representation of a value.
On <something>	Do something when whatever specified happens.
Open	Open file.
Option <something>	Set environment settings.
Or	Logical OR.
PI	3.14............
Print #<file>	Write values to a file.
Print	Send output to standard output.
Private	Set scope of variable to private.
Property Get	Get object member value.
Property Set	Set object property value.
Put	Write values to a file.
Randomize	Seed the random number generator.
Redim	Resize an array.
Rem	Comments
Reset	Close all open files.
Resume	Resume script execution.
Return	Return control to code that called sub/function.
Right/Right$	Return designated number of characters from rightmost portion of a value.
RightB	Same as Right, except return value is in bytes.
Rnd	Random number.
Round	Round a number.
RSet	Assign value to a string and right align it.
RTrim/RTrim$	Trim off trailing spaces.
Second	Seconds portion of a date/time.
Seek	Move pointer to a specified location in a file.
Select Case	Case statement.
Set	Instantiate new instance of an object.
SetFileAttr	Set file attributes.
Sgn	Return sign of a number.
Shell	Start another external program.
Sin	Mathematical sine function
Single	Declare a single variable.
Space/Space$	Assemble a string containing a certain number of spaces.
Spc	Insert certain number of spaces.
Sqr	Square root function.
Static	Declare the scope of a variable as Static.
Stop	Stop execution of a script; used in debug mode.
Str/Str$	String representation of a number.

Keyword	Description
StrCompare	Compare two strings for equality.
String	Declare a String variable.
Sub	Subroutine declaration.
Tab	Insert tab in print statement.
Time/Time$	Return system time.
TimeNumber	Convert numbers for hours, minutes, and seconds to a time value.
Timer	Time elapse since midnight.
TimeValue	Returns the time value represented by a string.
Today	Today's date/time.
Trim/Trim$	Remove trailing and leading spaces from a string.
TRUE	System variable for Boolean TRUE.
Type	Define a user-defined data structure.
Ubound	Number of elements in an array minus one.
Ucase/Ucase$	Convert string to all uppercase characters.
UChr/Uch$	Character represented by a Unicode numeric character code.
Uni	Unicode numeric character for first character in a string.
Unlock	Unlock a file.
Use	Include Script Library in your script.
UseLSX	Include LotusScript Extension file in your script.
UString/Ustring$	Create a string with the specified number of a character.
Val	Numeric value of a string.
Variant	Variant data type declaration.
Weekday	Returns the weekday associated with a date (as a number).
While	While..Wend loop.
Width	Output width to a sequential file.
With	Work with an object.
Write	Write values to a file.
Xor	Logical XOR.
Year	Returns the year portion of a date/time.

index

Symbols

! 216
"" 217
$File 176
$UpdatedBy 156, 161
%END REM 29
%INCLUDE 34
%Include 113
%REM 29
& 216
.lss 113
?CreateDocument 287
?OpenAgent 284, 287
?OpenDocument 287
@DBColumn 275, 295
@DBLookup 295
@function 215, 216
@Functions 275, 276, 283
@PickList 314
@ProperCase 276
@URLOpen 283
@UserRoles 276
_ 34
{} 209, 217
|| 209, 217
~ 162

A

Access Control List 143
accessor methods 54
ACL 142, 143, 145, 148, 149, 152
ACLEntry 304
action button 181, 295
Activate 185
ActivateApp 271, 274
activity logging 110
addElement 84
AddNewLine 166, 167
AddPageBreak 321
AddRow 248
AddTab 166, 167
AdjustDay 257
AdjustHour 257
AdjustMinute 257
AdjustMonth 257
AdjustSecond 257
AdjustYear 257
agent log 115, 117, 120, 121
agent.Run 297
Agents 134, 297
AllDocuments 48
AMString 264
AND 209, 210
API 271, 273, 282
apostrophe 29
Append 91
AppendParagraphStyle 321, 322
AppendText 166, 167
array 56, 61, 64, 65, 66, 68, 70, 71, 74, 79, 80, 81, 83
  multidimension 70
  of objects 55
As 13
Asc 196
attachments 174–179
AUTH_TYPE 281
Author access 143

B

back slash 104
back-end classes 57
base class 53, 60
beep 114
binary 87, 89, 97
binary access 86, 97–98
body 176
Bold 167, 170
Boolean 73, 83, 126, 128, 230
braces 209
breakpoints 6
browsers 280, 287
  checkbox 4
  pane 4
button 132
byte 309

C

Call 41
CanCreateDocuments 148
CanCreatePersonalAgents 148
CanCreatePersonalFolders 148
CanDeleteDocuments 148
carriage return 196
CCur 16
CDat 16, 253
CDbl 16
CGI environment variables 288
ChDir 100
ChDrive 100
checking objects 112
ChildCount 324
Chr 28
CInt 16
class 46, 48, 49, 50, 51, 52, 56, 59, 61, 309
ClearAllTabs 322
Click 132
CLng 16
Close 88, 107
closing a database 137
collection 75, 76, 78, 82
color 170
Comment 297
commenting code 29
CommonOwner 297
ComposeDocument 57
ComputeWithForm 295, 296, 301
Connection 241
ConnectTo 240
CONST 14
constants 14, 34
constructor 51, 61
contains 160
CONTENT_LENGTH 281
CONTENT_TYPE 281
continuation 34
Continue 126, 128
converting
    data types 16
ConvertToZone 257
cookies 280
CopyAllItems 159
CopyItem 159
CopyItemToDocument 158, 159
CreateACLEntry 146, 149
CreateDocument
    method 204
CreateDocuments
    property 149
CreateItem 201
CreateLog 117
CreateNewsLetter 232
CreateObject 181, 182, 204
CreatePersonalAgents 149
CSng 16
CStr 16
CurDir 100
CurDrive 100
Currency 13
CurrencyDigits 264
CurrentAccessLevel 144
CurrentDatabase 47, 58, 314
currentDay 260
CurrentDocument 57
CurrentView 313
CutOffDelete 319
CutOffInterval 319
CVar 16

D

DATABASE 102
database script 131
DataType 17, 72
DateNumber 253
Dateonly 255
DateSep 264
DateTimeValue 162
Day 253
DBstsSuccess 244
debugging 5, 113, 118
DecimalSep 264
Declare 272
Delete 51, 53, 61
delete 148
delete objects 185, 186
DeleteDocuments 149
DeleteRole 151
Depositor access 143
derived classes 49, 53, 60
destructor 51, 61
detach 177
Dim 13, 84
dimension 65
Dir 93, 98, 98–100
directories 98–102
Disabled 319
DisableRole 152
Do 20, 78, 91, 92, 93, 106
doclinks 231
Document 58
DocumentCollection 76, 80
DocumentContext 282
Domino.Connect 236, 248
DoNotCatalog 319
DoScore 231, 232
DoSubject 231, 232
Dot notation 47, 61
Double 13
drive letter 175

E

EditMode 129
Editor access 142
ElseIf 22
EMBED_OBJECTLINK 184
embedded object 165, 176, 177, 184
EmbeddedObject 182
embeddedobject 166
EmbeddedObjects 186
embeddedobjects 177
embedding 180, 199

EmbedObject 183, 184
encapsulation 46
End 23
EndDateTime 260
Entering 130, 131, 293
environment variables 281, 286
EOF 90
  random access 90
  sequential access 90
Erase 73
Erl 113
Err 113
errors 5, 113, 119
  checking 122
  handling 116, 244
  messages 113, 120
  numbers 111
  trapping 110
  user-defined 112
Evaluate 270, 275, 276
events 124
  Click 132
  entering 130
  exiting 130
  Initialize 124
  ObjectExecute 132
  PostDocumentDelete 132
  PostModeChange 129
  PostOpen 125, 131, 133
  PostPaste 134
  PostRecalc 128
  QueryAddToFolder 133
  QueryClose 128, 132, 134
  QueryDocumentDelete 131
  QueryDocumentUndelete 132
  QueryModeChange 128
  QueryOpen 126, 133
  QueryOpenDocument 133
  QueryPaste 134
  QueryRecalc 133
  QuerySave 127, 159, 292
  Terminate 124–125
  user-defined 134
  WebQueryOpen 129, 287
  WebQuerySave 130, 287
Excel 199
Excel spreadsheet 197
Excel.Sheet.8 197
Exit 23
Exit Sub 111
Exiting 130, 293, 301
explicit declaration 14
export 7
  options 8
ExtractFile 178

F

field events 131
field exit event 293
FieldGetText 293
fields 130
file 86, 92
  open 87, 314
  separator 104
file access 90
  Get 89, 90
  Input 89
  Line Input 89
file attachments 165, 174
File Not Found 111
FileCopy 101
FileDateTime 101
FileLen 101
FileOpenDialog 304
filepath 182
files 101
FileSize 176
FindFreeTimeDialogEx 316
FindString 316
FirstLineLeftMargin 322
folder 133
font 170
FontSize 168
For 19, 65, 68, 71, 76, 95
Forall 22, 65, 66, 68, 71, 72, 80, 81, 83, 127, 177, 186, 204, 222, 226, 297
format 33, 264
FormatDocument 231
FormatMsgWithDocLinks 231
forward references 308
forward slash 104
freefile 87
FROM 238
front-end classes 56
FTSearch 75, 78, 211
full-text index 75, 78, 208, 216
function 38, 39, 40, 41, 42, 44, 49, 226

G

garbage collection 54
GATEWAY_INTERFACE 281
GenerateHTML 318, 322
GenerateHTMLString 318, 322
Get 89, 90, 94, 98
get 54
GetAgent 298
GetAllDocumentsByKey 211, 212, 213
GetAttachment 178
GetDatabase 204
GetDocumentByKey 211, 213, 295
GetDocumentsByKey 74
GetEntry 149
GetError 242
GetErrorMessage 242
GetExtendedErrorMessage 242

GetFirstDatabase 102
GetFirstDocument 76, 77
GetFirstEntry 323
GetFirstItem 161
GetFormattedText 166
GetItemValue 161
GetLastDocument 77
GetNextDatabase 102
GetNextDocument 76, 77
GetNextEntry 148, 311
GetNthDocument 44, 76, 77
GetObject 186
GetPrevDocument 77
GetSelectedText 316
globals 42
Gmttime 255
Goto 24
GrantAccess 144

H

handle errors 244
HasEmbedded 179
HasItem 81, 112
hexadecimal 283
HideDesign 319
hotspot 132
Hour 255
HTML 283, 285, 286, 287, 304, 318
HTTP_ACCEPT 281
HTTP_REFERER 281, 283, 285
HTTP_USER_AGENT 281, 283
HTTPS 281

I

IDE 2, 305, 328
If 22, 78, 83, 106
IgnoreDeletes 319
IgnoreDestDeletes 319
implicit declarations 14, 19
import 7
indentifiers 18
InfoView 305
inheritance 46
Initialize 41, 44, 106, 124, 135, 140
Input 89, 98
input mode 87
Input Validation 127, 131, 292
InputBox 28, 223
Instr 30, 32, 195
Integer 13
InterLineSpacing 322
InternetLevel 326
Is 53
IsA 53
IsArray 66
IsAuthors 162
IsCurrencySpace 265
IsCurrencySuffix 265
IsCurrencyZero 265
IsDateDMY 265
IsDateMDY 265
IsDateYMD 265
IsDST 255, 265
Isdst 255
IsElement 73, 221
IsEnabled 297
IsEncrypted 162
IsFTIndexed 208, 217
IsList 73
IsNames 162
IsNewDoc 126
IsObject 53
IsProtected 162
IsPublic 297
IsReaders 162
IsRoleEnabled 152
IsSigned 162
IsSummary 162, 170, 222
IsTime24Hour 265
italics 167, 170
Items 79

K

Kill 101

L

label 111
LastRun 297
layout regions 327
Lbound 66
LCase 29, 30
Left 30, 32
LeftMargin 322
Len 29, 31, 95
Level 148
line feed 196
Line Input 89
linked object 180, 184
lists 71, 72, 74, 82, 84
ListTag 71, 72, 74
LOC 90
    random access 90
    sequential access 90
Localtime 255
LOF 90
Log 114, 116
LogAction 115, 118, 119, 120
LogError 115, 119, 120
logging 110, 119
    activity 114
    email 118
    errors 118
    Notes database 117
    script activity 120
    text file 118
logical operators 209
Long 13
looping 19
Lotus SmartSuite 174
LotusScript
    Data Object 236
    Extensions 113, 236
LS:DO 191, 236, 237, 246, 248
LSCONST.LSS 34, 343
lsconst.lss 113
LSERR.LSS 34, 345
lserr.lss 113, 114

Lsgmttime 255
LSLocalTime 255, 260
LSX 239, 240, 248
LSXBEERR.LSS 350
lsxbeerr.lss 113
LSXODBC 239
LSXs 236
LSXUIERR.LSS 356
lsxuierr.lss 113
LTrim 29, 31
lxbeerr.lss 114

M

Manager 144
Me 49, 50
MessageBox 25, 27, 28, 34, 224
methods 46, 49, 51, 56, 61, 102
Microsoft
  Access 237
  Excel 174, 179, 190, 196, 198
  Office 174, 180, 190
  Office 97 191, 197
  Outlook 190, 200
  PowerPoint 190, 200
  Word 181, 182, 190, 191, 193, 194, 275
Mid 29, 30, 196
Minute 254
MkDir 100
Month 253
MQSeries 248
MsgBox 25, 40
mulitdimensioned array 70
multidimensional array 69
multivalued arrays 84

N

NeverReplicate 319
New 52, 61
newsletter 215, 230
NextRow 245
No Access 143
NOI 46
NOT 209
Notes 5.0 303–328
NotesACL 143, 145, 146, 148, 149, 150, 151, 153, 304, 326, 358–360
NotesACLEntry 145, 147, 148, 150, 151, 152, 153, 326, 360–363
NotesAgent 296, 297, 298, 301, 304, 325, 364–366
NotesColor 169
NotesDatabase 43, 58, 68, 74, 75, 117, 143, 145, 146, 157, 208, 214, 216, 297, 298, 313, 314, 320, 366–377
NotesDateRange 260, 266, 377–378
NotesDateTime 216, 252, 255, 256, 258, 259, 262, 265, 378–380
NotesDBDirectory 102, 103, 381
  methods 102
NotesDocument 58, 68, 77, 79, 81, 112, 157, 161, 163, 177, 178, 223, 282, 284, 288, 295, 324, 382–390
NotesDocumentCollection 44, 48, 68, 74, 77, 78, 208, 211, 213, 215, 216, 315, 317, 323, 390–393
NotesEmbeddedObject 164, 174, 175, 178, 179, 184, 185, 197, 393–395
NotesFont 168
NotesForm 395
NotesInternational 252, 264, 397–400
  creating object 265
NotesItem 79, 81, 155–171, 247, 400–404
NotesLog 115, 116, 118, 119, 120, 121, 404–407
NotesName 407–410
NotesNewsLetter 220, 230, 231, 233, 411–412
NotesOutline 304, 309, 311, 312, 314, 328, 412–415
NotesOutlineEntry 304, 311, 312, 313, 415–417
NotesPump 329–341
NotesRegistration 417–422
NotesReplication 304, 318, 319, 422–425
NotesRichTextItem 163, 164, 165, 166, 170, 171, 176, 179, 183, 205, 425–427
NotesRichTextParagraphStyle 304, 321, 427–429
NotesRichTextStyle 167, 170, 171, 429–431
NotesRichTextTab 321, 431
NotesSession 57, 68, 117, 204, 232, 313, 432–437
NotesSQL 236, 248, 249
NotesTimer 437
NotesUIDatabase 304, 314, 320, 325, 438
NotesUIDocument 57, 58, 80, 126, 127, 128, 129, 135, 181, 182, 184, 186, 293, 294, 295, 316, 439–447
NotesUIView 133, 304, 324, 447

NotesUIWorkspace 57, 288, 304, 313, 315, 316, 448–454
NotesView 58, 74, 212, 295, 313, 323, 454–460
NotesViewColumn 460–465
NotesViewEntry 304, 323, 324, 465–467
NotesViewEntryCollection 304, 323, 324, 467–470
NotesViewNavigator 470–473
Nothing 78, 186
Now 252
NPActivity 331
NPConnect 332
NPField 336
NPFieldList 333
NumActions 119
NumErrors 120

O

Object 204, 309
object browser 190
ObjectExecute 132
object-oriented 46, 48, 54
ObjectView 305
ODBC 236, 237, 239, 240, 244, 249
  LSX 248
ODBCConnection 237, 239, 240, 241, 242, 244
ODBCQuery 237, 241, 242
ODBCResultSet 237, 242, 245, 248
OLE 164, 171, 179–184, 190, 191, 194, 199, 201, 202, 203, 205
  Automation 180
  object 186, 192
  registry 182
On Error 111, 114, 244
On Error Resume 151
On Event 134, 136, 140
onHelpRequest 327
Open 86, 113
Open AgentLog 120
Open DataBase Connectivity 236
OpenFileLog 118
opening a database 137
OpenMailLog 118
OpenNavigator 325
OpenNotesLog 117
OpenView 325
Option Base 15
Option Compare 15
Option Declare 16
Option Explicit 14
Option Public 16
Options 15, 113, 300
OR 209, 210, 228
Oracle 236, 248
outline 310
Outlook 201, 202
Output 91

P

parameter 39
PassThruHTML 321
PATH_INFO 281
PATH_TRANSLATED 281
PickList 304, 314
PickListCollection 315
PMString 265
position 322
PostDocumentDelete 132
PostDragDrop 327
PostModeChange 129
PostOpen 125, 131, 133, 134, 135, 136
PostPaste 134
PostRecalc 128
PostSave 327
Preserve 56, 67, 71, 84
Print 7, 25, 89, 280
printing 8
  scripts 305, 307
Priority 319
Private 18, 39, 49, 54, 61, 226
Prompt 304, 315
property 46, 47, 49, 54, 56, 61
Property Get 54, 55, 61, 226
Property Set 54, 55, 226
Public 19, 39, 49, 54, 61
Put 90, 94

Q

Query 297
Query_String 280, 281, 283, 284, 285, 287
QueryAccess 145, 146
QueryAddToFolder 133
QueryClose 128, 132, 134, 136
QueryDocumentDelete 131
QueryDocumentUndelete 132
QueryDragDrop 326
QueryExecuteTimeOut 241
QueryModeChange 128, 129
QueryOpen 126, 133, 135
QueryOpenAgent 287
QueryOpenDocument 133
QueryPaste 134
QueryRecalc 133
QuerySave 127, 134, 135, 159, 292, 301
QuerySaveAgent 287

R

random 87, 89
random access 86, 88, 90, 94–96, 97, 106
  versus sequential 94
Read 87
Reader access 143
reading files 89, 98
Redim 67, 68, 69, 71, 84
REMOTE_ADDR 281
REMOTE_HOST 281

REMOTE_IDENT 281
REMOTE_USER 281
remove 185
RemoveItem 158
REPLICA_CANDIDATE 102
replication 318, 320
reports 220, 222, 226, 230
  generation 224
REQUEST_METHOD 281
Reset 319
response documents 76
Resume 111
Resume Next 111
RevokeAccess 145
Rich Text 81, 84, 164, 165, 166, 167, 170, 174, 175, 183, 184, 193, 198, 199, 205
RichTextItem 164
RichTextStyle 164
Right 30, 32
RightMargin 322
RmDir 100
Roles 150, 153
Round 38
RTrim 30, 31
RunOnServer 298, 299, 301

S

SAP 248
Save 146, 319
SaveOptions 222, 224
scope 42, 49, 61, 114
script libraries 42, 224, 299, 300, 306
SCRIPT_NAME 281
search 78
  database 213
  string 209
Second 255
Seek 94
SELECT 238
Select Case 23
Send 205
sequential 87, 88, 89, 96
  access 89, 90, 91–94
SERVER_NAME 281, 285
SERVER_PORT 282
SERVER_PROTOCOL 282
SERVER_SOFTWARE 282
SERVER_URL_GATEWAY_INTERFACE 282
ServerName 297
Set 52, 61
set method 54
SetAnyDate 257
SetAnyTime 257
SetNow 256, 258
SetTabs 322
Shared 87
Shell 270, 271
Single 13
source 131
SpacingAbove 322
SpacingBelow 322
SpellCheck 316
SQL 236, 238–239, 241, 244, 247, 248
StartDateTime 260
static 18, 19, 39, 54
StdR4AgentLog 117
Stop 6
strikethrough 168, 170
strings 13, 29–33, 222
STYLE_NO_CHANGE 169
subclassed 53
subform 125
SubjectItemName 231, 232
Submit 287
subroutine 38, 40, 41, 42, 44, 49, 50

T

Tabs 322
TEMPLATE 102
TEMPLATE_CANDIDATE 102
Terminate 41, 44, 124, 140
Text 260
text files 91
ThousandsSep 265
threads 309
tilde 162
Time 252
TimeDifference 258
TimeNumber 253
Timeonly 255
TimeSep 265
TimeValue 253
Timezone 255, 265
Today 252, 265
Tomorrow 265
Trim 29, 31
Type 177
TypeName 17, 72

U

Ubound 66, 79
UCase 29, 30
UML 48
underline 167, 168, 170
UnderScore 34
UniformAccess 153
UnprocessedDocuments 75
UnprocessedFTSearch 75, 213, 214, 216
UnprocessedSearch 75, 215, 216
UpdateAll 215
UpdateFTIndex 216, 217
Use 300
Uselsx 244
Uselsx "*LSXODBC" 239
user-defined
  errors 112
  events 136

V

value arrays 84
variant 13, 14, 17
VBA 201
vertical bars 209

view 133
visibility 42
Visual Basic 180, 190, 192, 204

W

watching variables 6
web events 130
Web Navigator 287
WebQueryOpen 129, 280, 287
WebQuerySave 130, 280, 287
WeekDay 254
wend 21
WHERE 238
While 21, 148
Windows API 274
Windows/DOS separator 105
With 50, 51, 53, 56, 61, 106, 204, 205, 319
With/End 50
Word 193, 196
Word.Document.8 192
Write 87, 89
writing 89

Y

Y2K 252, 261, 266
Year 254
Yesterday 265

All source code for the examples presented in this book is available to purchasers from the Manning web site. The URL http://www.manning.com/Patton includes a link to the source code files. Purchase of *Practical LotusScript: Programming in the Lotus Notes/Domino Environment* also includes free Author Online support. For more information on this feature, please refer to page *xx*.